Thomas Rawson Birks

The Bible and Modern Thought

Thomas Rawson Birks

The Bible and Modern Thought

ISBN/EAN: 9783337100186

Printed in Europe, USA, Canada, Australia, Japan

Cover: Foto ©Lupo / pixelio.de

More available books at **www.hansebooks.com**

THE BIBLE

AND

MODERN THOUGHT.

BY

REV. T. R. BIRKS, M. A.,
RECTOR OF KELSHALL, HERTS.

CINCINNATI:
CURTS & JENNINGS.
NEW YORK:
EATON & MAINS.

PREFACE.

THE present volume was written last Spring, in compliance with a request from the Committee of the Tract Society, in order to supply some antidote, in a popular form, to that dangerous school of thought, which denies the miracles of the Bible, explains away its prophecies, and sets aside its Divine authority. Various circumstances have occasioned some unexpected delay in its publication. Though suggested by the appearance of the Essays and Reviews, which have gained so wide a notoriety, it is not, of course, a direct and formal reply to them. It is designed for the use of thoughtful Christians, or serious inquirers, who may have been perplexed by modern speculations, and not for scholars and learned divines. My aim has been to treat the subject of the Christian evidences and the authority of the Bible in a simple, clear, and solid style of argument, logically connected and continuous; and to deal with recent objections only so far as they lie directly in the way, and, like the lions in the allegory, block up the road of the Christian pilgrim to the palace of heavenly truth. At the same time, the fourth chapter, on the Reasonableness of Miracles; the eighth, on the Prophecies of the Old Testament; the twelfth and thirteenth, on the Interpretation of Scripture, and on its Alleged Discrepancies; the fourteenth and fifteenth, on Modern Science; and the sixteenth, on the Bible and Natural Conscience, contain a full discussion of the principles advanced in the Third, the Second, the Seventh, the Fifth, and the First Essays. But my desire has been not so much to detect and expose error as to unfold the truth, and guide the minds of sincere inquirers into a well-grounded faith in the truth, wisdom, harmony, and Divine authority of the Gospel, and of the written Word of God. May it please the Holy Spirit, the Lord and Giver of life, to use it, however humble in itself, for a help to the faith of the people of Christ in these latter days!

KELSHALL RECTORY, OCT. 10, 1861.

EDITOR'S PREFACE.

Mr. Birks has evidently well studied the skepticism of his own day and country; and in the following work has ably discussed the questions which have come before him. Modern infidelity is of course characterized by the spirit of the age in which we live. It is not coarse, daring, open, blasphemous; it does not attack by ridicule, scurrility, or misrepresentation. The ribaldry of Voltaire and Paine would offend and disgust our age, and their works are no longer read. The infidelity of our day is refined, respectful, subtile, analytical; it wears the appearance of candor and sincerity; the writer seems to be ingenuously searching after truth; he claims to be "an honest skeptic." He does not level his heavy artillery against the outer intrenchments; these have so long and so effectually hurled back his attacks that their invulnerability seems to be conceded. With guns of much longer range, and with much more accurate aim, he attacks the citadel itself, and hopes to find some weakness in its inner works.

Laying aside the figure, infidelity no longer contends against the historical evidences of the Bible; it no longer charges the sacred writers with imposture, dishonesty, and collusion; it accepts the antiquity, the genuineness, and almost the authenticity of the Scriptures. It concedes to the Bible a high degree of historical value and antiquarian interest; it extols its poetical beauties; it praises its lofty aim and pure morality; it even recognizes in the sacred penmen deep religious feeling; yet can not acknowledge their Divine inspiration, nor accept their teachings as the only and infallible messages of truth. In brief, the Bible is to the modern infidel a most excellent book in every respect—literary, historical, moral, and religious—but is not a revelation from God.

To meet these new and subtile attacks we need new champions. The attack comes from a new quarter; it must be met on new ground. It shows its true character best in Great Britain; in England, therefore, we expect to find its ablest opponents. Our author ranks in this class. He sees clearly, understands his work well, and writes forcibly. He does not evade the real points at issue, but enters fully and fairly into the subtile and delicate questions which lie back of all questions of mere historical credibility, and, conceding to a considerable extent the honesty of modern inquiry, he candidly meets and discusses the real difficulties which the skeptic presents. We bespeak for this work a cordial reception in this country.

I. W. WILEY.

CINCINNATI, JULY, 1864.

CONTENTS.

	PAGE
INTRODUCTION	15

Infidelity defined, 13; its changing forms, 13; covert infidelity, 14; its praise of the Bible, 14, 15; need of spiritual discernment, 17; questions to be answered, 18, 19.

CHAPTER I.

THE NATURE OF DIVINE REVELATION............ 20

Truths implied—1. The being of God, 20; 2. Reality of creation, 21; 3. Divine Nature capable of being revealed, 22; 4. Man capable of Divine knowledge, 24; 5. The fallen condition of man, 25; theory of the "Absolute Religion," 27; doctrine of the Fall, the key to supernatural revelation, 29.

CHAPTER II.

MAN'S NEED OF DIVINE REVELATION............ 33

Objection of the Theist, 33; the need proved by facts, 34; due to man's corruption, 35; no disparagement of natural religion, 36; kinds of inspiration distinguished, 37; a true revelation no burden, but a blessing, 38.

CHAPTER III.

THE SUPERNATURAL CLAIMS TO CHRISTIANITY............ 40

The main question—is Christianity human or Divine? 40; first appeal to the Bible itself, 40; midway position untenable in the presence of its claims, 41; St. Matthew's Gospel, 42; St. Mark and St. Luke, 46; St. John's Gospel, 47; Book of Acts, 50; Apostolic Epistles, 53. Conclusion, a supernatural claim of the essence of Christianity, 60.

CHAPTER IV.

THE REASONABLENESS OF MIRACLES.................................. 61

(Examination of Third Essay.)

Appeal to miracles by Moses, 61; our Lord himself and the apostles, 61; recent objections, 63. I. Charges against Christian advocates, 63; reply, 64; an inquirer not a judge, 65; reasoning consistent with moral guilt of unbelief, 67; historical and moral evidence rightly mingled, 68; belief not a simple act of will, 68; right order of honest inquiry, 69; moral preparation needed, 70. II. Objections to miracles stated, 73; Scripture view of their origin, 75; imply a false view of induction, 76; false view of the constancy of natural law, 77; false definition of miracles, 79; contradictions of the skeptical argument, 80. III. Objections to miracles as evidence, 82; definition of miracles, 84; their main use, 87; relation of external and internal evidence, 88; result of the inquiry, 91.

CHAPTER V.

THE HISTORICAL TRUTH OF THE NEW TESTAMENT................ 95

Historical character of the Bible, 95; assaults on the Gospels and Pentateuch, 96; preliminary remarks, 98; the Book of Acts to the death of Herod, 103; to St. Paul's voyage, 107; internal harmony, 112; the four Gospels—times, 114; places and persons, 117; reconcilable diversity, 119.

CHAPTER VI.

THE HISTORICAL TRUTH OF THE OLD TESTAMENT................123

I. From the Captivity to Christ—Limits in time, 123; absence of miracle, 126; chronological distinctness, 127; fullness of detail, 129; Book of Esther, 130. II. From Solomon to the Captivity. Chronology, 132; heathen history, 133; Kings and Chronicles, 136; prophetic books, 137. III. From the Conquest to Solomon. General remarks, 139; Book of Joshua, 142; Book of Judges, 147; its chronology, 150. IV. The Pentateuch, 152; results of induction, 153.

CHAPTER VII.

THE MIRACLES OF THE BIBLE..155

Circular reasoning of modern skeptics, 155. I. Infrequency of miracles, 156. II. Their publicity, 160. III. Their consistent plan, 162. IV. Their moral purpose, 167.

CHAPTER VIII.

THE PROPHECIES OF THE OLD TESTAMENT.................169

(*Remarks on the Second Essay.*)
Christianity, an appeal to miracles, 169; and to prophecy, 169; examples in the Gospels, 170; their wide range, 170; recent objections examined, 176; prophecy, Isa. vii-ix, 179; later prophecies of Isaiah, 184; Book of Daniel, its genuineness, 192; conclusion, 201-203.

CHAPTER IX.

CHRISTIANITY AND WRITTEN REVELATION.....................204
Reception of the Bible, a corollary of Christian faith, 204; general outline of the argument, 206; stage of doubt, 208; faith in the Gospel, and in the inspiration of the Bible, distinct, though closely united, 210; inspiration, a positive idea, 213; entrance of written revelation, a great era, 214; its uses and reasons, 215; its original perfection inferred, 217.

CHAPTER X.

THE INSPIRATION OF THE OLD TESTAMENT.....................220
Solemn introduction of written revelation, 220; testimonies of our Lord himself—1. The temptation, 221; 2. Galilean ministry, 222; 3. Sermon on the Mount, 223; 4. Charge to the leper, 225; 5. Testimony to the Baptist, 225; 6. Matthew xii, 3-7, 226; 7. Teaching in parables, 227; 8. Tradition, Matthew xv, 1-9, 227; 9. The Transfiguration, 228; 10. Divorce, 229; 11. Entrance to Jerusalem, 229; 12. Answers to Sadducees, 231; 13. Matthew xxiii, 232; 14. The passion, 233; 15, 16. St. Luke's Gospel, 234, 235; later books, 237; general conclusion, 238.

CHAPTER XI.

THE INSPIRATION OF THE NEW TESTAMENT......................240
Evidence less direct, 240. I. Analogy of the Old Testament, 241; II. Special nature of the new dispensation, 242. III. Resemblance in structure of New and Old Testament, 244. IV. Promises to the apostles, 245. V. Their rank compared with the prophets, 247. VI. Testimonies in St. Paul's Epistles to their own inspiration, 248. VII. And to the Gospels and Acts, 251. VIII. Epistles of St. Peter and St. Jude, 254. IX. Writings of St. John, 257. Conclusion, 260.

CHAPTER XII.

THE INTERPRETATION OF SCRIPTURE..................................261

(*Remarks on the Seventh Essay.*)

Amount of Biblical literature, 261; temptation thus occasioned, 261; recoil from the maxim of Vincentius, 262; counter maxim of the Seventh Essay delusive, 263; Bible to be studied *naturally*, 264; its inspiration not mechanical, 265; *reverently*, as the voice of the Spirit, 267; confusion of the negative criticism, 271; contrast in two examples, 273; value of human helps, 276; real certainty of Bible theology, 280.

CHAPTER XIII.

ON ALLEGED DISCREPANCIES OF THE BIBLE......................282

Theory of partial inspiration, 282; its difficulties, 283; divergence not contradiction, 284; variety one element of the true definition, Heb. i, 1, 285; Scriptures a condensed record, 286; silence, no proof of ignorance, 287; inferences not assertions, 288. I. Discrepancies alleged in the Essays, 290. II. Prolegomena to the New Testament, 295.

CHAPTER XIV.

THE BIBLE AND MODERN SCIENCE....................................308

(*Examination of the Fifth Essay.*)

Question stated, 308; its true limits, 309; astronomical objection, 310; based on three errors, 311; geological difficulties, 316; optical representation, 318; break in Gen. i, 2, 324; events of fourth day, 330; the firmament, 331; true relation of Genesis and geology, 333–335.

CHAPTER XV.

THE SAME CONTINUED..336

All the Bible of Divine authority, 336; contains materials of sciences, not sciences themselves, 340.

CHAPTER XVI.

THE BIBLE AND NATURAL CONSCIENCE............................350

(*Remarks on the First Essay.*)

Question stated, 350; direct authority of Scripture, 352; conscience not absolute or supreme, 358; its true nature, 360; no mediator, 361; needs to be corrected and purified by the Word of God, 362; the Gospel, an external authority, 368.

CHAPTER XVII.

THE HISTORICAL UNITY OF THE BIBLE..........371

I. The historical character of the Bible a mark of the Divine Wisdom, 372. II. Its unity of purpose a proof of its Divine origin, 375. III. Continuity of outline a distinctive feature, 377. IV. Simplicity of style, 379. V. Condensation of the Bible histories, 381. VI. The Pentateuch, 383. VII. Later historical books, 387. VIII. The Gospels, 392. IX. The Acts of the Apostles, 397. Conclusion, 401.

CHAPTER XVIII

THE DOCTRINAL UNITY OF THE BIBLE..........402

I. Doctrinal harmony in all the main topics of religious faith, 403. 1. The creation, 404; 2. The unity of God, 406; 3. The Fall and corruption of man, 407; 4. The doctrine of a Redeemer, 408; 5. Salvation by Faith, 409; 6. The need of an atonement, 410; 7. Need of regeneration, 411. II. Harmony in many other particulars, 412; contrast between the Old and New Testaments, 413; no real difference, 413; the Law and the Gospel, 415; their essential unity, 420; contrast no contradiction, 421.

CHAPTER XIX.

CHRISTIANITY A PROGRESSIVE SCHEME..........423

Object of the Bible, 423; the scheme of redemption, 423; not a scheme for the World's education, 424; redemption of the world a progressive scheme, 425; spurious theories of progress, 425; the Bible opposed to all such theories, 426; the true progress, 427; the promise and Divine forbearance 428; the incarnation of Christ, 430; the final triumph, 432; the Word of God, 434.

THE BIBLE AND MODERN THOUGHT.

INTRODUCTION.

CHRISTIANITY claims to be a Divine revelation, or a message of truth from the living God to the children of men, contained, embodied, and recorded in the Scriptures of the New Testament. It claims, further, to be the sequel and completion of earlier messages from the same Divine Author, contained and recorded, in like manner, in the Scriptures of the Old Testament. Christian faith, in the widest sense of the term, consists in the admission of this double claim. Infidelity consists in its rejection and denial.

This denial may assume very different forms. It may be coarse, arrogant, and abusive, or polite, modest, and refined in its tone. It may load the Bible with abuse, as a gross imposture, or admire its poetical beauty, extol its pure morality, and treat it with the reverence of the scholar and the antiquarian, as containing some of the choicest products of human intelligence. While one type of infidelity repels and disgusts by its open blasphemy, another allures and fascinates ingenuous minds by an air of caution and candor, and puts on the garb of philosophical research, moral sensibility, and religious reverence. But these, after all, may be only varieties of the same unbelief. The question between the Christian and the infidel does not turn upon the degree of merit or demerit assigned to the Scriptures, viewed as merely human compositions. It depends on the admission or rejection of their Divine authority. Is Christianity a supernatural message from the living and true God, or a mere product of the natural powers of the human mind? Is the Bible the voice of God, or only the voice of some Hebrew historians, poets, and moralists—the word of God, or the word of man?

The form of infidelity which prevailed at the close of the last century was daring, open, and blasphemous. It was bred amid the rottenness of a corrupted Church and a dissolute society; and ascribing to Christianity all the worst abuses of both, it kept no terms with "the wretch" it labored to destroy. The experience of seventy years has wrought a great change in the tactics of this moral warfare. The hopes of an ungodly and blaspheming philosophy were quenched speedily, under the reign of terror, in a sea of blood. The liberty, equality, and philanthropy, which had trodden the Bible under foot, were replaced, in a few years, by the heaviest yoke of military despotism. At the same time Christian faith received a fresh impulse, and began to win new trophies, by the revival of missionary zeal, the increased circulation of the Word of God, and the spread of the Gospel, through the self-denying labors of faithful men, in almost every part of the heathen world.

In consequence of these changes, the spirit of unbelief has revealed itself, of late years, in features less repulsive but more insidious. It rejects the Divine authority of the Bible, but is willing to extol its poetical beauty, and to recognize in it a high degree of historical value and antiquarian interest. It acquits the sacred writers of willful imposture, and even gives them praise for high religious feeling, for deep thought, and lofty imagination, though it refuses to own that they are the messengers of God. Its motto is no longer that of the unbelieving Pharaoh—"Who is the Lord, that I should obey his voice?" It resembles more nearly the "Hail, Master" of the false apostle, or the attempt of the spirit of divination to enter into partnership with the truth, when it cried—"These men are the servants of the Most High God, which show unto us the way of salvation."

This varied and more subtle form of assault on the authority of the Gospel requires increased discernment and watchfulness on the part of all the true disciples of Christ. Open blasphemies are more easily repelled. They revolt us by their gross impiety, put the conscience at once on its guard, and may often produce a powerful reaction in favor of the truth which they assail. But the sapping and mining process of a covert infidelity, which borrows the very phrases of the Gospel, to give them a philosophical meaning, and will own almost every kind of excellency in the Scriptures, except the authority of a Divine message, is far more perilous and seductive to thoughtful and serious minds. The chasm which separates faith from unbelief, submission to God from the rejection of his authority, is bridged over by a thin layer of ambiguous phrases, and thickly strewn with flowers of fancy, and a sentimental piety, till it disappears totally from view; and those who are thorough unbelievers at heart, mistake themselves for the genuine disciples of a pure and enlightened Christianity.

Let us contrast, for example, the ribaldry of Paine and Voltaire with the following eulogy on the Bible by a modern ringleader in the attempt to replace Christian faith by deism or natural religion. It will be evident at once how total a change has occurred in the weapons of assault; and what discernment and caution are required in the friends of truth, that they may not be deceived by smooth and complimentary phrases, while the foundations of their faith are silently, but vigorously and daringly assailed.

"This collection of books," Mr. Parker writes, "has taken such hold of the world as no other. The literature of Greece, which goes up like incense from that land of temples and heroic deeds, has not half the influence of this book from a nation despised alike in ancient and modern times. It is read in all the ten thousand pulpits of our land. In all the temples of Christendom is its voice lifted up week by week. The sun never sets on its glowing page. It goes equally to the cottage of the plain man and the palace of the king. It is woven into the literature of the scholar, and colors the talk of the street. It enters men's closets, mingles in all the grief and cheerfulness of life. The Bible attends men in sickness, when the fever of the world is on them. The aching head finds a softer pillow, when the Bible lies underneath. The mariner, escaping from shipwreck, seizes it the first of his treasures, and keeps it sacred to God. It blesses us when we are born, gives names to half Christendom, rejoices with us, has sympathy for our mourning, tempers our grief to finer issues. It is the better part of our sermons. It lifts man above himself. Our best of uttered prayers are in its storied speech, wherewith our fathers and the patriarchs prayed. The timid man, about to awake from his dream of life, looks through the glass of Scripture, and his eyes grow bright; he does not fear to stand alone, to tread the way unknown and distant, to take the death-angel by the hand, and bid farewell to wife and babes and home. Men rest on this their dearest hopes. It tells them of God and of his blessed Son, of earthly duties and heavenly rest. Foolish men find in it the source of Plato's wisdom, of the science of Newton, and the art of Raphael.

"Now, for such effects there must be an adequate cause.

It is no light thing to hold, with an electric chain, a thousand hearts, though but an hour, beating and bounding with such fiery speed; what is it, then, to hold the Christian world, and that for centuries? Are men fed with chaff and husks? The authors we reckon great, whose articulate breath now sways the nation's mind, will soon pass away, giving place to other great men of a season, who in their turn shall follow them to eminence, and then to oblivion. Some thousand famous writers come up in this century, to be forgotten in the next. But the silver cord of the Bible is not loosed, nor its golden bowl broken, as Time chronicles his tens of centuries passed by. Fire acts as a refiner of metals: the dross is piled in forgotten heaps, but the pure gold is reserved for use, and is current a thousand years hence as well as to-day. It is only real merit that can long pass for such; tinsel will rust in the storms of life; false weights are soon detected there. It is only a heart can speak to a heart, a mind to a mind, a soul to a soul, wisdom to the wise, and religion to the pious. There must then be in the Bible, mind, heart, and soul, wisdom and religion; were it otherwise, how could millions find it their lawgiver, friend, and prophet? Some of the greatest of human institutions seem built on the Bible; such things will not stand on chaff, but on mountains of rock. What is the secret cause of this wide and deep influence? It must be found in the Bible itself, and must be adequate to the effect." *

Such a school of infidelity, which assumes the garb, and borrows the phrases of Christianity, requires us to look below the surface, before we can discern its real nature, and guard against the inroads of its subtile delusions. All these praises of the Bible, in the writer just quoted, and others

---

* Parker's "Discourse of Religion," pp. 237-239, 242.

of the same type of thought, are followed by a distinc' and deliberate rejection of its Divine authority. "The conclusion," we are told, "is forced upon us that the Bible is a human work, as much as the 'Principia' of Newton or Descartes. Some things are beautiful and true, but others no man in his senses can accept. Here are the works of various writers, thrown capriciously together, and united by no common tie but the lids of the bookbinder—two forms of religion which differ widely, one the religion of fear, and the other of love."

The same spirit evidently pervades other writings, which profess to set Christianity free from the trammels of a traditional orthodoxy, and to bring it into harmony with the discoveries of modern science. It is essential, then, to look beneath the surface of the inquiry, and to examine the foundations themselves. A course of argument, like that of Paley, may be triumphant and complete against a direct charge of imposture, dishonesty, and collusion. But the form of temptation which now assails the Church requires some previous questions, more subtile and delicate in their nature, to be examined. What do we mean by a Divine revelation? What are the conditions on which its possibility, its probability, or its certainty depend? What need is there that such a revelation should be given to mankind? How far can miracles, prophecies, or moral excellence, separately or in combination, furnish decisive evidence of its reality? How may we infer the Divine authority of the Bible from the statement of the Bible itself, without a vicious circle in our reasoning? How are we to explain alleged contradictions between the language of Scripture and the results of antiquarian research, and the real or supposed discoveries of modern science? How can we reconcile the doctrine of Divine inspiration, and the claim of the Bible to a supernatural origin, with the innumerable signs of human authorship, with seeming discrepancies in its historical statements, and the diversity of manner and style in its different writers? Such questions as these require to be carefully examined, if a bulwark is to be reared against the tide-wave of skeptical thought, which threatens, at this moment, to bury the old landmarks of Christian faith.

CHAPTER I.

THE NATURE OF DIVINE REVELATION.

WHAT do you mean by a Divine revelation? What are the conditions on which the possibility of its occurrence depends? These are among the first questions which must be answered, that our acceptance of Christianity under the character of a message from God may be a well-grounded and reasonable faith.

The first truth, plainly implied, is THE BEING OF GOD as a personal and conscious intelligence. "He that cometh to God must believe that he is." Atheism by its very nature excludes all possibility of revelation. If there be no God there can be no communication from God to man. A blind, mechanical, unconscious Fate can never be the source of intelligible messages to intelligent beings. All faith in Divine revelation must imply a previous conviction that "there is a God in heaven who revealeth secrets"— an unseen lawgiver who is capable of making known his will to mankind.

That faith in God, however, which must precede our belief in a Divine message may be exceedingly dim, vague, and imperfect. It need not be more than a strong impression that there is some unseen intelligence higher, greater, and wiser than men. The true character of this unknown Being may remain concealed in thick darkness till it is learned from his own messages. Atheism makes the acceptance of a Divine revelation a contradiction and an impossibility. A full and adequate knowledge of God, apart from such a revelation, and before it is received, would degrade it into a useless and unmeaning superfluity.

A second truth, equally implied in the fact of revelation, is THE REALITY OF CREATED EXISTENCE. Those who receive a Divine message must be distinct from him who sends it. It may seem needless at first sight to dwell even for a moment on a truth so clear and self-evident. Philosophers, however, both in ancient and modern times, have often stumbled at the very threshold of true science, and have mistaken a denial of the earliest lessons of self-consciousness for superiority to vulgar prejudice, and a proof of their own more profound wisdom. The Maya or illusion of the Brahman, the absorption of Buddhism, the theories of Spinoza, the skeptical philosophy of Hume, and some later forms of German speculation, agree in denying the distinct reality of created existence. Whenever the Scriptural idea of creation is replaced by one of emanation or development, such a result seems naturally to follow. Pantheism in all its forms, no less than mere atheism, excludes revelation, and makes it impossible. If the souls of men are only parts of the Infinite Soul of the universe, there may be strange pulsations of life in this complex universe of being; but revelation, or the conveyance of truth from a Creator to his own creatures, becomes a logical contradiction. We must believe that WE are, as well as that God is, before we can believe that God has made to his erring and sinful creatures a true revelation of his own will.

A Divine message, like a mediator, is "not of one." It requires evidently two distinct parties—a giver and a receiver. The existence of the rational creature must be real, or there can be no manifestation of the Creator. This fundamental truth of our consciousness, without which all revelation would be impossible, is confirmed and ratified by the very first utterance of revealed religion when it tells us that "in the beginning God created the heavens and the earth," and that man himself was formed "in the image of God."

A third truth, also implied in the acceptance of a Divine revelation, IS THE·POWER OF GOD TO MAKE KNOWN HIS NATURE AND WILL TO HIS OWN CREATURES. His absolute dominion and infinite greatness do not make it impossible for him to reveal himself to men. The conception would indeed be strange, of a Being condemned by his own perfection to an eternal solitude; able to give life and reason to finite and intelligent creatures; but unable, because he is infinite, to bridge over the immense chasm which separates him from his own works, or to make known to those creatures his mind and will. On the contrary, one of those perfections which reason plainly requires us to ascribe to him, is the capability of revealing himself to all the rational creatures he has made. We may here apply the decisive reasoning of the Psalmist: "He that planted the ear, shall he not hear? he that formed the eye, shall he not see?" The argument, when carried a step further, is equally cogent. He that fashioned the tongue, shall he not be able to make his voice heard in clearest accents, and to communicate his mind and will to the children of men?

It is quite possible, in recoiling from the proud claims of natural reason, while it pretends to form *a priori* systems of the universe, to fall into error no less dangerous on the opposite side. The finite can not comprehend the infinite. Hence the inference may be drawn that the nature of God must remain forever inaccessible and wholly unknown. But this would be an illusion contradicted by every analogy in every field of science. In all subjects, from the lowest to the highest, partial but real knowledge is the essential condition of a created and finite intelligence. Created existence is a middle term between nonentity and absolute being. The knowledge of rational creatures, in like manner, is a middle term between pure nescience and perfect omniscience. That a real, genuine, though, of course, an imperfect knowledge of God is attainable, and ought to be attained, is one of the fundamental doctrines both of natural and revealed religion. It ranks side by side with the doctrine of creation, that is, faith in the reality of our own existence as the rational and intelligent creatures of God.

In every subject of thought knowledge may be real without being exhaustive or complete. The landscape may be spread beneath our eye in clear outline, though parts near the horizon are seen dimly, and all that lies beyond that horizon is wholly hidden from our view. The knowledge that two and two are four is within the reach of a child: it is a definite truth contrasted with a falsehood, in excess and defect, on either side; but to comprehend all the properties and relations of any one number—even *two*, the simplest of them all—would require omniscience. There is no room for a contrast, in this respect, between the knowledge of God and any other kind of knowledge whatever. The maxim, "We know in part," applies impartially to every field of natural, moral, and theological science. The degrees of our knowledge or ignorance may differ widely. Fallen man knows much of nature, little of himself, and least of his Maker. But even where his knowledge is greatest, far more than he has learned remains still unknown; and even where his ignorance is deepest, some traces remain, though in broken characters, of "the work of the law written in the heart."

Such is the third truth implied in the idea of a revelation, that the will and character, the ways and purposes of

God, are capable of being made known to his intelligent creatures. But when we speak of a revelation to mankind, a further doctrine is implied—that MAN, IN HIS ACTUAL STATE, HAS A CAPACITY FOR LEARNING AND KNOWING THE TRUTH OF GOD.

If we had no faculty of reason distinguishing us from the brutes, it would be unmeaning to address to us any message that requires the exercise of intelligence. There must be powers and capacities receptive of Divine truth, or else revelation would be impossible, and the claim of Christianity to be a message from God to mankind would be convicted of absurdity. It could no longer have any reasonable foundation on which to rest.

This truth, however plain, has been often obscured, and perhaps sometimes even denied, by overzealous advocates of Christian orthodoxy. The strong statements of Scripture respecting the moral disease and inability of man may be so combined and isolated as to engender a dull, passive fatalism, and turn into an idle mockery that earnest appeal to the human conscience which runs throughout the whole course of the Word of God. The heart of sinners, we are told, is gross; their ears are heavy; their eyes are blind; they are "dead in trespasses and sins." Such passages, taken alone, might appear to teach a natural incapacity for discerning any moral and religious truth rather than deep moral aversion from the messages of God. But other statements, equally strong and clear, restore the balance of truth. There is a frequent appeal to the conscience of the sinner himself on the equity of the Divine commands: "Come now, and let us reason together, saith the Lord." "And now, O inhabitants of Jerusalem and men of Judah, judge, I pray you, betwixt me and my vineyard." "O, my people, wherein have I wearied thee? testify against me." "Yea, and why even of your own selves judge ye not what is right?" The corruption of the sinful heart of man, and its averseness from the messages of God, is vividly portrayed in striking metaphors; but the presence of a natural capacity to discern the authority of those messages and to recognize their equity is also stated in the most emphatic and decisive terms.

These four main truths—the being of God, the reality of created existence, the communicableness of Divine knowledge, and the capacity of men for apprehending spiritual truth—are fundamental conditions and prerequisites of all faith in revealed religion. They separate the Christian believer at the outset from the atheist, the pantheist, or philosophical Buddhist, the skeptical idealist of the transcendental school, and the skeptical materialist of the positive philosophy. One further truth, however, is required, which distinguishes Christian faith from the most subtile and specious variety of unbelief—the doctrine of spiritual theism, with its admission of a constant, universal, unintermitted revelation of the will of God to the whole race of mankind. This further truth, on which the doctrine of supernatural revelation, when viewed practically, will be found to rest, is THE FALLEN CONDITION OF MAN, which requires special interpositions of Divine love and wisdom in order to effect his recovery.

Let us conceive a world of perfect moral purity, where no cloud of sin has ever dimmed the light of the Divine presence, or concealed the Holy One from the view of his own creatures. There might still, no doubt, be precepts and commands of the Creator, the reason of which was not explained, and which might retain the character of outward messages, communicated directly by the Word and the Spirit of God to sinless beings, willing subjects of the Divine authority. But where all was light the only contrast would consist in various degrees of the same heavenly brightness. The heavens would declare the glory of their Maker, and the firmament would show his handiwork. Every breath, every pulse of life, in every creature, would be referred instinctively to its Divine Author. His presence would be felt and his praise would be sung in the wonderful workmanship of the human frame, and in every exercise of the higher faculties of the soul within. All nature would be redolent of worship; all creatures would reflect, like unsullied mirrors, some ray of the Divine goodness. Life, in all its forms and in all its activities, would be one series of ceaseless revelations of the goodness and wisdom of the Creator. The world itself would be bathed in the light of the Divine presence. Revelations, ever new and endlessly varied, would be imparted to the souls of men by every sunrise and every sunset, by the song of the birds and the fragrance of the flowers, by the joys of childhood and the ripened wisdom of age, by all the beauties of the earth and all the glories of the sky. There might still be, from time to time, special manifestations of God's gracious presence, and more signal communications of his truth and love, by the visits of angels, or direct appearance of the Son of God. But where all was light and love the sense of contrast between these special revelations and the ordinary course of Providence, since this itself would be a continual and conscious revelation of God's presence and love, would almost disappear. A crystal palace, whose transparent walls admit the full daylight on every side, may receive a richer splendor when the sun breaks forth from a cloud and lights it up with noonday brilliance; but there was no darkness before, and that fuller light, however pleasant and joyful it may be, scarcely receives the name of a revelation. But let one such ray of sunlight, through some narrow crevice, visit the low dungeon whose massive walls exclude the least beam of day; whose narrow **window** choked with dust, can do no more than make darkness visible, and where some unhappy prisoner is pining in hopeless gloom, and then it is a revelation indeed. The light becomes more conspicuous and more joyful by the sudden contrast with the previous darkness.

Pure theism or spiritualism is the most subtle and plausible rival of Christian faith. It approaches nearest to it, adopts its phrases, borrows its morality, and nestles, as it were, close to its side. It rejects the open blasphemies of atheism, and the misty dreams of a pantheistic philosophy It allows, and even asserts, that God is able to make himself known to his creatures, and that man has faculties capable of receiving Divine communications. So far the spiritualist, the disciple of "Absolute Religion," and the Christian believer, travel side by side; but here their paths diverge from each other. Christianity affirms the doctrine of the fall, or a moral degeneracy and corruption of all mankind, which makes a supernatural provision of mercy desirable, and even essential, for their recovery. The spiritualist sets the doctrine aside, as degrading to human nature, and a mere dream of melancholy superstition. On this rejection he builds his own theory of revelation; and the following extract from the eloquent writer already quoted will show its total contrariety to the lessons of Christian faith:

"We have direct access to God through reason, conscience, the religious sentiment, just as we have direct access to nature through the eye, the ear, or the hand. Through these channels, and by means of a law, certain, regular, and universal as gravitation, God inspires man, makes revelation of truth. This inspiration is no miracle, but a regular mode of God's action on conscious spirit, as gravitation on unconscious matter. It is not a rare condescension of God, but a universal uplifting of man. To obtain a knowledge of duty, man is not sent away, outside of himself, to ancient documents, for the only rule of life and practice; the word is very nigh him, even in his heart; and by this word he is to try all documents whatever. Inspiration, like God's omnipresence, is not limited to the few writers claimed by the Jews, Christians, or Mohammedans, but is coextensive with the race.

"This theory does not make God limited, partial, or capricious. It exalts man. While it honors the excellence of a religious genius—of a Moses or a Jesus—it does not pronounce their character monstrous, as the supernatural theory; but natural, human, beautiful, revealing the possibility of mankind. Prayer is not a soliloquy, not an address to a deceased man, but a sally into the spiritual world, whence we bring back light and truth. There are windows toward God as toward the world. There is no intercessor or mediator between man and God; for man can speak, and God can hear, each for himself. He requires no advocate to plead for men, who need not pray by attorney. Each soul stands close to the omnipresent God, may feel his beautiful presence, and have familiar access to him—get truth at first hand from its Author. Is inspiration confined to theological matters alone? Is Newton less inspired than Simon Peter? . . . Plato and Newton, Milton and Isaiah, Leibnitz and Paul, Mozart, Raphael, Phidias, Praxiteles, and Orpheus, receive into their various forms the one spirit from God most high."*

This theory of inspiration, it must be plain, is based on a silent assumption of the unfallen and sinless condition of mankind. Christianity, in its claim to be a supernatural revelation, special and distinctive in its messengers and messages, though world-wide in its aims, starts from the

---

* Parker's "Discourse," pp. 160-165.

opposite assumption, that mankind have fallen from original uprightness, and that means more powerful than the voice of nature alone are needed for their recovery.

The doctrine of the fall, once received, explains all the special features of supernatural revelation. Nature, in all her works, in the rain from heaven, and fruitful seasons, may still bear witness to the bounty of her Maker. The heavens may still declare the glory of God, and the firmament may show his handiwork. But sin has made the eyes of men dim, and their ears deaf, that they seldom heed the message; and it has rendered deeper revelations of God's character than mere bounty and general benevolence essential to man's recovery from a state of guilt, alienation, and moral ruin. It fills the conscience with terrors, and the understanding with strong and strange delusions. It turns men into tempters and deceivers, each to the other, instead of multiplying mirrors, reflecting brightly upon each other the beams of the Divine goodness. Its universal tendency, and, in dark times, its actual result, is to pervert human society into a gigantic system of moral falsehood, in which men are "foolish, disobedient, deceived, serving divers lusts and pleasures, living in malice and envy, hateful, and hating one another." Tit. iii, 3. The light from God's natural works still shines upon this land of mist and darkness; but "the darkness comprehendeth it not:" it is too feeble to penetrate the thick gloom. Every field of nature is either peopled with phantom gods—the mere reflections of human lust and appetite—or second causes alone are seen, and the great First Cause is thrust out of sight and forgotten. It becomes needful, then, by signs and wonders, to break through the monotony of nature, and to force on reluctant hearts the conviction that there is a living God, the Lord of nature, higher and nobler than the laws he has ordained for his creatures, the true Sovereign of the universe. Since men have become mutual deceivers, unable to discern even the simpler lessons of natural religion, and still more to anticipate the mysteries of redemption, and to devise, or even to understand, the means required for their own recovery, special messengers of truth must be provided, if the work of mercy is to be carried on. The Word of God, whether before his incarnation, or incarnate in human flesh, may thus have to become the messenger to sinners of his Father's will. Angels, whose vision of God has been dimmed by no fall, though their intercourse with a fallen race is almost wholly suspended, may still be sent, from time to time, on errands of mercy or of judgment, at the bidding of their Lord. Holy men, the choice firstfruits of redemption, in whom the work of moral recovery is more advanced than in their fellows, may be raised, from time to time, above themselves, and shielded from the influence of remaining infirmity and error, in order to become the vehicles of Divine messages to their fellow-men. And thus by prophets, by angels, and the Son of God himself, attested by miracles and by prophecies, a system of Divine revelation may be carried on, which meets the necessities of a fallen race, speaks to mankind in louder and clearer tones, and with wider and deeper truths, than a mere religion of nature can attain; secures at every step of its progress some partial victories of truth and righteousness over sin, error, and delusion; and moves on with firm and measured step toward a long-promised consummation of restored holiness, when the tabernacle of God shall be with men, and his will be done on earth as it is in heaven.

To decide, then, between the high-sounding dreams of spiritualism, with its pretensions to universal inspiration, and the modest claims of Christianity, with its specialities of miracle, prophecy, and sacrifice, we need only read the history of the world, and its long ages of sin and sorrow

The voice of nature might well suffice for an unfallen race; or if it were supplemented by special messages from heaven, these angels' visits need not be "few and far between," and would lose their strange and miraculous character amid the unclouded sunshine of a sinless world. But when mankind have turned their backs on the light, and plunged themselves into thick darkness; when habits of sin have blunted the conscience, and tainted and defiled every faculty of the soul; when the laws of a holy God have been broken, and denounce a curse against the rebels who have trampled them under their feet; when the pall of death broods over the whole race, and the daily spectacle of its ravages, with no return from the grave, has almost blotted out all faith in the soul's immortality; when life is short, and death is near, and judgment at hand, and conscience accuses, and the law of God condemns, and dark clouds of fear and remorse have separated the souls of men from their God,—it needs a clearer and stronger voice than that of nature alone, to restore peace to the troubled heart, to subdue the inveterate power of sin, and open the pathway of life to the trembling sinner. For Nature herself has solemn messages, and can terrify the guilty with the fear of judgment to come, no less than delight the children of innocence with her tones of gentleness and peace. Clouds and thick darkness, the volcano and the earthquake, the lightning, the whirlwind and the hurricane, the spreading fever, and the destroying pestilence, all have their own voice of fear and alarm to the guilty consciences of men. They echo in loud accents the warning of the Bible itself, that "the wrath of God is revealed from heaven against all ungodliness and unrighteousness of men."

Christianity, then, in claiming to be a special and supernatural revelation, implies and presupposes the great doctrine of the fall of mankind. Whenever this truth is de nied, the need for any such special interference of God, to make known his ways, will cease to be recognized, and the sufficiency of the mere light of nature will be maintained. The specialities of revealed religion will then be held for so many proofs of its arbitrary and capricious character, so as to make it unworthy a God of universal benevolence. The whole provision of supernatural evidence, in miracles and prophecies, will seem a laborious superfluity; and then, by natural consequence, an incredible deviation from the fixed and usual laws of Divine Providence. When a whole neighborhood are enjoying perfect health, the arrangements of a hospital, with its nurses and physicians, its wards and couches, its medicines and surgical instruments, however complete or skillfully devised, may seem to be only a complicated and laborious folly. "They that be whole need not a physician, but they that are sick." An unfallen and sinless race would have little need for a long series of miraculous messages and supernatural revelations.

Once admit, however, the truth that man is fallen and apostate, and needs rescuing from moral degradation and spiritual danger, and the seeming anomaly disappears. Christianity, with its miracles and prophecies, and mysterious doctrines, is no longer an inexplicable paradox, a strange, incredible excrescence on the simpler creed of pure theism and universal philanthropy—a creed maintained to be complete and effective, without this higher aid, to meet every want of the souls of men. On the contrary, the truth of its own descriptions of its blessed office commends itself at once to the burdened conscience and the sorrowing heart. The salvation it brings to sinners is "the power of God, and the wisdom of God;" and the Savior in whom it centers is "the Dayspring from on high," sent on a visit of mercy to a race of wandering prodigals, " to give light to them that sit in darkness and the shadow of death."

CHAPTER II.

MAN'S NEED OF DIVINE REVELATION.

"I DEEM it unnecessary to prove that mankind stood in need of a revelation, because I have met with no serious person who thinks that, even under the Christian revelation, we have too much light, or any degree of assurance that is superfluous."

The objection, which Paley has thus pithily dismissed in his opening sentence, has been revived by some late writers in a more paradoxical form. A supernatural revelation, they affirm gravely, instead of a help, would be only a hinderance to the souls of men. It would charge the scheme of Providence with an inexcusable defect. Its admission disparages and sets aside natural religion, and denies the ceaseless activity of the Divine goodness. It would lay a heavy yoke upon the reason and conscience, and subject them to a degrading and oppressive tyranny. The charge has been made in these words:

"This theory makes inspiration a very rare miracle, confined to one nation, and to some score of men in that nation, who stand between us and God. We can not pray in our own name, but in that of the Mediator, who makes intercession for us. It exalts miraculous persons, and degrades men. Our duty is not to inquire into the truth of their word; reason is no judge of that: we must put faith in all which all of them tell us. It sacrifices reason, conscience, and love to the words of the miraculous men; and thus makes its mediator a tyrant who rules *over* the soul by external authority, not a brother who acts *in* the soul by awakening its dormant powers. It says the canon of revelation is closed; God will no longer act on man as heretofore. We have come at the end of the feast, are born in the latter days and dotage of mankind, and can only get light by raking among the ashes of the past. The religion of supernaturalism is worn-out and second-handed. Its vice is to restrict the Divine presence and action to towns, places, and persons. It overlooks the fact, that if religious truth be necessary for all, then it must either have been provided and put within the reach of all, or else there is a fault in the Divine plan. If the two main points—a knowledge of the existence of God, and of the duty we owe to him—be within the reach of man's natural powers, how is a miracle, or the tradition of a miracle, needed to reveal the minor doctrines involved in the universal truth? Where, then, is the use of miraculous interposition?"*

I. The first objection is here made to lie against the notion itself, that a supernatural revelation could be needful, or even desirable, for mankind. It would imply, it is said, a serious fault in the plan of Providence. That scheme must be perfect; and could not be perfect if men stood in need of any supernatural light. No matter what the historical evidence may be, that men, without such aid, have groped for ages in thick darkness, the whole must give way, in the view of such confident theorists, to this one aphorism of *a priori* reasoning, and is refuted by their own conception of what a perfect scheme of Providence inevitably requires.

The simplest reply, then, to this first objection, is an appeal from dreams to facts, from the fancies of rash and ignorant speculation to the stern realities of the world's

---

* "Discourse of Religion," pp. 156, 158.

history. Whatever the means of natural light which, in the view of such theorists, *must* have been provided, the great bulk of mankind have been steeped for long ages in gross religious darkness. The same writers who assure us that a miraculous revelation is needless, or else the Divine plan would be imperfect, map out the religious history of the past into three stages, which they describe as follows: The first is Fetichism, in which "the saint is a murderer, and the fancied God presides over the butchery." The second is Polytheism, in which "the gods were to be had at a bargain;" and the priesthood " separated morality from religion, life from belief, good sense from theology," and the story is "a tragedy of sin and woe." The third and latest is a corrupt Monotheism, whose disciples "make earth a demon-land, and the one God a king of devils." Men have groped, it seems, in such blindness for thousands of years; but they must be held, on *a priori* grounds, to have lived all the time in clear daylight, rather than skeptics will own that there could be any real need for a supernatural revelation.

But the objection is no less faulty and worthless in its reasoning, than opposed to the plainest facts in the religious history of the world. Miraculous messages imply no fault in the Divine plan, but only sin and corruption on the part of men. Means of religious light, adequate to the wants of sinless creatures, have been provided from the first, in the works of nature and the rich bounties of Providence, and have never been withdrawn. It is sin and rebellion alone which have dulled the understanding, and perverted the will, so that nature no longer avails to lead the souls of men "through nature up to nature's God." This same apostasy has also called into exercise deeper attributes of the Godhead, and has made it needful for men to apprehend higher truths than nature alone could teach them, before they can be recovered to the lost favor and image of their Maker again. Even in the outward world, the food of health is far more abundant than the medicines which are required in sickness. The profligate, who has ruined his health by vice and intemperance, has no right to blame the constitution of nature, if the remedies of the physician, unlike his daily bread, are costly in price, and possibly difficult to procure. Christianity, on the face of it, professes to be a Divine remedy for a dangerous moral disease. The Savior, to whom it points, is the physician of souls. The disease which needs an effectual cure, is guilt, disobedience, and rebellion against the Divine will. Those who are suffering from such a malady only prove its depth and malignity, when they claim that the Great Physician shall consult their notions of equity, rather than his own wisdom and holiness, in the means he may graciously devise for restoring guilty and rebellious sinners to moral health and happiness again.

II. The second charge against miraculous revelation is, that it would be positively hurtful, because it disparages and sets aside natural religion, and confines inspiration to a few persons only, in a remote age of the world's history.

The reply to this strange indictment is very simple. The gift of revelation withdraws from mankind nothing which they really possessed before. Instead of blotting out the lessons of God's natural works, it revives them, and makes all those works speak in clearer accents than ever to the souls of men. The only sacrifice it involves is that of mischievous delusions, by which men indulge in vain fancies of light and knowledge, while they are really sunk in gross darkness. It forbids the guilty rebel to say "Peace, peace" when there is no peace. It forbids the cruel savage, "his hands smeared all over with the blood of human sacrifice," to think that he needs no mediator or advocate, but "stands close to God, may feel his beautiful presence, and have familiar access to him," and, without change or repentance, may "sit down" with prophets and saints "in the kingdom of God." All the means of instruction which nature without or conscience within supply to men, remain as before, or rather their efficacy is largely increased. The only loss is that of the moral delirium, which boasts of health amidst the symptoms of a raging fever; and extols man's higher capacities for knowing and loving his Maker, amidst the wide-spread ruin of a moral desolation which has reached from the first dawn of history down to our own days, making every page of the world's history resemble the roll of the prophet, full of "lamentations, and mourning, and woe."

Again, the charge that inspiration is thus confined to a few individuals, and the presence of God restricted to particular times, places, and persons, has no other ground than a palpable abuse of terms. Inspiration, in the sense in which the Christian claims it for prophets and evangelists, instead of being made universal by the skeptic, is denied and rejected altogether. In the sense affirmed by the skeptic himself, or as a common gift or capacity of all men, it is not denied by the Christian, but is only freed from an absurd and mischievous exaggeration. It is the constant and daily prayer of the Church of Christ, to the God of the Bible, that "by his holy inspiration we may think those things which be good; and by his merciful guiding we may perform the same," and that he would "cleanse the thoughts of our hearts by the inspiration of his Holy Spirit, so that we may perfectly love him, and worthily magnify his holy name." The double doctrine of a natural action of the Spirit of God on the souls of all men, in sustaining and upholding their various faculties, and of a special action on the souls of the good and holy, to renew and sanctify them from day to day, is a main and fundamental part of the orthodox Christian faith. The belief in a more special inspiration, usually confined to "holy men of God," but given in some rare cases to others, and designed to fit them for the special work of transmitting pure truth from God to their fellow-men, does not interfere in the least with those wider statements of the Gospel which are confirmed by the daily experience of all pious Christians. There is thus a natural, a moral, and a prophetic inspiration. The natural belongs to all mankind. Gen. ii, 7; Job xxxii, 8. The moral is the privilege of holy and regenerate souls. The prophetic belongs to those whom the sovereign will of the Supreme Lawgiver has singled out to convey and record his own messages, with Divine authority, for the general benefit of the human race.

III. The third objection brought against Divine revelation is, that it lays a yoke upon the reason and conscience, and makes them subject to a degrading tyranny.

The true relation between the Bible and human conscience needs a distinct inquiry, since it is this point which forms the main divergence between Christian faith and a negative or semi-infidel theology. As a preliminary objection, this indictment against the word of God in the Bible only calls for a brief reply. Assuming the claim of a supposed revelation to be false, and its contents to be unworthy of that God in whose name it is given, there can be no doubt that the admission of its Divine authority will impose a heavy burden upon the conscience and reason of all whom it has deceived. They must either lower their conceptions of the Almighty to the level of a human forgery, or else put a force upon language, and submit to an immoral practice of disingenuous and forced interpretations of the messages they profess to receive as Divine. At least this result must follow, unless we ascribe a moral wisdom and excellence to the pretended revelation, which it seems incredible that a mere imposture should attain.

On the other hand, if the God of truth and wisdom has really been pleased to make known his will to men, and has given them messages sealed with clear marks of their Divine origin, then the obligation to receive these messages in their true character, and to use them for gaining insight into the ways and works of God, can never be felt as an oppressive yoke by the wise, the humble, and the pious. Such a gift can be irksome and oppressive only to the proud, the self-willed, and the profane. It is not reason and conscience, but rather a satanic pride, which refuses to sit humbly at the feet of our Lord; and instead of wondering at "the gracious words which proceed from his lips," and treasuring them in the heart with gladness and reverence, sees in them a usurpation on its own fancied right to speculate, without restraint and without a guide, on the character, the works, and the providence of the Most High. The mere fact that such an objection could be made to the reception of the Bible, as endued with Divine authority, by those who have been reared in a Christian land, and have had means of acquainting themselves with its treasures of grace and holiness, is only a new illustration of the truth of one of its inspired warnings. The God of the Bible, in every age, hides his truth from the wise and prudent, and reveals it to babes. "He hath filled the hungry with good things, and the rich he hath sent empty away."

CHAPTER III.

THE SUPERNATURAL CLAIMS OF CHRISTIANITY.

The contrast between Christian faith and that school of thought which professes to introduce a more free and rational theology, lies much deeper than the question whether the canon of Scripture be perfect, and its inspiration verbal, plenary, and complete. It relates to that main feature of the whole message on which its practical worth and excellency entirely depends. Is Christianity itself human or divine? Is it simply a product of imposture or superstition, or at best of the unaided wisdom of imperfect, prejudiced, and fallible men? Or is it the voice of the living God speaking to his creatures by prophets, whom he has himself commissioned and inspired, and by his only begotten Son? Is it a message, every part of which must stand or fall separately, according to our private opinion of its merit? or one which he has ratified, in all its parts, "with signs, and wonders, and divers miracles, and gifts of the Holy Ghost, according to his own will?"

Here the first duty of every honest inquirer is to learn what the writers of the Bible themselves affirm respecting the nature of their message. Their statement, of course, will not of itself prove the reality of their Divine mission. "If I bear record of myself," our Lord said to the Pharisees, "my record is not true." The mere assertion of high claims, unsustained by any further evidence, is always suspicious. It may often be a mark of imposture or of fanatical delusion. But still an important end is at once fulfilled when it is seen that the Law and the Gospel, as recorded by Moses and the Evangelists, do manifestly claim for themselves a supernatural character as the proof of their Divine origin. The controversy is greatly narrowed. Men will be saved from the delusion of supposing that they are genuine Christians of a more enlightened school, while they submit the Gospel piecemeal to the tribunal of their own private reason, and admit or reject in its pages just whatever pleases them. If the Bible *is*, or even if it *contains*, a Divinely-attested message, then our first duty is to ascertain to what part, whether more or less, the attestation is to be given, and to receive all such portions with the docility of a childlike faith. But a book, every part of which is to be received or rejected independently, according as we judge its histories to be true or faulty, its doctrines reasonable or foolish, its morals sound and true, or unsound and erroneous, differs in no respect from any other book whatever. Miraculous attestations to such a message are a ridiculous superfluity, since we can not tell what it is they are meant to attest. There would thus be an apparatus of special interferences for no practical end; a miraculous derangement of the course of nature, and a singular change in the usual laws of Providence, completely wasted and thrown away.

Every midway position between belief and disbelief becomes untenable, in the presence of a distinct claim by our Lord and his apostles to a miraculous commission. If this claim be true, then a merely eclectic Christianity is an absurdity in logic, and, in morals, a direct rebellion against the authority of God. If the claim be false, those who make it must be either impostors or fanatics; and hence they must rank lower, either in simple honesty, or in wisdom and good sense, than good men of an ordinary stamp, who have never been guilty of so great an extravagance.

The mere existence of this claim on their part, when once proved, shuts out every compromise. Those can not be safe guides, as mere human teachers and moralists, who have either feigned or fancied a direct commission from Heaven they never received. It is absurd in this case to deny the authority of the message, and still to look up to the messengers with high admiration and peculiar deference. We ought rather to abhor them for their dishonesty, or else to pity them for their delusion. The remark of a modern skeptical writer has a wider application than to the doctrine and the moral virtue directly named in it. "When the New Testament attributes humility to Christ, it is manifestly under the notion of him as a Divine Being, who has descended from a celestial condition into this lower state of human suffering and degradation. As soon as Jesus is regarded as a real [mere] man, the reversed condition of necessity requires the corresponding reversal of the moral characteristic into one or another phase of lofty daring and unmeasured aspiration."

Let us turn, then, to the New Testament, and inquire what is its own evidence. Are the miracles and alleged fulfillments of prophecy a mere excrescence, which may be entirely pruned away, leaving behind them a system of pure morality unaltered and unimpaired? Or do they form the woof of the whole narrative, so that almost every page, and every main fact, receives the stamp of a Divine authority, or else is tainted with a hopeless leprosy of fraud and delusion? Let us examine in succession the Gospels of St. Matthew and St. John, the Book of Acts, and the Apostolic Epistles.

I. The Gospel of St. Matthew.

Out of the twenty-eight chapters of the first Gospel, three-fourths contain the mention of some miracle, or some asserted fulfillment of prophecy. But this fact alone would give a very imperfect impression of the way in which the supernatural element forms the texture of this Divine biography.

Let us begin with the narrative of our Lord's birth and infancy. The first verse alludes evidently to two leading prophecies, ten and fifteen centuries old, as being fulfilled in the whole course of the sacred narrative. The birth of our Lord is next declared to be a miracle, and also to be the fulfillment of a third prophecy in Isaiah. The wise men are led to Jerusalem, miraculously, by the star which appears to them in the east. They, along with Herod, learn the birthplace of Christ from the prophecy of Micah, also seven centuries old. The star reappears, and guides them to the very place. A dream from God warns them not to return to Herod. An angel, by a dream, directs the flight of Joseph into Egypt. The angel reappears to direct his return, and a fifth dream from God instructs him to leave Judea and return to Galilee.

The opening of the public ministry, in the next two chapters, has the same character. We have first, at our Lord's baptism, the opening of the heavens, the descent of the Spirit, and the miraculous proclamation from heaven— "This is my beloved Son, in whom I am well-pleased." Next follows a supernatural fast of forty days, a direct conflict of the Redeemer and the tempter, a miraculous transfer of our Lord to the pinnacle of the Temple, and a record of the ministration of angels. A prophecy of Isaiah is shown to be fulfilled in the chosen theater of our Lord's ministry, and his work is affirmed to be the cure of "all manner of sickness and all manner of disease."

The Sermon on the Mount is mainly a code of Christian morality, but still it contains the strongest assertions of our Lord's supernatural mission. Near its opening the Divine authority of the law and the prophets is stated in most emphatic terms; while a claim of like authority on the part of our Lord was the main impression his words left on the mind of his hearers. "They were astonished at his doctrine, for he taught them as one having authority, and not as the scribes." Miracles, also, are represented as so closely linked with his message that many counterfeits would arise. "Many will say to me in that day, Lord, Lord, have we not prophesied in thy name? and in thy name have cast out devils? and in thy name done many wonderful works?"

In the six chapters that follow, the miraculous element is conspicuous from first to last. They begin with the healing of the leper, of the centurion's servant, and the mother-in-law of Simon Peter. Many miraculous cures are then dismissed in a brief sentence: "When the even was come, they brought unto him many that were possessed with devils, and he cast out the spirits with his word, and healed all that were sick." Then follows the stilling of the tempest, and the dispossession of the demoniacs of Gadara, the cure of the palsy and of the issue of blood, the resurrection of the ruler's daughter, the healing of the two blind men, and of a dumb man possessed with a devil. The eighth and ninth chapters, in short, are filled almost entirely with the mention of these miracles, and close with the more general statement that Jesus went through the cities and villages "healing every sickness and every disease among the people."

The commission of the twelve apostles confers on them miraculous gifts. "He gave them power over unclean spirits to cast them out, and to heal all manner of sickness and all manner of disease." The words of Christ are recorded by which the power was given: "Heal the sick, cleanse the lepers, raise the dead, cast out devils; freely ye have received, freely give." The reply to the Baptist's message alludes to the number of the miracles and their notoriety: "Go and show John again those things which ye do hear and see. The blind receive their sight, and the lame walk, the lepers are cleansed, and the deaf hear, the dead are raised up, and the poor have the Gospel preached to them; and blessed is he whosoever shall not be offended in me." The Baptist's own mission is next declared to be a distinct fulfillment of prophecy. Chorazin, Bethsaida, and Capernaum have solemn judgments denounced, because of the greatness of the miracles they had witnessed, and of their own stubborn unbelief. The next chapter contains the cure of the withered hand, and a signal dispossession attended by a double cure of dumbness and blindness, which fills the people with amazement. The following discourse is occasioned by an admission of the truth of the miracles on the part of the Pharisees, and their attempt to elude the evidence, thus supplied, of our Lord's divine mission. The visit to Nazareth, at the close of the next chapter, gives two indirect assertions of the same general fact. The Nazarenes exclaim, "Whence hath this man this wisdom and these mighty works?" while the Evangelist adds to his account of their perplexity the brief and simple comment, "He did not many mighty works there because of their unbelief."

The next division of the Gospel—chapters xiv-xx—is equally full of statements of miracle and fulfilled prophecy. It begins with the attempt of Herod to account for our Lord's mighty works by the supposition that the Baptist was risen from the dead—xiv, 2. Then follow, in quick succession, the healing of many sick on the further side of the Sea of Galilee—verse 14—the miraculous feeding of the five thousand—verses 15-21—the walking of Jesus on the sea—verses 22-27—the attempt of Peter, its partial success and speedy failure—verses 28-32—the healing of many sick after the return to the western side—verses 34-36-the dispossession of the daughter of the woman of Canaan—chapter xv, 21-28—multiplied cures of "the lame, the dumb, the blind, the maimed, and many others"—vs. 29-31—and the second miracle of the seven loaves and the four thousand—chapter xv, 32-39—a rebuke of the disciples for their forgetfulness of the two successive miracles of the loaves—chapter xvi, 9—a prophecy of our Lord's resurrection—verse 21—the transfiguration—chapter xvii, 1—the cure of the demoniac child—verse 14—the procurement, miraculously, of the tribute-money—verse 27—and, last of all, the healing of the two blind men in the neighborhood of Jericho. Chapter xx, 30-34.

The last portion, occupied with the events of passion-week, begins with the fulfillment of a prophecy of Zechariah, the healing of the blind and lame in the Temple, and the curse on the barren fig-tree, speedily fulfilled; while it is chiefly occupied with two main subjects—the accomplishment of many prophecies in our Lord's betrayal and crucifixion, and the last and crowning miracle of his resurrection from the dead.

It is needless to enter into the details of the second and third Gospels, which agree very nearly with that of St. Matthew. St. Mark has thirty-five or thirty-six records of miracles, or allusions to their occurrence, and the number is still higher in St. Luke. Out of the few incidents peculiar to St. Mark, two are records of fresh miracles, unnoticed by St. Matthew—the cure of the deaf man who had an impediment in his speech, and of the blind man at Bethsaida. St. Luke, also, in addition to the miracles of the first Gospel, contains the vision of Zechariah, his miraculous dumbness and his recovery, the visit of the angel to the Virgin, the appearance to the shepherds, the prophecy of Simeon, the mission of the seventy with miraculous gifts, like those of the twelve, and their return with the joyful exclamation, "Lord, even the devils are subject to us through thy name." The mention of the miracles, also, in each of these Gospels, reaches from their first opening to their common close in the history of the resurrection.

II. The Gospel of St. John.

The fourth Gospel has so plainly a doctrinal aim, and is composed so largely of our Lord's discourses, that we might expect to find in it only a sparing mention of the miracles. This is true of the number of them, but not of their prominence in the history. On the contrary, all the main divisions of this Gospel, and all its chief discourses, depend on some miracle of our Lord.

The opening chapters proclaim his Divine glory, and recount his first entrance on his public ministry. And how are they introduced? By a signal testimony of the Baptist, our Lord's forerunner, to the sign by which the Messiah would be made known to him. "I saw the Spirit descending like a dove, and it abode upon him." And this sign concurred with a previous message to the Baptist himself. "And I knew him not; but he that sent me to baptize with water, the same said unto me, Upon whom thou shalt see the Spirit descending, and remaining on him, the same is he which baptized with the Holy Ghost. And I saw, and bare record that this is the Son of God." The call of the apostles is marked by a miraculous revelation to Nathanael; and the opening of our Lord's ministry by the miracle at Cana, and other works in Jerusalem at the feast. The conversation with the Samaritan woman ascribes to our Lord prophetic insight, plainly supernatural, which forced from her the exclamation, "Come, see a man which told me all things that ever I did: is not this the Christ?" The return into Galilee is marked by the cure of the nobleman's son at Capernaum. The fifth chapter forms a distinct portion of the Gospel, separated in time from what precedes and follows; and the whole is based upon the cure of the impotent man at the pool of Bethesda. The sixth is another distinct portion, about the time of the last Passover but one. It repeats, with some variations of detail, the miracles of the five thousand and the walking on the sea, recorded in the earlier Gospels. It adds also a full mention of the discourse at Capernaum, which arose out of the miracle, and alludes to it from first to last. The visit at the Feast of Tabernacles contains various discourses at Jerusalem—chaps. vii–x—but the central fact is the cure of the man blind from his birth, which is given in this Gospel alone. Then follows the remarkable history of the raising of Lazarus, in the eleventh and part of the twelfth chapter, which links itself, by the allusion—xi, 17—with the great concourse at our Lord's last entry into Jerusalem. In the midst of the discourses, again, at the Last Supper, we find this striking summary of our Lord's ministry, and the guilt of Jewish unbelief: "If I had not done among them the works which no other man did, they had not had sin; but now have they both seen and hated both me and my Father." To complete the series, in the closing chapter of this Gospel, we have the record of a miraculous draught of fishes, which followed our Lord's resurrection—a counterpart, but with important differences, of an earlier miracle recorded by St. Luke, which took place near the commencement of our Lord's public ministry.

This Gospel also, in harmony with its later date and more reflective character, not merely recounts various miracles, but suggests and unfolds the connection between these tokens of our Lord's divine mission, and the truth of which they were the public confirmation and evidence. Thus we read in chap. ii, 11, "This beginning of miracles did Jesus in Cana of Galilee, and manifested forth his glory; and his disciples believed on him." In the same chapter we are told once more that "many believed on his name, when they saw the miracles which he did." Nicodemus opens his interview with the simple statement—"Rabbi, we know that thou art a teacher come from God, for no man can do these miracles that thou doest, except God be with him." The sluggish faith which craves perpetually for fresh marvels is reproved in the words, "Except ye see signs and wonders, ye will not believe." Yet a sign is given to the nobleman by the speedy and sudden cure of his son, and "himself believed, and his whole house." In the discourse which follows the cure of the impotent man, our Lord assigns his miracles a middle place among the proofs of his Divine mission. "I have a witness greater than that of John; for the works which the Father hath given me to finish, the same works that I do bear witness of me that the Father hath sent me." In the discourse at Capernaum, he blames the sordid interest in the outward meal provided, instead of their thoughts being fixed on the miracle itself, and on the proof which it supplied of his true character. "Ye seek me, not because ye saw the miracles, but because ye did eat of the loaves, and were filled." In the narrative of the blind man, the same lesson is put into his own lips. "Since the world began was it not heard that any man opened the eyes of one that was born blind. If this man were not of God, he could do nothing." In the case of Lazarus, the conclusion appears from the lips of the Pharisees themselves: "What do we? for this man doeth many miracles. If we let him alone, all men will believe on him: and the Romans will come and take away both our place and nation." Our Lord's condemnation of the Jews, because of the greatness of his own works, has been already quoted from his parting discourse before the crucifixion.

The apostle himself sums up these brief but instructive comments, in his own statement of the scope of his whole narrative: "And many other signs truly did Jesus in the presence of his disciples, which are not written in this book. But these are written that ye might believe that Jesus is the Christ, the Son of God, and that believing, ye might have life through his name."

III. The Book of Acts.

The book of Acts forms the transition from the long series of Bible histories to those of later times, after the canon of Scripture was closed, where the supernatural element ceases to appear. In time it occupies more than thirty years—A. D. 30-63—and includes the reigns of four emperors, Tiberius, Caligula, Claudius, and Nero, one of whom is mentioned by name. In place it includes nearly all the main centers of civilization in the brightest days of the Roman empire—Jerusalem, Cæsarea, the Syrian and Pisidian Antioch, Philippi, Athens, Corinth, Ephesus, Alexandria, and Rome. It includes also the mention of two Jewish kings, and four Roman governors—two of Judea, one of Cyprus, and one of Achaia; of the asiarchs of Ephesus, the chief man of Melita, and the military prefect of Rome; and thus links itself at every turn with the most familiar elements of classical and Jewish history. Yet the miraculous element continues throughout its whole course, and is not less prominent than in the Gospels themselves. Let us briefly notice the successive passages. A series of simple references, with a few words of occasional comment, will perhaps exhibit this feature in the clearest way:

Chap. i, 9-11—The ascension, with the appearance and message of two angels.

Chap. i, 16-21—Fulfillment of prophecy in the death of Judas.

Chap. ii, 1-12—The miraculous descent of the Holy Spirit, and the gift of tongues.

Chap. ii, 43—Many wonders and signs done by the apostles.

Chap. iii, 1-11—The healing of the lame man at the gate of the Temple. The rest of the chapter is an address founded entirely upon this public miracle.

Chap. iv, 13-18—The confession of the miracle by the Jewish council, with their charge to the apostles to speak no more in the name of Jesus.

Chap. iv, 21, 22—"So when they had further threatened them they let them go, finding nothing how they might punish them; for all men glorified God for that which was done. For the man was above forty years old on whom this miracle of healing was shown."

Chap. iv, 31—The place is shaken where the disciples were assembled, and they are all filled with the Holy Ghost.

Chap. v, 1-11—The miraculous judgment on Ananias and Sapphira.

Chap. v, 12—Many wonders and signs done by the hands of the apostles.

Chap. v, 15, 16—The sick are cured by the shadow of Peter passing by, and the multitudes resort for healing to Jerusalem.

Chap. v, 19-26—The apostles are miraculously freed from prison by an angel.

Chap. vi, 8—Stephen works great wonders and miracles among the people.

Chap. vii, 55, 56—A miraculous vision to Stephen before his death.

Chap. viii, 5-8—Great joy in Samaria from the miraculous cures wrought by Philip the Evangelist.

Chap. viii, 14-19—Gifts of the Spirit bestowed by imposition of the apostles' hands, and money offered by Simon Magus to purchase the same power.

Chap. viii, 26—Philip sent by the message of an angel to meet the Ethiopian eunuch.

Chap. viii, 39, 40—Philip miraculously caught away after the baptism of the eunuch, and found at Azotus.

Chap. ix, 1-9—The conversion of Saul by a miraculous vision.

Chap. ix, 10-18—The vision of Ananias, and miraculous cure of Saul's blindness.

Chap. ix, 32-35—The cure of Eneas by St. Peter. 36-42—The raising of Dorcas from the dead.

Chap. x, 1-8—The vision of the angel to Cornelius. 9-16—The vision to St. Peter.

Chap. x, 44-48—Miraculous gifts of the Spirit bestowed on Cornelius and other Gentiles.

Chap. xi, 1-18—Rehearsal to the Church of the miraculous conversion of Cornelius.

Chap. xi, 28-30—The prophecy of Agabus fulfilled under Claudius.

Chap. xii, 1-17—The deliverance of St. Peter from prison by the message of an angel.

Chap. xii, 22, 23—The sudden judgment on Herod ascribed to the angel of the Lord.

Chap. xiii, 6-12—Blindness miraculously inflicted on Elymas by St. Paul.

Chap. xiv, 3—Signs and wonders done at Iconium by the hands of Paul and Barnabas.

Chap. xiv, 8-18—Cure of the impotent man at Lystra, and Divine honor offered to the apostles.

Chap. xv, 12—Barnabas and Paul report in the council at Jerusalem "what miracles and wonders God had wrought among the Gentiles by them."

Chap. xvi, 8-10—St. Paul guided into Europe by a miraculous vision.

Chap. xvi, 18—The damsel dispossessed of the spirit of divination.

Chap. xvi, 25-34—The earthquake at Philippi, the loosing of all the prisoners, and the jailer's conversion.

Chap. xvii, 31—St. Paul at Athens bears witness to the fact of Christ's resurrection.

Chap. xviii, 9, 10—St. Paul at Corinth has a miraculous vision and message from the Lord.

Chap. xix, 6—Gifts of the Spirit are bestowed on twelve disciples at Ephesus.

Chap. xix, 11, 12—Special miracles are wrought by St. Paul at Ephesus.

Chap. xix, 13-17—Vain attempt of Jewish exorcists to copy the miracles of the apostle.

Chap. xx, 7-12—Miraculous recovery of Eutychus. 23—St. Paul claims to know by the Holy Ghost the bonds and imprisonment which await him.

Chap. xxi, 9-12—Prophecy of Agabus.

Chap. xxii, 6-16—St. Paul's account of his own conversion, (17-21,) and his vision in the Temple at Jerusalem.

Chap. xxiii, 11—A vision to St. Paul, and a prediction of his journey to Rome.

Chap. xxvi, 8-23—St. Paul's account of his conversion before Agrippa and Festus.

Chap. xxvii, 10—St. Paul's prediction of the shipwreck, (23-26,) angelic vision, and further prophecy.

Chap. xxviii, 3-6—St. Paul's miraculous escape from the viper, (7,) and cure of Publius's father, (9, 10,) and many others.

Chap. xxviii, 25-27—Prophecy of Isaiah fulfilled in the unbelief of the Jews.

This brief list of references will show how intimate and inseparable is the union of the miraculous element with the whole course of this apostolic history. From the resurrection and ascension in the first verses, to the gifts of healing exercised by St. Paul at Melita, after his escape from shipwreck, this feature gives its coloring to every main event in the narrative. To borrow the phrase of the able author of "The Restoration of Belief," the relation is one of intimate cohesion, and not of mere adhesion. Once attempt to remove it and "the vitality of the writer is gone, though much that he has recorded might still be true. We have slain the man, but if he carried about with him any thing that is valuable, we take it to ourselves." Or rather, we may go still further, and say that, when the miraculous element is rejected, nothing of real value is left behind. The historical fragments that would remain would be too few, and too suspicious, to save the bandit's occupation of rifling the dead from being a pure waste of learned labor.

IV. The Apostolic Epistles.

When we turn from the historical books of the New Testament to the letters of the apostles to individuals, or to the Churches they had founded, a marked change occurs in the frequency with which any direct mention of miracles occurs. The fundamental doctrine, indeed, of the resurrection of Christ meets us in almost every page, and is the constant basis alike of the doctrinal statements of the apostles, and of their practical appeals to the conscience. Setting this aside, however, out of twenty-one epistles, there are only seven in which the topic of miracles is directly introduced. In the other fourteen they are passed by in total silence, or if there be allusion to them, it is so delicate and unobtrusive as to require the most careful search to find any trace of it. Out of a hundred and twenty-one chapters, there is only one which contains a formal and distinct statement of the existence and nature of miraculous gifts in the early Churches; and out of nearly three thousand verses, there are, besides that one chapter, only about twenty scattered up and down which contain distinct allusions to the same truth. The fact has been made, by the writer just quoted, the ground of a powerful argument, to confirm the honesty, the moral uprightness of aim, the practical soundness of judgment, remote from all false or blind enthusiasm, of the apostolic writers. It is doubly striking, when we observe that the Churches where St. Paul's authority was most fully allowed, and in which he placed the most confidence, are the same with whom this topic is omitted; and that he appeals to it only in those cases, like the Churches of Galatia and of Corinth, where he had to administer strong rebuke, or where his authority was encountered by some evil influence. The prominence, then, of the moral element in the Epistles, and the comparative fewness of their direct allusions to miracles, form a striking pledge of the uprightness, veracity, and practical wisdom of the apostles of Christ.

But when we view the subject from the opposite side, it will be clear that the assertion of a miraculous element in the Gospel, whether directly made, or indirectly implied, runs throughout the Epistles, no less than the historical books of the New Testament. Let us review them briefly in the probable order of time. The contrast of supernatural and non-supernatural epistles refers only to the explicit character of allusions to present miraculous powers exercised by the apostles themselves. But with regard to Christianity itself, the direct assertion or indirect assumption of its supernatural evidence and authority is common to every one of these writings, without a single exception.

The two Epistles to the Thessalonians hold the first place in order of time. They are earnest and warm outpourings of the apostle's heart to young converts in a time of severe persecution. No direct assertion of his own miraculous gifts is therefore found in them. They are reminded, however, that the Gospel came to them "not in word only, but also in power, and in the Holy Ghost, and in much assurance;" which, when compared with the history, contains a scarcely-doubtful allusion to the δυναμεις, or miraculous gifts of the Spirit, which accompanied his preaching. They are reminded that their new hope was "to wait for his Son from heaven, whom he raised from the dead," a passing affirmation of the crowning miracle of the Gospel history. The apostle associates himself and his fellows with the prophets of the Old Testament, and with the Lord Jesus himself, under the common character of messengers from God, whom the Jews had persecuted because of their messages. He speaks to them—1 Thess. iv, 1—as one endued with a Divine authority, and announces to them the order and circumstances of the resurrection, with the significant preface, "This we say unto you by the word of the Lord." The double charge, "Quench not the Spirit, despise not prophesyings," when collated with other epistles, includes evidently an allusion to miraculous gifts. In the second Epistle even this indirect allusion is not found. Still, the first chapter is a warning of judgment, ready to light on those "who obey not the Gospel," which clearly implies its authority as a direct message from heaven; and the second contains a further warning of a strong delusion, with signs and wonders of falsehood, to which those would be abandoned who had rejected the truth of God. No stronger assertion could be made, by mere implication, that true signs and wonders had been notoriously given to attest the truth of the Gospel.

The Epistle to the Galatians, unlike the two earlier ones to Thessalonica, is a polemic against Judaizing teachers, with strong rebuke of the Churches addressed for their fickleness and inconstancy in the faith. The authority of the apostle was questioned or denied, and he begins his letter by asserting it in the plainest terms. He calls himself "Paul, an apostle, not of men, neither by man, but by Jesus Christ, and God the Father, who raised him from the dead." His reference to miracles, accordingly, becomes distinct, repeated, and earnest. He appeals, first of all, to the notorious fact of his own miraculous and sudden conversion, giving no details of the vision, it is true; but still with the plainest reference to the supernatural character of the revelation. Then, in the midst of the keenest censure and rebuke, he reminds the Galatians of gifts of the Spirit they had themselves received, and follows it by a reference to his own apostolic credentials. "He that ministered to you the Spirit, and wrought miracles among you, was it by the works of the law, or by the hearing of faith?"

The Epistles to the Corinthians are addressed to a Church where the apostle had much to blame, and where his own authority had been depreciated and opposed. But instead of avoiding, on this account, all reference to miracles, the allusions to them are unusually full and various. He begins by reminding them that they come behind in no spiritual gift by which the testimony respecting Christ had been visibly confirmed among them. He appeals to the notorious fact of his own miraculous conversion. "Am I not an apostle? have I not seen Christ Jesus our Lord?" He occupies a whole chapter with a statement of the spiritual gifts, some directly miraculous, others more purely spiritual, which were in exercise among them; and he gives the palm of excellence, not to those which were most startling to the outward senses, but to those which referred to the minds and hearts of Christians, and, above all, to the crowning grace of charity or love. He resumes the subject in another chapter, and gives rules, with Divine authority, for the mode in which these wonderful gifts were to be exercised. He describes, in passing, their probable effect upon strangers who might be present in their assemblies. "And thus are the secrets of his heart made manifest; and so, falling down on his face, he will worship God, and report that God is in you of a truth." 1 Cor. xiv, 25 Amidst this clear recognition of their miraculous endowments, he firmly claims for himself a superior degree of them, and a Divine authority which it was their plain duty to allow. "I thank my God I speak with tongues more than you all." "If any man account himself to be a prophet, or spiritual, let him acknowledge that the things I write unto you are the commandments of the Lord." Verses 18, 37. He refers to five distinct appearances of the Lord after his resurrection as to notorious facts, which needed no proof or comment, and closes with a striking reference to the vision he himself had received. "Last of all he was seen of me also, as of one born out of due time." With a calm and unaltered tone he turns from description of the most striking miracles to a course of earnest reasoning on the doctrine of the resurrection, and from this returns to minute details with regard to collections for the poor, and the arrangement of his own journeys.

In the second letter, after the tidings of their repentance had reached him, three-fourths are without any clear allusion to miraculous gifts, and are occupied only with a rich variety of moral lessons and exhortations, based on the doctrinal truths of the Gospel. But toward the close the mention of those gifts recurs in various forms. "I suppose I was not a whit behind the very chiefest apostles." "I will come to visions and revelations of the Lord." "In nothing am I behind the very chiefest apostles, though I be nothing. Truly the signs of an apostle were wrought among you in all patience, in signs, and wonders, and mighty deeds." "If I come again I will not spare, since ye seek a proof of Christ speaking in me." "I write these things, being absent, lest being present I should use sharpness, according to the power which the Lord hath given me, to edification, and not to destruction." Words could not more plainly express a claim to authority, received directly from the Lord himself, and ratified by miraculous powers, which had been exercised already in the midst of the Corinthian converts.

The Epistle to the Romans is occupied throughout with a full statement of Christian doctrine, and of the practical lessons based upon it. Nine-tenths of it are complete before there is any distinct allusion whatever to miraculous attestations of the Gospel. But at the close it appears, though briefly, in the most decisive form. "I will not dare to speak of any of those things which Christ hath not wrought by me, to make the Gentiles obedient, by word and deed, through mighty signs and wonders, by the power of the Spirit of God; so that from Jerusalem, and round about unto Illyricum, I have fully preached the Gospel of Christ." The assertion is doubly striking, from its association with this precise geographical limit, and the mention of a province named no where else in Scripture, so as to bring out the strictly historical character of the statement into full and bold relief.

The Epistles from Rome during the first imprisonment, are addressed to prosperous Churches, and contain praise and encouragement, rather than rebuke. Accordingly they have only the slightest and most general allusions to Christian miracles. Traces of them, however, do appear. The Ephesians, after they believed, had been "sealed with the Holy Spirit of promise." The mystery of the Gospel had been made known to St. Paul "by revelation," and was revealed unto all the "holy apostles and prophets by the Spirit." The Lord, when he ascended on high, "gave gifts unto men," and foremost among these the endowments of apostles and prophets, where even the second and lower title implies a supernatural claim. In the Pastoral Epistles similar allusions are found. The Spirit had spoken expressly of a great departure from the faith. 1 Tim. iv, 1. Timothy is charged not to neglect the gift that was in him, and given by prophecy, meaning, apparently, by the voice of some inspired prophet, before or at the time of his first public separation for the work of God. He is charged, again, to stir up the gift of God, received by imposition of the hands of the apostles, a spirit of power, as well as of love. The allusion to Jannes and Jambres compared with Acts xiii, 7, 8; xv, 12, seems also to imply that signs and wonders like those of Moses accompanied the preaching of the Gospel. The statements in the Epistle to the Hebrews, on the other hand, where rebuke and censure are needed, become explicit and full once more. "How shall we escape, if we neglect so great a salvation, which at the first began to be spoken by the Lord, and was confirmed to us by them that heard him; God also bearing them witness, with signs and wonders, and divers miracles, and gifts of the Holy Ghost according to his own will?" "It is impossible for those who were once enlightened, and have tasted the good word of God, and the powers of the world to come, if they shall fall away, to renew them again to repentance." "He that despised Moses' law died without mercy under two or three witnesses: of how much sorer punishment shall he be thought worthy who hath done despite to the Spirit of grace?" Heb. ii, 3–5; vi, 4; x, 28.

It is needless to pursue the inquiry further. The claim to a miraculous and supernatural character, on the part of our Lord and his apostles, runs clearly through the whole of the New Testament, and coheres inseparably with its historical narrative, its doctrinal teaching, and practical exhortations. It appears conspicuous in the whole course of the four Gospels, from the birth of our Lord to his resurrection and ascension into heaven. It continues, with the same frequency and fullness, throughout the apostolic history, from the hour of the ascension to the voyage and shipwreck of the apostle of the Gentiles, and his arrival at the metropolis of the Gentile world. In the Epistles it is present throughout, but usually as a latent assumption, which needed no express and direct statement. But in proportion as the authority of the apostle is resisted, or sinful practices have to be rebuked, or doctrinal declensions exposed, the claim reappears; and it is made most strongly in those very cases where the assertion would be evident madness, if it were not undeniably true. It is a weapon sheathed in the presence of friends, but drawn from its scabbard whenever vice has to be rebuked, error resisted, or doubts of the apostle's authority reduced to silence.

The result of this review must be plain. A supernatural claim is of the essence of Christianity. Whenever this is rejected, the nature of the message is changed; the heart is torn out from it, and its life expires. It ceases to be the Word of God, and acquires, by fatal necessity, the very opposite character. It becomes a system of human fraud and imposture, or a strange, inexplicable mass of lunacy and mental derangement. Our Lord and his apostles must either have been messengers with a direct commission from God, or else they can have no title to retain the character even of honest, upright, and reasonable men. They must either be condemned to an asylum, or else obeyed with reverence, because they are seen to be clothed with supernatural and Divine authority.

CHAPTER IV.

THE REASONABLENESS OF MIRACLES.

THE prophets of the Old Testament, and the apostles of the New, and One greater than both—the Lord Jesus Christ himself, agree in appealing to miracles to prove themselves teachers and messengers sent from God. The commission of Moses, as recorded in the law, began with a formal statement of this principle of Divine revelation. "It shall come to pass, if they will not believe thee, nor hearken to the voice of the first sign, that they will believe the voice of the latter sign." The rejection of this evidence is declared to be the reason why an unbelieving generation were shut out from the land of promise. "Because all those men which have seen my glory, and my miracles which I did in Egypt and in the wilderness, have tempted me now these ten times and not hearkened to my voice; surely they shall not see the land which I swore unto their fathers." The language of our Lord in the Gospels is exactly the same: "Woe unto thee, Chorazin; woe unto thee, Bethsaida; for if the mighty works which were done in you, had been done in Tyre and Sidon, they would have repented long ago in sackcloth and ashes. But it shall be more tolerable for Tyre and Sidon in the day of judgment than for you." The lesson taught in these direct and solemn warnings to the cities of Galilee is repeated in his secret instructions to his own disciples on the eve of his departure. "If I had not done among them the works which no other man did, they had not had sin; but now have they both seen and hated both me and my father." So also St. Paul writes to the Corinthians, appealing to the same proof of Divine authority. "Truly the signs of an apostle were wrought among you in all patience, in signs, and wonders, and mighty deeds." In another epistle the same truth appears once more in its aspect of solemn warning. "For if the word spoken by angels was steadfast—how shall we escape, if we neglect so great salvation, which at the first began to be spoken by our Lord, and was confirmed to us by those that heard him; God also bearing them witness, with signs, and wonders, and divers miracles; and gifts of the Holy Ghost, according to his own will?"

This view of miracles, as the proper and reasonable tests of a Divine message, though affirmed by prophets and apostles, and our Lord himself, and consequently received by all the advocates of Christian faith, both in ancient and modern times, has been recently questioned or contradicted by some who have not openly renounced the Christian name. They allege that the progress of science has introduced insuperable difficulties into the admission of any suspense or reversal of the laws of Nature.* Miracles, in their opinion, are no longer the evidence, but rather the stumbling-blocks and incumbrances of a professed revelation.† The faculty of faith has now turned inward, and can not accept any outer manifestations of the truth of God.‡ Narratives inherently incredible can not change their nature, or become credible, by the supposition that they fulfill some religious purpose.§ The region of physical change, then, must be given up to the unbroken and undisturbed dominion of natural laws; and our faith in spiritual truth must rest on moral grounds, or acts of pure reason, without the least dependence on external testimony.

---

* Essays and Reviews, Essay iii, p. 104.   † P. 140.
‡ Essay i, p. 24.   § Essay ii, p. 83.

It has thus become needful to examine whether these modern Christians, by means of their superior attainments in physical science, and metaphysical speculation, have really been able to convict their Lord and his apostles of direct falsehood or grievous folly, in that appeal to the evidence of miracles, as conclusive tests of a Divine mission, which they have plainly and repeatedly made.

The objections which have been lately urged against the usual view of the Christian evidence are of three kinds. They relate, first, to the temper, style, and tone of the advocates of Christianity; secondly, to the credibility of miracles in themselves; and, thirdly, to their suitableness and sufficiency, as proofs and tests of a Divine revelation. Objections of the first kind are preliminary, but still deserve some notice and reply. The others enter into the heart of the whole subject, and involve the whole controversy between Christian faith and a spirit of utter and hopeless disbelief. I will examine each of them in order.

I. The tendency of objections of the first class is to prejudge the whole subject, by creating an impression of habitual unfairness and insincerity, or of secret doubt, on the part of the defenders of Christianity. Their usual tone, we are informed, is that of "the special partisan and ingenious advocate," and not of the unbiased judge. It is one of polemical acrimony, and settled and inveterate prejudice. There is a disposition to triumph in lesser details, rather than to grasp comprehensive principles. While infidel objections may have been urged in an offensive manner, there is often, in Christian writers, a want of sympathy with difficulties which many inquirers seriously feel in admitting the evidences of the Gospel. An appeal to argument implies perfect freedom to receive or reject the conclusion. It is absurd to reason with men, and anathematize them if not convinced by the reasoning, to make honest doubts a proof of moral obliquity, and denounce men as skeptics because they are careful to discriminate truth from error. The distinction between questions of external fact and of moral truth has been extensively overlooked and kept out of sight. Advocates of historical evidence inconsistently make their appeal to conscience and feeling; while upholders of faith and moral conviction, with equal inconsistency, regard the external facts of revelation as not less essential truth, which it would be profane to question.*

It is alleged further, that it is the common language of orthodox writings to advise men not to seek for precise answers to objections and difficulties, but to regard the whole subject as one which ought to be exempt from scrutiny, and received with silent submission. Their frequent reply is, that we are not to expect demonstrative evidence, that we must be content with probabilities, that exact criticism is always sure to rake up difficulties, that cavilers find new objections when the first are refuted, and reason can not be convinced unless the conscience and will are disposed to accept the truth. Thus the inquiry is removed from the ground of truth and honesty to one of practical expedience; objections are treated as profane, and exceptions dismissed, as shocking and immoral, without an answer.†

Now, it can not be doubted that on this subject, just as in many others of inferior moment, the zealotry of unscrupulous partisans, bent only on silencing an opponent, or gaining a cheap reputation for orthodoxy and controversial ability, may sometimes counterfeit the earnestness of a genuine faith. The description, however, when applied generally to the modern advocates of Christianity, is a se-

---

* Essays and Reviews, Essay iii, pp. 95-98. † Essay iii, pp. 96-100.

rious calumny. The arrogance which partially disfigures the writings of a Bentley or a Warburton is the exception, and not the rule. An opposite charge may be made with more truth against Paley and other apologists of the last century. Their treatment of an inquiry so vital to the highest interests of men, however clear, is, perhaps, too cold and passionless. Though mere earnestness is a bad substitute for strict reasoning, yet on a subject which involves the welfare of souls and issues of eternal life and death, we can not be reasonable unless we are earnest—so earnest as to shock the taste of mere intellectual theorists, and disturb the deathlike placidity of their speculations. The tone of calm, cold, abstract philosophizing, which the objection seems to prescribe to such discussions, has no sanction in the practice of the apostles. Their maxim was widely different—"Knowing, therefore, the terrors of the Lord, we persuade men." St. Paul, it is clear, had not made the modern discovery that it is absurd to appeal to men's reason, and still to warn them of their guilt and danger, when they refuse to yield to the force of evidence, and thus reject the message of the Gospel. His own practice was based on the opposite maxim, that in proportion to the strength of the reasons which prove the reality of a Divine message, must be the guilt of those who, under any pretext whatever, set aside its authority and reject its claims.

It is no doubt a serious fault, and a great stumbling-block to inquirers, when professed champions of revealed religion betray the tone of unscrupulous advocates, who are contending for victory alone. But it is no less unseemly, either for the inquirer or the believer, to affect the character of an unbiased judge. Such a pretension betrays in itself a bias of the worst kind, because it involves a plain denial of one of the simplest truths of the Gospel. Christianity does not appeal to us as a culprit, to be cleared from a charge of imposture and mendicancy before the tribunal of our superior wisdom. We have to plead at the bar of Christ, not Christ at ours. He appeals to our reason; but from above, not from beneath; as a judge, a physician, a father pleads with a culprit, a patient, or a child. For any of these parties to claim the character of an unbiased judge, because their obedience requires some exercise of judgment on their own part, would be a ridiculous affectation. If the Gospel be true, no one to whom it is fully made known can reject it, unless from the strong bias of "an evil heart of unbelief;" and no one truly receives it unless by the expulsive power of a new affection. They must have yielded to an influence still more powerful than sensual appetite or the pride of false reason—the mighty attraction of the Cross, and the constraining power of the love of Christ.

An appeal to argument implies a natural capacity in those to whom it is made to apprehend the force of sound reasoning. But it does not imply a state of entire equilibrium and strict moral indifference. It would then have to be confined to some distant world, and could have no place in our intercourse with sinful men. Even among philosophers and metaphysicians, since their speculations began, there has never been a case of pure, abstract, colorless indifference to the truth or falsehood of Christianity. The words of Christ make no exception either for skeptics, philosophers, or divines. "He that is not for me is against me, and he that gathereth not with me scattereth abroad." Neutrality here is strictly impossible. It is quite consistent and reasonable, then, to set before the inquirer or the unbeliever the evidences of the Christian revelation; and still, when these are rejected after their full exhibition, to ascribe that rejection to a moral obliquity, possibly quite unsuspected by themselves, and thus to refuse the flattering title of honest doubt to their culpable unbelief. This implies, it is true, that the skeptic, in many cases, is "no judge of his own mind;" but it does not imply, on the part of the Christian advocate, any claim to omniscience and infallibility. It simply proves that he has more faith in the true sayings of Christ than in the self-knowledge of those who reject the messages of their Maker, and flatter themselves that the only reason is their scrupulous care to avoid imposture and delusion. The disclaimer of all moral bias by the skeptic who refuses to own the authority of Christ, however sincerely made, is only one ingredient in his unbelief. The Christian advocate who admits the claim, in order to acquire a reputation for superior candor, only shares in the guilt, since he disowns a truth which is clearly revealed in the Word of God.

A second charge brought against many advocates of Christianity is a neglect of the wide distinction between questions of external fact, and of internal, moral, and religious truth. They digress irregularly, it is said, from one subject into the other. They mingle a moral element with their treatment of the evidence for the facts of Christianity; or when they urge the moral claims of the Christian faith, they include in their view of it the historical facts of the creed along with ideas of the pure reason.* The fact must be allowed that such a union and interchange of topics does continually occur. But the question remains whether it is the advocates of Christian faith or their critic and censor who betrays a grievous blindness to the lessons of daily experience, of sound philosophy, and of Christian truth.

---

* Essays and Reviews, Essay iii, pp. 97, 98.

Let us begin with the simple analogy which is suggested by the very form of the objection. The Christian religion has external facts and internal principles; it has a body and a soul. Is it a great error to treat them as if joined together in closest union? Christianity must be slain before we can turn it into a disembodied spirit. Is it a fault in the psychologist who treats of the human mind to spend chapters on the five senses—on touch, and taste, and hearing, sight, and smell—all of which involve a direct reference to the body, and are inseparable from it? Is it a fault in the physician who prescribes for a dangerous fever to direct that the mind of the patient should be kept free, if possible, from causes of excitement that would aggravate the disease, and make it more dangerous? Is it confusion of thought when a treatise on the preservation of bodily health is connected with moral lessons on the benefit of chastity and temperance? Or is it a culpable irregularity when the connection is traced, either by the physician or the moralist, between the indulgence of vice and exposure to fatal disease? If not, then analogy alone refutes the objection so hastily and superficially brought against the advocates of revelation.

Let us examine the subject, next, by the light of reason. Is it unreasonable to introduce a moral element at all in discussing the external evidences of Christianity? To justify this view, three assumptions must be made: that there are no moral obstacles to be overcome in those to whom these evidences are addressed; that no moral feature enters into the miracles of Christ and his apostles, or into the predictions of the Bible, and adds immensely to their force as evidence; and, finally, that there is no moral aim in the message itself, to which the outward evidence is entirely subordinate. Unless all these assumptions were true, the objection is clearly baseless and unreasonable. But every one of them is exactly the reverse of the truth. The only wonder is how any one with the lowest pretensions to the faculty of reasoning could impute a fault to a number of able and thoughtful writers, which implies his own ignorance or neglect of the simplest analogies of daily life, and of the most prominent feature in the miracles of the Gospel.

There is still a third, and a higher test, which may be applied to this strange censure of so many Christian writers, because they have yielded to a clear necessity of commonsense and sound reason. We may appeal to an authority which all Christians are bound to revere. How did Christ and his apostles treat the external evidences and the moral elements of the message they delivered to mankind? Did they part them from each other by a wall of separation? Did they jealously avoid any mixture of a moral element in their statement of the outward facts of the Gospel, or any mention of the outward facts in their moral appeal to the conscience? Plainly and notoriously, their conduct was just the reverse. Far from being at pains to separate these two elements, as the objection prescribes, they labor to unite them closely together. Their intermarriage is a feature conspicuous on almost every page both of the Old and New Testament. There is scarcely a fact announced, but some great moral truth beams out from beneath it, and lights it up with a deeper significance. There is scarcely a precept or a promise, a doctrinal statement, or an utterance of devotion, but some historical allusion is mingled with it, so as to give it a firmer hold on the affections, and translate it from a mere abstraction into a living reality of Divine Providence. The Sermon on the Mount, for example, abounds in every part with distinct and specific historical allusions. Its usual title is borrowed from the place where it was uttered, a mountain in Galilee. It was addressed to the disciples, and to multitudes "from Judea,

Decapolis, and Tyre, and Sidon." It refers to all the persecutions of the prophets under the Old Testament, to the giving of the law by Moses, and a variety of precepts, therein contained, to the daily facts of providence, the sunshine and the rain from heaven, to the tax-gatherers of Palestine, to the long and pretentious prayers of the Pharisees, to the birds of heaven, and the lilies of the field, to the natural habits of the dogs and the swine, to the whole range of earlier revelations in the law and the prophets, to the number of the unbelieving and profane, and the fewness of the faithful, to trees and their fruits, to outward miracles wrought by false disciples, to the wonder of the people at our Lord's teaching, and its contrast with the teaching of the Jewish scribes. All these are external elements, united inseparably with one of the purest and simplest exhibitions of moral and spiritual truth.

The union, then, of external facts with moral elements, in writing on the Christian evidences, is justified by the clearest analogies, by sound reason, and by examples which every Christian is bound to revere. The only ground of surprise is how any one, claiming the character of a philosopher or a Christian, can make a charge against the judgment of others which implies his own equal rejection of the plainest lessons of natural reason and of Christian faith.

The objection brought against many advocates of revelation, that they counsel an evasion of difficulties rather than an attempt at their solution, and a willingness to rest on probable evidence alone, with a certain submissiveness of the conscience and will, is less easy to answer; and there are cases in which it has a foundation in justice and truth. It is clear that, in subjects of this kind, a willingness to be taught, and the absence of a settled purpose to find excuses for unbelief, is a moral prerequisite for the acceptance of the message of the Gospel. It is also certain that where strict demonstration is not attainable, we are bound to act upon mere probability; and that whenever there is a desire to multiply difficulties, occasions for cavil and objection will never cease to be found. They are like the heads of the fabled hydra, and when one is cut off, a dozen more will appear in its stead. But still it can not be denied that som professed antidotes of skepticism are not unlikely to aggravate the disease they seek to cure, by seeming to transfer their advocacy of revelation from the ground of definite and intelligible reason to a vague, undefined religious sentiment. Men are urged to believe, simply because unbelief leaves a painful vacuum in the heart; with a faith arising from no calm conviction of the judgment, but from a mere effort and determination of the will. A faith so produced can scarcely be genuine. It does not meet difficulties in the face, but merely shuts its eyes, and endeavors not to see them. The effect of such a tone, in the advocates of Christianity, on the minds of thoughtful but perplexed inquirers, can hardly fail to be pernicious. Advice to cast off skeptical doubts and suggestions by a mere effort of will may sometimes only aggravate the disease which it attempts to cure.

On the other hand, no sounder advice can be given to those whose faith is unfixed, but who profess a sincere desire after religious truth, than to fix their thoughts, first of all, on the direct and central evidences of Christianity. They do well to delay any attempt at solving particular difficulties, or settling knotty questions as to the correctness of the Scripture canon, the mode and degrees of inspiration, the seeming discrepancies of the Gospels, or the propriety of New Testament quotations; till they have come to a clear and firm decision on the main subject, whether Christ is indeed a teacher come from God, and the Bible, at least in substance, a true record of real messages from the God of heaven. There is no difficulty in detail for which the humble and thoughtful Christian may not expect to find a solution, partly even in this life, and wholly in the life to come. But in the pursuit of Divine knowledge, just as in natural science, there is an order and discipline which must be observed, and the neglect of which will be punished with total failure. The student would vainly strive to master the Principia of Newton, or the Mecanique Celeste, who has not first stooped to learn Euclid and the Elements of the Differential Calculus. Even when these elements have been mastered, the ascent must be gradual, or real knowledge will elude the grasp, and the demonstrations that bring delight and conviction to the well-prepared student, become a heap of incomprehensible verbiage to those who strive to enter into their meaning without submitting to the needful preparation. The case of Christian inquirers is exactly similar. A humble and patient spirit brings the key which will unlock, by degrees, a thousand mysteries, and solve a thousand enigmas in the Word of God, or in the course of providence. But pride and impatience are like a picklock, and the wards are so constructed by Divine art as to resist and defeat all unlawful violence. Even those who bring the key with them must often be content to wait; and the solution of each particular doubt or difficulty may depend on the previous solution of others, which come earlier in the pathway of truth. The ways of heavenly wisdom "are all plain to him that understandeth, and right unto them that find knowledge." But, however obnoxious the truth may be to the pride of philosophy, without a moral preparation, without a humble and teachable spirit, mere intellectual cleverness is here of little avail The death-knell of its presumptuous hopes may be heard in that solemn utterance of the Son of God: "I thank thee, O Father, Lord of heaven and earth, because thou hast hid these things from the wise and prudent, and hast revealed them unto babes. Even so, Father, for so it seemed good in thy sight."

From these preliminary objections let us turn to the two main topics, which have been involved in no little mist— the credibility of miracles in themselves, and their sufficiency and limits as real proofs and tests of a Divine revelation.

II. The difficulties respecting miracles in general, or suspensions of natural law, have assumed, it is said, a much deeper importance in our own time. The credibility of alleged events, and the value of testimony, must be estimated by a reference to the fixed laws of belief, and our convictions of established order and analogy. In appreciating the evidence for any events of a wonderful kind, our prepossessions have an enormous influence. We look at them through the medium of our prejudices. The more remarkable any occurrence, the more unprepared we are to view it calmly. Disbelief of an event by no means implies a denial of the honesty or veracity of the impression on the minds of its witnesses. It means merely that the probability of some mistake, somewhere, is greater than that of the event happening in the way or from the causes assigned. What is alleged is a case of the supernatural; and on testimony reaches to the supernatural, but only to apparent sensible facts. That these are due to supernatural causes depends on the previous belief or assumption of the parties who observe them. If any strange, unaccountable fact were observed at the present day, an unbiased, educated person would not doubt for a moment, if a physical student, that it was due to some natural cause, and might at some future time be explained by the advance of discovery. Miracles therefore, are now discredited, and have become really incredible. This result has arisen from growing study of the phenomena of the natural world. The inductive philosophy is based on one grand truth, the universal order and constancy of natural causes. This is a primary law of belief, so firmly fixed in the mind of every truly-inductive inquirer, that he can not even conceive the possibility of its failure. An opposite view can arise only from want of power to grasp the positive scientific idea of the order of nature. Its boundaries exist only where our present knowledge places them; to-morrow's discoveries will enlarge them. The progress of research will unravel what seems now most marvelous, and what is now least understood will hereafter be familiarly known.

"A miracle," it is continued, "means something at variance with nature and law. There is no analogy between it and a mere unknown phenomenon, or an exceptional case of a known law included in a larger, still unknown. Arbitrary interposition is wholly different in kind. Imagined suspensions of the vast series of dependent causation are now inconceivable, from our enlarged critical and inductive study of the natural world. These are the principles we should apply to marvelous events in common history and at the present day. But the attempt to claim an exceptional character for the Gospel records forfeits or tampers with their historical reality. Those who would shield them from the criticism, to which all history and fact are amenable, force upon us the alternative of a mythical interpretation."

An appeal here to the Divine Omnipotence, it is said, is out of place. "That doctrine is an inference from the language of the Bible, and is founded on the assumption of our belief in revelation. And besides, it admits of being applied in an opposite way. Our ideas of Divine perfection tend to discredit the notion of occasional interference. It is derogatory to infinite power and wisdom to suppose an order of things so imperfect that it must be interrupted and violated to provide for the emergency of a revelation. All such reasonings, if pushed to their limits, must lead to a denial of all active operation of the Deity, as inconsistent with unchangeable and infinite perfection."*

Such is the philosophical objection against the miracles of the Law and the Gospel in its more recent and popular form. In the eyes of the thoughtful Christian, it lies open at once to a *prima facie* suspicion of entire falsehood, of the most formidable and decisive kind. It agrees punctually with an apostle's definition, eighteen centuries ago, of the form of presumptuous unbelief that would mark the last days of the Church of Christ, and ripen scoffers for the severest strokes of Divine judgment. He even requires us to place this truth very early in our list of Christian lessons, to be treasured up for our own guidance. "Knowing this *first*, that there will come in the last days, scoffers. walking after their own lusts, and saying, Where is the promise of his coming? for since the fathers fell asleep, all things continue as they were from the beginning of the creation. For this they willingly are ignorant of, that by the Word of God the heavens were of old." The theory, as thus described to us long ago, has by no means an attractive genealogy. It is born, according to the apostle, from willful ignorance of the Creator; its twin children are sensuality and scoffing; and its final issue is a solemn and terrible judgment.

Let us inquire, however, apart from the testimony of apostles, what claim this doctrine has to be received on the ground of philosophy alone. It is made up of mere assumptions, and even self-contradictions, of the most unphil-

---

* Essays and Reviews, Essay iii, pp. 107–114.

osophical kind. It involves a false view of induction, a false conception of the order of nature and the constancy of its laws, a false definition of miracles, and a denial of special features which plainly attach to every real or supposed message of religious truth, immediately conveyed from God to man.

First, the view of induction which this objection implies is unphilosophical and untrue. Inductive research and mathematical deduction are different, and even contrasted. both in their processes and results. The deduction of pure science is the development of truths, or results of a hypothesis, which are necessarily true, or the contrary of which involves a self-contradiction. Such are the truths that the three angles of a triangle are equal to two right angles, or the rectangles of the segments of intersecting chords equal, or that every prime number of the form $4n+1$ is the sum of two squares. But induction ascends from observed facts to generalizations of fact, or actual laws. It includes three stages: the accumulation of observed phenomena; the development of some hypothesis for their explanation; and the correction or confirmation of the hypothesis, by collating its results with the whole series of observations. The middle step is here borrowed from pure, or deductive reasoning. But the two others are of an opposite kind. The observations are known to be true, simply by testimony, or the evidence of our senses, and contrary or different facts are equally conceivable. The law obtained, being merely the sum and integration of the separate phenomena, shares in the same character. It is true, but not necessary. We believe it on the joint evidence of testimony to certain facts, and of deductive reasoning from a proposed hypothesis; but the result can not rise higher in certainty than the weaker of its two components. It is credible on the ground of repeated or multiplied testimonies to the facts which agree with it. But the deviation of other facts from it is equally conceivable, equally credible upon due evidence, and our faith in the law would receive at once a new limitation. In short, all such laws are provisional, not necessary truths, a summation of facts which might have been different. We can easily believe, on credible testimony, of their apparent suspension or reversal, in particular cases, either by the intersection of some higher law, or by some directly spiritual and supernatural agency. We can even conceive, without much difficulty, of their total replacement by other laws entirely different.

It is thus a wholly false view of the nature of inductive science that it is occupied with the investigation and discovery of laws which are necessary and unalterable. The exact reverse is the truth. Deductive science alone is occupied with the development of necessary truth; but applied or inductive science deals with phenomena, and through these with laws, of which the essential feature is that they are not necessary, however real, and that they repose on the basis of multiplied testimonies; so that deviations from them, and even their reversal, are quite conceivable, and would demand our faith, if sustained by due evidence, on the very same principle on which the laws themselves are believed to exist.

Again, the objection involves a total misconception of the order of nature and the constancy of natural laws. It is true that the progress of physical science enables us, in these days, to refer many phenomena to some law or property of matter which were once inexplicable. We can not doubt, also, that further advances in the same direction will still be made. Other laws, hardly less wide than that of gravitation, may be discovered; and many things now mysterious, like the phenomena of comets, and the subtile and delicate movements of light and electricity, will be more clearly understood, and enlarge greatly the field of human knowledge. But this movement, by which the horizon of science perpetually recedes and enlarges, instead of proving the inflexible constancy of natural laws, in the sense which the objection requires, proves exactly the reverse. It transfers the certainty from the physical laws of nature, as now defined by our present knowledge, to the scheme of universal providence, as it lies open to the view of Omniscience, and thus resolves itself into a philosophical rendering of the great doctrine of the Bible, that "known unto God are all his works from the beginning of the world," and that in the counsels of Infinite Wisdom there is "no variableness, nor the shadow of turning." Our own experience reveals the constant action of the human will upon the human body, and upon all portions of matter that lie within the range of the muscular strength and physical powers of man. These are small, indeed, compared with the forces ever at work in the great cosmical system; but still their action, through successive ages, has wrought sensible effects even on the physical condition of whole regions of the earth. We should count it absurd to speak of mere physical law deciding the movements of the ball, the marble, or the orange, when once placed within the grasp of a human hand. Once let us conceive of spiritual beings whose power over matter bears the same proportion to ours as the orange to the mass of the earth, and the seeming immutability of physical law, even in the case of the planetary movements, would equally disappear. It would resolve itself at once into some higher law of the spiritual world. But we can have no proof from reason alone that no such creatures exist in the universe. Our proof is limited to the fact that for a certain number of years, as far as human testimony can reach, there has been no such gigantic interference with the regularity of the celestial motions, though the will of man interferes ceaselessly with all the products of nature on the surface of our own planet. But this contrast between the vastness of the starry world, and the narrow range of human volition, however conspicuous in fact, has no semblance whatever of being a necessary truth. We have no proof whatever, on grounds of pure reason, that the constancy for thousands of years of the planetary courses, undisturbed by spiritual agencies immensely more potent than the human will, is more than a counterpart, on a larger scale, to the quiet and silent growth of the corn in the harvest-field, till the hour when the husbandman "puts in his sickle because the harvest is come."

Thirdly, the objection involves also a false definition of miracles themselves. They are defined to be "something at variance with nature and law," suspensions of a known law, arbitrary interpositions, and events "isolated and uncaused." But none of these descriptions are correct. They are not, in the view of the Bible or of Christians, mere arbitrary interferences, but acts of Divine power, exerted for a special purpose, in harmony with a scheme of moral government, to which all physical laws whatever are also subordinate. They obey a moral and spiritual law of the Divine Wisdom, higher and nobler, but possibly no less clear and definite in its own sphere, than the law of gravitation itself. They are suspensions of known law, just as the law that bodies fall toward the earth is suspended when wood floats in water, or a balloon mounts toward the sky; or the law that a bell is sonorous is intercepted and suspended when it is rung in an exhausted receiver. The difference is not in the principle, but in the special cause of the suspension. In one case a lower physical law is intersected and reversed by another law, equally physical, but more extensive. In the other the same law is suspended and reversed by some spiritual agency, or a direct act and purpose of the Supreme Will.

The objection denies further that any special features of the Christian records will justify our departure from the general incredulity, with which the ascription of a miraculous character to any strange event would be regarded in the present age of scientific attainment. To regard them as an exceptional case, it is alleged, transfers them from the domain of genuine history to that of mere legend. But it is hard to understand by what obliquity of judgment an assertion so preposterous could be made. The exact reverse is self-evidently true. A professed message from God, which barely affirmed its own Divine origin, and was accompanied by no credentials worthy of its Author, such as the signs and wonders of the Law and the Gospel supply, would be open, without defense, to the charge of being a mere dream of the imagination, and might be transferred at once from the region of fact and real history to that of mere legend. Miracles answer here to the crucial tests of the inductive philosophy, and form the contrast between a tissue of mere human fancies and authentic messages from heaven, sealed with the royal signet of the King of kings.

Besides these errors, there is a deeper charge of self-contradiction, which lies against the whole tenor of this skeptical argument. Writers of this school, the disciples of the positive philosophy, when they would free physical science from the intrusion of metaphysics and religious faith, insist on the doctrine that our task, as students of nature, is confined to the discovery of laws, the mere generalization of classes of phenomena, and that causes lie completely beyond our reach; that their existence is doubtful, and their nature inconceivable. We know a series of events, of antecedents and consequents; but of secret links, named causes, which have been supposed to bind them together, we know, and can know, nothing. On this basis is raised a theory of negative atheism, that God may possibly exist, but that his existence must forever be uncertain, and is also needless for all the wants of human science. But when the miracles of the Gospel are to be set aside, and the supernatural banished from the thoughts of men, this reasoning is suddenly and completely reversed. These laws of nature, which before were nothing else than a summation of observed facts, are transformed into real causes, inflexible and unalterable as the fates of the old heathens, which admit neither God, nor angel, nor man, to interfere with their absolute and supreme dominion. What contradiction can be more gross and intolerable? The heathen, who cut down the cypress or the oak of the forest, hewed and squared it into decent shape, and, after using part to cook his food, turned the rest into an idol, and bowed down before it, was only a type of the more pretentious, but not less foolish, course of this unbelieving philosophy. Its disciples hew and carve the phenomena of nature, and turn the chips and parings, the secondary laws of art and of applied science, into passive instruments that minister to the comfort of human life. All the rest of those laws, though equally perishable in themselves, but a little more firm and massive in appearance, they invest with the attributes of Divinity. These are fixed, unalterable, eternal, incapable of being varied by the will of man, or by the power of the living God. The worship of such speculators, so far as they worship at all, is paid to this system of physical law, and to that alone. They fall down before it, like the old heathen before his wooden idol or molten image, and say, "Deliver me, for thou art my god." And there is little doubt, if one of the old prophets were to rise again, that he would pronounce over them once more that indignant sentence, "They have not known nor understood; for he hath shut their eyes, that they can not see, and their hearts, that they can not understand."

III. The third class of objections refer to the sufficiency of miracles as the proofs and tests of a Divine revelation. And here it is urged that their force must be only relative, and depend on the knowledge or ignorance of those to whom they appeal. The miracle of an ignorant age ceases to be such in an age of greater light. Columbus's prediction of an eclipse was supernatural to the islanders of the Antilles. Some have, therefore, applied to them the Greek proverb, that they are "marvels for fools," and supposed it equivalent with the rebuke of the evil generation, who sought after a sign. Schleiermacher held them to be only relative to the notions of the age. The Pharisees ascribed them to evil spirits, and the later Jews to a theft of the ineffable name. Signs may thus be suited to one age or one class, and not to others. Miracles, which would now be incredible, were not so in the age when they are said to have occurred. Evidence, which might be convincing and powerful to an age of ignorance, may have only an injurious influence when urged in these days, with whose scientific conceptions it is at variance. Where there is an indiscriminate belief of the supernatural, or where it is wholly disbelieved, the allegation of particular miracles will be equally in vain. Some recent writers have held that revelation ought to be received, though destitute of strict evidence either internal or external. Others have strongly denied that historical testimonies can be justly styled the evidences of Christianity. Whenever, instead of miracles being the sole certificate of the message, the force of evidence is made to lie in their union with the internal excellence of the doctrine, the latter becomes the real test for the admission of the former. Such a principle appears in the Bible itself, since false prophets might predict signs and wonders, which might also come to pass; and false Christs and false prophets, under the Gospel, by similar miracles, almost deceive the very elect. What is the value of faith at second-hand? Many Christian writers have held a right of appeal, superior to all miracles, to our own moral tribunal, as De Wette, Doderlein, and others. Thus all outward attestation would seem superfluous, if it concur with these moral convictions, or to be rejected if it oppose them. And hence the general conclusion is reached, that "the more knowledge advances, the more Christianity, as a real religion, must be viewed apart from connection with physical things."

There are here two important questions, much controverted even among Christian divines, which need some patient thought before they can receive a distinct answer. How far is the evidence of miracles real and absolute, or only relative to the ignorance of those who witness them? What is the connection, also, between external and internal evidence? Do miracles alone, and apart from every moral test, form a complete attestation of a Divine message? Or do they need rather to be joined with some moral evidence before they can be received as decisive? Christian writers, as Wardlaw and Trench, have given opposite replies to these questions. It becomes the more needful to use caution in seeking to answer them. The truth, if once clearly defined and explained, will, perhaps, spare the necessity of sifting the divergent statements of Christian apologists. It will then be needless to pursue the skeptical argument in detail through the pages of an essay, which pretends to throw new light on the study of the evidences, and seems only to wrap the subject in mist and confusion, that it may securely undermine the old foundations of the Christian faith

The reply to the first of these questions must plainly depend on the true definition of a miracle. If it be simply the suspension or reversal of the known laws of nature, then it must clearly be relative to our varying knowledge of those laws; and events miraculous in one age, or to one class, may cease to be so in a later age, or among better-instructed men. If it be a direct act of God, in contrast to all agency of second causes, and by an exercise of power strictly and exclusively Divine, then its nature is absolute and not relative, and must remain the same to all classes, and in every age of the world.

The latter view has been adopted by many Christian writers in their works on the evidence of revelation. It seems to have the advantage of simplifying the argument; since miracles, thus defined, must plainly be a decisive proof that the message they accompany is Divine. But this seeming benefit is more than counterbalanced by the loss. On such a view it must be impossible to know when a miracle has been wrought, unless we could know all the possible results of second causes, in their most unusual combination, or define the limits of power which may belong to superhuman, but created intelligence. Now this is a knowledge which no one has ever attained, even with our actual advances in science, and amidst all the light of revelation. How much less can it be the condition on which the evidence for the truth of that revelation is made to depend! No definition of miracles can leave them available as the proper tests of a Divine message, which requires a knowledge, both of God and of nature, quite beyond the attainments of those to whom the message is given.

The following view is free from this fatal objection. Miracles, as evidence, may be immediate, mediate, or improper. Immediate miracles are those which satisfy the last definition, or distinct and immediate actings of the

THE REASONABLENESS OF MIRACLES. 85

Great First Cause, apart from all second causes whatever. The resurrection of our Lord is an instance which seems clearly to belong to this first and highest category. Mediate miracles are those wrought by some unusual and supernatural power bestowed on a Divine messenger. The miracles of our Lord himself, as the Son of man, may be correctly referred to this class, and still more undeniably those of his apostles. They were not immediate acts of the Divine power alone, but are distinctly ascribed to a gift imparted to them as God's messengers. "He gave them power over unclean spirits, to cast them out, and to heal all manner of sickness and of disease." "Behold, I give unto you power to tread on serpents and scorpions, and on all the power of the enemy." A deputed and real power, then, can not be denied without contradicting Scripture, and the adoption of a line of reasoning which destroys the distinction between miracles and common events, by resolving all alike into the ceaseless operation of the First Cause alone. Improper miracles are those which result from rare and unusual combinations of second causes. In these foresight, and not power, is the really-supernatural element. The plague of the locusts, the feeding with quails, and even the destruction of the cities of the plain, may probably be referred to this class. In each case second causes, already in being, were clearly employed; and it is not certain that more was needed than a prearrangement, by Divine Wisdom, of special conditions for their combined action. The effect on those who saw the events would be equally miraculous, and create a full persuasion of the presence of the mighty hand of God.

These three kinds of miracles, however distinct in their definition, it may be impossible in many cases to distinguish from each other. Their value, as evidence, can not then depend upon such a discrimination having been previously made. We need a practical definition which shall include them all, and bring into relief that common feature on which their strength as evidence for a Divine revelation depends.

Miracles, then, viewed as evidences for revelation, are "unusual events not within the ordinary power of man, nor capable of being foreseen by man's actual knowledge of second causes, and wrought or announced by professed messengers of God, to confirm the reality of their message." The definition has a negative and a positive element. There must be no second causes, or at least none within human knowledge, that will account for the event; and there must be an apparent connection with some plain moral object or some professed message from God. Whenever these two conditions meet, we have a case of miraculous evidence. Some of these, by the progress of science in later times, might come within the range of man's actual power over nature, or his insight into natural changes, and would then cease to be miraculous; while others may surpass not only human, but superhuman power, and imply a direct exercise of the Divine Omnipotence.

The use of miracles as evidence, like the need itself for supernatural revelation, depends on the doctrine of the Fall. It results from the dimness and blindness of the heart of man in all spiritual things. In a perfect state, all second causes would be referred instinctively to the will of God, and all nature be translucent with the Maker's presence. Miracles, in their strangeness and peculiarity, would cease to exist. All we behold would be miracle. Even the direct converse of the Word of God with his sinless creatures would only be the crown and top-stone of one harmonious system of communion among men and angels, and all the holy creatures of God. But when, through the power of sin, creation has grown opaque to the eyes of men, and the physical course of nature has concealed the presence of the great Lawgiver, miracles are needed, to form an antidote to blind nature-worship, and undo the subtile spell of unbelief. This end may be secured, either by acts of Divine power, suspending or reversing the laws of nature; or else by combining these in such an unusual way, and with so clear a moral purpose, as to force the conviction on reluctant minds that Nature is only a servant and handmaid of the living God, who is the moral governor of the universe.

The evidence, then, of miracles, in the widest sense of the term, may in some cases be only relative to the knowledge of those who witness them. Still there are few, if any, of those recorded in the Bible, which lie so near to this inferior limit as to be really affected in their evidential power by the discoveries of modern science, and the increase of man's power over the works of God. Even supposing some of the plagues of Egypt to have been effected simply by a preadjustment of second causes, no reach of science, even now, could enable the wisest philosopher to rival Moses, and to predict the coming of the scourge and the time of its removal. Our chemistry, with its immense discoveries, leaves the miracle at Cana as purely miraculous as in the hour when it was wrought; and the feeding of the five thousand remains till now, as clearly as ever, a work truly supernatural and Divine.

The evidence derived from miracles to confirm the truth of revelation needs thus no intrusion into the deep things of God, no exact discernment of limits which separate all created power and second causes from acts of Divine Omnipotence, in order to give it force and validity. It depends simply on the union of two conditions; that second causes, adequate to the result, either do not exist, or are hidden from view; and that a moral cause, as the exhibition of Divine power and holiness, or the confirmation of a Divine message, shall be plainly conspicuous. The words of the conscience-stricken magicians will then be applicable—"This is the finger of God." And the reasoning of our Lord will apply—"If I by the finger of God cast out devils, no doubt the kingdom of God is come upon you."

This leads to a second inquiry of equal importance. What is the relation between the external and internal evidence, between the miracles which attest a message, and the moral features of the alleged revelation? The path of truth seems here, as in many other cases, to lie almost midway between opposite extremes.

First, it is not the doctrine of Scripture that miracles alone, simply as miracles, are decisive proofs that any message or teaching they accompany is from God. The marvels of the Egyptian sorcerers who withstood Moses, the caution in the law against teachers of idolatry, whose signs and wonders should come to pass, the account of our Lord's temptation, his own warning against false prophets, whose great signs and wonders might almost deceive the elect, and other passages in the Epistles and Book of Revelation, conspire to teach an opposite lesson. It avails nothing to allege that wicked spirits can never attain to works properly Divine. Revelation would be needless, if men were already so wise as to know the highest possible reach of all created power, and instinctively to discern it from the workings of real Omnipotence. Indeed we have no proof that most of the miracles in the Bible require a higher power than its own promises assure to saints and angels in the kingdom of God; and the contrary may perhaps be implied, where miraculous gifts of the early Christians receive that impressive title—"the powers of the world to come."

The opposite extreme, however, that the goodness of

the message, discerned by the light within, is the real test of the admissibility of miracles, instead of miracles being the tests of the message itself, is still more remote from the truth. A conscience so enlightened beforehand as to decide at once on the wisdom or folly, the truth or falsehood of every part of a message that claims God for its author, can stand in no need of a direct revelation from heaven. The same moral blindness, which alone calls for the remedy of a supernatural message, unfits men entirely for the perilous task of sitting in judgment on the words of their Maker. To see truth in the light of God is not the state of those to whom either the Law or the Gospel is first given. It is the best and highest attainment of those who have received in faith the words of their Maker, and been trained by them to the full enjoyment of his presence; where faith is lost in sight, and provision for their journey through a land of moral pitfalls is exchanged for the gladness and glory of a heavenly inheritance.

Miracles of themselves simply attest the presence and working of a superhuman power. They do not, without some further test, prove that this power is that of the true and only God. The Bible affirms the existence of spirits of evil superior to men in natural power and wisdom, who must, therefore, be capable of working wonders, or predicting events and revealing secrets, beyond the range of mere human ability. Some further element, then, is required beyond mere signs and wonders, though apparently supernatural, to prove the doctrine or message to be Divine. And this test may be twofold—the greatness of the miracles themselves, or the moral features of the message when viewed as a whole. The first is the simplest; the second, the most decisive. Both of them rest alike on the voice of reason, and distinct examples in the Word of God. The Divine power must surpass the power of all spirits of evil; and if they are permitted to work seeming wonders, it seems reasonable to expect that the Lord of heaven and earth will merely suffer it so far as to illustrate more brightly his own supremacy and omnipotence. Again, though revelation would be useless, if men were able to pass judgment safely in detail on every part of a Divine message, such a degree of moral discernment as would enable them, on the whole, to discern good from evil, the message of a holy and benevolent Deity from the lying voice of spirits of darkness, must surely belong to all mankind who have not reached the worst and lowest stage of judicial blindness.

Now, both of these tests, which alone are needed to make the evidence of miracles adequate and complete, are distinctly recognized in the Bible history itself. The magicians of Egypt, so far as the words of Scripture are any guide, rivaled outwardly the signs of the first plagues and the previous wonders, with an inferiority in degree alone. After this limit their permitted power, or that of the false gods whose servants they were, failed them, and they were compelled to own, "This is the finger of God." Again, when a prophet spoke in the name of the Jehovah, the success or failure of the signs he gave was declared to be the test of his sincerity or falsehood in his claim to a Divine commission. But if a prophet or dreamer showed a sign or wonder to persuade the Israelites into idol-worship, even the success of the sign was to be no proof of his authority. On the contrary, it is declared to be merely permitted for the trial of their fidelity, and the teacher of falsehood and idolatry was to be put to death for his crime.

The words of Nicodemus in his secret interview with our Lord are quite consistent with the same view. The conclusion rested apparently not on the mere fact of miracles, but on their number or their greatness. "No man can do these miracles which thou doest, except God be with him." Our Lord himself assigns the same reason for the guilt of the Jews in rejecting him. It was not simply because miracles had been wrought, but greater miracles than by any of the prophets, and therefore in fullest harmony with the rank and character of the true Messiah. "If I had not done among them the works which no other man did, they had not had sin." The presence of miracles, then, simply and in itself, is not a completely-decisive proof of a Divine message. They may, in rare cases, accompany the permitted delusions of spirits of darkness. But miracles, striking and impressive in themselves, and not confronted by others still more miraculous, or when joined with a general impress of holiness in the message they attest, do form a complete and decisive evidence that the teaching is from God, and the revelation truly divine.

Let us now sum up the general result of this inquiry.

All science tends toward unity; but the true source of that unity can not be found within the boundaries of physical science alone. This vast ocean has its tides secretly controlled by a higher law than the currents and rippling of its own waves. The real unity consists in a scheme of moral government, guided and disposed in every part by the wisdom of the great Lawgiver, of which only a small part is disclosed to us in our present state. There is a partial unity in every compartment of nature, but this is limited by its subordination to a greater whole. Mechanical laws, which govern solid matter, are modified by the subtile influences of heat and electricity. These higher laws again are modified by vital action in all the forms of vegetable and animal life. All the lower forms of life upon earth, as well as all material objects, are controlled in various degrees by the reason and will of man. At this point in the ascent higher laws begin to appear—not of mechanical agency or physical sequence, but of moral government. Ideas force themselves upon our notice, of right and wrong, duty and disobedience, of sin and holiness, of reward and punishment. Beyond these there emerges to the view of faith, when enlightened by the Word of God, and by its echoes and reflections in the purified conscience, the glorious vision of a scheme of creation, providence, and redemption, which spans eternity in its range; begins from the foundation of the world; stretches forward into the ages to come; includes all events, small and great, within its own capacious bosom; and makes all the outward works of the Creator, from the stars of heaven to the cedar of Lebanon and the hyssop on the wall, subserve the mysterious counsels of Infinite Wisdom and Love.

The knowledge which man has attained, in any age of the world, of the laws of nature, is like an islet in the midst of this vast, undiscovered ocean of the counsels of the Most High. It gives him a firm standing-place for the active duties of his daily life, while its narrow limits teach him the duty of owning a higher power, and adoring with reverence at the footstool of his Almighty Creator. In a perfect moral state this limited and imperfect knowledge would never be a vail to hide from his eyes the presence and dominion of the Unseen King. But sin has darkened the human conscience; and ages of the world in which "many run to and fro, and knowledge is increased," may blind the eyes of men to the limitations of physical law, and its dependence on the higher purposes of God's moral government. They mistake this ocean islet—this narrow region of discovered physical laws, reared by the insect labors of thousands of men of science in successive generations—for that mightier world to which the islet itself, and the ocean that girdles it, equally belong. It becomes needful, then, either by the unexpected inference of other physical laws still undiscovered and unknown, by signal and secret arrangements of Providence, or by the direct agency of spiritual messengers higher than men, to break through the thick crust of atheism which has begun to darken the conscience; and to force on it anew the conviction that man is a creature subject to the control of an all-wise Creator, and that higher laws than the dull mechanism of unconscious matter, or the low instincts of animal life, enter into the mighty scheme of God's universal providence. This is the first and immediate effect of the τέρατα, or wonders, that herald and accompany the message of God.

But to arouse the attention, and disperse the atheistic blindness which worships dead nature, is only their first effect. They are signs as well as wonders, or significant attendants of some message from heaven, some moral truth which they partly convey of themselves, and partly confirm, as it flows from the lips of God's appointed messengers. The miracles of the Bible startle men from their apathy, but they also teach and signify some celestial truth. The Flood, the destruction of the cities of the plain, were messages of solemn anger against abounding sin. The smitten rock, from whence the water flowed at Rephidim, and the manna in the wilderness, were signs of a higher provision for the souls of men. The healing of the sick, the cleansing of lepers, the unstopping the ears of the deaf, the opening the eyes of the blind, the draught of fishes, the feeding of the multitudes, in our Lord's ministry, had all of them a deep moral significance. The little islet of known natural laws was invaded, its dull monotony was disturbed, and its tenants wakened up to wonder, curiosity, and eager inquiry, by a ship of heaven, laden with good news from a far country. But the ship had a firmness of its own, not less complete in its kind than the islet it was sent to visit, and its treasures were the products of a continent, far more rich in its extent than the self-satisfied but ignorant islanders could ever have dreamed of, before it anchored on their distant shore. The miracles of revelation are that ship of heaven. They have a system and structure of their own, adapted wonderfully to convey heavenly truth to the dwellers of earth, although the visit breaks through their contented slumber within the narrow region of sensible things. They seem, then, in themselves, like infractions on the dominion and permanence of the lower laws of nature, already known to men. But in truth they convey to them the products of a nobler and higher world of thought, of which the laws are equally firm, and even firmer, than those which the miracles seem to reverse, and are larger, wider, deeper, and nobler, unchangeable and everlasting. That higher world is the vast scheme and counsel of redeeming love. Its foundations are the attributes of Him who is unchangeable. Its hills and valleys are the wide range of moral and spiritual truth. Its rich productions are all those various lessons of duty, laws of holiness, and instincts of purity, wisdom, and grace, which will nourish and gladden the souls of the redeemed forever. Physical laws may be firm, but the moral laws of the Divine government are still firmer. The pillars of earth may tremble and be astonished; but no change can assail that city "which hath foundations, whose builder and maker is God."

CHAPTER V.

THE HISTORICAL TRUTH OF THE BIBLE.

THE Bible differs from all other ancient books, which have claimed a sacred origin, by its historical character. In this respect it stands alone. The Koran of Mohammed is simply a series of monologues; only a few Scripture narratives rhetorically disguised, or Arabian legends, interrupt the wearisome monotony of its religious appeals, invectives, and exhortations. The Hindoo Vedas are equally unhistorical. Learned students, with their utmost efforts, can only just infer from them, indirectly, the age when they were written. The same feature appears in the Zendavesta, and the Egyptian sacred writings and Ritual of the Dead. All of these flit before us like ghosts or disembodied spirits, and the garment of historical fact or allusion with which they are clothed is of the most thin and shadowy kind.

The Old and the New Testament agree in a common character precisely the opposite to these pretended revelations. They include the history of a long and connected series of events, of great, public, and notorious acts of Divine Providence. In each of them four-sevenths of the whole is simple narrative; and the other books also, whether didactic, devotional, or prophetic, with hardly one exception, are fixed by clear and internal marks to their own place in the history. This is the stem which supports them all, the Psalms, Proverbs, Canticles, and Prophets in the Old Testament, and the Epistles and Book of Revelation in the New. The Bible narrative, so simple and unadorned in itself, seems here, like the rod of Aaron, to bud and bring forth blossoms and yield almonds. In these other books only a few chapters are direct history; but still their connection with the historical portions is intimate, unbroken, and complete.

This character of the Bible is most favorable to the detection of its falsehood, or to the establishment of its truth. It multiplies greatly the tests which separate faithful testimony from the impostures of fraud and the mere illusions of fancy. Unreal history is too sandy a foundation on which to rear, with the least hope of success, a temple of pure and everlasting truth. Sincere and honest narratives, though slightly discordant or imperfect in a few minor details, might certainly be the means of conveying to us Divine messages of the highest worth and authority. But it is incredible that histories which would be condemned in all other cases as dishonest or worthless, legendary and deceptive in their broad outlines, should be the stem upon which are found to grow the blossoms and richest fruitage of heavenly wisdom. Men do not gather grapes of thorns, nor figs of thistles. A pure morality and theology can never be the fruit of dishonest and deceptive history. Once let the conviction spread that whole books of the Bible, and main portions of its narratives are gross, strange, and monstrous distortions of the real facts, or else mere legends containing no real facts whatever, and Christianity will have received a fatal death-wound in the minds of educated and thoughtful men.

The Pentateuch and the four Gospels are the historical basis, on which all the other Scriptures of the Old and of the New Testament entirely depend. Each has been exposed, of late years, to repeated and persevering charges of historical falsehood. Early forms of skepticism ripened at length, in Strauss's "Leben Jesu," into an attempt to dissolve the whole of the Gospels into a heap of fables, due entirely to the dreaming and inventive imagination of the early Christians. The cool audacity of the hypothesis, with the laborious minuteness of its detailed criticisms, created a momentary sensation; just as the tale of a lunatic may be so minute and particular in its various inventions as to make us almost forget for a time how preposterous it is. But this tide-wave has gone by, though some traces of it may be left behind. The Gospels are too recent in their date, too intensely real in their tone, too fruitful in historical consequences, to make it possible for so wild a theory to have more than a brief popularity among unbelievers themselves. The oscillation from naturalism into mythicism was followed inevitably by a backward movement into naturalism again. And indeed this uneasy alternation can never cease till the eyes of the soul are opened, like those of the blind man in the Gospel, and it learns to bow the knee in reverence and worship before the Son of God.

The attacks on the Pentateuch began earlier, and have been still more persevering. Skepticism had here many advantages which were entirely wanting in its assaults upon the Gospel history. The period itself is more remote by nearly two thousand years. The law, being a revelation originally for the Jews alone, has a much weaker hold than the Gospel on the faith and sympathy of the great body of modern Christians. Till quite lately, there were few collateral sources of information to be found, either in ancient monuments or heathen records. The efforts of unbelieving criticism were thus confined mainly to a dissection of the books themselves. From the time of Astruc onward, a long series of writers have labored to detect inconsistencies, to disprove the Mosaic authorship, and to transfer the broken fragments of the Pentateuch to various legend-makers, or compilers of loose tradition, under the Jewish kings. More recently the progress of discovery in the remains of Egypt, Assyria, Persia, and Babylon, has supplied far more copious materials for comparison with the histories of the Old Testament. Its later books have gained singular and unexpected confirmation from results of Assyrian and Babylonian research. But the effect of Egyptian discovery, in the comparison of the monuments with the books of Moses, is more controverted and ambiguous. Here also many facts, usages, and details in the sacred narrative are confirmed by the monuments in a striking manner. But on the main question of the general outline of the early history some learned students, while differing by whole centuries and millennia in their own reckonings, agree to set aside the book of Genesis as legendary and unhistorical, that they may replace it by their own views of the immense antiquity of Egyptian civilization. An attempt has lately been made to bring these supposed discoveries within the general reach of English readers in a popular form; and thus to destroy their faith in the veracity of those books of Moses, which form the historical basement of the whole series of the Jewish and Christian revelations.

It would be impossible, in a few pages, to enter into the details of an inquiry so immense and various. The Bible histories occupy seventeen books of the Old, and five of the New Testament, and spread over a space, at the lowest reckoning, of nearly four thousand years. Within this wide range, and with all the various materials amassed by modern research, hundreds, and almost thousands of questions may be raised, that would each require a chapter or small volume for their full discussion. Our knowledge of the earliest period is still so obscure, and the views both of those who reject the authority of the Pentateuch, and of those who maintain it, are so diverse, that a suspense of judgment on several important questions may be still the wisest course, even after the most careful use of all the existing evidence But a way lies open by which, in spite of some questions still unsolved, and confident assertions by a few men of science, agreed in rejecting Moses, but still at variance among themselves, we may come to a full assurance, in agreement with the plainest maxims of inductive philosophy, on the massive strength and solidity of the historical foundations of the Christian faith.

The great question which requires an answer is this: Have we any clear and full warrant for believing the veracity of the Bible historians, and the substantial truth of their narratives, however plainly intermingled with statements of supernatural events, and whatever minute discrepancies may seem at first sight to be detected by a rigid and searching inquiry? And here two prefatory remarks seem desirable before we proceed to consider the direct evidence of their truth.

First of all, the veracity of these writers is closely linked, in the general faith of Christians, with the doctrine of their special inspiration, and an implied belief of their freedom from all error in delivering the messages of God. This intimate union of two distinct ideas, however natural and desirable for the uses of practical piety, may become a snare and a source of perplexity in tracing out the reasonable grounds of our Christian faith. We may be charged with a circular and sophistical mode of reasoning; as if we believe the Scriptures inspired and infallible because a few texts seem to affirm it, and reckon these texts decisive evidence because all Scripture is true and inspired. Faith, however, in the exact limit and extent of the Scripture canon, and in a mode of inspiration so complete as to exclude the slightest error or discrepancy, is rather the crown and top-stone than the basis of a reasonable belief in Christianity. It could not have been essential while the canon was unfinished, nor for centuries afterward, when several books were widely but not universally received; while in modern times a less rigid view of the effect of inspiration can claim many advocates of deep and earnest piety, and of general soundness in the faith. On the other hand, a conviction that the sacred writers, especially the Evangelists, are sincere, honest, and credible witnesses of the facts they record seems a first essential of all real faith in Christianity. For surely no one can hold the Evangelists and apostles to have been fraudulent historians and dishonest witnesses, and still receive the Gospel itself as a message truly Divine.

There is here an important distinction between the doctrinal and prophetic books or passages of Scripture and the historical books themselves. In the former there is generally a direct or virtual claim of Divine authority. Their character is totally changed when we view them as purely human. We must accept them as Divine, or own them to be an immoral experiment on the credulity of mankind. But the historical books, with the exception of prophetic passages or doctrinal discourses, require no such alternative. The claim to inspiration is not made by each historian on his own behalf. It is not plainly implied by the mere existence of the record. No one without a special commission can reveal heavenly truth so as to claim with full authority the obedience of mankind; but every honest witness may give a true report of discourses he has heard, or events he has seen, or of which copious evidence has been placed within his reach, without special and supernatural inspiration. If St. Luke had not written, and the accounts to which his preface alludes had survived, they might have been disfigured by some mistakes and errors, and have obscured the due proportion of the events they contained; but they would doubtless have agreed in the main with our present Gospels, and might have nourished for ages the spiritual life of the whole Church. Entire freedom from the least error, if proved by distinct evidence, is a superadded perfection of the sacred narratives, which increases their practical value, and simplifies the acting of Christian faith; but their honesty, as the work of upright witnesses, and careful and well-informed historians, is the first condition on which all reasonable faith in Christianity must depend.

The life, death, and resurrection of Christ—the bases of Christianity—are recorded by four distinct writers in the four Gospels. This agrees with the maxim of the law of Moses, and the lesson of common-sense, that "in the mouth of two or three witnesses every word should be established." The plurality of the witnesses is thus made one chief element in the strength of their united testimony. Every view, then, of the inspiration of these books which sets aside or obscures the individuality of the four writers, and reduces them to fingers of the same hand, used mechanically by the Spirit of God, defeats one main purpose for which the message was conveyed to us in its actual form. No further truth respecting the special inspiration of the Evangelists ought to cloud from our view the fact, so conspicuous in itself, and so important in reference to the great object of the revelation, that we have a concurrence of four distinct and separate witnesses to all the main facts and many details of the Gospel history.

Secondly, the veracity of the Bible has been often questioned and denied on the simple ground that it contains miraculous events and prophecies. A whole series of German critics base their rejection of its histories, in their actual form, entirely on this principle, that the mention of a miracle is "evident proof of a later narrator, who was no eye-witness of the event." The great question is thus prejudged in the gross before any attempt is made to confirm this general disbelief by detailed criticism. But such a line of argument bears its condemnation on its face; for the claim of the Bible is plainly that it contains a series of messages from God to man, attested by signs, wonders, and prophecies. To make the presence of these in the narrative a disproof of its reality is therefore a flagrant contradiction of all common-sense. Two demands alone can be reasonably made: that the history, setting apart its miraculous character, shall possess all the other marks of honesty and truth; and that the testimony to these miracles and prophecies, in its strength and clearness, shall correspond with their importance as public and solemn credentials of a revelation from God.

Again, the improbability of miracles, which evidence has to overcome, depends entirely on their association with some great religious object, or their independent occurrence. In the former case they can not be more unlikely than one or other of these affirmations: that there is a God; that men stand in need of fuller light from their Maker; and that a God of wisdom and love has made provision for this wide and deep want of mankind. In the latter case their occurrence is just as unlikely as the supposition that an all-wise Governor will abrogate the laws he has ordained, in mere caprice, and with no apparent motive whatever. Thus in one case we have a high probability that they will, and in the other that they will not occur. The proposal to test the Bible, in this respect, by the rules applied to common histories, is therefore a logical absurdity of the most glaring kind. We have been told, for instance, that the outward evidences of Scripture are "not adequate to guarantee narratives inherently incredible," and that our investigation "forfeits its historical character" unless we scrutinize the Christian miracles "on the same grounds on which we should investigate any ordinary narrative of the supernatural or marvelous." This amounts, in fact, to an assertion that it is just as unlikely an all-wise Creator should work signs and wonders with the highest reason conceivable for such an exercise of his omnipotence, or out of mere caprice with no reason whatever.

The way is now open for a brief review of the direct evidence which attests the historical truth of the Old and New Testaments. We may distinguish six main periods: from Creation to the Exodus, from the Exodus to the Temple, from thence to the Captivity, and from the Captivity to Christ; and, in the New Testament, from the Birth of our Lord to his Ascension, and from thence to the close of the history, or St. Paul's arrival at Rome. The earliest period is lost in the shades of remote antiquity, where, till of late, few outward materials for comparison could be found; but the last answers to the palmiest days of the Roman Empire, and the most public and conspicuous era of classical history. The sacred history, however, from first to last, is recorded on the same general scale, with a marked harmony of character, style, and tone. The natural course is to ascend from the last period, where the means for testing its reality are most abundant, to the earlier ones, where they are of recent discovery, and still comparatively uncertain and obscure.

I. The Book of Acts is a whole, complete in itself, distinct in character from the Gospels, and not less distinct from the histories of the Old Testament. It abounds in testimonies to the resurrection and ascension of Christ, and to the fact of numerous miracles wrought during its course by the apostles to confirm their message. Apart from these features, has it all the marks of genuine history?

Does it satisfy the various tests by which an authentic record of facts may be discerned from the tales of imposture, from deliberate fiction, or from the dreams of excited fancy? The evidence may clearly be of three kinds: derived from its allusions to a real geography and the actual history of the times, from its coincidences with the rest of the New Testament, especially St. Paul's Epistles, and from the internal keeping and harmony of its own narrative. In each of these it is unusually full and copious, and space will not allow more than an enumeration in the briefest form.

1. From the Ascension to the death of Herod Agrippa. The book opens with an allusion to a former treatise by the same author, containing the events of our Lord's ministry till his ascension. This treatise is still extant in our third Gospel, and agrees with the description, and also with several features of style in the later narrative. Conf. Luke iii, 1-4; ii, 1-6; Acts v, 37; xi, 28; xviii, 12; xxiv, 27. It alludes next to forty days from the resurrection to the ascension, followed by a few days of earnest and continued prayer before the day of Pentecost. This is the usual name of the second Jewish festival in Philo, Josephus, and other Greek writers; and its meaning—the fiftieth day from the Passover—corresponds with the double definition of the intervals of time. The disciples are called, in the first and second chapters, Galileans. This agrees both with the Gospel account of the chief scene of our Lord's ministry, and with the nickname of the Christians, as late as Celsus, Porphyry, and Julian. Olivet is called "a Sabbath day's journey from Jerusalem." This is confirmed by the known topography, and by Jewish authorities on the distance allowed to be traveled on the Sabbath. Aceldama is said to be the name of the field of blood in "the proper dialect" of Jerusalem. This agrees with the

local use of Syriac in Judea. Joseph, called Barsabas, was also surnamed Justus. This indicates the presence of the Romans in Palestine, leading to the occasional acquisition, by Jews themselves, of Latin surnames. The countries from which the Jews are said to have been present on the day of Pentecost agree with the known state of intercourse in the Roman world, and with their wide dispersion through all those lands and provinces, as confirmed by Josephus and other testimonies. Mesopotamia and Judea come together; for the grouping refer to dialects, and the Chaldee and the Syriac of Palestine were near akin to each other. Both Jews and proselytes are mentioned as numerous, and the number of Gentile proselytes in that age is confirmed by all historians. In the sermon of St. Peter the sepulcher of David is said to be among the Jews at Jerusalem to that day. It still occupies a leading place in plans, views, and descriptions of Mount Zion and its vicinity. Williams's Holy City, Front. and p. 417. The Beautiful Gate of the Temple and the Porch of Solomon are named as places of especial resort. The latter is described by Josephus—Antiquities, xx, 9—and the former, though the Greek name does not seem to occur, answers, both in position and meaning, to the gate called Susan by the Jews from its beauty. The captain of the Temple is named, in passing, along with the chief-priests. The same officer is mentioned by Josephus—Ant., xx, 6, 2; B. J., ii, 12, 6; and vi, 5, 3—and under the kindred name of "overseer of the Temple," in 2 Mac. iii, 4. The rivalry of the Sadducees and Pharisees, which runs through the history, and the special opposition of the former to the preaching of the resurrection, agrees fully with larger details in Josephus. Annas is named as high-priest, and Caiaphas associated with him. The former, under the name of Ananus, is noted by Josephus as "most fortunate; for he had five sons, and all of these had the high-priesthood, and he himself, first of all, held the same honor a long time, which happened to no other of the high-priests." The appointment and deposition of Caiaphas is also named—Ant., xviii, 2, 2, and 4, 3—the latter just after Pilate was removed from his office. The cotemporary rule of Herod Antipas and Pilate—Acts iv, 27—appears, also, both in Josephus and Suetonius. The surname Barnabas, given to Joses, and its interpretation, agree with the relative use of the two languages in Judea and Syria. The celebrity of Gamaliel agrees with the mention in the Mischna of Rabbin Gamaliel, son of Rabbi Symeon, and grandson of Hillel. The statement that those who were with the high-priest were of the Sadducees, answers to the statement—Ant., xx, 9, 1—where Ananus, the son of Annas, is said to follow the "sect of the Sadducees, who were fierce, with reference to legal judgments, beyond all the Jews." The passing use of the title, "the taxing or census," applied to that under Cyrenius or Quirinus, agrees with the account in Josephus of its political celebrity, as a main era in Jewish and Syrian history. The mention of Hebrews and Hellenists at Jerusalem, the prevalence of Greek names among Hellenist Jews, as in the seven deacons, and the existence of national synagogues, as that of the Libertines, or Jewish freedmen, are all features of instructive correspondence with the actual circumstances of the times. The road to Gaza is called "desert," in agreement with the topography. The name Candace, according to Pliny—vi, 29—was taken in succession by the queens of Upper Egypt, or the district of Meroe. Other features of correspondence with general history are: the resort of worshipers to Jerusalem from remote countries at the feasts; the relative position of Gaza, Azotus, and Cesarea; the temporary dominion of Aretas over Damascus—Acts ix, 23-25; 2 Cor. xi, 32, 33—the rest of the churches, explained by Caligula's persecution of the Jews in the last years of his reign; the nearness of Lydda and Joppa; the use of the name Tabitha by the apostle, and Dorcas by the Greek historian; the mention of the Italian band; the military force at Cesarea; the rigid practice of the Jews about eating with Gentiles; the importance attached to the distinction of food, as lawful or impure; the greater freedom shown by the Jews from Cyprus and Cyrene; the place and occasion when the name Christian was introduced; the mention of the reign of Claudius in contrast to that of Caligula, when Agabus gave the prophecy, and that of Nero when the history was written; the reign of Herod Agrippa over Judea, under Claudius; his quarrel with Tyre, his reconciliation, and his sudden death after a public oration at Cesarea.

2. From the death of Herod to St. Paul's voyage to Rome.

The number and variety of these external allusions and confirmations of the history seems only to increase when the Gospel is formally spread among the Gentiles by the first missionary journey. Seleucia is mentioned familiarly, in passing, as the port of Antioch. Salamis and Paphos are placed on opposite sides of Cyprus, the first nearer Antioch, the second more remote from it. The Jews were numerous in the island, and had many synagogues there, in agreement with the mention of their expulsion from it in the time of Trajan. A proconsul, not a propretor, is named. Suetonius mentions that Cyprus was at first an imperial province, when Augustus shared the provinces with the senate, but that he restored it to the senate again. The sorcerer had an Arabic as well as a Hebrew name, and the apostle a Roman. This agrees with the extensive intermixture of the Jews, by residence, with other nations, and with St. Paul's birth as a Roman citizen. The site of Antioch in

Pisidia has been lately re-discovered, "with an inscription, Antiocheæ Cæsare." Iconium is assigned by Xenophon to Phrygia—Anab., i, 2, 19—but by Strabo, Cicero, and Pliny to Lycaonia, and by Ammianus Marcellinus to Pisidia Here no province is named for it, and it seems at the time to have been a distinct territory, ruled by a tetrarch—Plin. Nat. Hist., v, 27—Lystra and Derbe are called cities of Lycaonia, and it is said to have a distinct dialect. So we read in Stephanus Byzantinus, "Derbe is a garrison and port (?) of Isauria; but some call it Derbea, which is, in the dialect of Lycaonia, the juniper bush." Attalia is mentioned as near to Perga, and a seaport. It lies on the opposite side of a large plain, and was built by Attalus for trade with Syria and Egypt, and is still called Satalia. The land route from Antioch to Jerusalem is briefly described as passing through Phenice and Samaria. The law of Moses is affirmed by St. James to be read in the synagogues every Sabbath throughout the Eastern cities. This wide extension of Jewish synagogue worship, and its constant character, is confirmed by Jewish and classic writers. Phrygia, Galatia, Asia, Mysia, Bithynia, and Troas are named incidentally, but in their natural order, in the apostle's journey to the coast. The voyage to Philippi takes three days, with a notice that the wind was favorable. The return, with no such notice, is said to have been in five days. Samothracia and Neapolis are made the two stages of these voyages in their due order. Philippi is termed "the first city of that part of Macedonia, and a colony." The province has been broken into four districts, in its conquest by Æmilius Paulus. Philippi was the first city of importance within the province on the line of route. It was also a Roman colony, and the inscription is still found on coins: "Colonia Augusta Julia Philippensis." The Jewish place of prayer was by a river side. A small stream, Gangites, ran by the town, and such proseuchæ were near running streams for convenience in Jewish purifications. Lydia was "a seller of purple, of Thyatira." Inscriptions still remain of "the guild of dyers" of Thyatira. The names of the magistrates and officers, and the mode of punishment, beating with rods, agree with the character of the city as a Roman colony. The apostle "journeyed through Amphipolis and Apollonia to Thessalonica." The great Egnatian road (ὁδός) connects these towns, and an ancient itinerary reckons these three stages at thirty-three, thirty, and thirty-seven Roman miles. Thessalonica was a free Greek city. The mention of the Demus and the politarchs, or rulers, corresponds. They are Greek rather than Roman names. The original "where was *the* synagogue of the Jews," implies that one was found here only, and not in the three other towns. Thessalonica was the capital of the province, and hence was a natural place for this preference on the part of the Jews. Athens is said to be "wholly given to idolatry;" and Xenophon calls the city "one entire altar, altogether an offering to the gods." Pausanias calls the Athenians "more devout toward the gods than other persons." The sects of the Epicureans and Stoics, and the curious, inquisitive, talkative character of the Athenians, are other features of strict historical reality. Altars, also, ἀγνώστῳ θεῷ to an unknown God, are affirmed by Pausanias and Philostratus to have been reared in several parts of the city. Mention is made of a decree of Claudius, that all Jews should depart from Rome. Suetonius writes of that emperor: "Judæos, Chresto impulsore assidue tumultuantes, Roma expulit." It is named, in passing, that Gallio was deputy of Achaia while St. Paul was at Corinth. Tacitus gives particulars of his appointment through his brother Seneca, and the time agrees punctually with the date inferred here from the rest of the history, or A. D. 52–54. He is called

Proconsul; and the province had been imperial for a time under Tiberius, but was transferred by Claudius to the senate. The allusion to St. Paul's vow, and his haste to reach Jerusalem by Pentecost, agrees with the customs of the Jews. The phrases "he went up, and saluted the Church, and went down to Antioch," answer to a time when Jerusalem was still the sacred metropolis even of Gentile believers, since the place is implied, but not named. Asiarchs are mentioned at Ephesus, and also the worship of Diana, as the tutelar goddess of the city. A passage occurs with the phrase, "I swear by our country's deity, the great Artemis of the Ephesians," and also an inscription with the words, "the great goddess Artemis before the city." The ruins of the theater, and its site, indicate it to be the largest of any known in the remains of antiquity. The name of Asiarchs is also given, in many inscriptions, to officers chosen by the cities of Asia to preside over their festivals. The title of the "town-clerk," or "$\gamma\rho\alpha\mu\mu\alpha\tau\varepsilon\acute{u}\varsigma$," occurs in existing Ephesian inscriptions. So also the description of the image $\Delta\iota o\pi\varepsilon\tau\acute{\varepsilon}\varsigma$, or Jove descended, and the title of the city, $N\varepsilon\omega\kappa\acute{o}\rho o\varsigma$, or temple-keeper, are confirmed as in actual and frequent use at Ephesus. The intervals of the return voyage from Philippi correspond minutely with the known distances, and with the interval from the Passover to the Pentecost—Acts xx, 6, 16; xxi, 8—Philippi, Troas, Assos, Mitylene, Chios, Samos, Trogyllium, Miletus, Ephesus, Coos, Rhodes, Patara, Cyprus, Tyre, Ptolemais, Cesarea, are all mentioned on the route in the most rapid manner; but the presence of an eye-witness is apparent in every part, and is also implied, in the most unobtrusive way, by the transition to the first person—"We sailed away from Philippi after the days of unleavened bread." Acts xx, 6. We have, next, the mention of the Egyptian, and of the Sicarii, both of them named more fully by Josephus; of the Stairs of Antonia, where was the Roman garrison; of the preference, by the Jews, of their native dialect, while Greek was still widely intelligible; of the privileges of Roman citizens, and the fear of the captain who had violated them; of the feud of the Pharisees and Sadducees; of the recent change of high-priest, after the death of Jonathan, mentioned in Josephus, which accounts for St. Paul's ignorance that Ananias held the office; and of the letter of Lysias to Felix, so characteristic of a Greek, holding office under a Roman governor. We have a further harmony with facts, otherwise known to us, in the government of Felix at this time, his covetous spirit, his marriage with the Jewish Drusilla, and his removal, when Festus was his successor; in the frequent appeals from Judea to the emperor at Rome; in the royal dignity of Agrippa and Bernice, though they had plainly no authority at Jerusalem; and in the whole course of procedure of a Roman provincial governor, when conducting a cause of public importance. In all these numerous particulars every conceivable test of genuine history is satisfied and fulfilled.

3. The voyage and shipwreck of St. Paul.

These two closing chapters, when minutely examined, with all the light which can be thrown upon them by modern knowledge of the Levant, and by classical accounts of the ships and navigation of the ancients, become a striking and impressive demonstration of the truth of the whole narrative to which they belong. The subject has been fully treated by Mr. Smith in his "Voyage and Shipwreck of St. Paul," to which the reader must be referred; or to the brief abstract of its chief results in Dean Alford's Notes, or in Supplement G to Paley's Evidences.* It is

---

* School Edition, Religious Tract Society.

almost impossible to conceive how a narrative of the same length, without any loss of perfect simplicity, could be more densely crowded with decisive tokens of its being the result of ocular testimony, and in every part historically true.

4. Coincidences with the Epistles of St. Paul.

These have been traced at length in the Horæ Paulinæ, and placed in so clear a light that it seems impossible to conceive how more convincing proofs could be given of the genuineness of the letters and of the historical truth of St. Luke's narrative, from the first missionary journey to the arrival of St. Paul at Rome. The indirect nature of the coincidence, in almost every instance, creates an impression of reality, which no honest and candid mind can resist. A few remarks require correction, and other particulars of the same kind may be added, as in my own supplement;* but the effect of Paley's own work must be so decisive, on minds open to conviction, as scarcely to admit of sensible increase.

5. Another class of evidence may be found in the internal harmony of the history itself. Amidst the simplicity and truthfulness of tone in the separate narratives, there is a unity of design in the successive steps of the progress of the Gospel, which leads our thoughts to the perception of a Divine plan, steadily fulfilled, while it only confirms the historical reality of each separate portion. The opening words of our Lord are like a key to the structure of the treatise: "Ye shall be witnesses to me, both in Jerusalem and Judea, and Samaria, and to the uttermost parts of the earth." This order is observed in the accounts that follow. Seven chapters record the spread of the Gospel at Jerusalem and in Judea. After the death of Stephen it is

---

* Horæ Apostol., Religious Tract Society.

preached with great success in Samaria. The conversion of the eunuch is a first step in its diffusion to the ends of the earth. An apostle for the Gentiles is then provided. Their formal and public admission into the Church follows next, in the history of Cornelius. A central post among the Gentiles is gained at Antioch, and a Gentile name replaces that of Nazarenes. The persecution of Herod and the murder of an apostle sever the link which bound the Church so closely to Jerusalem. Then the first missionary journey begins, with Antioch for its starting-point and goal of return. The freedom of Gentile believers from the law of Moses is secured by the council at Jerusalem. Then the Gospel, set free from its Jewish moorings, speeds swiftly forward through the heathen provinces—Phrygia and Galatia—to Troas, Philippi, Thessalonica, Athens, Corinth, and Ephesus, where the apostle receives a prophecy of that visit to Rome with which the Bible history comes to its final close. "Paul purposed in the spirit when he had passed through Macedonia and Achaia to go to Jerusalem, saying, After I have been there I must also see Rome." Acts xix, 21. His arrival there marks the close of the narrative, which begins with the acceptance of the Gospel by Jews at Jerusalem on the day of Pentecost, and ends with its rejection by Jews and acceptance by Gentiles in the metropolis of the heathen world.

When all these various kinds of evidence have been summed up together, and weighed in an impartial balance, it may be safely affirmed that there is no extant history of the same age, and of similar length, which can claim to approach the book of Acts in full, various, and decisive proofs of historical veracity. Coins, inscriptions, nautical records of ancient and modern times, Jewish and classic authors, the Epistles of St. Paul, and the truest and deepest chords of the human heart, all conspire to stamp it, from first to last, with the plainest signature of reality and truth.

II. The four Gospels.

The four Gospels and the book of Acts form two distinct portions of New-Testament history. The space of time is probably just the same, or thirty-three years. Their structure, however, is very different. In the former we have four parallel biographies, but in the latter one continued narrative. The account in the Gospels, also, is confined to our Lord's childhood and his public ministry; and twenty-eight years, or six-sevenths of the whole interval, are passed by in almost total silence. All is here centered on the person and public work of the Messiah. This simple and sublime unity of object distinguishes them not only from common histories, but from the other historical books of Scripture themselves. They seem only to echo in every page the Baptist's message: "Behold the Lamb of God! who taketh away the sin of the world."

This character of the Gospels, so different from the book of Acts, hinders them from offering numerous points of contact with general history. Their theater is Palestine, and not the Roman world. The persons and places named in them are less numerous, and Josephus is almost the only writer with whom a direct historical comparison can be made. On the other hand, the concurrence of four historians supplies marks of reality of a different and most impressive kind. The vital connection, also, of the life of Christ, both with all the prophecies of the Old Testament and with the later history of the New, forms a peculiar and most weighty proof of the deep and intense reality of the whole narrative. We may consider the evidence under the heads of Time, Place, Persons, Reconcilable Diversities, and the double reference to the Old Testament and to the later history of the Church of Christ.

1. The time to which the Gospels refer is historically well defined. The possible variations amount only to three or four years at either limit. They are due mainly to the fact that Josephus is the only writer who affords very full data for comparison, and that some of his statements appear slightly inconsistent with each other. The limits of the date of our Lord's birth are B. C. 6 and 3, and those of the date of his death, A. D. 29 and 33. The direct statement of Josephus places the death of Herod between the Summer of B. C. 4 and of B. C. 3. But from his mention of an eclipse before that death, many have inferred that it took place earlier, or in March, B. C. 4; and others that it was three years later, or January, B. C. 1, when an eclipse took place about three months, instead of one month, before the Passover. The direct statement of Josephus, being reckoned from a double date of the reign, is probably the safest guide. In this case Herod's illness must have lasted the greater part of a year after the eclipse of March 13, B. C. 4; and the birth of our Lord, if referred to December, B. C. 5, would be nearly a year before Herod's death. His baptism would then be in A. D. 27, when he would be one or two months above thirty years of age; and his first Passover, soon after, would be in the forty-sixth year of Herod's rebuilding the Temple. His death, after a three years' ministry, would be in A. D. 30, when Thursday would naturally be the Passover day.

The notes of time which serve to fix the chronology are indirect and various, and lie scattered through the different Gospels; and their agreement, with only a very slight degree of uncertainty, is a striking evidence of their common truth. The birth of our Lord, and his flight into Egypt, are fixed by St. Matthew to the reign of Herod, and the return from Egypt to the accession of Archelaus. St. Luke, again, places just six months between our Lord's birth and that of the Baptist, and assigns the annunciation to the reign of Herod, and the nativity itself to the time of a census, either made by Cyrenius, or before his government of Syria began. It places the preaching of the Baptist in the fifteenth year of Tiberius, under the government of Pilate, states the age of our Lord at his baptism to be about thirty years, notices one Passover in the course of his ministry, and assigns it indirectly, by one of its parables, a length of about three years. The Gospel of St. John makes our Lord's ministry begin very soon after his baptism, at the time of a Passover, when the Temple of Herod had been forty-six years in building; implies a second Passover at or near the time when the cure took place at the pool of Bethesda, and a third about the time of the miracle of the five thousand; and specifies visits to Jerusalem at the Feasts of Tabernacles and Dedication in the last year. In its notice of the last Passover it seems at first sight to vary from the other Gospels, and to place the Jewish festival a day later, as referred to the week days; and the solution of this difficulty has divided the judgment of critics and expositors from the earliest times.

Now, if we retain the direct statement of Josephus on the length of Herod's reign, confirmed by the coins of Herod Antipas, and the account in Dio of the exile of Archelaus; and also accept his date for Herod's rebuilding the Temple; if we suppose that our Lord's birth was nearly a year before Herod's death, as St. Matthew seems to imply; and that St. Luke, a writer of Antioch, dated the years of Tiberius by a provincial reckoning from his association with Augustus in power over the provinces, two or three years before his sole reign, as attested by Suetonius; and also that our Lord was just about thirty years old at his baptism, the due priestly age; if we assume, further, that his ministry lasted three full years, as implied in the parable of the Fig-Tree, and inferred with strong likelihood from the feasts in St. John; and, finally, if we expound the statements of St. John on the last Passover, as is both possible and reasonable, so as to agree with the joint evidence of the first three Gospels; then all these notes of time, so widely dispersed, so indirect and various, will agree perfectly together, and with the proper age of the moon at the time of the Passover, and thus become accumulative evidence to the reality of the events and the historical accuracy of the record. Even if we were led, by a different view of the testimony of Josephus, to place the death of Herod part of a year earlier, or more than two years later, which is the limit of possible variation, the agreement will be only affected in a small degree, if we raise the crucifixion to A. D. 29, or place it lower in A. D. 33; and in every alternative the evidence of reality, from the concurrence of notes of time so widely scattered, will scarcely receive a sensible abatement.

2. The places named in the Gospels are about fifty in number, or half as many as in the book of Acts. They include the province of Syria, the tetrarchies or districts of Judea, Samaria, Galilee, Iturea, Trachonitis, Abilene, the regions of Perea, of Tyre and Sidon, of Gennesaret, Dalmanutha, and Decapolis, and the land of Gadara. Besides these, we have the following towns or localities, partly with Old Testament, partly with Syriac, and partly with classic names: Bethlehem, Bethabara, Bethany, Bethphage, Bethsaida, Chorazin, Capernaum, Cana, Nazareth, Nain, Jericho, Jerusalem, Sychar in Samaria, and Ephraim near the border, Aenon, Salim, Emmaus, Olivet, Arimathea, Tiberias, and Cesarea Philippi, Bethesda, Gabbatha, Golgotha, Gethsemane, the Pool of Siloam, and the Brook Kidron. All these local allusions have only had their truth and accuracy confirmed by the assiduous research of modern

travelers. Bethany, Nain, the probable site of Capernaum, Cana of Galilee, Sychar, and the well of Jacob, have all been brought to light once more; or new points of coincidence discovered in the mention of places and scenes already known.

3. Besides our Lord and his apostles, about thirty other persons are named in the course of the Gospel history. These include the two emperors, Augustus and Tiberius, Herod the Great, Archelaus, Herod Antipas and Herodias, Pontius Pilate, Annas and Caiaphas, the Syrian governor Cyrenius or Quirinus, and the tetrarchs Philip and Lysanias. In every one the statement is in agreement with the known facts of Roman, Syrian, and Jewish history; while in some of them there is a special and minute coincidence. The birth of our Lord is placed under Herod the Great; but it lies, from the other notes of time, so near to his death, as placed by Josephus, that when the latter is removed only half a year backward, some difficulty begins to arise; and a shortening of his reign by only three years would involve the Gospels in direct contradiction to other facts of history. Again, the return of Joseph into Galilee has a reason assigned, that Archelaus was reigning in Judea. The reign of Herod himself was over both provinces; but Galilee was separated and placed under Herod Antipas as tetrarch, at the accession of Archelaus; while the latter, we find from Josephus, gained a character for cruelty from the slaughter of the Jews at the very first Passover in his reign. The marriage of Herod with Herodias after her divorce from Herod's brother, is also related at some length in Josephus; and was the occasion of a great reverse in a battle with Aretas, whose daughter, his former wife, was dismissed for her sake. Josephus adds that this defeat was looked upon by the Jews as a Divine judgment for the murder of John the Baptist, which con-

firms, incidentally, another main fact in the first three Gospels. The government of Pilate, again, is said to have lasted ten years, and his removal by Vitellius is placed at the Passover in the year before the death of Tiberius, or A. D. 36. That government will thus include the opening, as well as the whole course, of the joint ministries of our Lord and his forerunner. The high-priesthood of Caiaphas yields another coincidence of a similar kind.

4. The reconcilable diversity of the Gospels, with substantial unity amidst their variation in details, is a powerful evidence of their common truth. The resemblance of the first three is so extensive, as to have led many critics to the hypothesis that they are varieties of one original document. The fourth has all the marks of a later and supplementary narrative. All of them agree in their mention of the Baptist as the forerunner of Christ, in their allusions to our Lord's baptism, in the account of the miracle of the five thousand, and in the closing scenes of the crucifixion and resurrection. The agreement of the first three is much more extensive, and includes about thirty leading incidents of the Savior's ministry. Still each has its own distinct character, and there is considerable diversity in arrangement and minor details.

There are two opposite ways in which the testimony of witnesses to the same events may be rendered suspicious or proved false. Their agreement in details, or in phrases, may be so complete as to seem an artificial result of collusion, or there may be extensive and irreconcilable contradiction. On the other hand, the combination which gives the strongest impression of reality and truthfulness is when substantial agreement in the main facts is joined with freedom and variety in the tone and method of the description, and with slight discrepancy, real or apparent, in secondary details.

Now this is precisely the character of the four Gospels. The agreement, in a few passages, is verbally complete, and in all the main outlines it is full and clear. In other cases, the difference is such as almost to give the impression of being irreconcilable. The historical unity is so apparent that scores of harmonists have endeavored, with considerable success, to combine them all into one continuous narrative. On the other hand, the differences have occasioned many disputes, among the most skillful harmonists, on the exact order of several events, and the most probable method of reconciliation. Side by side with their labors, a deep conviction is felt by the most careful critics and students, that each Gospel has a plan, style, and purpose of its own, and justly claims the rank of a distinct and unborrowed testimony.

These two opposite tendencies, in the criticism of the Gospels, began early, and have continued down to our own days. At the close of last century, the document hypothesis was in much favor. From the amount of agreement, extending often to the very phrases, an attempt was made to resolve the first three or synoptic Gospels into a kind of literary patchwork, formed in each case by combining three or four shorter documents, no longer extant, in a particular way. The principle, after being espoused by some eminent critics, was at length elaborated into such a complex scheme, to account for all the observed diversities, that its triumph proved its ruin. The documents required were so numerous, and the conjectural processes so complex, as to disprove effectually the hypothesis out of which they arose. An opposite view is now in vogue, that the Gospels were derived from oral tradition, but in all other respects strictly independent of each other. This hypothesis has perhaps equal difficulties on the other side. The writer of the last, it is plain, must have known of and seen the earlier ones, unless we contradict equally its traditional authorship and its internal features. Yet the diversity here is the greatest of all. There is nothing, then, in the smaller differences of the others, to preclude the idea that each knew the writing of his predecessors. Whether this were the case or otherwise, the actual measure of divergence is the same, and effectually disproves the notion of any attempt at collusive and artificial agreement. No one of them is a mere echo of any other. St. Mark, who narrates only two or three incidents that are not given in St. Matthew, is the most original and copious of all the four in the minute details. St. Luke, who seems through several chapters—chaps. iv-ix—to follow closely in the steps of his two predecessors, diverges from them almost entirely throughout nine chapters that follow; and thus forms a midway transition to the Gospel of St. John, which consists almost entirely of new and distinct matter. But the simple fact that two extreme hypotheses have been widely maintained, of a common documentary origin, and of total and entire independence, is a convincing proof, on the large scale, that there is just that union of substantial agreement and partial diversity, which imparts to the concurring testimony of different witnesses the most decisive evidence of honesty and truth.

Viewed in this light, the difficulties of harmonists on several points in the Gospels, whatever perplexity they may occasion as to the exact nature and extent of the inspiration of the Evangelists, are a striking confirmation of their historical fidelity. The four distinct witnesses whom the Lord has provided for his Church, that its faith in the great facts of his life and death may rest on a sure foundation, can not by any effort be fused and melted down into one. They offer us stereoscopic views of their great object. You can not simply superpose them without producing a sense of partial confusion. The lines overlap, and seem here and there to interfere; though the great resemblance is plain at once. But combine them rightly, as views taken from points of sight slightly different, but of the same glorious object, and the combined picture has a depth, massiveness, and solidity which no single outline, however full and clear in itself, could ever attain.

A comparison of the Gospels with the predictions of the Old Testament, and with the later history of the Church, would supply still further evidence of their historical truth. The facts they record are so deeply and closely interwoven with the whole course of Providence, both in earlier and later times, that no amount of violence can rend them away without destroying the entire texture of the world's moral history. But it is needless to dwell on further proofs, where the marks of truth and reality are so deeply impressed on every page.

CHAPTER VI.

THE HISTORICAL TRUTH OF THE OLD TESTAMENT

THE Old-Testament history is naturally parted by the Exodus, the Building of the Temple, and the Captivity into four distinct portions. In inquiring into the evidence of its reality, the proper order is to begin with the latest and nearest portion, and to ascend successively to those which are more remote.

I. From the Captivity of Babylon to the Birth of Christ.

Three books of sacred history—Ezra, Nehemiah, and Esther—belong to this fourth period; but their joint length barely equals the average of the six books which come before them, four of which belong wholly to the third period. These three books, however, offer many features of great interest in considering the evidence for the genuineness and veracity of the Bible histories.

1. The first feature worthy of notice in these books is their chronological limitation. The fourth period reaches from the Captivity or the Return to the Birth of Christ. Now, the course of the Bible history is unbroken and continuous from the Creation to the Captivity, and no blank of a single century is found through a range of not less than three thousand five hundred years. Even the fifty years from the Fall of the Temple to the Return are bridged over by historical chapters in Ezekiel and Daniel, and by the last verses of Jeremiah, and the book of Kings. The thread is resumed after the Return in these three books, and continues through a whole century, down to

the thirty-second year of Artaxerxes Longimanus. But here the canon closes abruptly. There is a space of more than four centuries of which no Bible history is given. The broken thread is resumed, however, in the New Testament, and then continues unbroken through two generations till the arrival of St. Paul at Rome, only seven years before the total dissolution of the Jewish polity. The books of Maccabees, it is true, belong to the interval; but they range over only two generations at most, and also it is clear that they never formed a part of the Hebrew Scriptures or Jewish canon.

This break, then, of four centuries is quite unique. It is a solitary exception to the continuity of a history which ranges through more than four thousand years. Sacred prophecy in Malachi, and sacred history in Nehemiah, cease almost at the same moment; and both reappear together, in tenfold effulgence, in the history of St. Matthew's Gospel and the prophecy on the Mount of Olives.

This sudden suspension, also, of the Bible history is attended by other circumstances which add to its significance. The interval is four hundred and thirty years, or exactly the same which is noted prominently as closing at the Exodus, that conspicuous type of the Christian redemption. It is also spanned by two prophecies of Daniel in successive chapters, one of which serves to fix and define its length, while the other predicts its political changes so clearly as to have suggested the solution, from Porphyry down to Dr. Williams and the modern skeptics of Germany, that it must certainly have been composed after the events had occurred. Viewed as parts of a Divine plan, the relation of all these facts to each other is clear and intelligible. Sacred history and prophecy ceased together four centuries before the coming of Messiah, that there might be a clearer mark of the dying out of the old covenant, and that the dawn of the new—the predicted rising of the Sun of Righteousness—might by contrast be rendered more deeply impressive. But still the faith of the Jewish Church needed support and guidance during this long interval of delay. Therefore, while sacred history and actual prophetic messengers were withdrawn, the light of prophecy was given with peculiar clearness. These visions of Daniel well supplied the place of direct history. The prophecy of the Seventy Weeks, beginning from one of the decrees in Ezra and Nehemiah, defined a space of sixty-nine weeks, or four hundred and eighty-three years, to the appearance of "Messiah the Prince" in his public ministry; and the later prophecy of the Scripture of truth described the main events of Persian, Syrian, and Egyptian history, in connection with the Jews, through nearly four of the five centuries which make up the whole period from the Return to the Nativity. The concurrence of this double clearness of prophetic light with the suspense of Bible history, both of them facts unique and without a parallel, marks clearly the presence of a Divine plan. On the skeptical hypothesis with regard to Daniel both facts are alike inexplicable. Why should Jewish writers at this moment have suddenly ceased to compose their own annals, and to add them as fresh books, equally sacred, to the earlier histories? Or why should some unknown Jew, in the days of Antiochus, instead of openly assuming the upright and honorable character of a simple annalist, usurp the prophet's mantle in order to write a mere syllabus of Persian and Syrian reigns already past; and then impose it on his countrymen, under the name of Daniel, for a true prediction, with the audacious title, for a shameless forgery, of "the Scripture of Truth?" Nothing can be more meager and threadbare than Dan. xi, 2–30, when taken for history written after the event; but when viewed as genuine prediction it stands alone, even in the Bible, in the clear testimony it yields to the Divine foreknowledge, and in its fullness of prophetic light, vouchsafed at the exact moment when prophetic inspiration and sacred history were withdrawn together.

2. A second feature of these three books is the entire absence of the supernatural. No trace of an alleged miracle occurs in any one of them. The old covenant, which the earlier books of Exodus and Numbers usher in with signal wonders, seems here to be indeed waxing old, and "ready to vanish away." This character belongs equally to the three books, though in other respects there is a singular and total contrast. Ezra and Nehemiah are loaded with details that seem almost trivial, and their outline appears fragmentary and unfinished. The book of Esther, on the contrary, has such a striking dramatic unity, that the suspicion might easily arise, in some minds, of its being a purely-artificial composition. But the entire absence of direct miracle is a feature common to it with both the others, while the contrast in other respects is complete.

This negative character, besides the deeper truth it conveys with regard to the decay of the Jewish dispensation, has plainly an important bearing on the reality and truth of the whole Bible narrative. The inspired annals close abruptly, but there is no abruptness in the transition from sacred to common history. We have an easy stepping-stone by which the mind may rise from the level of ordinary events, and find itself, unawares, in the outer court of the temple of God. There is no shadow of a plea in these books for doubting their entire truthfulness, because of the presence of a miraculous element in the narrative; yet, when once received in simplicity, they lead us by the hand, upward and onward, by the decree of Cyrus which fulfilled the prophecy of Jeremiah; by the mention of the

Urim and Thummim as a former means of supernatural guidance then withdrawn; by the Feast of Tabernacles, referring back to the history in the wilderness; and, above all, by the prayer and song of the Levites to all the earlier miracles of the old covenant: "Thou didst divide the sea before them, so that they went through the midst of the sea on dry land; and their persecutors thou threwest into the deep, as a stone into the mighty waters. Moreover, thou leddest them in the day by a cloudy pillar, and in the night by a pillar of fire, to give them light in the way they should go. Thou camest down also upon Mount Sinai, and spakest with them from heaven, and gavest them right judgments and pure laws, good statutes and commandments; and gavest them bread from heaven for their hunger, and broughtest forth water for them out of the rock for their thirst."

3. Chronological distinctness is a third character which is very conspicuous in two of these books, by which the main line of the history is continued and brought to its close. They occupy just a century under the Persian kings, the dates are expressly given, and the reigns can be identified, without difficulty, in full agreement with the canon of Ptolemy and other authorities. The reign of Cyrus dates in the canon from the capture of Babylon, B. C. 538, and no place is there left for Darius the Mede. But the book of Daniel, which places his reign after the capture, almost implies its short duration by the mention of his age; and, by a further allusion—xi, 1—implies that this short reign was secured by a special Divine interference against a strong current of Persian supremacy which had now set in. Thus, a comparison of texts restricts it to two years. The decree of Cyrus is thus referred to B. C. 536, his first year in Scripture, but his third in the canon. The setting up of the altar is referred to the seventh month

of the same year, and the foundation of the Temple to the second month, or early Spring, of the year following. We have, next, a brief mention of two reigns before Darius, during which the building was delayed by vexatious opposition. The beginning of this interval answers to the time of Daniel's fasting and humiliation, when he received his last and fullest prophecy of the future history of his people. History supplies just two reigns before Darius Hystaspes: Cambyses, who, from his cruelty and passion, and Smerdis, who, from his character as a Magian impostor, adverse to Cyrus and his race, would be likely to reverse the policy marked by the decree of restoration. The work is then resumed in the second year of Darius, or B. C. 520, and the Temple is finished in Adar of the sixth year, that is, February or March, B. C. 515; while in the fourth of Darius, agreeably with Zech. vii, 1–5, exactly seventy years were complete from the destruction of the former Temple. The reign of Xerxes is here passed over, though clearly described in Daniel's prophecy; and the history resumes with the mission of Ezra in the seventh of Artaxerxes Longimanus, or April, B. C. 458; while his arrival at Jerusalem is referred to the first day of the fifth month, or August in the same year. The history closes with the separation of the strange wives, complete by the first day of the next year, March or April, B. C. 457. An interval of "seven weeks and threescore and two weeks," or four hundred and eighty-three years, seems to lead exactly to the first month of the Baptist's ministry, and to the baptism of our Lord, followed by his first Passover; after which he began his preaching with the message, "The time is fulfilled, and the kingdom of heaven is at hand."

The book of Nehemiah comes a little later under the same reign. It begins with the month Chisleu, of the twentieth of Artaxerxes, and continues with the month Nisan, or the first Jewish month, in the same twentieth year This agrees with the indirect evidence of classic history, which refers both the true and nominal accession of Artaxerxes to December, and not to the early months of the Julian year, in which case these two notices would have contradicted each other. The history closes in the thirty-second year, or soon after—Neh. xiii, 22—or B. C. 433; exactly four hundred and thirty years before the Exodus of our Lord himself from Egypt after Herod's death. Thus we have plainly, in these last two books of Bible history, a high degree of clearness and consistency in the notes of time.

4. Another feature of these books is the multitude and variety of personal and local details. The sacred history gives here, at first sight, a strong impression of being tediously and superfluously minute. We have, first, an enumeration of the vessels restored from Babylon: "Thirty chargers of gold, a thousand chargers of silver, nine-and-twenty knives, thirty basins of gold, silver basins of a second sort four hundred and ten, and other vessels a thousand; all the vessels of gold and silver five thousand four hundred." Next follows a list of the captives who returned with Zerubbabel, in thirty-three companies of the people, each distinctly named and numbered; four companies of priests, and one of Levites, one of singers, and one of the porters, thirty-five companies of Nethinims, and eleven of Solomon's servants, of which only the total is given—three hundred and ninety-two. We have then two Persian decrees, one of Smerdis, and another of Darius Hystaspes, given at length. A third decree of Artaxerxes follows. The chiefs of the fathers are then named, and particulars are given of Ezra's journey. The minuteness of the account is like a pre-Raphaelite drawing. "Then we departed from the river of Ahava, on the twelfth day

of the first month, to go unto Jerusalem; and the hand of our God was upon us, and he delivered us from the enemy, and such as lay in wait by the way. And we came to Jerusalem, and abode there three days. Now, on the fourth day was the silver and the gold of the vessels weighed in the house of our God, by the hand of Meremoth, son of Uriah the priest; and with him was Eleazar the son of Phinehas, and with them Jozabad son of Jeshua, and Noadiah son of Binnui, Levites; by number and by weight of every one and all the weight was written at that time. Also the children of those that had been carried away, which were come out of the captivity, offered burnt-offerings unto the God of Israel; twelve bullocks for all Israel, ninety and six rams, seventy and seven lambs, and twelve he-goats for a sin-offering; all a **burnt-offering** unto the Lord."

The book closes with a list of those who put away their strange wives, in which a hundred and nine names are separately given. About double this number occur in the book of Nehemiah, which gives copious and minute details of the various parties, who joined in rebuilding the walls of Jerusalem. The fibers are thus multiplied at the close, by which the sacred canon strikes root downward into Jewish history. Simplicity, grandeur, dramatic unity seem all to be in some measure sacrificed, to secure the highest possible assurance of thorough reality and historical truth.

5. The book of Esther differs widely from these two other works. History meets us here in its most ideal, as in the others in its most real, form. The poetry of the opening description, the doomed race of Haman the Amalekite, the beauty of Esther, the law of the golden scepter, the sleepless night of the king, which forms the crisis of the drama, and the greatness of Mordecai at the close, all conspire to throw around it the air of a dramatic composi-

tion. The entire absence of the name of God from first to last is another remarkable feature, which only deepens the moral significance of the whole. Even the reign to which it belongs is not quite clear. It must plainly be later than Cyrus, since Persia and Media, not Babylon, are in power, and Persia takes the precedence; but opinions are still divided whether Xerxes or Artaxerxes is the true Ahasuerus. An internal coincidence, however, of a delicate and unobtrusive kind, makes it very probable that Josephus is right in referring the narrative to the latter of these two kings.

But if any should infer, from the dramatic features of this book, that it is rather a poetical fiction than a real history, there is one plain and decisive argument, besides many others, which proves its unquestionable truth. The Feast of Purim, on the fourteenth and fifteenth of Adar, is affirmed at the close to have been appointed, by Esther and Mordecai, for a yearly memorial of this great deliverance. This festival was observed in the days of Josephus, and has been ever since, throughout the long dispersion of the Jewish people. It still keeps its place in their calendar, along with the Passover, Pentecost, the Feast of Tabernacles, and the Feast of Dedication. No testimony could be more decisive and complete to the reality and greatness of this national deliverance.

The sacred history, then, in this closing portion, the fourth and latest period of the Old Testament, diverges on one side into the greatest minuteness of detail, and on the other, into the highest degree of dramatic unity and power; but in both alike exhibits the clearest and fullest evidence of historical reality and truth. The overruling hand of Providence is placed in striking relief, but no trace of miraculous intervention is found in it; as if these books were designed to form a stepping-stone of transition from common history to the miraculous story of the previous works, and every hinderance were purposely removed, which might prevent skeptical minds from recognizing at once the undeniable truth of the sacred history.

II. From Solomon to the Captivity.

This third period occupies a space of about four hundred and thirty years from the accession of Solomon to the destruction of the Temple, or four hundred and eighty years to the fall of Babylon. It occupies the two books of Kings, and also the second of Chronicles, and includes the period of all the prophets, except Haggai, Zechariah, and Malachi. The greater part of it consists of the record of the divided kingdom, from the death of Solomon to the fall of Samaria. The proofs of its historical reality may be ranked under these heads—a clear and distinct chronology; relations with heathen history; the harmony of the accounts in Kings and Chronicles; the multiplied allusions in the writings of the prophets; and the internal harmonies and marks of truth in the narrative alone.

1. The chronology of this period, compared with other histories, is very full and complete. The notes of time are numerous, and occupy about forty verses in Chronicles, and eighty in Kings. With one or two very slight exceptions, where an error has probably entered in the numbers—such as the thirty-seventh instead of the thirty-ninth year of Joash, 2 Kings xiii, 10—they are all consistent with each other. The interval fixes itself accurately by the data which the text supplies, so that the latitude of reasonable doubt amounts only to about three years. Baron Bunsen, it is true, in his work on Egypt, devotes twenty pages to the subject, and professes to have found just as many inconsistencies and errors in the notes of time in the second of Kings. These, however, are due entirely to his own strange incapacity to discern the simple and uniform law, which guides the notation of the synchronisms. When

this is once perceived, and it is very simple, the alleged confusion disappears, and the intervals can be traced, from first to last, with the greatest ease. Even Usher and Clinton seem to have adopted a less natural view, which renders the process of comparison more subtile and laborious, though the final result is hardly affected at all by the difference in the two modes of computation. Those cross references, which Baron Bunsen seems to regard as full of error, and a source of hopeless perplexity, are in reality a series of strict and severe tests of the consistency of the whole narrative. The most erratic and illogical minds are thus almost compelled, in spite of their own instincts, to keep close to the true chronology. His own labors are a striking example. After contracting the space, in his first edition, to ten years less than the true period, he returns in the second to the received chronology, with a slight variety, which may probably give the true year of Solomon's accession; though he has only reached this result by the help of conjectural emendations, which rest on no external evidence, and which falsify a large number of the plainest and most consistent notes of time. In fact, a chronology which depends on the reckoning of a double series of reigns, like those of Israel and Judah, of kings sometimes at war, sometimes in alliance, sometimes joined in actual affinity, is itself a condensed history, and forms by its own consistency a most powerful evidence for its own historical truth.

2. The various references to heathen history in this period are another sign of reality, which alone is enough to prove the history real. Mention is made in its course of Hiram and Eth-baal, or Ithobalus, kings of Tyre; of Shishak, Zerah, So, Tirhakah, Necho, and Hophra, kings of Egypt or Ethiopia; of Pul, Tiglath Pileser, Shalmaneser, Sargon, Sennacherib, Esarhaddon, kings of Nineveh; and

of Merodach Baladan, Nebuchadnezzar, Evil Merodach, and Belshazzar, kings of Babylon. These allusions are spread over the whole period. Under the reign of Solomon mention is made of Hiram of Tyre and Shishak of Egypt; and under his son Rehoboam, of Shishak alone. Under Asa the invasion of Zerah occurs, and is repelled. Jezebel, the wife of Ahab and cotemporary of Jehoshaphat, is the daughter of Eth-baal, king of Tyre. Pul, the king of Assyria, exacts tribute from Menahem in the reign of Uzziah. Under Jotham and Ahaz, Tiglath Pileser invades Israel, and a second stage of captivity begins. Hoshea makes a compact with So or Sevechus, king of Egypt, and is carried away captive by Shalmaneser. Sennacherib invades Judea under Hezekiah, and is checked in his career of conquest by tidings of the approach of Tirhakah, king of Ethiopia. He is slain after his return to Nineveh, and Esarhaddon reigns in his stead; to whom, under the name of Asnapper, the transfer of the Apharsites and other settlers, the fathers of the Samaritans, is ascribed in the book of Ezra. Ezra iv, 2, 9, 10. Merodach Baladan, king of Babylon, sends messengers to Ezekiel after the repulse of Sennacherib. Pharaoh Necho slays Josiah in the battle at Megiddo, and conquers Jerusalem. Nebuchadnezzar's reign extends through those of Jehoiakim, Jeconiah, and Zedekiah, and extends to the thirty-seventh year of Jeconiah's captivity. Evil Merodach then succeeds to the throne, and Belshazzar is in power at the time when the kingdom is numbered and finished—when the reign of the Medes and Persians begins. It is thus plain that the links of connection with heathen monarchs and dynasties belong to the whole period, from its commencement to its close.

Now, in all these allusions to the history of four or five distinct nations—Tyre, Assyria, Babylon, Egypt, and Ethiopia—and to eighteen or twenty kings—all mentioned by name—the palpable agreements are many, while not one contradiction or error has ever been shown to exist. If there be any defect in this branch of the evidence, it is due to the uncertainties and variations of the heathen dynasties or annalists, which require us, in some cases instead of treating them as independent witnesses, to adjust their uncertainties by the clearer light and stricter chronology of the sacred writings. Thus the two lists of Egyptian dynasties, from Shishak to Amasis, who answer to Solomon and Zerubbabel, as given by Africanus and Eusebius, differ from each other, in excess or defect, above a whole century, and each falls nearly a century short of the true interval. In the proposed restoration of Baron Bunsen, six reigns out of twenty-two, and three dynasties out of five, have their length altered by mere conjecture, and half a century is added to the longer reckoning so as to gain the desired result of making the reign of Shishak correspond with the Scriptural date of Solomon's death. The recent discoveries in the remains of Assyria and Babylon have added greatly to the strength of this external evidence. Monuments disinterred, after being buried for ages, and deciphered slowly and laboriously out of languages of which the very letters were previously unknown, have risen up to bear witness to the truth and accuracy of the inspired narrative. Thus the exact amount of the tribute of gold—thirty talents—imposed by Sennacherib on the kingdom of Judah, has been found and deciphered from an Assyrian obelisk in the British Museum in full agreement with the passage in the book of Kings. The name of Belshazzar has in like manner been discovered in the monuments of Babylon, and a minute and delicate coincidence brought to light. It appears from the decipherment that he was a joint ruler with his own father, who seems to be the Labynetus or Nabonadius who fled to

Borsippa; and this explains the contrast that Joseph was made second ruler in Egypt, but Daniel was promised to be "the third ruler in Babylon."

3. The double account in Kings and Chronicles supplies strong additional evidence of the historical fidelity of the whole narrative. The writer of Chronicles, it is true, must have been familiar with the books of Kings; and many passages in both are verbally the same. We can not, therefore, ascribe to them the character of two testimonies wholly independent. The later account, however, differs in several important features from the first. It is confined almost entirely to the history of Judah, and overlooks the cotemporary events in the kingdom of Israel. A prediction of Elijah is recorded, but his miracles and those of Elisha, which form one of the main features in the earlier history, are entirely unnoticed. No miraculous incidents occur except the sudden infliction of leprosy on Uzziah, and the destruction of Sennacherib's army, and possibly the mutual destruction of the enemies of Jehoshaphat may be referred to the same class. In general, we have a signal series of providential mercies and judgments in connection with prophetic messages; but signs and wonders, in the strict sense of the words, do not appear.

When we compare the two histories in detail we find that the later one gives many incidents of which there is no mention in the former, but which cohere intimately with the common portion of the narrative. Some of these notices are very minute—others refer to events of high importance. Of the former class are the notices that "Solomon went to Hamathzobah, and prevailed against it," and that "he went to Eziongeber and to Eloth at the seaside of the land of Edom." The book of Kings mentions the preparation of the navy, but not the visit itself of the king. Again, that Rehoboam built "cities of defense in

Judah, Bethlehem, and Etam, and Tekoa, and Bethzur, and Shoco, and Adullam, and Gath, and Mareshah, and Ziph, and Adoraim, and Lachish, and Azekah, and Zorah, and Aijalon, and Hebron, fenced cities in Judah and in Benjamin." That one of these—Lachish—was a fenced city in the time of Hezekiah is mentioned both in Kings and Chronicles, and is recently confirmed by the Assyrian remains. Of the same character is the mention of the three chief wives of Rehoboam, and of seven of his sons; the mention of Adnah, Johahanan, Eliada, and Jehozabad, the chief captains of Jehoshaphat; the help given to Uzziah "against the Philistines, the Arabians that dwelt in Gurbaal, and the Mehunims," and the towers he built in Jerusalem "at the inner gate, and at the valley gate, and at the turning of the wall." Of the other class are the battle between Abijah and Jeroboam, with the immense loss of the Israelites; the invasion and defeat of Zerah, the Ethiopian; the covenant in the fifteenth year of Asa; the publication of the law under Jehoshaphat, and his victory over the confederates near Engedi; the sin and judgment of Jehoram; the repairs under Joash; the murder of the prophet Zechariah; the prosperity of Uzziah, and his leprosy; the restoration under Ahaz of the captives of Judah; the reformation and passover of Hezekiah; and the captivity and repentance of Manasseh. On the other hand, the histories of Elijah and Elisha, and of the captivity of the ten tribes, and even most of the names of the kings of Israel, are passed by in silence. We have thus plainly two distinct testimonies to the portions common to both histories, and a direct confirmation by this means of their historical truth.

4. Thirteen prophetic books belong to this period, and abound throughout with direct or indirect allusions to the history. In Isaiah we have mention of Uzziah, Jotham,

Ahaz, and Hezekiah, and allusions to all the main events of the three later reigns. In Jeremiah there is an equal fullness of reference to the reigns of Josiah, Jehoiakim, Jeconiah, and Zedekiah. Ezekiel dates all his prophecies by the years of Jeconiah's captivity, and refers to the chief events of Nebuchadnezzar's reign. The book of Daniel ranges throughout the seventy years, from the beginning of the Captivity to the third year of Cyrus. In Hosea there is mention of Joash, king of Israel; in Amos of Jeroboam, son of Joash, and of an earthquake under his reign, also mentioned by Zechariah. Obadiah alludes to the events at the beginning of the Captivity; Micah to the reigns of Jotham, Ahaz, and Hezekiah; Nahum to the invasion of Sennacherib; Habakkuk to the near approach of the Chaldean armies; and Zephaniah to the reign of Josiah, and the judgments then close at hand. These books contain, also, nearly thirty chapters of direct history, besides more than a hundred references and allusions to the events in Chronicles and Kings. The whole texture, indeed, of these prophecies is manifestly founded upon the truth of the narrative which the historical books of the Bible contain.

When the external evidence is so abundant and various it is needless to dwell on the internal harmonies, indicative of truth, which the history itself supplies. The reality of these Jewish annals, from Solomon downward, is so clear, the links of connection with the prophecies and with heathen dynasties are so multiplied and indissoluble, and the chronology itself so complete, that skepticism must degenerate into insanity before it can venture to deny their substantial truth.

In one respect, however, this third period, from Solomon to the Captivity, is plainly contrasted with the period that follows. It includes, interwoven throughout the narrative, both miracles and miraculous predictions. Such are the prophecy of Ahijah the Shilomite, the rending of the altar at Bethel, the withering of Jeroboam's hand and its restoration, the prediction of Josiah by name three centuries before his birth, the death of the prophet from Judah, the famine under Elijah; the widow's cruse and the raising to life of her son, the fire from heaven at Carmel, and the abundant rain after Elijah's prayer, the vision at Horeb, the destruction of the two captains and their fifties, the rapture of Elijah, the parting of Jordan, the healing of the waters, the raising of the Shunamite's child, the healing of the pottage, and multiplying of the loaves by Elisha, the blindness inflicted on the Syrians, the deliverance of Samaria, the man raised after Elisha's death, the cure of Naaman and the leprosy of Gehazi, the leprosy of Uzziah, the reversal of the shadow on the dial of Ahaz, and the sudden destruction of the Assyrian army. The historical footing is just as firm as in the later period; but we are plainly within the borders of a sacred history, where the special presence of the God of Israel is revealed "in signs and wonders according to his own will."

. III. From the Conquest to Solomon.

This period, from the entrance of Canaan under Joshua to the accession of Solomon and the building of the Temple, answers to the books of Joshua, Judges, the first and second of Samuel, and the first of Chronicles. Two of these, however, belong to the last forty years, or the reign of David alone. For the rest of the period, or about four centuries—if we accept the date in 1 Kings vi—we have only one record of the events, in Joshua, and the book of Judges, and the first of Samuel. We have here, also, no collateral prophecies, though many of the Psalms refer to the events of David's reign, and the book of Ruth is a short episode of the time of the Judges. There are no references either to Assyrian, Babylonian, or Egyptian reigns. The truth of the Bible history in this period rests, therefore, almost entirely on its internal consistency, and on the constant reception of these books, as sacred and authoritative records of their own history, by the whole Jewish nation from the earliest times.

Now, first of all, it is plain that these books cohere most intimately with those which follow, both in their structure, style, and scale of composition, and in their external evidence. They form one continuous series of national Jewish history through a space of nine hundred years. They have been received by the Jews, without distinction, as the sacred annals of their nation from the death of their lawgiver till open prophecy was withdrawn. Even the scale on which the two portions are constructed is the same. The periods of time are nearly equal from Joshua to David's accession, and from that of Solomon to the Fall of the Temple; and the collective length of Joshua, Judges, Ruth, and the first of Samuel, and again of the second of Chronicles, and first and second of Kings is also nearly the same. The only difference is that in the earlier period we have fuller details of its beginning and its close, and the middle is passed over more rapidly. But the general harmony, both in the scale and the style of the history, leaves instinctively the impression that they are parts of one consistent whole.

In the next place, these books are national annals of such a nature that their national reception as true and genuine is inconceivable on the hypothesis of their spurious origin. The book of Joshua contains a record of the allotments of the twelve tribes and their separate possessions, on which the whole fabric of Jewish law and family inheritance would plainly depend. Along with this we have the singular economy by which the tribe of Levi were dispersed among the others, and separate cities with their suburbs allotted for their exclusive possession. The six cities of refuge were a still more peculiar institution. It is incredible that the origin of such laws, so definite and peculiar, should have been forgotten within a few generations, or that there should have been no public and national record to confirm and sustain their authority. The first of Samuel, again, contains the origin of the kingly form of government, and is linked throughout with three names so conspicuous and so dramatic in their interest—Samuel, Saul, and David—as to exclude the possibility of later fictions being accepted for real history.

The book of Judges is the only one to which these proofs of authority do not apply; but here we have another quite distinct and equally strong. For this book, from first to last, is one record of national sin, humiliation, and punishment. It is the very last work by which an unprincipled forger could seek to gain public favor, and a place among the historians of his own people. From first to last it is like an expansion of the later song of Moses, a witness against the people on behalf of God, a humbling record of repeated and persevering apostasy. No external pledge of its veracity could be more decisive than this moral feature which runs through the whole narrative.

Thirdly, these books abound, even more than those which follow them, with geographical details. This results at once from the nature of the book of Joshua, as a national record of the inheritance of all the tribes of Israel. Nearly three hundred names of places occur in it, and a large proportion of them are linked with events locally defined in the subsequent history.

Since, however, the books of Joshua and Judges have been assailed, like the Pentateuch, by a school of negative criticism, and a late origin and fragmentary character assigned to them, it may be useful to point out briefly, with regard to each of them, the strong internal proofs of their historical reality.

Now, the book of Joshua bears on its face a character of unity and completeness. It describes, in succession, the passage of Jordan, and four main steps by which the land was conquered; the destruction of Jericho and of Ai, and the defeat of two successive confederacies in the south and the north. Then follows a detailed list or catalogue of twenty-nine kings who were subdued. After the conquest we have an account of the settlement of the tribes. There is, first, a retrospective statement of the territory assigned by Moses himself to two tribes and a half on the east of Jordan. There is then a description of the boundaries and possessions of the two leading tribes of Judah and Ephraim, including the other half tribe of Manasseh. We have next a statement of the districts allotted to the remaining seven tribes, Benjamin, Simeon, Zebulun, Issachar, Asher, Naphtali, and Dan. After this are mentioned, in order, the appointment of the cities of refuge and the selection of the forty-eight cities for the Levites out of all the tribes. There is, next, the dismissal of the two tribes and a half to their own possessions on the east, and the controversy which it occasioned, from their erection of an altar of witness near the fords of Jordan. Last of all, there are the two successive interviews of Joshua with the people before his death; the first, apparently, at Shiloh, where the tabernacle was set up; and the other at Shechem, sacred by the memory of their forefather, where the covenant was solemnly renewed. The history closes with three events, all marking the termination of a distinct era—the death of Joshua, the burial in Shechem of the bones of Joseph, which had been brought out of Egypt, and the death of Eleazar the high-priest.

Again, the composition seems fixed by internal marks to the generation after Joshua's death, and agrees well with the supposition that Phinehas, the son of Eleazar, was its author. The words, "until we were passed over," suit best with the view that the writer actually took part in the first entrance into the land. So again the statement about Rahab, "she dwelleth in Israel unto this day," naturally implies that it was written during her lifetime. Her age was probably less than fifty at Joshua's death, and she might easily survive him twenty or thirty years. On the other hand, the conquest of Leshem by the Danites took place after the death of Joshua, as we learn from the fuller account in Judges. It was, however, during the lifetime of Phinehas, since a still later event, the conflict with the Benjamites, was during his high-priesthood. The last event mentioned in the book of Joshua is the death of Eleazar, whom Phinehas succeeded in that office.

The separate statements, again, are confirmed indirectly in every part of the book by later allusions of the most incidental kind. The first is the charge to the Reubenites and Gadites to share the campaign with their brethren—i, 12–18—which is referred to again, iv, 12, 13, and corresponds with the mention of their dismissal to their own possessions at the close of the work. The mention of the "stone of Bohan the son of Reuben," in the border line of Judah and Benjamin, seems probably an indirect allusion to the same event. The most natural explanation would be, that it was a stone or pillar set up by one of the leading Reubenites to mark his participation in the campaign of Israel, since it was placed not far from Gilgal and the banks of the Jordan. The history of Rahab and the spies is confirmed by the mention of her—vi, 25—as still alive when the book was written, and by the statement in St. Matthew, that she was married to Salmon, and the mother of Boaz. The place where the miracle was wrought, in staying the waters of the Jordan, is said to be near the city of Adam, beside Zaretan; and the latter is mentioned incidentally in the book of Kings, with reference to the brazen vessels in Solomon's Temple: "In the plain of Jordan did the king cast them, in the clay ground between Succoth and Zarthan." The place, Gilgal, where the stones were set up, and the Israelites encamped after the passage, besides other places where it is named, is referred to by Micah in a prophetic appeal to Israel after seven hundred years: "O my people, remember what Balak king of Moab consulted, and what Balaam the son of Beor answered him from Shittim unto Gilgal; that ye may know the righteousness of the Lord." Mic. vi, 5. The curse of Joshua upon Jericho is mentioned, when it was fulfilled after six hundred years, but only in one passing sentence in the book of Kings: "In his days [Ahab] did Hiel the Bethelite build Jericho; he laid the foundation thereof in Abiram his first-born, and set up the gates thereof in his youngest son Segub, according to the word of the Lord which he spake by Joshua the son of Nun." The sin of Achan is alluded to in the genealogy in Chronicles: "The sons of Carmi, Achan the troubler of Israel, who transgressed in the thing accursed." The valley of Achor is also mentioned again by Hosea, after seven hundred years, and in the most incidental way: "I will give her her vineyards from thence, and the valley of Achor for a door of hope; and she shall sing there as in the days of her youth, when she came up out of the land of Egypt." The mention of the blessings on Mount Gerizim—viii, 33—agrees with the high veneration shown to it by the Samaritans in later times, and its selection for the site of a temple to rival the Temple at Jerusalem. The narrative respecting the Gibeonites is confirmed by the later mention of their destruction by Saul "in his zeal for the children of Israel and Judah," and the retribution and judgment of the people: "There was a famine in the days of David three years, year after year, and David inquired of the Lord. And the Lord answered, It is for Saul and for his bloody house, because he slew the Gibeonites." Gibeon is also named as the place where the tabernacle was pitched in the times of David and Solomon, before the building of the Temple, and where Solomon received a vision. 1 Chron. xvi, 39; 2 Chron. i, 3, 6, 13. Beeroth is named among the five cities of the Gibeonites, included in the lot of Benjamin. The murderers of Ishbosheth were sons of Rimmon a Beerothite, and we have this incidental notice: "For Beeroth also was reckoned to Benjamin, and the Beerothites fled to Gittaim, and were sojourners there unto this day." No further light is thrown on this incident, so simply recorded as to speak its own reality. Once in Nehemiah, and there only, we find mention of their new residence among the towns of Benjamin after the Captivity: "The children of Benjamin dwelt at Michmash, and Aija, and Bethel, and their villages; at Anathoth, Nob, Ananiah, Hazor, Ramah, *Gittaim*, Hadad, Zeboim." Of the five confederate kings, two of the towns, Jerusalem and Hebron, continue to this day; and a third, Lachish, is prominent in the history to the time of Sennacherib, and his siege of it seems depicted in the sculptures recently found. Bethhoron, the upper and the nether, are also prominent places in the later history, and their site is still identified by travelers. Azekah is named again in the war with the Philistines, who pitched "between Shochoh and Azekah" before David's victory. Libnah, one of the cities destroyed by Joshua, occurs in two incidental notices in Kings. First, in the reign of Jehoram: "Yet Edom revolted from under the hand of Judah unto this day. Then Libnah revolted at the same time." It was a city of the priests—Josh.

xxi, 13—and its revolt might be occasioned by Jehoram's open apostasy, through his affinity with Ahab. One wife, also, of Josiah was "a daughter of Jeremiah of Libnah." 2 Kings xxiii, 31. The list of the thirty-one kings in Joshua—xii, 9-24—by the admission of negative critics themselves, "is either a cotemporaneous, or what is equivalent to a cotemporaneous authority."

The confirmations of the local notices that follow, in the later history, are too numerous to be specified. The following are a few examples. "The children of Israel expelled not the Geshurites nor the Maachathites"—xiii, 13; and Absalom "fled for refuge to Talmai son of Ammihud, king of Geshur." Hebron and its environs were given to Caleb, and Maon and Carmel are named next to it in the list of the cities of Judah; and Nabal was "of the house of Caleb," and is called "a man in Maon, whose possessions were in Carmel." Ziklag is named among "the uttermost cities of Judah, toward the coast of Edom southwards;" and the history of David's sojourn there answers perfectly to the description. Shochoh and Azekah are joined together in the list—xv, 35—and also in the account of the Philistine army—1 Sam. xvii, 1. Achzib is found in the list—xv, 44—and no mention of it recurs till after seven centuries, in Micah i, 14, "The house of Achzib shall be a lie to the kings of Israel." The same is true of Mareshah; while Adullam, a third place in the list and in the prophecy, occurs repeatedly in David's history, and its caves are known and explored to this day. Giloh is known only by one later allusion, but in connection with a striking and public event. "And Absalom sent for Ahitophel the Gilonite, David's counselor, from his city, even from Giloh, while he offered sacrifices." Gezer is connected with two notices, at long intervals, but mutually consistent. "Neither did Ephraim drive out the Canaanites that dwelt in Gezer, but the Canaanites dwelt in Gezer among them." Judges i, 29. "And this is the reason of the levy which king Solomon raised—to build the house of the Lord, and his own house, and Millo, and the walls of Jerusalem and Hezor and Megiddo and Gezer. For Pharaoh king of Egypt had gone up and taken Gezer, and burnt it with fire, and slew the Canaanites that dwelt therein, and given it for a present to his daughter, Solomon's wife." The cities and villages of the tribe of Simeon are reported, in Chronicles, with a very slight change in two or three names; but two facts are added, of an extension in the days of Hezekiah, when some of them "went to the entrance of Gedor, the east side of the valley, to seek pasture for their flocks," and others "went to Mount Seir, and smote the rest of the Amalekites that escaped, and dwelt there unto this day." Bethlehem, again, is mentioned in the tribe of Zebulun: and besides the contrast implied in the two names Bethlehem Ephratah or Bethlehem Judah, applied to David's birthplace, we are told that "Ibzan, a Bethlehemite, judged Israel, and was buried at Bethlehem;" and his place between Jephthah the Gileadite and Elon the Zebulonite shows that a northern Bethlehem is intended, while the other is called, for distinction, a few chapters later, Bethlehem Judah.

The marks of unity in the book of Judges are equally plain. It begins with a review of the state of the Israelites at the time of the conquest, and after Joshua's death, which forms the historical basis of the later narrative. It then gives a moral summary of the whole period, which it describes as one series of national apostasies, followed by merciful deliverance. We have then a brief, but connected history of the whole period, from the death of Joshua to that of Samson, after whom the double series of prophets and kings began, with Samuel, Saul, and David. The book then reverts to the earlier part of the whole period, and describes the first public entrance of idolatry, in the tribe of Dan, and the narrow escape of the tribe of Benjamin from extinction, through unnatural vice and crime. This event is alluded to long after, by the prophet Hosea: "They have deeply corrupted themselves, as in the days of Gibeah." "O Israel, thou hast sinned from the days of Gibeah: there they stood: the battle in Gibeah against the children of iniquity did not overtake them." By these episodes, the practical aim of the whole narrative is brought out at last more clearly into view; that a firmer government was needed for the welfare of the people—a king whom the Lord himself should provide for them. "In those days there was no king in Israel: every man did that which was right in his own eyes."

The allusions to the history of this period in the later Scriptures are not few, and some of them are so indirect as to lend it all the confirmation of an undesigned coincidence. The statement about Gezer—i, 29—is confirmed by the mention of it as conquered by Pharaoh in the time of Solomon. The family of Othniel is traced downward in Chronicles for several generations. The overthrow of the Canaanites is alluded to in Psalm lxxxiii: "Do unto them as to Sisera, as to Jabin, at the brook of Kishon, which perished at Endor, and became as dung for the earth." So also the victory over the Midianites: "Make their nobles like Oreb and Zeeb, and all their princes like Zebah and like Zalmunna." The triumphal song of Deborah lends its language to Psalm lxviii: "Thou hast led captivity captive." The truthfulness of the history, in all the local circumstances of the battle, and the ravine of Kishon, has been shown, in a most graphic manner, in a recent work on Palestine, "The Land and the Bible." The successive deliverances are appealed to by Samuel, when the people chose Saul for their king. "He sold them into the hand of Sisera, captain of the host of Hazor, and into the hand of the Philistines, and into the hand of the king of Moab. And the Lord sent Jerubbaal, and Bedan, [Barak,] and Jephthah, and Samuel, and delivered you out of the hand of your enemies." Again, in Isaiah ix, 4, "Thou hast broken the yoke of his burden, and the staff of his shoulder, the rod of his oppressor, as in the day of Midian." Ophrah, the city of Gideon, is named again in the account of the Philistine incursions. "The spoilers went out of the camp of the Philistines in three companies, and one company turned to the way to Ophrah, to the land of Shual." Penuel is mentioned among the cities which were fortified by Jeroboam. Succoth, in Joshua, is placed in the valley. The Psalmist speaks of "the valley of Succoth," and the brazen vessels of the Temple were cast in the plain "between Succoth and Zaretan." "The pillar that was in Shechem" where Abimelech was made king, answers to the "great stone" by the sanctuary of the Lord which Joshua had set up for a memorial, and would seem especially suited for the scene of a royal contract. The land of Tob is named in the history of Jephthah, as the scene of his exile, and the men of Ishtob are among the Syrians hired by the Ammonites in the time of David. A great slaughter of the Ephraimites, forty-two thousand, was made by Jephthah near the fords on the east of Jordan; and a wood of Ephraim, probably named from this conspicuous calamity of the tribe, since it was not in their territory, is the scene of Absalom's defeat, also on the east of Jordan, not far from Mahanaim, or in the land of Gilead. Timnath is placed on the border of Judah, near to Ekron, and is named, in the account of Samson, as a city of Philistines. The expedition of the Danites, after being mentioned briefly in Joshua, is recorded more fully in Judges. Beth-rehob, where Laish lay, occurs in 2 Sam. x, 6, where the Syrians of Beth-rehob are hired by the Ammonites. Dan, the city, is mentioned in the numbering of the people under David, and more generally, in descriptions of the limits of the country "from Dan to Beersheba." The conflict with the Benjamites, for the crime of the men of Gibeah, is named repeatedly in Hosea, and it was the city of Saul, where seven of his sons were put to death, because of his cruelty to the Gibeonites. "We will hang them up in Gibeah of Saul, whom the Lord did choose." The resemblance of the conduct of the Israelites, when sin was suspected in the Reubenites, and when it actually occurred among the Benjamites, illustrates the reality of the whole history. For, though separated in appearance by the whole period of the judges, the real interval of time was short; since Phinehas, who took part in the first message, was still alive, and high-priest, when the Israelites assembled at Mizpeh. The sense of national unity was still strong, and had not been weakened by declensions and apostasies of three hundred years.

The chronology of this period offers some difficulty. If all the separate intervals are successive, the total from the Exodus to Solomon will be about six hundred years, and the incidental mention of four hundred and fifty years for the time of the Judges, in Acts xiii, seems to confirm this view. On the other hand, 1 Kings vi, 1, assigns four hundred and eighty years for the interval from the Exodus to the fourth of Solomon, and this seems to agree better with the genealogies, and with the mention of three hundred years from the conquest to Jephthah's war with Ammon. But even the shorter reckoning disagrees with Baron Bunsen's hypothesis on the Egyptian place of the Exodus, and the lengths of the dynasties. He has, therefore, devised a singular expedient for setting it aside altogether. The book of Judges, he affirms, is not a history at all, but only has a historical basis. "It is an epos, midway between mythos, or fable, and genuine history. It is a strictly-popular epic in shape, by generations of forty years." When we inquire wherein this poetical character consists, we find that it is solely in the substitution of four false dates—three of forty and one of eighty years—for what he supposes to be the correct intervals—three of seven and one of ten years. There is happily a simple test by which every one may judge whether the Bible epos or the "history" framed out of it by this simple process agrees best with "the fundamental principles of historical criticism." According to Judges vi–ix, Gideon before his call was "the least in his father's house," and his eldest son Jether was a youth of eighteen or twenty years. The country "was in quiet forty years in the days of Gideon." After his victory "he had many wives," and in all seventy children. After his death Abimelech, one of them, slew all the others; and Jotham, the youngest, alone escaped, and made the celebrated address to the men of Shechem from the top of Mount Gerizim. Now, according to Baron Bunsen's revised version, by which the poetical element is removed, Gideon survived his victory just ten years; so that within that space sixty sons at least must have been born to him. Abimelech must have been less than ten years old when he slew his infant brothers; and Jotham, the youngest, a mere babe when he addressed the Shechemites from Mount Gerizim, and "then ran away and fled to Beer." Clearly, it is not the Bible narrative, but the modern substitute, which has here the best claim to be styled an epical fiction. The superiority of the sacred text to the learned criticism which assails it, and pretends to detect its errors, could scarcely receive a more striking illustration. For in all particulars, except the chronology, the book is untouched by the ordeal of criticism, and no smell of fire has passed upon it.

IV. The history of the Pentateuch.

The books of Moses contain a connected narrative from Creation to the conquest of Canaan, and are by far the oldest written history now extant. In consequence of their antiquity no direct materials for comparison exist, except the half-deciphered remains of Egyptian monuments brought to light within the last thirty years. The direct evidence of their authenticity is of the strongest kind. They have been accepted as the writings of Moses by the followers of three different and rival creeds — the Christians, the Samaritans, and the Jews — as far back in each case as their own history extends, or any record of their belief can be found. Their character, as the code of laws of a whole nation, entering into the minutest details of daily life, and involving the whole constitution of the state, and the local arrangements of all the tribes, would make a late forgery incredible and inconceivable. Apart from its record of miracles, and its views of the Divine character and holiness, which are so opposed to the whole spirit of an unbelieving philosophy, there can be no doubt that its claims to the title of true and credible history would have been received without the least difficulty, and owned to rest upon the most solid grounds. Since, however, the tests which can be directly applied are few, and at present ambiguous and controverted in the conclusions drawn from them, we are bound to apply the maxims of the inductive philosophy. These books contain a narrative of the first out of six successive periods of sacred history — four in the Old and two in the New Testament. The general character of the series, from first to last, is the same in its main features, though with important varieties of a secondary kind. Each portion seems to grow, by a natural development, out of those which precede. The mutual references, from first to last, are very numerous. We have one summary of the Pentateuch at the close of Joshua; a second, of the period of Exodus and the Judges in Samuel; a third and a fourth, from Abraham to David, or to the Captivity, in the Psalms and Nehemiah; a genealogical summary in the Gospels of St. Matthew and St. Luke; a historical summary from Abraham in the discourse of Stephen; a second, from the Exodus in that of St. Paul at Antioch; and a final outline from the beginning of Genesis to the Captivity, in the Epistle to the Hebrews.

Now, in all the five later periods the truth of the sacred history, as we have seen, is confirmed by a large variety of external and internal evidence. The tests are more various and abundant in the later portions, and in proportion as they are multiplied the evidence of reality becomes the more decisive. The period from Joshua to Solomon is internally consistent, but furnishes hardly any date for comparison, either with heathen dynasties or between parallel records of the same interval. Where these do occur, in the reign of David, in 2 Samuel, and 1 Chronicles, and the Psalms, the marks of consistency multiply in the same proportion. The period of the Kings supplies additional tests. We have two reports in Kings and Chronicles. We have thirteen books of prophecy belonging to the same interval, and we have the mention of eighteen or twenty foreign kings. The only result is to multiply the evidences of chronological accuracy and historical truth. The next period brings us within the early times of classic history. The minuteness and copiousness of the details is here carried to an extreme. There is no presence of miracles to awaken the doubts of skeptics, and the agreement with the best heathen records of the Persian reigns is complete. Similar confirmations are found in the history of the New

Testament, and especially in the book of Acts, its latest portion, which belongs to the brightest days of the Roman Empire, and is the period in which the elements for comparison are the most abundant in historical works, inscriptions, and existing remains.

The conclusion which results from this course of induction is plain. Wherever the tests are abundant they confirm in the strongest manner the truth of the Bible history. We are justified, therefore, and even compelled by the laws of sound reason to admit its truth, even in that earliest period, where, from its antiquity, it seems to stand alone in unapproachable dignity and preëminence. At least, we are bound to accept its *prima facie* claim to be real and genuine history, till counter-evidence can be found, so clear, distinct, and decisive, as to outweigh the collective strength of all those evidences of simplicity, consistency, and truth which meet the eye of the careful student through all its later course of fifteen hundred years. How far the revised chronology of the time of the Judges, of which a specimen has just been given; or hypothesis on the Hyksos period of Egypt, which Lepsius reckons at five, Bunsen at nine, and De Rouge at fourteen centuries, can affect this counterpoise, and, separating the early books of the Bible from their intimate, organic union with the later history, reduce them to epos or mythos, that is, narratives mainly or wholly fabulous, may be safely left to the judgment of every candid and thoughtful mind.

CHAPTER VII.

THE MIRACLES OF THE BIBLE.

MODERN rationalism, in its criticisms on the Bible histories, adopts, usually, a laborious process of circular reasoning. Unbelief is assumed in the premises, and, of course, reappears inevitably in the conclusion. It is affirmed, first of all, that miracles and real predictions are incredible and impossible. By the help of this doctrine the Bible is dissected, parted into imaginary fragments, resolved into loose traditions of some later age, or completely dissolved into mere legend. Immense labor is bestowed on this double process of dissection or sublimation; and the result is then announced that criticism has proved the history to be merely common events distorted by tradition, or the clothing of some abstract ideas of truth. This is the course adopted, alike by Strauss in the New, and Ewald and many others in the Old Testament. The same assumption is made openly in both cases, that a supernatural revelation, accompanied by miracles and prophecies, is "neither a fact nor a possibility." From infidel premises, of course, there can be reached no other than an infidel conclusion.

There are, on the contrary, only two questions which need an affirmative reply, that our acceptance of the Scriptures as a Divine revelation may be a reasonable faith. Has the Bible, setting aside, in the first place, the supernatural elements involved in it, every other sign and evidence of historical truth? And next, do the miracles or prophecies themselves agree in character with their alleged design as the credentials to a series of Divine revelations? The former question has now been briefly answered. It remains to inquire, next, whether the miracles satisfy the required conditions. These may be reduced, perhaps, to these four heads: a wise parsimony, general publicity, a consistent plan, and a moral purpose.

I. Miracles, to fulfill their great object of attesting and confirming messages from God, must retain an unusual and exceptional character. When they become habitual with any regular law of recurrence, they cease to be miraculous, and only add one more element to the immense number of natural laws. If they become frequent, but remain irregular and unaccountable, they will cease to startle or surprise, or fulfill any moral purpose, and will come to be classed with shooting-stars, or similar unexplained phenomena of the natural world. There is no conceivable limit to the invention of mere legends; but real miracles, it is plain, have strict and severe conditions to which they must conform. If too obscure and isolated, they will be insufficient for their professed object. If too numerous or constant, they forfeit the character of signs and wonders, and must lose a great part of their influence over the minds of those who may witness them. A wise parsimony is one main feature which must be expected, therefore, to characterize their actual occurrence.

Two causes have tended to create a false impression with reference to the number of the miracles in the Bible history. The first is its extreme compression, and the vast period of time which it embraces from first to last. The other is the religious tone of the whole narrative; so that common events, where there is no proper miracle, are ascribed habitually to the power and providence of God. When these two circumstances have been duly weighed, it will be seen, with surprise, how sparing, according to the

Bible itself, has been the use of miracles in the Divine economy. For the question is not what proportion they bear to the facts expressed in the record, but to those which are implied in it. Even without any inspired testimony, we know that the course of nature must have continued from day to day, and from generation to generation. But if miracles are declared to attest and confirm Divine messages, the mere omission and silence of the record amounts almost to a full proof of their non-occurrence.

The first period of Bible history reaches from the Creation to the Deluge, and occupies a space of more than sixteen hundred years. The record is very brief, but we may fairly assume, for the reason just named, that the chief events really miraculous have been included. Now, these are only five or six in number: the temptation of the serpent in Paradise; the expulsion of Adam and Eve, with the cherubic sword of fire at the east of the Garden; the vision to Cain after Abel's sacrifice; the translation of Enoch; the mixture, perhaps, of the sons of God with the daughters of men, and birth of the Nephilim; and, lastly, the Deluge itself, and its attendant circumstances. Six instances of miraculous interference — three at the very beginning, two during the course, and one at the close— of nearly two whole millennia of the world's history, are surely no lavish and extravagant amount of supernatural interference.

The second period reaches from the Flood to the Descent into Egypt, and is a space of six — but according to the Septuagint of fourteen—centuries. Only three main events of a public or a national kind occur in it which are miracles, or quasi-miraculous: the confusion of tongues at the Tower of Babel; the destruction of the Cities of the Plain; and the dreams of Pharaoh, with the seven years of plenty and seven of famine. Even of these the last belongs less naturally to miracles than to supernatural prophecy. But since the foundations of a new economy were now being laid, there is a considerable number of visions recorded of a more private and personal kind. We meet with about ten instances in the life of Abraham, three or four in that of Isaac, and eight in that of Jacob. Most of them are simply dreams or visions, and only three or four involve a distinct angelic appearance. This, also, is a frugal provision of signs and wonders for the first foundation of an economy of grace, by which all the families of the earth were to be blessed, and which was to endure to a thousand generations.

The third period is that of the Exodus and the Conquest, and lasted about forty-five years. It was the season when the Law was given, and written revelation first began. It forms, therefore, an exception to the character of the previous and the following periods, with regard to the number and frequency of the signs and wonders which attested the new economy, and that written law which was to be the foundation of all the later messages of God. All the other miracles of the four thousand years of the Old Testament are scarcely so numerous or so striking as those which are crowded into the limits of this single generation, though comparatively modern in its date; since Abraham, and not Moses, is about midway in the Old-Testament history.

The fourth period, from the Conquest to Solomon, occupies considerably more than four hundred years. But the miracles recorded in its course are comparatively few. The chief are: the angelic vision at Bochim; the call of Gideon; the double miraculous sign of the fleece; the angelic vision to Manoah; the wonders of Samson's strength, and its loss when his vow was broken; the vision to Samuel when a child; the judgments on the Philistines and the men of Bethshemesh; the prophesying of Saul; the thunder and nail after Samuel's rebuke of the people; the appearance of Samuel to Saul after his death; and the infliction of the pestilence and its removal; or scarcely more than twelve through a period of nearly five centuries.

In the fifth period, from Solomon to the Captivity, besides the number of prophets who were raised up, and whose writings are part of the canon, the direct miracles are more numerous. About forty distinct examples of them are recorded during this interval of four hundred and thirty years, and two or three others in the history of Daniel at Babylon. The signs and wonders approach in their striking character to those of the Exodus; but they are spread over a longer interval, while the others are all concentrated within one instead of ten or twelve generations. In the last period of the Old Testament, after the Return, and till the Birth of our Lord, there is an entire absence of all recorded miracles through more than five hundred years.

The whole range of New-Testament history is only sixty-six years, or two generations. It begins with miracles in the narrative of our Lord's infancy, and they are found in the very last chapter, after the shipwreck of the apostle, and before his arrival at Rome. They do not, then, shrink or disappear from the history, when it comes into contact with the broad daylight of Greek and Roman civilization. On the other hand, there are twenty-eight years of this period, or nearly one half of the whole, which are passed by in silence, and where the absence of miracles is clearly implied. This same feature, also, continues to mark the ministry of the Baptist, the forerunner of Christ. The contrast is brought out plainly in the fourth Gospel in the words of the Jews, "John did no miracle, but whatsoever John spake of this man was true."

Thus, on a review of the whole, we find that the Bible itself teaches clearly that miracles were a rare exception, and not the ordinary rule of Divine Providence, and this even among the chosen people. From the purpose expressly assigned to them we may infer, with great probability, that all such departures from the usual course of nature, of a signal character, would be put on record; and the whole number may be rather more than one hundred throughout the course of four thousand years from the fall of Adam to the coming of the second Adam, the Lord from heaven. The first condition, then, of true miracles, a wise parsimony in their exhibition, is clearly fulfilled in the Bible history.

II. Again, miracles, in order to fulfill their office, as proofs of a Divine message or commission, require a character of publicity. To use the words of St. Paul before Agrippa, it would contradict their great object, if they were "done in a corner," and there were no adequate witnesses of their reality.

This condition, again, is satisfied in the highest degree by the main body of the miracles, both of the Old and New Testament. The Flood, the confusion of tongues, the destruction of Sodom and Gomorrah, the plenty and famine of Egypt, were events of the most public kind, and on the largest scale. A public assertion of them, unless very remote in time, would involve a speedy and complete exposure of fraud and falsehood. The plagues of Egypt, the pillar of cloud and fire, the daily manna, the passage of the Red Sea, the supply of water from the rock, have all the utmost possible degree of publicity. The same is true of the passage of the Jordan, and is there additionally striking because of the memorial appointed at the time, to be a public testimony of the occurrence to later generations. The same character applies to several of Elijah and Elisha's miracles, and to the later overthrow of the Assyrian army. In the New Testament it is the common feature of all our Lord's miracles, and most of those of the apostles. The appeal is repeatedly made by our Lord himself, as well as his disciples, to this character of the miraculous works. John xv, 22–24; v, 36; xi, 47, 48; xii, 37; xviii, 20; Acts ii, 22; iii, 16; iv, 21, 16; v, 16; x, 37, 38; xix, 12; Rom. xv, 19.

But while this character of publicity belongs to the Bible miracles, as a whole, there are many exceptions in which they are exhibited in the light of a special privilege, and witnessed by a few only. Such were the visions to the three patriarchs; the appearance in the bush to Moses; the messages of the angel to Gideon, and afterward to Manoah and his wife; the support of Elijah by ravens, and again by the widow of Zarephath; and some others in the Old Testament. In the Gospels we see that our Lord, in several cases, enjoined silence on those who were healed, or chose out a few witnesses only. Thus three apostles alone were allowed to be present at the raising of Jairus's daughter, and at the Transfiguration; and the blind man at Bethsaida was led aside out of the town before his eyes were opened, and then charged not to tell it to any one in the town. The resurrection of our Lord holds in this respect a middle place. The number of witnesses was large, for "he was seen of above five hundred brethren at once;" and the appearances were numerous, for no less than ten are distinctly put on record, and they reached through an interval of forty days; but the privilege was reserved, in every case, for disciples alone. It is clear, then, that a second law intersects, and in some cases supersedes, the general rule of publicity; and that the moral aspect of such manifestations, as a special privilege which must not be wasted upon senseless and stubborn minds, mingles with and modifies their fundamental character, as "a sign to them who do not believe." 1 Cor. xiv, 22.

III. A third feature, which may be expected to distinguish real miracles, designed to fulfill some great object of the Divine government from the mere chance inventions of falsehood, or a fortuitous series of mere legends, invented by the caprice of imaginative minds, is the presence of a consistent plan in their actual distribution and occurrence.

It is common with skeptical writers to represent miracles, as maintained by the advocates of Christianity, to be "something at variance with nature and law," "arbitrary interposition" and acts of mere caprice, in "marvelous discordance from all law." But this is a gross misconception. The term law, instead of being confined exclusively to physical relations, is borrowed from a higher field of thought—the deliberate acts of intelligent wills—and is only transferred by analogy to the mere regularity of physical changes. Moral laws have a better claim to the title than the physical; the latter have borrowed it from them, and are merely, so to speak, undertenants at will. The highest and noblest kind of law of which we can have a conception consists of the moral and spiritual maxims by which the Supreme Lawgiver, the only wise God, disposes his own acts in the government of the creatures he has made. Viewed in this light, while miracles are either real or seeming infractions of some physical law of material sequence, they are, in every case, fulfillments of a higher law of God's moral government; which may be discerned in them, more or less clearly, when the understanding has been purified by faith and prayer, and has learned to meditate with reverence on the ways of the Most High.

The question between unbelief and Christian faith seems capable, then, of being brought here to a distinct and definite issue. If alleged miracles are the mere inventions of imposture, or the dreams of inventive fancy, we might reasonably infer that they would be ascribed most plentifully to periods most remote from historic knowledge, and diminish gradually as we come within the region of authentic history, tested by collateral evidence and a well-defined chronology. On the other hand, if they are the real credentials of Divine messages, we should expect them to abound at marked eras of revelation, when there is some conspicuous unfolding of the Divine will; and to be more sparingly exhibited in those intervals, when there is merely a continuation of former degrees of light, and no sign of any new message from God to man.

Now, it will be plain, on the least inquiry, that this latter character, and not the former, belongs to the whole series of miracles which the Bible records. Three or four miraculous events marked the close of the brief economy of Paradise, and introduced the sixteen centuries of the antediluvian world. One miracle alone occurs during their long course—the translation of Enoch; for the marriage of the sons of God with the daughters of men is either simply a natural event, or a marvel of sin, and not an interference of God. The Deluge and its attendant wonders ushered in a new dispensation, and a formal covenant with mankind in their new head. Two signal acts of judgment mark the long period from the Flood to the Exodus, when iniquity had reached its hight, in the building of Babel, and the Cities of the Plain; but all the other wonders are of a more private kind, connected with the persons of the three patriarchs alone, in whom the foundation was laid for all the later revelations of the Divine will. But with the Exodus a new dispensation began. The revealed will of God was now, for the first time, embodied in a written and permanent form. The books of Moses, which were written by the great lawgiver of the Jews, form the key to all their later history, and are the basement story of the whole edifice of revealed religion. Here, then, we meet in the sacred narrative with a profuse display of miraculous agency, contrasted equally with earlier and with later ages. This contrast is boldly drawn out in the law itself. "For ask now of the days which are past, which were before thee, since the day that God created man upon the earth, and from one side of heaven unto the other, whether there hath been any such thing as this great thing is, or hath been heard like it. Did ever people hear the voice of God speaking out of the midst of the fire, as thou hast heard, and live? Or hath God assayed to go and take him a nation from the midst of another nation, by temptations, by signs, by wonders, and by war, and by a mighty hand, and by a stretched-out arm, and by great terror, according to all that the Lord your God did for you in Egypt before your eyes?" This era of marvels lasts throughout the forty years of the Exodus, till Jordan is crossed, the book of the law complete, and the chosen people have entered into their promised inheritance. Its close is then hardly less marked than its commencement. The manna ceases as soon as the Jordan is passed. After the conquest is complete, except the solitary message of rebuke by the angel at Bochim, we have two whole centuries, to Gideon, in which no trace of a miracle is found, and only one prophetic message, that of Deborah to Barak. The few miracles that come later are of a personal kind, or messages to individuals, to fit them for some special work or service. Two public miracles occur, at intervals, in the later half of the period between the Conquest and Solomon, and each of them is connected with a main event in the tabernacle worship of Israel. The first was the rescue of the ark from the Philistines, which was never again restored to the tabernacle at Shiloh; and the other was the pestilence, which issued in the designation of a new site on Mount Moriah for the temple of God.

But as soon as the Theocracy, under the law, began to wane, and new revelations were to be given, permanently, by prophets to complete the old covenant, and link it with the Gospel that was to follow, not only prophetic messengers are multiplied, but public miracles reappear. Their place is not found amidst the dimness of uncertain history, or an obscure chronology, but precisely where the annals of Israel and Judah dovetail into each other with recurring notes of time, and link themselves with the records of Tyre, Assyria, Egypt, and Babylon. A signal prophecy by Ahijah the Shilonite, and three signal miracles in connection with the prophet from Judah, usher in the first separation of the kingdom of Israel, and are like an earnest of the new era that was to begin. In the two generations of Elijah's and Elisha's ministry nearly forty miracles are recorded in Chronicles and Kings. A series of prophetic messages was thus publicly inaugurated, which reached from Jonah, the earliest, a cotemporary of Elisha, to Jeremiah and Ezekiel at the time of the Captivity; when it was sealed once more by the two signal miracles, in which the faith of Daniel and his companions "stopped the mouths of lions, and quenched the violence of fire," in the interval between the Captivity and the Return from Babylon.

After this return the Sinaitic covenant was waxing old, and even the code of Old-Testament prophecy was nearly complete. Three shorter books of prophecy sustained the faith of the remnant who had been restored to Judea in a time of weakness and Gentile opposition, and renewed the promise of brighter days at hand. But miraculous interference is entirely withheld. No outward miracle is found in these last books, of Ezra, Nehemiah, Esther, Haggai, Zechariah, and Malachi. Signs and wonders first, and very soon the gift of prophecy itself, are withdrawn, through a long space of five hundred years. The old dispensation, with its code of Divine messages, was complete, and the fuller light of the Gospel was not come.

When this time of waiting was gone by, a series of marvels accompanies the dawning of a new dispensation, and ratifies the messages of the Gospel. They begin with the birth of our Lord, but their chief development attends the opening of his public ministry. Amidst the fullest light of classic literature, and in the hight of the Roman dominion, when the whole civilized world was linked by perpetual and daily intercourse, we are suddenly confronted once more with "signs, and wonders, and mighty deeds," less startling and terrible than those which sealed the sterner messages of the law, but still more numerous and varied, and reaching, like the others, through a space of forty years and upward, from our Lord's baptism to the very close of the Jewish polity. Their reality is attested, not only by the simplicity and truthfulness of the record, but by the admission of Celsus, Porphyry, and of the unbelieving Jews, and by their moral power in the formation of the Christian Church, and its growth and spread through successive ages. They are the rock on which it is built so firmly that the gates of hell have never prevailed for its overthrow. But when once the Church is founded, and the new dispensation of the Gospel established throughout the breadth of the Roman Empire, the sacred canon is brought to a close, and miracles, beyond that limit, either suddenly cease, or melt away insensibly, with the removal of the first believers and apostolic converts, and "fade into the light of common day."

The miracles of the Bible, it thus appears, are not scattered confusedly throughout the whole period, as, if they were due only to the accidents of legend-weaving, we should expect them to be. They follow a manifest law in their distribution, no less than the planets of the solar system in their settled orbits. They are grouped mainly around two great centers, the Law of Moses and the Gospel of Christ, the two known and essential components in one great, progressive scheme of revelation. An important but secondary series attends and introduces the teaching of the prophets, the connecting link between the two dispensations. When we add to these a few acts of solemn judgment, the Flood, the Confusion of Tongues, the Destruction of Sodom, the overthrow of the Assyrian host, and more private messages or visions to the three patriarchs, and a few judges and kings, we have nearly exhausted the whole range of recorded miracles. Every feature of their arrangement confirms the constant faith of the Church, that they are neither the inventions of imposture, nor the dreams of wayward fancy, nor unaccountable freaks of blind chance; but credentials, appointed by the Only Wise God, to confirm and ratify the authority of his own messages of holiness and grace to the children of men.

IV. The last feature which marks the Bible miracles, and severs them widely from the idle tales of marvels with which a skeptical criticism would confound them, is the presence throughout of a moral purpose. It is not merely true that they are shown by the law of their distribution to be the seals and certificates of the messages of God. They form themselves one part of the message which they seal.

This moral character of the miracles of the Bible has been often observed, and unfolded by several writers with rich and abundant evidence of its truth. It is the less needful, then, to dwell on it here at any length. The miracles of our Lord, with scarcely an exception, are parables also. Some deep spiritual truth shines out through the supernatural history. They are not, as the mythical theory pretends, mere ghosts or unembodied ideas, clothed with a shadowy vail of fiction. They have a body, real and true; but it is a spiritual body, like that which is promised to the children of the resurrection, translucent in every part with the powerful impress and energy of the living truth within. The plagues of Egypt partake of the severity and holiness of the legal dispensation. The works of Christ are gracious and gentle, though surpassingly wonderful, and answer well to the grace which was poured into his lips, and forms the essential spirit, the distinguishing glory, of the Gospel. There is a Divine harmony of character between the signs and wonders themselves, the healing of the sick, the unstopping the ears of the deaf, and opening the eyes of the blind, the stilling of the storm and tempest, and the truth which all of them were given to confirm and ratify—"the Gospel of the grace of God."

CHAPTER VIII.

THE PROPHECIES OF THE OLD TESTAMENT.

CHRISTIANITY, as a public message which claims the faith and obedience of mankind, rests evidently on a double foundation—the miracles of our Lord and his apostles, and the fulfillment of earlier prophecies of the Old Testament in the history of Christ, and the early progress of the Gospel. The appeal to the miracles is conspicuous in every part of the New Testament. "If I do not the works of my Father," our Lord said to the Jews, "believe me not; but if I do, though ye believe not me, believe the works." And to his disciples: "If I had not done among them the works which no other man did, they had not had sin." Nicodemus, even in the first twilight of his faith, had already learned the same lesson: "Rabbi, we know that thou art a teacher come from God; for no man can do these miracles which thou doest except God be with him."

But the appeal to the fulfillment of prophecy is no less frequent, both in the lips of our Lord himself, and in the teaching of his apostles. It is, equally with the miracles, made the ground of a direct and earnest claim that Jesus of Nazareth should be received as the true Messiah, and the Gospel believed to be the word and message of God. If this appeal be groundless and delusive, then Christianity, it follows by necessary consequence, is a system of delusion. Whatever elements of pure morality it may seem to contain, these too must be deceptive; since it would come with a lie in its mouth, to claim submission and reverence in the name of a God of truth and holiness. Whoever denies the reality of these predictions ceases, *de facto*, to be a Christian. For a Christian means a disciple of Christ; and those can not be disciples of our Lord who deliberately contradict and set aside many of the clearest and most emphatic sayings which proceeded from his lips. Christianity, it is evident, as a reasonable faith, nay, as a scheme of high morality, and not of false pretenses, must stand or fall with the acceptance or rejection of the fulfillment of Old-Testament prophecies, in the life, death, and resurrection of the Lord Jesus.

Let us review, first, the passages in which this claim is distinctly made.

1. Matt. xi, 10: "For this is he of whom it is written, Behold, I send my messenger before thy face, who shall prepare thy way before thee."

This prophecy of Malachi is here distinctly asserted by our Lord to belong to the Baptist, his own forerunner. It is implied with equal clearness that the following clause is a prediction of his own presence among the Jews, and in the Jewish Temple: "And the Lord whom ye seek shall suddenly come to his Temple, even the messenger of the covenant, whom ye delight in: behold, he shall come, saith the Lord of Hosts."

2. Matt. xii, 39, 40: "An evil and adulterous generation seeketh after a sign; and there shall no sign be given it, but the sign of Jonas the prophet: for as Jonas was three days and three nights in the whale's belly; so shall the Son of man be three days and three nights in the heart of the earth."

Here we have not only a prophecy of the resurrection on the third day, which lodged in the memory even of the unbelieving Pharisees — Matt. xxvii, 63 — but a distinct assertion by our Lord that the strange and unusual history of Jonah, which was a sign to the Ninevites, was a vailed prediction of his own resurrection from the dead. The same statement is repeated once more—Matt. xvi, 4.

3. Matt. xxi, 42: "Jesus saith unto them, Did ye never read in the Scriptures, The stone which the builders rejected, the same is made the head of the corner: this is the Lord's doing, and it is marvelous in our eyes? Therefore I say unto you, The kingdom of God shall be taken from you, and given to a nation bringing forth the fruits thereof. And whosoever shall fall on this stone shall be broken: but on whomsoever it shall fall, it will grind him to powder."

Here our Lord not only affirms that the verse in Psalm cxviii is a distinct prophecy of his rejection by the Jewish rulers, but infers from it the truth, soon fulfilled, of their own expulsion from the covenant of God, attended by heavy judgments. The apostle, who was present at the time, twice repeats and confirms the saying of his Lord. Acts iv, 11, 12; 1 Pet. ii, 7, 8.

4. Matt. xxii, 41, 46: "If David, then, call him Lord, how is he his Son?" The words of Psalm cx, 1, are here affirmed to be a prophecy of the exaltation of Messiah, which was fulfilled in the twofold nature of our Lord and his future exaltation to the throne of God.

5. Matt. xxiv, 15, 16: "When ye see the abomination of desolation, spoken of by Daniel the prophet, stand in the holy place, (whoso readeth let him understand,) then let those which be in Judea flee into the mountains." Here, when the words are compared with St. Luke, our Lord teaches his disciples that one of Daniel's predictions, instead of being written after the event in the time of Antiochus, was a true prophecy of desolation to be soon inflicted on Jerusalem by the Roman armies.

6. Matt. xxiv, 30: "And they shall see the Son of man

coming in the clouds of heaven, with power and great glory." These words are a plain reference to Daniel vii, 13, 14, and a distinct claim by our Lord to be the Son of man, of whom Daniel had prophesied, and announced his everlasting dominion and glory.

7. Matt. xxvi, 23, 24: "He answered and said, He that dippeth his hand with me in the dish, the same shall betray me. The Son of man goeth as it is written of him."

We have here our Lord's declaration that his sufferings were the express subject of prophecy. But the connection shows that he refers immediately to Psalm xli, 9, and affirms its fulfillment in his betrayal by one of his own disciples.

8. Matt. xxvi, 28: "For this is my blood of the new covenant, which is shed for many for the remission of sins." The declaration here, though indirect, is not the less decisive, that Jeremiah xxxi referred to our Lord's sacrifice on the cross, and to the Gospel covenant which it sealed.

9. Matt. xxvi, 31: "Then saith Jesus unto them, All ye shall be offended because of me this night; for it is written, I will smite the Shepherd, and the sheep of the flock shall be scattered abroad."

No statement could be plainer than this. The prophecy in Zechariah, our Lord tells his disciples, made it certain that they would abandon him in the hour when he was to be smitten, and lay down his life for the sheep.

10. Matt. xxvi, 53, 54: "Thinkest thou that I can not now pray to my Father, and he shall presently give me more than twelve legions of angels? But how, then, shall the Scriptures be fulfilled, that thus it must be?"

Here, also, nothing can be more distinct than our Lord's assertion, rendered stronger by its interrogatory form. The prophecies so truly foretold his sufferings as to make it essential for their truth and the faithfulness of God, that he should yield himself up without resistance into the hands of his enemies. The Scriptures would have failed and been falsified unless he suffered. The Evangelist presently repeats and reëchoes the same doctrine: "But all this was done that the Scriptures of the prophets might be ful filled."

11. Matt. xxvi, 64: "Hereafter ye shall see the Son of man sitting on the right hand of power, and coming in the clouds of heaven." Our Lord has once before applied the description in Daniel to himself, in his discourse to the disciples. He here repeats the same before the Sanhedrim. The saying, for which he was adjudged to be worthy of death, was simply a claim to be the express object of this prediction. If Daniel vii were merely a pretended prophecy, or referred to some one else, there seems no escape from the conclusion that our Lord was a deceiver, and his condemnation a righteous sentence.

12. Matt. xxvii, 46: "About the ninth hour Jesus cried with a loud voice, saying, Eli, Eli, lama sabachthani? that is to say, My God, my God, why hast thou forsaken me?"

This exclamation, if it stood alone, might be explained as a mere adoption of the Psalmist's words, because they suited his present experience of suffering; but when we compare them with the taunt in verse 43, which is a quotation from the same Psalm, and the quotation just before by the Evangelist in verse 35, they clearly imply a conscious appropriation by our Lord, on the cross, of the whole Psalm, as a distinct prophecy both of his inward experience and outward shame.

13. Luke iv, 17, 21: "And he began to say unto them, This day is this Scripture fulfilled in your ears." The prediction in Isaiah lxi, 1, is here expressly referred by our Lord to his own ministry, as its true and proper meaning.

14. Luke xviii, 31–33: "Behold, we go up to Jerusalem,

and all things that are written by the prophets concerning the Son of man shall be accomplished. For he shall be delivered unto the Gentiles, and shall be mocked, and spitefully entreated, and spitted on, and they shall scourge him, and put him to death, and the third day he shall rise again."

Nothing can be clearer than that the true and proper fulfillment of various predictions, such as Psa. xxii, 6, 7. 15; Isaiah l, 6, is here asserted by our Lord to center in his own person, and the sufferings he was about to undergo.

15. Luke xxii, 37: "For I say unto you, that this which is written must yet be accomplished in me, And he was reckoned among the transgressors; for even the things concerning me have their fulfillment."

16. Luke xxiv, 25, 26: "Then he said unto them, O fools, and slow of heart to believe all that the prophets have spoken! Ought not Christ to have suffered these things and to enter into his glory? And beginning at Moses and all the prophets, he expounded unto them in all the Scriptures the things concerning himself."

Luke xxiv, 44: "And he said unto them, These are the words which I spake unto you, while I was yet with you, that all things must be fulfilled which were written in the law of Moses, and in the prophets, and in the Psalms concerning me."

17. Luke xxiv, 45, 46: "Then opened he their understanding that they might understand the Scriptures, and said unto them, Thus it is written, and thus it behooved Christ to suffer, and to rise from the dead the third day, and that repentance and remission of sins should be preached in his name among all nations, beginning at Jerusalem."

18 John v, 39: "Search the Scriptures, for in them ye

THE PROPHECIES OF THE OLD TESTAMENT. 175

think ye have eternal life, and they are they which testify of me."

19. John v, 46, 47: "For had ye believed Moses, ye would have believed me; for he wrote of me. But if ye believe not his writings, how shall ye believe my words?"

20. John xiii, 18: "I know whom I have chosen; but that the Scriptures may be fulfilled, He that eateth bread with me hath lifted up his heel against me."

21. John xvii, 12: "And none of them is lost, but the son of perdition, that the Scripture might be fulfilled."

22. John xix, 28, 30: "After this, Jesus knowing that all things were now accomplished, that the Scripture might be fulfilled, saith, I thirst. . . . When Jesus, therefore, had received the vinegar, he said, It is finished, and he bowed his head, and gave up the ghost."

After these plain and repeated statements of our Lord himself, it is needless to dwell on the many passages where the same doctrine is echoed by the Evangelists and apostles. Twenty-five such passages, besides their parallels, occur in the Gospels, an equal number in the book of Acts, and still a larger number in the various Epistles.

The predictions, to which this appeal is publicly made by our Lord and his apostles, range through the whole extent of the Old Testament from Genesis to Malachi. Besides many indirect allusions, or applications of types in the history, they include two passages in Genesis, one in Exodus, two in Numbers, two in Deuteronomy, one in 2 Samuel, nearly twenty in the Psalms, more than twenty in Isaiah, two or three in Jeremiah, as many in Daniel, and in Hosea, one in Joel, two in Amos, one in Jonah, two in Micah, four in Zechariah, and two in Malachi. The claim is made throughout the whole of the New Testament, from the first chapter of St. Matthew to the last of Revelation—Matt. i, 22, 23; Rev. xxii, 6, 9, 16—and the prophecies to which it expressly belongs range equally throughout the Old Testament, from the third of Genesis to the last chapter of Malachi.

Of late years, however, some have ventured to renounce and contradict this uniform testimony of Christ himself and his apostles, and still to retain the name of Christians. How those can be disciples of Christ who reject some of his plainest and most emphatic sayings, it is hard to understand. We have been told, for instance, that in Germany there has been "a pathway streaming with light, in which the value of the moral element in prophecy has been progressively raised, and the directly predictive, whether secular or Messianic, has been lowered."* It is by no means evident how the moral element can have been enhanced, by turning the prophets from inspired messengers of God into successful practicers on the credulity and superstition of their countrymen. But unless our Lord spent his time, after the resurrection, in deluding his own followers, this light is merely a relapse into that darkness which brought on them his severe rebuke, and from which they were finally set free, when "he opened their understanding, to understand the Scriptures." A school of negative criticism, which translates Psalm xxii, 16, "For lions have compassed me, the assembly of the wicked have inclosed me, as a lion my hands and my feet," and then makes these hands and feet to be those of the whole Jewish nation, is more akin to lunacy than to real learning. A vast induction, composed of such elements, may prove to be only an accumulation of learned folly. A pathway of prophetic interpretation, streaming with such light, merely illustrates the words of our Lord. "If, then, the light which is in thee be darkness, how great is that darkness!"

---

* Essays and Reviews, Essay ii, p. 67.

Hebrew prophecy, in all its parts, was doubtless a witness to the kingdom of God, or to a scheme of moral government, exercised through successive ages over a sinful world. And the real question at issue is, whether it were a true witness to a real redemption, and a living Redeemer, promised from the beginning; or a series of dim and imperfect guesses, by fallible men, as to the future results of the events which were passing around them. In the view of Christian faith, it must contain, throughout, both a moral and a predictive element. It is neither bare and naked ethics, nor mere prediction of the future; but a conjoint revelation of the will and purposes of God. If its predictions are mere guesses of man, with no Divine authority, then the message becomes a public and notorious immorality. It is a fraud upon the faith of men, and a blasphemy against the God of truth. On the other hand, merely to enforce duty was never the sole or chief part of the prophet's message. The contrast between a high standard and actual experience would make such a work, if carried on alone, a source of despondency and darkness. But prophecy, from first to last, is a message of hope. Amidst the darkness of sin and sorrow, it reveals the prospect of a great redemption. Every gleam of light, which it threw upon actual sin and rebellion, was meant to awaken stronger desires for the rising of the day-spring from on high. It is a message from that God, who sees the end from the beginning, with whom a thousand years are as one day. While its precepts and warnings belong, of course, to the times when each message was given, its promises and encouragements are borrowed from that future, which lay hidden in the counsels of God, and which God alone could reveal. Hence its chief characteristic is a revelation, with increasing clearness, of "the good things to come." All centers in it around the person of the great Redeemer.

The prophecies are a landscape, bright in every part with a light which flows from the still unrisen Sun of Righteousness. "To him gave all the prophets witness," and "the testimony of Jesus is the spirit of prophecy."

Now, every message of prophecy will receive a different interpretation, as it is read with the face or the back turned toward this great hope of redemption, this sunrise in the eastern sky. One method results inevitably in the destructive criticisms of learned unbelief; but the other is that instinct of faith and hope which alone could profit aright by these messages when they were first given, or enable us, in the retrospect, to perceive their real fullness and Divine beauty. They must be read not as mere human guess-work by many authors widely remote in time, and brought together now by mere accidental causes, but as gifts from God to sinful men, pervaded throughout by the unity of common purpose. This is essential, according to the Scriptures themselves, in order to attain a just view of their meaning. "Knowing this first, that no prophecy of Scripture is of self-interpretation; for prophecy came not at any time by the will of man, but holy men of God spake as they were moved by the Holy Ghost."

It will be enough for our present object to examine two or three main examples of that vast induction on the destructive side, which begins by reversing this first essential of true interpretation, and then glories in having stripped the prophecies, one by one, of their Messianic character; as if it were a proud triumph of modern learning to resume the exact position of the first disciples, when their understanding was still darkened, and they were pronounced, by the Truth himself, to be "fools, and slow of heart to believe what the prophets had spoken." I will select three instances alone, the earlier and the later prophecies of Isaiah, and the visions of the beloved Daniel, doubly sanctioned by our Lord in his own prophecy on the Mount of Olives, and when he witnessed his good confession before the Sanhedrim of the Jews.

I. The prophecy—Isaiah vii–ix—according to the constant faith of the whole Church, and the express words of the New Testament, is a prediction of our Lord's supernatural birth, and announces the lasting continuance of his kingdom. The negative theology rejects this interpretation altogether. The phrase, Mighty God, it assures us, may only mean "strong and mighty one, father of an age." It "can never listen to one any who pretends that the maiden's child was not to be born, in the days of Ahaz, as a sign against the kings of Pekah and Rezin." In other words, the prophecy could only be read aright with the back turned upon the bright future, and the hope of the seed of the woman, who had been promised from the days of Paradise. The Jews were to fix their thoughts entirely on their trouble at the moment from the confederate kings; and the whole drift of the Divine message was a promise that they would soon have access to the pasturages from which they were then shut off by the siege, and would be able to indulge their infant children once more with curds and honey!

Now let us turn to the prophecy, and see whether it lends us no key to its own real meaning. It begins with a startling offer, made by God himself to the people and their unbelieving king. "The Lord spake again unto Ahaz, saying, Ask thee a sign of the Lord thy God: ask it either in the depth, or in the hight above." All nature seems here thrown open to his choice; as if no token of God's power, however wonderful, would be withheld in this hour of temptation, if it were needed to confirm his faith in the Divine protection. But the same unbelief, which made Ahaz tremble before his enemies, led him to reject the gracious offer, with the vain excuse that it would be tempting God to obey his own command. The choice of a sign then reverts from the faithless king to the Lord himself, by whom the offer had been made. We must, therefore, expect it to be determined, not by the selfish fears of the wicked Ahaz, but by the grandeur of the Divine counsels of mercy, and in the spirit of that later declaration: "As the heavens are higher than the earth, so are my ways higher than your ways, and my thoughts than your thoughts." With him a thousand years are as one day. The malice of Pekah and Rezin would be, in his sight, like dust in the balance, compared with his own thoughts of mercy to the chosen line of David, and through them to Israel and the whole race of mankind. "And he said, Hear ye now, O house of David, is it a small thing for you to weary men, but will ye weary my God also? Therefore the Lord himself will give you a sign. Behold, the virgin conceives and bears a son, and shall call his name Immanuel. Butter and honey shall he eat, that he may know to refuse the evil, and to choose the good."

The great object of the promised sign is clearly to give a full assurance of God's mercy toward the house of David, however great its own sin and perverseness, and however fierce the threats of its enemies. The sign, taken in its strictest meaning, fulfills this object; especially since it appears from chap. ix, 6, 7, that this promised child was to be the heir of David's throne. It implies three things: a supernatural birth, answering to the first promise of the seed of the woman; a superhuman character, so that in his person God would be truly present with his people; and freedom from human corruption, since, unlike all other children, Immanuel would know from his first infancy to refuse the evil, and to choose the good.

Such, then, is a double reason in favor of the Christian

interpretation. It agrees with the nature of the offer which introduces the prophecy, and with its return, after its rejection by Ahaz, to him who gave it. It supposes the sign to have been truly what the offer implied, "in the depth and in the hight above;" and it also ascribes to the terms of the promise their strictest, fullest, and most expressive significance.

Again, the whole force of the sign, on the opposite view, depends on the immediate birth of the child before Rezin and Pekah's overthrow. It would have no force till the actual birth, and its value would cease as soon as Damascus was taken by the Assyrians. It would be simply an ephemeral sign of a momentary respite, in the prospect of heavier and more lasting judgments. It would require such a paraphrase as this: "A child shall be born, in the course of nature, within a year, to Ahaz or Isaiah; and before it is three or four years of age, it will be possible for it to be fed on curds and honey, because these enemies will have been overthrown, and the pastures be accessible once more." Now, it is plain that, on this view, the sign really precedes the event as little as in the Christian interpretation, at least in its most essential feature. For the natural birth of a child from human parents is the most commonplace of events, and, standing alone, has scarcely any character of a sign whatever; while the circumstance marked as significant, the peculiar diet of this child, was not to precede, but to follow the wished-for deliverance from Ephraim and Syria.

A third reason for the same view results directly from the passage—Isaiah vii, 1–4—where the birth of a child to the prophet himself is announced for a sign. This son of Isaiah, Maher-shalal-hash-baz, besides the entire difference of the two names prophetically given, can not be the same with Immanuel, for a clear and simple reason, that the latter is declared to be the owner of the land—chap. viii, 8—and the destined occupier of David's throne. Chap. ix, 7. But the birth of the prophet's child evidently fulfilled every object required for the temporary purpose of being a pledge that the Syrian overthrow was close at hand. The birth of a second child, as a mere chronological sign, would have been a mere superfluity; and, in fact, Hezekiah, the immediate heir, was born several years before. It results, plainly, that the promise of Immanuel had a different object, and did not refer to one moment of time, but to the whole series of troubles which were coming on the house of David, from mightier foes than Rezin or Remaliah's son.

Again, on the naturalist view, the birth of Immanuel is simply a pledge of Rezin's speedy overthrow, and is subordinate in its importance to that deliverance of Judah and of King Ahaz, which must constitute the main scope of the prophecy. But the whole passage, when compared together, points to an exactly-opposite conclusion. This overthrow of Rezin is there made simply the preface to a long series of heavier troubles from the kings of Assyria, by which Israel and Judah alike would be brought to comparative desolation. But the promise of the child Immanuel takes the lead of the whole prophecy. It appears in the middle of it as the stay in the hight of the Assyrian conquests of desolations, and breaks out once more at the close as a full message of everlasting consolation: "He shall pass through Judah, he shall overflow and pass over, he shall reach even to the neck; and the stretching forth of his wings shall fill the breadth of thy land, O Immanuel. Take counsel together, and it shall come to naught; speak the word, and it shall not stand, for Immanuel. . . . For unto us a child is born, unto us a son is given, and the government shall be upon his shoulder; and his name shall be called Wonderful, Counselor, the Mighty God, the Everlasting Father, the Prince of Peace. Of the increase of his government and peace there shall be no end, upon the throne of David, and upon his kingdom, to order it, and to establish it with judgment and with justice, from henceforth, even forever. The zeal of the Lord of Hosts will perform this."

Even those words of chap. vii, 16, which form the stronghold of the naturalist interpretation, and which have led many Christian writers to admit a double fulfillment in a child of Isaiah or Ahaz, as well as in Messiah, will be found, I believe, on closer examination, to lend no real support to this view. The mention of "butter (or curds) and honey" as the food of the infant Immanuel, is the link by which alone his birth is here connected, in time, with the overthrow of Rezin. "For before the child shall know to refuse the evil and choose the good, the land thou abhorrest shall be forsaken of both her kings." But the passage does not terminate here; nor would the connection be at all clear unless we read the verses that follow. Now, these predict, along with, and *after*, the overthrow of Rezin, an Assyrian and Egyptian invasion, extending to Judah as well as Samaria. One result of these would be the general use of a diet of "butter and honey" from the desolation of the country. "In that day a man shall nourish a cow and two young sheep; and for the abundance of milk that they shall give he shall eat butter (or curds;) for butter and honey shall every one eat that is left in the land." These desolations were to extend to Ahaz himself, his people, and his father's house. Verse 17. And thus the real drift of the prediction must be, that before the promised Immanuel was of age to refuse the evil and to choose the good, not only would Rezin have been overthrown, but the land of Judah itself have been desolated by the Assyrian armies. Thus the sole argument in favor of the lower and temporary view of the prediction, when closely examined, disappears, and lends a further presumption to the nobler application to our Lord himself, the Son of the Virgin, the true Messiah, and the long-promised Heir of David's throne.

II. The later prophecies of Isaiah—chapters xl–lxvi—are another main object of assault to those modern critics who labor to dispense with all supernatural prediction. It is asserted boldly that they were not written by Isaiah himself, but nearly two centuries later, in the time of Zerubbabel, and are much rather a history of the present than prophecies of a distant future. The treatment of them in this spirit, so as to establish these conclusions, has been called the most brilliant portion of Baron Bunsen's prophetical essays. In this he only succeeds, it is said, to an inheritance of opinion derived from Gesenius, Ewald, Maurer, and earlier and later authorities in Hebrew criticism, to dispute whose decisions would be reckoned, in Germany, a suicidal and ridiculous folly.

In Germany itself, however, these views have by no means met with such a blind submission. On the contrary, there are critics of no inferior ability who have seen and proclaimed the hollow nature of the unbelieving assumption on which they rest. Thus, Keil remarks upon Ewald's treatment of Joshua, and the words apply equally to this portion of Isaiah: "In this dissection the only principle which guides him is the old rationalistic doctrine, that a supernatural revelation, accompanied by miracle and prophecies, is neither a fact nor a possibility; and that the theocratic view of Israelitish history is altogether a creation of poetic myths. . . . This foregone conclusion of common rationalism is both the chief assumption and the decisive rule in the determination of the original sources. The different passages are said to date from the periods to which, in his opinion, the predictions contained in them refer, since the prophecies are nothing but the vailed poetic method of picturing present events, or, at most, forebodings of future occurrences already involved in the present. Actual predictions do not exist. The entire theory is, therefore, built upon the sand. It has not the slightest objective truth in it, and does not admit of examination in detail, as it is not founded on any scientific principle."

Let us now examine the direct proofs of authenticity in these later chapters of Isaiah, and the nature of those critical objections which have been urged to set it aside.

1. First, the whole book has been received by the Jews, so far as evidence remains, from the very date of its publication as the genuine work of Isaiah. The inscription alone is a public testimony to the fact, and no trace of a contrary opinion can be found among them. The writer of Ecclesiasticus, also, in the second century before Christ, alludes distinctly to these later prophecies, and refers them without hesitation to Isaiah as their author.

2. The book of Ezra supplies a still stronger proof. It begins with a decree of Cyrus: "He made proclamation through all his kingdom, and put it in writing. Thus saith Cyrus, king of Persia, The Lord God of heaven hath given me all the kingdoms of the earth, and he hath charged me to build him a house in Jerusalem, which is in Judah." There is here a distinct reference to Isa. xliv, 28: "That saith of Cyrus, He is my shepherd, and shall perform all my pleasure; even saying to Jerusalem, Thou shalt be built; and to the Temple, Thy foundation shall be laid."

This explanation of the decree is not only plain in itself, but confirmed by the statement of Josephus, which proves that it was the current tradition of the Jews in the first century. "**These** things," he observes, "Cyrus knew through reading the book which Isaiah left of his own prophecies two hundred and ten years before. For he reported the message of God: 'I have chosen Cyrus, whom I have made king of many and great nations, to send my people into their own land, and to build my Temple.' These things Isaiah predicted a hundred and forty years before the Temple was destroyed. When Cyrus had read these words he wondered at the Divine message, and a certain impulse and ambition seized him to do what was written."

3. Our Lord and his apostles bear witness to the same truth. There are about fifty-four quotations from Isaiah in the New Testament, and nineteen in which he is mentioned by name. Thirty-three of them are from these later chapters of which the authenticity has been denied, and they are referred eleven times to Isaiah by name. Thus Isa. xl, 3, is ascribed to him by John the Baptist and all the four Evangelists. When our Lord opened his ministry at Nazareth, "there was given to him the book of Esaias the prophet." He turned to the sixty-first chapter, read its opening verses, closed the book and sat down, and then said, "This day is this Scripture fulfilled in your ears." This indirect testimony to the passage, as truly part of Isaiah's writings, and the direct acknowledgment of it as genuine prophecy, formed the starting-point of our Lord's Galilean ministry. Again, St. John accounts for the unbelief of the Jews in our Lord's miracles by referring to another of these predictions: "That the saying of Esaias the prophet might be fulfilled, which he spake, Lord, who hath believed our report?" "Therefore they could not believe, because that Esaias said again," etc. The two quotations—one from the earlier and one from the later chapters—are followed by the common statement, "These things said Esaias when he saw His glory and spake of

Him." The theory, then, which assigns these chapters to some later writer during the exile, is in flagrant contradiction to the teaching of our Lord and his apostles.

4. The structure of the work yields decisive internal evidence of its unity. Four chapters of simple narrative separate its two main portions. The book of Isaiah's prophecies can not be supposed to end with the first of these, or chapter xxxv; for then it would entirely omit the most impressive part of his personal history and message at the time of Hezekiah's sickness, and of the Assyrian invasion. A final close at chapter xxxix would be still more unnatural. How lame and impotent a termination would it be to all the warnings and promises even of the earlier portion alone—"Then said Hezekiah to Isaiah, Good is the word of the Lord which thou hast spoken. He said, moreover, For there shall be peace and truth in my days."

The book, on the contrary, as it now stands, has an almost dramatic unity. The earlier portion is grouped, in all its warnings and promises, around the great fact of the progressive desolations wrought in Palestine and the border countries by the kings of Assyria. The later portion has its basis and prophetical departure in the exile at Babylon and the deliverance under Cyrus. The ten tribes were to be utterly desolated by the Assyrian; but though the waters of the river, strong and many, would reach in Judah even to the neck, the adversaries were not to prevail, but to meet, on the contrary, a decisive overthrow. Under Babylon the two tribes also would be overthrown, and led away into a long captivity; but when the judgment had thus reached its hight, the mercies of the Lord would begin to return to the chosen people.

Now, the four chapters xxxvi–xxxix, exactly fulfill the purpose of effecting the transition from one of this double series of prophecies to the other. They begin with the invasion of Sennacherib, and describe the weakness of Judah, the alarm of the people, the insulting boldness of the Assyrian invader, and the faith of the pious king. The message of Isaiah follows, which forms the climax and culminating point of his personal ministry. Then follows the brief account of the sudden destruction of the Assyrian army, and the death of the proud king by parricide, after his return to Nineveh. The first woe from Assyria has now passed away, but another begins to dawn in the far horizon. Merodach-baladan, the king of Babylon, sends messengers and a present to Hezekiah, to congratulate him on his recovery. Under an impulse of vanity he shows them all his choicest treasures; and the prophet is sent to him at once with the humbling message, that all these treasures, and his own sons and successors on the throne, shall be carried away in captivity to Babylon. This new danger, prophetically announced, now becomes the starting-point of a new and still more glorious series of predictions. The former were marked by a tone of warning and judgment, but these are rich, from first to last, with promises of deliverance and blessing. The intermediate time of growing trial and distress, the more humbling details of the Captivity, and of the Return itself, are all passed over in silence. Two themes of hope and joy characterize the whole: the deliverance under Cyrus in the nearer distance, or prophetic foreground; and beyond it, the work, the sufferings, and the glory of the promised Immanuel, the true Israel, the Man of sorrows, the Anointed Prophet and Intercessor, the lasting inheritor of David's throne.

The book of Isaiah, then, in its actual form, has a symmetry of structure which the skeptical hypothesis completely destroys. The four historical chapters, by the nature of their contents, fulfill the purpose of linking together two contrasted series of prophecies. All the earlier ones converge toward the event narrated, chaps. xxxvi–xxxviii, the grand catastrophe of the Assyrian overthrow. All the later ones radiate from the warning to Hezekiah, chap. xxxix, and compose a treasury of hopes by which the faithful were to be sustained, through two centuries of sorrow and fear, till the Return, and through five centuries more of conflict and delay, till the coming of the promised **Immanuel** If we tear away this later portion from the rest of the book, instead of one consistent whole we have two broken fragments, equally unnatural and incomplete in their separate structure.

5. A comparison with the real prophecies of the exile will yield a further proof of the baseless nature of the novel theory Only five or six chapters of the book of Jeremiah are simply prophetic, and all the rest are either pure history, or abound with historical details. The last sixteen chapters of Ezekiel are simple prophecy, but the others, being two-thirds of the whole, have historical dates, or various particulars of actual history. The same is true of the books of Daniel and Zechariah. We have no single instance of a complete prophecy, without mention of the name of its author, or some statement of the time when he wrote, or some definite allusions to the actual events of the times. But these chapters, if not a part of Isaiah, would be a solitary contrast to this universal law of prophetic revelation. No name of a writer would be prefixed, no mention of the place where, or the time when he wrote. No single detail occurs in them with regard to a single person among the Jewish exiles, no name of one king or noble of Babylon, or any thing which has the air of historical narration. The passages which approach the nearest to this character, are not only prophetical in tone and style, with a constant use or intermixture of the future tense,

but are joined with distinct assertions that they are the words of that God who "declareth the end from the beginning, and from ancient times the things that are not yet done." With such a concurrence of external and internal evidence for their authenticity, as the best and noblest portion of Isaiah's prophecies, it seems impossible to account for the acceptance of an opposite view, but from a spirit of settled unbelief in the possibility of supernatural revelation.

6. The special reasons alleged for this view are either of no force, or else prove exactly the reverse. First, in chap. xlvi, 1, "Bel boweth down, Nebo stoopeth;" the present tense is used, as it is very frequently in most prophecies. But the inference that the events were passing at the time is both inconsistent with the supposed date, before the close of the exile, and with the words which immediately follow, verses 10, 11, which teach us to read in this clear prediction a proof of the Divine foreknowledge. Again, in chap. xlviii, 20, "Go ye forth from Babylon," the appeal is no less unfortunate. For the same chapter supplies this distinct explanation: "Because I knew that thou art obstinate, and thy neck an iron sinew, and thy brow brass; I have even from the beginning declared it unto thee, before it came to pass I showed it thee." The argument from the presence of a few Chaldee forms or phrases is only a curious illustration of the perversity of these skeptical criticisms. For the book of Daniel, when viewed as genuine, was written by Daniel, a Jewish exile, dwelling in Chaldee; and accordingly one half of the book is Chaldee, and the rest is Hebrew. The negative critics, however, stoutly deny its authenticity, and ascribe it to some Jew of Palestine, in the time of Antiochus Epiphanes, when neither Chaldee nor Hebrew, but a Syriac, distinct from both, was the usual language. On the other hand, these chapters of Isaiah, which are Hebrew throughout, and where not a single verse

is Chaldee, as in Jeremiah, are referred to a Jew toward the close of the time of the exile, when the displacement of Hebrew by Chaldee would probably have reached its hight. One of the very few words on which the argument is based, also, is *sagan* for prince in the verse, "I have raised one from the north, and he shall come; from the rising of the sun he shall call upon my name, and he shall come upon princes as upon mortar, as the potter treadeth clay." Now, certainly, the sixty years which had passed from the first Assyrian invasions to the fifteenth of Hezekiah—since the Chaldeans were included among the dependencies of Nineveh—were an interval quite long enough for the prophet and the Israelites to have learned the Chaldean names for their princes; and it would be only natural and significant to make use of it in a prediction of their overthrow by the Persian conqueror. Hezekiah, besides, had received an honorable embassy from the King of Babylon, and it is most probable that one or more *sagans* might have been the messengers; so that nothing can well be more ridiculous than to found an argument on this solitary word for lowering the time of the prophecy two hundred years.

7. It is needless to dwell, in detail, on the violent and even monstrous glosses which have accompanied this hypothesis; and which are necessary—even when its date has been lowered to the time of Zerubbabel, in defiance of all testimony and all internal evidence—to purify it completely from the character of a Divine and supernatural prophecy. Such is that brilliant discovery that Isaiah liii is no prophecy, but a historical sketch of the life of the prophet Jeremiah. After nine distinct and explicit applications of clauses of this prophecy to Christ in the New Testament, including the discourse of Philip to the eunuch under the express teaching of the Spirit, when he "began

at the same Scripture and preached to him Jesus," and the words, still more weighty, if possible, of our Lord himself: "I say unto you that this which is written must yet be accomplished in me: and he was numbered with the transgressors, for even the things that concern me must be fulfilled"—the acceptance of such a view by any one who calls himself a Christian can hardly be explained, unless by another passage of the same prophet: "Stay yourselves and wonder: they are drunken, but not with wine; they stagger, but not with strong drink; for the Lord hath poured out upon them the spirit of deep sleep, and hath closed your eyes; the prophets and rulers, the seers hath he covered, and the vision of all is become as the words of a book that is sealed." Truths, which are plain as the daylight to simple and honest hearts, become wrapped in mist and darkness when the pride of fancied learning usurps the place of lowly reverence for the oracles of the living God.

III. The prophecies of Daniel are another object of determined hostility to the negative critics of modern times. In fact, a belief in their genuineness is fatal at once to their whole theory. The unusual fullness and clearness of the predictions in chapters viii and xi forces us to accept the alternative that they are either due to the Divine foreknowledge, or else forged prophecies, written after the vents which they pretend to foretell. Accordingly, the latter view is adopted by Celsus and Porphyry, the open adversaries of the Gospel in early times, and by all those critics in our own days who strive to reconcile the name of Christian with a rejection of all the most essential features of the Christian revelation.

Now, here it is well to remember, at the outset, the real nature of the question at issue between unbelieving criticism and Christian faith, and which it is sought to disguise by smooth and flattering words where real compromise is impossible. We have been told, for example, that although the writer lived after the events, and only borrowed the name of the true Daniel, he was a "patriot bard," who used it with no deceptive intention, as a dramatic form, to encourage his countrymen in their struggle against Antiochus. But this hypothesis, on the face of it, is incredible and absurd. If ever there were a history which clearly and undeniably was meant to be received as real, it is these chapters of Daniel. If ever there were prophecies which, if not real prophecies, are a series of blasphemous profanations of the name of God, it is these visions. The real meaning, then, of the hypothesis is this, and can be nothing else, that the book of Daniel consists of false and fraudulent history, invented at will by an unprincipled and profane Jewish forger, to be the vehicle of pretended prophecies written after the events they seemed to predict; and where the name of the God of truth and holiness is profaned in every chapter, and almost in every verse, to give greater currency to an infamous lie. It means, also, that the unknown writer, though our Lord himself has called him "Daniel the prophet," was really one of the foremost in the class the apostle describes, who say, "Let us do evil that good may come; whose damnation is just." Once accept the premises of these critics, and it is impossible to escape the conclusion that a book more immoral, more recklessly profane than this book of Daniel has scarcely been written since the beginning of the world. The evidence must indeed be strong which would persuade any pious mind to acquiesce for a moment in so hateful and hideous a conclusion.

Let us now examine the direct evidence for the authenticity of these prophecies, and the nature of the objections which have been alleged to prove them spurious.

1. First, the book has been received without opposition by the Jewish Church and people, from the time when the canon was finished as the genuine work of Daniel himself. It rests, therefore, on the same internal evidence on which the Christian Church, from the beginning, has received every other book of the Old Testament, the constant and uniform tradition of the Jewish people, whose jealous care of their Scriptures has been confirmed by tests of peculiar severity, both before and after the time of the Gospel.

It has been urged, as some abatement of this testimony, that Daniel is placed among the Hagiographa, between Esther and Ezra, and is not numbered with the other prophets. But it seems a simple explanation that the book was not only composed out of Palestine, and partly in a Gentile dialect, but that a considerable part is pure history, and forms a historical link between the book of Kings and those of Esther, Ezra, and Nehemiah. It is quite easy, then, to understand that its place might be fixed with reference rather to its histories than its prophecies, especially since two of the last are expressly sealed, and when the canon was formed their meaning would be still an unopened mystery. As a history the book forms the natural transition from the close of Kings or Chronicles to the books of Ezra, Nehemiah, and Esther; and its association with these in the canon is, therefore, very simply explained without the least impeachment of its authority.

2. Next, we have a distinct testimony of Josephus that the book was extant in the time of Alexander, that one part of it was read to him when he visited Jerusalem, and that it was the occasion of public and especial favors being granted to the Jews. "And when the book of Daniel the prophet was shown to him, in which he revealed that some one of the Greeks would destroy the Persian dominion, judging that he himself was pointed out, he was rejoiced,

and dismissed the multitude; and summoning them the next day, bade them ask for what gifts they chose. And when the high-priest requested that they might use their national laws, and be free from tribute every seventh year, he granted the whole. And when they further besought that he would allow the Jews in Babylonia and Media to use their own laws, he readily promised to do what they desired." The appeal is here made to facts which must have been notorious, of privileges given by Alexander to the Jews. There could be no stronger testimony to the full and undoubting conviction of Josephus and the Jews of his days, that the prophecy of Daniel was in the hands of Jaddua in the time of Alexander, or nearly two hundred years before Antiochus.

3. A testimony still more decisive, by far, in the eyes of every Christian is that of our Lord himself, as recorded in the first two Gospels: "But when ye see the abomination of desolation, spoken of by Daniel the prophet, standing in the holy place, (let him that readeth understand,) then let them which be in Judea flee into the mountains." Soon after there follow these impressive words: "Heaven and earth shall pass away, but my words shall not pass away."

One of the words of Christ, then, attested by this solemn sanction from the lips of Him who is the Truth, is the statement that the prophecy in the hands of the disciples, which they were charged to read with intelligence, and where the abomination of desolation is repeatedly named, is truly that of "Daniel the prophet." The theory, then, broached by those modern critics who would make it a forgery in the days of Antiochus, gives the lie direct to the Lord of glory, in one of his clearest averments, which is followed by a most explicit and solemn attestation. It is hard to understand how those who embrace it can still dare to call themselves disciples of Christ.

4. The testimony of the apostle in the Epistle to the Hebrews is more indirect, but hardly less powerful and complete. Among the list of the victories of faith in the worthies of the Old Testament, we find the two particulars, that they "stopped the mouths of lions, quenched the violence of fire." The allusion is plainly to the two histories, Dan. iii and vi. These are placed in the same rank of historical certainty with all the other facts in the brief summary, and the conclusion is drawn: "These all, having obtained a good report through faith, received not the promise: God having provided some better thing for us, that they without us should not be made perfect. Wherefore, seeing we are compassed about with so great a cloud of witnesses, let us run with patience the race that is set before us." But if some of these witnesses, and the asserted triumphs of their faith, are mere inventions of an unscrupulous forger, the earnest appeal that follows is robbed entirely of its moral power, and becomes ridiculous and absurd. The truth of the facts is the basis of all the force and strength in this glowing exhortation to diligence, fidelity, and patience.

5. The internal evidence from the historical facts alone is strong and clear. The chronology falls in with the statement of the other Scriptures, and also with the canon of Ptolemy. The name of Belshazzar, after being looked for in vain in heathen writers, has now of late been detected in the deciphered remains of Babylonia, as a joint ruler with his own father at the time of Babylon's fall. This accounts, also, as remarked already, for the minute contrast, that while Joseph was made second ruler in Egypt, Daniel was only promised by Belshazzar, in the hour of his terror, to be the third ruler in his kingdom.. The madness of Nebuchadnezzar toward the close of his reign is attested by a fragment of Megasthenes. The supplication of Daniel, in

the first year of Darius the Mede, corresponds punctually with the near approach of the expiration of the seventy years from Jehoiachin's captivity; and the earnestness of his later prayer, with fasting, in the third of Cyrus, equally corresponds to the crisis in the book of Ezra, when adverse counsels first interrupted the progress of the work at Jerusalem, and brought the Jews into disfavor once more at the court of Persia. An unprincipled inventor of fables in the days of Antiochus was little likely to form by accident, or to produce by artifice, such undesigned coincidences as these. The mention that Darius was sixty-two years old when he took the kingdom, while it agrees with all probability, if he were the uncle of Cyrus, is one of the clearest signs of a cotemporary and well-informed writer. No other explanation is possible, except we impute to him a deliberate fraud in order to produce a false impression, and clothe mere fiction with a mask of historical reality.

6. The language of the book, and the mutual relation of its histories and its visions, are another proof of its genuineness. The character of the whole, in these respects, is peculiar and complicated. The first six chapters are historical; the other six are a series of prophetic visions. The first chapter, three verses of the second, and the last five are in Hebrew, but the rest, from ii, 4, to vii, 28, is in Chaldee. Again, the third person is used in the six historical chapters, and the first person in all the rest. Nothing could show more clearly the unity of the whole, and the claim, throughout, to be the writing of Daniel himself. If the separation of the languages had coincided with that of history and prophecy, there might be some excuse for a hypothesis which would ascribe the two parts to different authors. Their interlacing together, where one chapter of history alone is in Hebrew and one of the four successive visions alone in Chaldee, proves that the whole forms

one connected work, the parts of which can not be severed But it discovers also a secret relation between the actual contents and the languages employed, which marks the wisdom of an inspired prophet and not the capricious narration of an unprincipled forger. The history begins in Hebrew, so as to link itself both in form and substance with the canonical history at the close of Kings. It changes to Chaldee as soon as the Chaldeans are introduced in the dialogue, and continues in Chaldee throughout the time of the seventy years' Captivity to its close. The first vision, also, is in Chaldee; since it does not refer specifically to Jewish history, but to the series of Gentile monarchies, and is an enlargement of the vision, already recorded in Chaldee, which was given to the king Nebuchadnezzar. But the other prophecies, since they all refer to the later history of the Jews, and the time of their restoration, are in Hebrew only. In all these delicate and complex relations we have a distinct harmony with the character and position of the true Daniel, a Hebrew of the royal stock, but an exile from his childhood, who remained in Babylon through the whole course of the seventy years. Instead of these secret harmonies of Divine wisdom, the skeptical theory offers us the blind chance-medley of a Jewish forger, who chose, in the times of Antiochus, to indite his own inventions in the shape of history, and then to garble real history by turning it into pretended prophecy; who adopted a false name in two different ways, and constructed his forgery in two different languages, both of them distinct from the vernacular of his own days, and one of them without precedent in a canonical book of prophecy.

7. The objection from the alleged presence of Greek words, or late forms of expression, has been abundantly refuted in Germany itself by scholars of accuracy and learning. In fact, our own earlier writers against the deists

of last century, Samuel and Bishop Chandler, had already done it with substantial force of reasoning. Hengstenberg and Havernick, and others, have treated it more fully. It is enough to observe here that of the two Macedonian words, *symphonia* and *psanterion*, referred to—Essays, p. 76—as decisive proofs of a late composition, the second is neither a Macedonian word nor occurs in the book of Daniel, while the other occurs in two forms, *sumponya* and *syponya*, neither of which corresponds exactly with the Greek word; that only one known instance occurs, in Polybius, where this Greek word is used for a musical instrument; that in the case of a third musical instrument, the *sambuca*, equally relied on by earlier opponents of the authenticity, both Strabo and Athenæus expressly refer the instrument itself and its name to an eastern source. Besides, it is highly probable that some intercourse of Greeks with upper Asia dates from the time even of Sennacherib, as we may infer from Polyhistor and Abydenus. The whole objection, once held to be so formidable, after reducing itself to three names of musical instruments alone, has at length been abandoned by some of the latest opponents in Germany as untenable and worthless. On the other hand, the broad fact, already noticed, of the twofold language in which the book is written, agrees perfectly with the supposition that it is the genuine work of the prophet Daniel, and with no other view.

8. It has been urged, as a further objection, that the prophecies are clear and full to the time of Antiochus Epiphanes, about B. C. 169, and then suddenly cease, or become vague and ambiguous. No assertion, however, could be more grossly untrue. There is no pretense whatever for making three out of the five prophecies close with Antiochus; and a comparison with the New Testament will prove that we can only accept that view, in a fourth pre-

diction, by directly contradicting and rejecting the authority of an inspired apostle. The reference of the fourth part of the image and of the fourth beast—chapter vii—to the Roman Empire is confirmed by an immense preponderance of external authority and internal evidence; and the contrary hypotheses of the negative critics are not only mutually destructive, but each of them is loaded with some palpable absurdity. Such is the view which makes the Medes and Persians to be two of the four empires, in direct opposition to the book itself—chapter viii—where they form conjointly the Ram, or one empire only; and that which makes Alexander and his successors two distinct empires, in equal contradiction to common-sense and the language of the prophecy. But the prophecy of the seventy weeks offers a shorter and more distinct proof of the entire falsehood of this confident assertion. It is quite impossible, without a critical torture like that of the Inquisition, to make it agree in any way with the asserted date under Antiochus; for, not to insist on the total period, sixty-two weeks of years are four hundred and thirty-four years. The earliest decree to rebuild Jerusalem was that of Cyrus, B. C. 536. Hence, this shortened and imperfect period, applied to the earliest possible date, would bring the close to B. C. 102, or nearly seventy years after the Dedication under the Maccabees, when the persecution of Epiphanes reached its close.

On the other hand, the Christian application of the prophecy, in its main outlines, is simple, easy, and consistent. The seventy weeks are broken into three compo nents of seven, sixty-two, and one single week, or forty-nine, four hundred and thirty-four, and seven years. The close of the first is not distinctly defined, but it seems implied that the street and the wall were to be rebuilded during its progress. In B. C. 458 was the decree of Artaxerxes, which formally reconstructed or rebuilt Jerusalem as a civic corporation, or a provincial metropolis under the Persian Empire. Within forty-nine years, or before B. C. 409, the book of Nehemiah was complete, the street and the wall were rebuilt, and the canon of Scripture apparently closed. Sixty-two weeks from this limit, or four hundred and thirty-four years—four hundred and eighty-three from the first decree—bring us to A. D. 26-27; the exact year and date, it is almost certain, of the Baptist's ministry, and of those words of our Lord which allude probably to this very passage: "The time is fulfilled, and the kingdom of heaven is at hand: repent and believe the Gospel." Then follow three and a half years of the Baptist's and our Lord's ministry till his crucifixion, when Messiah was cut off, and none were on his side; the confirmation of the new covenant with many disciples; and, lastly, the prediction repeated and applied by our Lord himself when Jerusalem was compassed with armies, and the desolating abomination stood on holy ground, and the city and the sanctuary were both destroyed. To those skeptical critics who resist so plain and consistent an application, and strive to wrest the prediction to the times of Antiochus, the words of another prophet may well be applied: "We grope for the wall like the blind, and we grope as if we had no eyes; we stumble at noonday as in the night." The folly of this fancied learning, which sets itself boldly against the clearest authority of Christ and his apostles, and achieves after all such bare and impotent results, can only deserve profound commiseration.

The books of the Old Testament, then, from first to last, contain multiplied and various prophecies, which have been fulfilled in the person and work of the Lord Jesus, and in the later spread of his Gospel. The seed of the woman has been miraculously born, and has begun to bruise the head of the serpent, by casting down heathen idolatry in the chief nations of the world, and planting the standard of the cross victorious upon its ruins. The race of Japheth have been enlarged, and dwell now in the tents of Shem, by the reception of the nations of the West into the visible Church of the God of Israel. The seed of Abraham has been born, and has begun to be a blessing to all the families of the earth. The true Shiloh has appeared, before the scepter had departed from Judah; and his later sentence by a Roman governor proved that it had been then departed or was just passing away. A prophet like Moses has appeared, rescued in his infancy from the malice of murderous enemies, and rejected, when he first came to them, by the very people whom he sought to deliver. The Virgin has conceived and borne a Son, and his name is called Immanuel, by the consenting worship of one-fourth of the world's population. His name is called by these countless millions, in every Christmas celebration, "Wonderful, Counselor, the Mighty God, the Everlasting Father, the Prince of Peace." He has come in the character ascribed to him by the same prophet, "a man of sorrows and acquainted with grief." The Jews, his own people, "hid their faces from him; he was despised and they esteemed him not." That which was written was strictly accomplished in him: "He was numbered with the transgressors," for even the sufferings of the Son of God, being predicted in Holy Scripture, must be fulfilled. Less than seventy weeks of years elapsed after Artaxerxes's decree of restoration to Jerusalem, when "Messiah the Prince appeared." He was cut off, none were on his side, but even his disciples forsook him and fled; and the people of the Roman prince, within forty years, destroyed the city and the sanctuary, and their desolation has continued even to the present day. But the unbelief of the Jews has only confirmed the prophecies, and insured the fulfillment of a further promise made to Messiah in the prospect of their rebellion. "It is a light thing that thou shouldst be my servant, to raise up the tribes of Jacob, and to restore the preserved of Israel; I will also give thee for a light to the Gentiles; that thou mayest be my salvation to the ends of the earth." He who can compare the history in the Gospel, and the later progress of Christianity, with the series of Old-Testament predictions, and still continue blind to their correspondence, and the proof it supplies of the Christian revelation, falls under the stern rebuke of that sentence of our Lord himself: "If they hear not Moses and the prophets, neither will they be persuaded though one rose from the dead."

CHAPTER IX.

CHRISTIANITY AND WRITTEN REVELATION.

Christian faith consists in an acknowledgment of the Divine mission of our Lord and his apostles, and an acceptance of their testimony to the person and work of Christ, as the Son of God, and the Savior of the world. The natural means in our days for attaining this faith is an acceptance of the Gospels, Acts, and Epistles, as credible and truthful records of the first rise of the Christian religion. But a reception of the whole Bible as inspired and authoritative, is a corollary of Christian faith. It holds the first place among the subsidiary doctrines of the Gospel. It does not enter distinctly into the creeds of the early Church; but still it penetrates the whole range of Christian literature, and is the chief security for a steady and firm progress in the knowledge of Divine truth. In the minds of common Christians it is now so closely united, both by habitual association and spiritual instinct, with their faith in the Gospel itself, that they find it hard to view the two truths as separable. It is chiefly when we have to deal with unbelievers, or perplexed and doubting inquirers, that it is needful to distinguish clearly two successive stages in the growth of a reasonable faith; which must rest, first of all, on the person of our Lord, and his supernatural mission and Divine authority; and will afterward embrace the inspiration of the written Word and the Divine authority of all the Scriptures, both of the Old and the New Testament.

The previous chapters refer to the evidence of Christianity itself, in contrast to that more open infidelity which rejects the Divine authority of the Lord Jesus. Those which follow relate to the further truth, assailed by a lax and semi-infidel school of professed Christianity, that the Old and New Testaments are, throughout their whole extent, the words of the Holy Ghost, and authoritative messages from the God of truth to the children of men. It seems desirable, then, to offer here a brief outline of the general course of argument, by which our faith in the Gospel and in the Scriptures is sustained; since a laborious effort has lately been made to involve the whole theory of Christian belief in confusion and darkness.

"Whoever would take the religious literature of the present day as a whole, and endeavor to make out clearly on what basis revelation is supposed by it to rest, whether on authority, on the inward light, on reason, on self-evidencing Scripture, or on the combination of the four, or of some of them, and in what proportions, would probably find that he had undertaken a perplexing but not altogether profitless inquiry."* Such is the contribution to the guidance of young and unsettled minds, which forms the close of nearly eighty pages of disquisition on the "Tendencies of Religious Thought in England," and of a review of the whole series of English works on the evidences of Christianity. But if all past arguments by the ablest men, on behalf of Christianity, are inconsistent and almost worthless by the admission of clergymen and Christian divines themselves, the skeptic may well conceive that his cause is gained, and that the Gospel of Christ is worn-out and effete in the view of its own official guardians. The idea, also, of sending young students to the religious literature

---

* Essay vi, p. 329.

of the present day, "as a whole," in order to solve for themselves a difficult problem of theology, which their teachers seem to abandon in despair, is much the same as it would have been, at the beginning, to recommend a dip into chaos in order to guess out the nature of the coming world.

A healthy eye is required for perfect vision. But it is not needful, happily, to know whether our sight depends on the cornea or the crystalline lens, on the aqueous or the vitreous humor, or "on a combination of the four, or of some of them, and in what order and proportion," before we can discern and rejoice in the presence of a beloved friend. A humble heart and a healthy conscience will lead the most unlettered Christian to a firm belief in the Gospel, and in the truth of the sacred Scriptures, though he may never have cared to settle what share each kind of evidence may have had in this result. Such inquiries may be objects of lawful curiosity to spiritual anatomists; and when humbly and cautiously pursued, like the dissection of the natural eye, may enrich our Christian theology with deeper views of the Divine wisdom; but they leave the actual processes of spiritual vision wholly unaltered. The simplest cottager and the most subtile metaphysician stand here on the same level; and those who are quite unable to describe the steps of the mental process, may be able to discern with fullest certainty "the light of the knowledge of the glory of God, in the face of Jesus Christ."

The steps by which the early disciples were led to Christian faith stand out before us in clear and full relief in the New Testament. The miracles of our Lord and his apostles made a first and simple appeal to their senses and to their hearts. The most thoughtless who witnessed them were arrested by the sight; and all who were not withheld by strong Jewish prejudice, or the debasing power of idol atry, owned at once the finger of God, and the authority of his chosen messengers. But where strong Jewish prejudices had to be overcome, the next appeal was to the word of prophecy. The apostles reasoned with their Jewish adversaries out of their own Scriptures, "opening and alleging that it was needful that the Christ should suffer, and should rise again from the dead, and that this Jesus" whom they preached "was indeed the Christ." There was thus a striking example of what has been aptly termed in physical science, "the Consilience of Inductions." The results separately derived from the occurrence of many miraculous signs, and from the plain fulfillment of many predictions, in which the prophets had announced a despised, rejected, and suffering Messiah, led to the same conclusion—that Jesus of Nazareth, though rejected and despised by his own countrymen, was truly the Christ of God. This truth was further established to the early believers by miraculous gifts which many of them received, by their own joyful experience of the pardoning love of God in Christ, by their consciousness of the sanctifying power of the Gospel in their own hearts, and by the abundant fruits of it which they witnessed daily in the lives of their fellow-believers.

This order, so clear in the case of the first disciples, is varied a little, and only a little, in the case of modern disciples, born amidst the institutions and traditions of a Christian land, who have the Bible placed in their hands from childhood as the Word of God. First of all, they receive the Scriptures with a human faith, on the authority of parents and teachers, and of an almost unanimous assent of good and wise men, whose conversation and writings are like an atmosphere of Christian thought that surrounds them on every side. When they read the New Testament they find in every page the signs of its general truth and credibility. They are thus brought at once face to face within view of the same double evidence of miracles and prophecy, which compelled the faith of the early disciples. The miracles of our Lord and his apostles stand revealed to them with full historical proofs of their reality; and the agreement between Jewish prophecies and the life and death of Christ is no less clear than when appealed to by the apostles themselves in the synagogues of Palestine and of the Roman world. Distance of time, in the case of the miracles, may have made the impression less vivid, but can not affect the substantial force of the argument. But there are further confirmations of the Gospel, not shared in those early days, from the fulfilled prophecies of the New Testament, in the spread and permanence of the Gospel, the overthrow and ruin of the Temple, and the long-lasting desolation and dispersion of the Jewish people.

When once the truth of Christ has been practically embraced still fuller evidence dawns upon the heart of believers. They feel the power and comfort of its gracious promises. Their conscience, taught by the Spirit of God, responds with delight to the beauty of its Divine morality. They perceive with growing clearness the harmony of its doctrines, both with the wants of man and with the attributes of God. And thus their experience, while they submit with reverence and humility to the Divine messages, illustrates the truth of their Lord's promise: "To him that hath shall be given, and he shall have more abundance;" while borderers and theological triflers, who keep the truth at arm's length from their own conscience, for subtile and curious speculation alone, fall too often under the edge of the solemn warning: "From him that hath not, even that he hath shall be taken away."

There may be a stage, however, in the course of serious and thoughtful inquirers, in which their faith in the Gospel itself is unshaken, but their traditional trust in the Bible is sorely tried, and in some measure gives way. With growing thought and knowledge, difficulties once overlooked start out into sudden relief, and may seem for a time to be unsurmountable. They have been accustomed from childhood to hear the Bible spoken of as one book—the Word of God. They examine it more closely, with the help of classical knowledge since acquired, and see that it consists of many works, in two different languages, written by many different writers at remote periods of time; and bears traces in every part of its human authorship—in language, grammar, idiom, style, historical features, and even in some cases in its doctrinal tone. They have been accustomed, again, to hear it defined by entire freedom from all error. But they find that errors of translation, errors of transcription, and readings probably defective, though comparatively slight in amount, are admitted almost universally by well-informed scholars to exist within its pages; so that the ideal perfection once ascribed to it seems to disappear. They find numbers, here and there, which seem plainly to need emendation; and details which appears more or less contradictory in different accounts of the same event. Quotations from the Old Testament in the New do not seem always strictly to correspond, even in words; and the meaning assigned, in some cases, does not appear, on the first glance, to be the natural and genuine interpretation. Again, large portions in some of the books of the Old Testament seem to be useless details, that bear no stamp of Divinity, and are difficult to reconcile with the theory of a direct, miraculous, and all-perfect inspiration. These perplexities, and a few others of the same kind, when they first dawn upon the young Christian student, without destroying or, perhaps, sensibly weakening his faith in the Gospel itself, may easily induce him to imitate the Alexandrian mariners, when they cast out the wheat into the sea with their own hands, to lessen or avert the danger of total shipwreck. The plenary inspiration of the Scriptures may then be regarded as a superstitious accessory, a needless incumbrance of the Christian faith, which, in an hour of peril, out of love to that faith itself, it may be needful to sacrifice and cast away.

A looser faith in the inspiration of the whole Bible, when it arises from such causes, ought not to be confounded with a settled spirit of unbelief. It may be only like froth and scum on the surface in a process of fermentation, by which a passive and merely-traditional belief is passing into a more powerful, active, and living faith, the new wine of the kingdom of God. Men may profess to believe the whole Bible without an effort, when they have never appropriated or applied one single truth. But when some doctrines, or some books, begin to live intensely in their hearts, others may seem, by contrast, to be like dead branches, which it would be a gain, rather than a loss, to prune away.

Faith in Christianity, and a belief in the inspiration of the whole Bible, may either be confounded together and identified, or too widely dissevered. One error involves some degree of superstition; the other produces a dim and misty faith, with some tendency to a dangerous rejection of the truth of God.

The words of Christ in the Gospels, the facts of his death and resurrection, and the great truths and doctrines derived from them, might have been transmitted by oral tradition alone, or by honest writers under no especial guidance and control of the Spirit of God. The truth, in this case, would have been earlier and more largely mingled with partial error. It must have been liable, in a few generations, to a more rapid degeneracy and corruption, and the means of later reformation and recovery would be almost wholly removed. Still, facts have shown that even the presence of inspired writings has been no full safeguard, either to Jews or Christians, against the entrance of wide and mischievous corruptions of the faith. They simply exclude one inlet of error, but many others still remain. Humble and earnest hearts, in all ages of the Church, have often found the way of salvation by oral teaching alone; and those discourses of Christ, or words of his apostles, which have formed the chief nourishment of Christian faith and piety, might plainly have been recorded and preserved by honest witnesses, even though the rest of the works in which they were preserved bore many traces of infirmity and error.

The relation between the writings of the New Testament and the Gospel they reveal resembles closely that of the apostles to the Lord who sent them forth. All of them bore the stamp of his authority and commission. Two or three of them are rather prominent in the course of the history; but of the greater part little more is recorded than their names alone. All seem to delight to vail themselves in obscurity, that the name of their Lord and Master may stand out in fuller relief.

Now, the same remark applies to the separate books of the New Testament. All are full of one great subject—Jesus Christ; but they speak almost nothing of themselves and of each other. The three earlier Gospels were all composed before many of the Epistles, and yet these contain only two or three allusions to one of them only. No mention is made of the name of their authors, and there is no quotation from any of them, except one very brief clause. St. Paul himself, in his last Epistle, gives no list of those he had previously written, which were to be included in the canon. The four other apostles give no list of the written Gospels. Only one clear allusion occurs in their letters even to St. Paul's Epistles, where St. Peter gives a highly important testimony to these writings of his brother apostle, and places them in the same rank with the earlier Scriptures, but supplies us with no catalogue of their names. 2 Pet. iii, 16. Thus the New Testament contains no hint that a correct knowledge of the limits of its own canon, without excess or defect, was a leading essential of the Christian faith. Such an article could not enter the creed while the canon was still unfinished, and has not been added in later times. Even the warning at the close of the Apocalypse—Rev. xxii, 18, 19—while it enforces the guilt and danger of willfully corrupting the Word of God, either by subtraction or addition, directly applies to that book alone; and it is accompanied by no list of the completed canon, so as to enrol this knowledge among the essentials of Christian faith. On the contrary, every Church was left to acquire it, slowly and gradually, by receiving those books or epistles which were proved to be written by apostles, or had received distinct, apostolic attestation; and the actual canon had its birth out of the agreement of these results in different Churches. An error on this point would simply leave the Christian with a less pure or less complete medium for acquiring Divine knowledge, but would not affect the main outline of the facts of the Gospel, or the grand and essential doctrines of Christianity.

Again, the inspiration and authority of the Bible are not synonymous with entire freedom from the intrusion of the slightest error. We can not conceive, indeed, that messages from the God of truth should contain the least error, flaw, or contradiction, at the moment when they issue from their heavenly Source, and before their actual transmission to mankind. It seems the simplest view, therefore, to ascribe absolute perfection and freedom from error to each autograph, as it proceeded at first from its inspired penman and this simplest view may be the truest also. But it is unwise to place the essence of the doctrine in a circumstance which is no where distinctly revealed, and which does not apply to the chief practical difficulty; for the autographs of the Bible have never existed together: the earliest had doubtless perished long before the later ones were written. A Bible, then, gifted with this ideal and mathematical perfection, has never been in the hands of a single human being. The Bible, which alone has been accessible to the great body of the Church from the earliest times till now, is, either in whole or in part, a translation from copies of the first originals; and possible and even actual errors, both of copyists and translators, must be allowed to exist in its pages. The narrow limits of such mistakes is, practically, of the highest importance; but questions of degree disappear, and one slight or solitary corruption of the text becomes as fatal as the most extensive or the most numerous, when once we define Bible inspiration by the negative character of entire freedom from all error.

The only true and safe definition of Bible inspiration must be of a positive kind. These books were written by accredited messengers of God, for a special purpose, in order to be a standing record of Divine truth for the use of mankind. They are thus stamped throughout with a Divine authority; and this authority belongs to every part, even in that form in which the message reaches every one of us, till clear reasons can be shown for excepting any portion from the high sanction which belongs naturally to the whole. There are two ways in which such an exception may arise. It may be shown by historical evidence that such a verse, or clause, or construction, is due to wrong translation, or a defective reading, and is disproved by exact criticism, or by earlier or more numerous manu scripts; or else, the mere fact of a discrepancy may prove in itself the presence of a slight error, though we may be unable to point out, historically, when or how it first entered into the text. Such flaws, however, few in number, and chiefly in numerical readings or lists of names, can not affect, in the least, the direct evidence which affixes a Divine sanction to all the Scriptures of the Old and New Testaments. But when errors are asserted to exist which can not be referred, with any show of reason, to changes due merely to the transmission of the message, as when the narrative of Genesis i is pronounced to be scientifically false in every part, or the genealogies of the patriarchs are affirmed to be a mere disguise of national migrations, then a blow is aimed at the very root of the authority of the Scriptures. They are plainly degraded from being faithful messages of God to the level of erroneous and deceptive writings of fallible men.

Let us now turn to the other aspect of the inquiry, and see what are the conclusions we may fairly gather from the simple fact that God has been pleased to embody his own messages in a written form.

First of all, there is nothing accidental in the gift of written revelation. It marks the entrance of a new and remarkable era in the history of the world. Nearly three thousand years had passed before we have any proof or sign that any Divine message was embodied in a permanent record. But when the chosen people were brought out of Egypt, the gift of a written law was plainly designed, from the first, to be one especial feature of the new dispensation. The old Mosaic economy centered in the revelation of the Law on Mount Sinai; and this law was not only proclaimed miraculously by the voice of God out of the clouds and thick darkness, but it was miraculously placed on record by the hand of God himself: "The tables were the work of God, and the writing was the writing of God, graven on the tables." These tables of stone, engraven a second time by the finger of the Almighty, were afterward inclosed in "the ark of testimony" under the mercy-seat, in the most sacred recess of the tabernacle of God. But the whole series of Divine laws, enshrined in the facts of sacred history, was also from the first committed to writing at the command of God. This is taught in the ordinance of the Passover, and the later directions concerning it, which imply that a permanent record was to be made for use after entrance into Canaan. It is implied, again, at the waters of Marah, and after the gift of the manna; and is distinctly affirmed at the time of the conflict with Amalek: "And the Lord said unto Moses, Write this for a memorial in the book, and rehearse it in the ears of Joshua, for I will utterly put out the name of Amalek from under heaven." When the sacred code was complete, just as the two tables, miraculously graven, were already placed within the ark, so this book of the Law, the national code of Israel, was given to the Levites, and placed "in the side of the ark of the covenant of the Lord." Deut. xxxi, 26. After twenty-five centuries, during which the world has been without a written revelation, ever since the miraculous gift of the Law in flames of fire on Mount Sinai, and onward through more than three thousand years to the present day, such revelations have formed one main feature in the history of the moral government of mankind.

Now, if we ask the reasons of this great change, they seem at once to suggest themselves to a reflective mind. While laws are very few and simple, and the facts which it is desired to register are also few, mere oral tradition may well suffice without any written record. Such a tradition, in early times, when confined to a small number of particulars, might be preserved and handed down with great tenacity, and even appear doubly sacred to those who were its depositaries, because it was intrusted to the fidelity of their memory alone. But when facts and laws are multiplied, a written record is necessary, or the truth will rapidly be obscured and lost. There are millions who could remember twenty or thirty lines of verse, but only a few, here and there, who could recollect and repeat twenty or thirty thousand. Now, with the lapse of time, those facts of Divine Providence, which it was desirable to keep before the minds of men, were continually multiplied; and, with the entrance of the legal economy, the great moral precepts were unfolded into a large variety of personal and national duties, and increased by a system of typical ordinances and ceremonial commands. These reasons, while they account for the transition from merely oral to written revelation, would lead us to infer that this new and higher mode of revelation, after being once introduced, would never cease to the end of time. For the facts of Providence worthy of memorial, and the precepts and promises, the doctrines and examples, based upon them, must naturally go on increasing in later generations of mankind.

Revelations from God to man, when reduced to writing, secure plainly a double object. They are more definite and more permanent. They are less liable to be varied, and thus gradually corrupted, by erroneous additions; and they are also less liable to die out and be forgotten. After a season of decay and apostasy their power may be revived anew by a fresh appeal to the original documents. Such was eminently the case with the Jews in the reigns of Jehoshaphat and of Josiah, and still more remarkably on their return from Babylon. It was a feature equally conspicuous in the Protestant Reformation. This double purpose is seen in the Divine message, when the Law was repeated: "Ye shall not add unto the word which I command you, neither shall ye diminish aught from it, that ye may keep the commandments of the Lord your God which I command you."

Now, it is plain that the first of these two objects, instead of being secured, would be frustrated and reversed, if these written messages, from the very first, were loaded and disfigured by any sensible incrustation of human error. We may assume that, if God conveyed his messages through human agents, all the characteristics of those agents, except moral defect and falsehood, would be permitted to appear in the record, and thus become a further pledge of its reality and historical truth. But if this condescension were to extend still further, so as to allow their mistakes and ignorances, their sins and follies, to stain and disfigure communications which claimed to be Divine; then the means devised to secure the permanence of God's truth would, so far, exactly reverse its office, and would give permanence to error and falsehood, under the apparent sanction of the God of truth. Such a view of the Scriptures is therefore exposed to an objection, on *a priori* grounds, which it would require no slight amount of direct evidence to overcome. A means devised by the wisdom of God to give permanence, through all later ages, to his own truth, would be strangely diverted, so as to produce a result precisely opposite, and stereotype historical misconceptions and religious falsehood.

These reasons, which apply with great force to the first gift of a Divine revelation in a written form, do not warrant any expectation of a series of miracles to preserve its later transmission from every trace of carelessness and error. Even where documents are of no special importance, the usual mistakes, in a single transcription, are comparatively few; and the comparison of several copies, at first hand, will enable us, almost without a shade of doubt, to restore the exact original. In the course of many successive copyings the risk of error will be slightly increased; and it may be impossible, after some lapse of time, to be quite certain with regard to every letter and word of the original document. But still, these variations, at the worst, are of a very limited and subordinate nature. They are like straws or specks upon the surface of the writing, and do not penetrate its inner and vital texture. The same would be true if the prophet, as a prophet, were secured from all error; but, as a simple amanuensis, were left, like later copyists, to the natural results of his own care in recording a message felt to be of high and sacred importance.

The case, however, is widely different, if errors are interwoven into the message itself. There is, then, no means by which it can be eliminated, without tearing the whole to pieces, and destroying its authority. There is, also, in this case no assignable limit to the amount of error which may have entered in. The whole edifice of revealed religion would only rest upon a quicksand. No one would be able to say how much was true, how much was false; where human corruption reached its limit, and gave place to the tones of Divine truth and wisdom. Instead of stooping to the actual ignorance and blindness of man, to raise him once more into the light of heaven, such mingled messages would require almost a superhuman sagacity to discern good from evil, and light from darkness, even in words apparently sealed with God's own signet. We may, therefore, well apply the question of Luther to such a view of Scripture and its inspiration: "Are we not ambiguous and uncertain enough already, without having our ambiguity and uncertainty increased to us from heaven?" The great end for which the messages of God are conveyed to mankind in a written form, seems of itself to be a pledge of their Divine perfection, and echoes back to thoughtful Christians the sayings of their Lord, that "the Scripture can not be broken," and that "till heaven and earth pass, one jot or one tittle shall in no wise pass from the law, till all be fulfilled"

CHAPTER X.

THE INSPIRATION OF THE OLD TESTAMENT.

The great change in the public relation between God and man, implied in the gift of written revelation, marked the opening of a new and nobler era in the history of the world. It was attended with signal displays of the Divine power in the plagues of Egypt and the thunders of Sinai, and in great and terrible works of the God of Israel. Revealed religion was now to outgrow the narrow limits of human memory, and required a firmer and fuller record than oral tradition alone. The special acts of Divine power and wisdom in former generations were to be noted down and faithfully preserved for the instruction of every succeeding age. The great truths of religion and morality were to receive a larger development, and to be embodied in laws, and statutes, and ordinances, which required the study of a lifetime, rather than the recollection of a moment, and were to be handed down, in all their width and fullness, to many generations.

All the circumstances which attended this change were such as to attest its high importance. The ten commandments, the sum and center of the whole legal economy, were uttered, first, amidst thunder, lightning, smoke, and fire, from the sacred top of Sinai, by the lips of Jehovah himself. They were twice miraculously graven on tables of stone by the finger of God, deposited within the ark of the covenant, in the most holy place of the tabernacle; and again transferred, after five hundred years, to the most holy place in the Temple of Solomon. Every reason which prompted this new form of revelation seems to require us to believe that the written Word of God, when first bestowed on his people, was free from all sensible intermixture of human infirmity, moral imperfection, or historical falsehood Such, accordingly, is the view of the law of Moses, which meets us continually in the later writings of the Old Testament. All their testimonies agree in tone with the words of the Psalmist: "The law of the Lord is perfect, converting the soul: the testimonies of the Lord are sure, making wise the simple: the statutes of the Lord are right, rejoicing the heart: the commandment of the Lord is pure, enlightening the eyes: more to be desired are they than gold, yea, than much fine gold; sweeter also than honey, and the honeycomb." "Thy Word is true from the beginning: every one of thy righteous judgments endureth forever."

It is needless, however, to multiply quotations from the Old Testament to prove the high veneration in which the written law was held by Jewish believers, and by the prophets who were also commissioned to speak the words of God to his people. The testimony of our Lord himself ought alone to be decisive with every Christian. We may apply his own words to the Jews with regard to the authority of Moses and the prophets, and say with truth of professing Christians, If they believe not Christ and his apostles in their testimony to the earlier Scriptures, "neither will they be persuaded, though one rose from the dead." Let us examine some of the chief passages in which this decisive evidence is given.

1. The history of our Lord's ministry begins, in two of the Gospels, with his temptation in the wilderness. The event, it is plain, unless the narrative were a gross imposture, must either have been personally reported by our Lord

himself to his disciples, or made known by a supernatural revelation of the Spirit of God. In either case its details come plainly to us with a Divine sanction, even if the other parts of the Gospels were uninspired history.

Now, the main feature of this narrative is the signal honor paid by the Son of God himself to the written Word. By this sword of the Spirit every onset of the mighty and subtile tempter is repelled. "It is written," is the one reply, thrice repeated, which has power to quench in a moment "all the fiery darts of the wicked one." Even when Scripture, shortened and garbled, is used in the temptation, still Scripture is the only reply. The kingdoms of the world and all their glory are weighed by our Lord and Savior against one single sentence of Scripture, one word of the law of Moses; and they are only like dust in the balance in the eyes of Him who was filled with "the spirit of wisdom and understanding, the spirit of counsel and might, the spirit of knowledge and of the fear of the Lord." It is a startling lesson, which fallen sinners are slow to learn, but which stands out in clear relief in this wonderful narrative, sealed by the testimony of the Son of God, that obedience to one sentence of the law of Moses is a treasure more to be desired than all the riches and glories of the outward universe.

2. After the temptation our Lord began his public ministry, and soon transferred it from Judea to Galilee, and from Nazareth to Capernaum, by the Lake of Tiberias. One main and striking feature of his whole ministry was its Galilean theater. This gives a tinge and coloring to almost every later allusion in the book of Acts. "Ye men of Galilee, why stand ye gazing up into heaven?" "Behold, are not all these which speak Galileans?" "That word ye know which began from Galilee, after the baptism which John preached." "He was seen many days of them

which came up with him from Galilee to Jerusalem, who are his witnesses unto the people."

What now, by the testimony of the Evangelist, was one chief motive which led our Savior to transfer his ministry from Judea to Galilee? A distinct reply is given: "That it might be fulfilled which was spoken by Esaias the prophet, saying, The land of Zebulon, . . . Galilee of the Gentiles, the people that sat in darkness saw a great light; and to them which sat in the region and shadow of death light is sprung up." The force of the prediction lies in the simple opposition between the especial scene of sorrow and desolation in the early stages of the Captivity, and the first appearance of the light and joy of Messiah's presence. Still, the link was so real and powerful that to fulfill this prophecy the Lord of glory forsook Judea, and chose the shores of the Sea of Galilee for the chief and most favored scene of all his earthly ministry. A single sentence of the prophet, being a Divine message, had thus power to impress its distinctive character on the whole public life of the Son of God.

3. Our Lord, in the Sermon on the Mount, assumes his appointed character as the great lawgiver; and, first, near its opening, he defines his relation to the Scriptures of the Old Testament in these words: "Think not that I am come to destroy the law and the prophets: I am not come to destroy, but to fulfill. For verily I say unto you, till heaven and earth pass, one jot or one tittle shall in no wise pass from the law till all be fulfilled. Whosoever, therefore, shall break one of these least commandments, and shall teach men so, shall be called the least in the kingdom of heaven; but whosoever shall do and teach them, the same shall be called great in the kingdom of heaven."

Several things require careful notice in this passage.

And, first, our Lord ratifies the truth and sacredness of the law of Moses by the same emphatic phrase which he applies elsewhere to his own weightiest sayings: "Heaven and earth shall pass away, but my words shall not pass away." Secondly, he extends his full sanction to every "jot and tittle" of the written law of God. Thirdly, since he addressed a Jewish audience, there can be no doubt that his hearers understood by this "law" the whole Pentateuch at least, or the five books of Moses. Fourthly, the words were spoken to remove a probable misconception, arising from a certain perceptible contrast of tone between this law and our Lord's own sayings. He assures his disciples that the seeming contrast was no real contradiction. His teaching was an expansion and supplement of that contained in the law of Moses, but did not abrogate it or set it aside. Fifthly, the statement seems plainly inconsistent with the notion that this law, as first given, in one jot or tittle, contained any real error; or that it had contracted any error in its actual form which a sincere and humble learner might not easily separate from the law itself, so as to leave the latter in its real purity. Sixthly, the prophets are included, along with the law itself, in a common recognition. The tone of the whole statement, so solemnly made, is wholly adverse to the theory of an intermittent, mongrel, and imperfect inspiration, which leaves part of the contents of the Old Testament to be Divine, and other parts to be the mistaken words of fallible men.

Toward the close of the discourse a similar allusion recurs: "Therefore all things whatsoever ye would that men should do unto you, even so do unto them; for this is the law and the prophets."

Here the reason given by our Lord for this simple aphorism of moral duty is deeply instructive. He does not point out its agreement with instincts of natural equity.

He does not rest it simply on his own Divine authority. The reason which enforces it is of another kind. It is the sum of "the Law and the Prophets." It concentrates the various lessons of social duty, which God had given in such various forms and portions throughout the range of the Old Testament. No statement could more plainly imply the binding authority of the written Word, of the Law and the Prophets, over the disciples of Christ as true messages from heaven.

4. The charge is given to the leper, after his cure, "Go thy way, show thyself to the priest, and offer the gift that Moses commanded, for a testimony unto them."

The quotations in the narrative of the temptation are all from Deuteronomy. But here our Lord refers to the book of Leviticus, and to a chapter full of ceremonial details. He enforces their authority by his own command to the leper, and, at the same time, gives direct testimony to their Mosaic authorship. No statement could prove more clearly that, in the view of our Lord, the Pentateuch was of Divine origin, and still binding in its precepts on the Jewish people.

Again, in his reply to the Pharisees, he says: "Go and learn what that meaneth, I will have mercy, and not sacrifice." Here he quotes a brief clause from Hosea, one of the minor prophets, appeals to it as a message of God, and ascribes the sin and folly of his opposers to their neglect of its true meaning.

5. After the message of the Baptist, our Lord speaks to his disciples as follows:

"But what went ye out to see? A prophet? yea, I say unto you, and more than a prophet. For this is he of whom it is written, Behold, I send my messenger before thy face, who shall prepare thy way before thee . . . . For all the prophets and the law prophesied until John. And if ye will receive it, this is Elias, which was for to come."

This passage is full of attestations by our Lord to the authority of the Old Testament, as composed, from first to last, of the true sayings of God. First, he quotes from Malachi, the very latest of the prophets, and affirms that in the coming of the Baptist one of that prophet's predictions was fulfilled. Next, he affirms that, in a certain sense, another prediction of the same prophet about Elias also applied to the Baptist, and had a fulfillment in him. Thirdly, he implies that all the prophets were God's messengers, but that John was honored above them, because of his nearness to Messiah, who was the great object of hope in all their messages. Fourthly, he arranges the course of Providence, not by a reference to worldly empires, but to the series of these Divine revelations, as if they formed the true key to all history. First came the Law, then the Prophets, the sequel of the Law; and, last and greatest of these, the Baptist; then the first days of the kingdom of heaven. The words imply a series of Divine messengers, completed by Christ himself, the great Messenger of the Covenant, with whom a new era of light was to begin. The close of the chapter alludes to the history, in Genesis, of the overthrow of Sodom, and bears a solemn testimony to its historical truth.

6. Matt. xii, 3, 7: "Have ye never read what David did when he was a hungered, and they that were with him? . . . But if ye had known what this meaneth, I will have mercy, and not sacrifice, ye would not have condemned the guiltless."

The appeal is here made to a simple history in the first book of Samuel; from which, compared with the words of Hosea, an inference is drawn that the act of his disciples was quite lawful. But there is also a reference to the law of Moses with regard to the tabernacle or temple service of the priests. Thus we have, in this one passage, a threefold testimony of Christ that the Old-Testament history is trustworthy in its facts, and a Divine record from which moral inferences may be safely and certainly drawn; that the minor prophets are inspired Scripture, in which the separate clauses are the words of God; and that the Law, as a whole, including, evidently, the whole Pentateuch, was worthy of full confidence, so that an appeal might be safely made to its implied facts, no less than to its direct statements, as a basis for moral and religious reasoning.

7. In Matt. xiii, 13–17, our Lord explains to his disciples the reason why he spoke to the multitude in parables, because of their spiritual blindness and indifference to the truth. He proceeds to say that the prophecy of Esaias was fulfilled in them—"By hearing ye shall hear, and not understand, and seeing ye shall see, and not perceive." The same prophecy is afterward applied by St. Paul, at Rome, to the same unbelief of the Jews, at the very close of the sacred history, and is there styled the voice of the Holy Ghost. It is quoted a third time by St. John in the fourth Gospel, with the same reference. No testimony could be more complete, on the part of our Lord and his two apostles, that the book of Isaiah contains the words of the Holy Ghost; and that the prophecy in Isaiah vi is a true prediction of that Jewish blindness which found its climax in the rejection of the Gospel during the apostolic age.

8. In Matt. xv, 1–9, we have another testimony to the Divine authority of the law of Moses, and of the prophecies of Isaiah. "Why do ye also transgress the commandment of God by your tradition? For God commanded, saying, Honor thy father and mother: and, He that curseth father or mother let him die the death." Here the commands in the Decalogue and in the twentieth of Leviticus are equally quoted as Divine. A broad moral contrast is also drawn between the written Word, of which the binding authority is affirmed, and those pharisaic traditions which had obscured

its meaning, and practically destroyed its authority. The words of Isaiah, chap. xxix, are also quoted as being an undoubted voice of the Spirit of God. But if the Old-Testament Scriptures, in any part, were purely human writings, and not Divine messages, then our Lord, by his constant appeal to them, without making any distinction between them, would be guilty of the very sin he condemns so strongly in the Pharisees, and would be included under his own censure—"In vain do they worship me, teaching for doctrines the commandments of men."

9. The history of the Transfiguration, as recorded by St Mark, offers another explicit testimony of the same kind. "And he answered and told them, Elias verily cometh first, and restoreth all things; and how it is written of the Son of man, that he must suffer many things, and be set at naught. But I say unto you that Elias is indeed come, and they have done unto him whatsoever they listed, *as it is written of him.*"

The exact reference of these last words is not perfectly clear. But this makes the appeal of our Lord to the written Word, not only with reference to his own sufferings, but those of the Baptist, doubly striking. His deeper wisdom, when contrasted with the knowledge of his early disciples, or modern half-disciples, instead of leading him to discern errors and imperfections in the Old Testament, only revealed to him in its pages definite predictions of specific events in distant ages, where only a dim haze might be visible to common eyes. His own sufferings were all "as it was written," and those of his forerunner, who came "in the spirit and power of Elias," were also "as it was written of him." His words teach us distinctly to rest upon the truth of Scripture, and the certainty of its prophetic intimations, even where we see through a glass dimly, and its meaning by no means stands out to us in clear and full relief.

10. The reply to the question of the Pharisees on divorce is of peculiar interest. Our Lord bears witness in it to the Divine authority of that early part of Genesis which has been assailed of late by so many unbelieving doubts and criticisms. "Have ye not read, that he which made them at the beginning made them male and female, and said, For this cause shall a man leave father and mother, and cleave to his wife, and they two shall be one flesh? Wherefore they are no more twain but one flesh. What therefore God hath joined together, let not man put asunder."

Now, here, first of all, the very form of the appeal shows that what the Pharisees read in their own Scriptures, in Moses, the Psalms, and the Prophets, they were bound to receive as the words of God. "Have ye not read?" This implies, evidently, whatever you read in those Scriptures which you habitually receive, you are bound to regard as Divine truth, and of decisive authority in all moral questions. Next, our Lord does not fall back on his own authority. He rests his answer on a decision already given. A single verse in the second of Genesis, which critical anatomists would transfer from Moses, the inspired prophet, to some unknown patcher-up of ancient documents hundreds of years later, is, in the view of Christ, a Divine statute, of binding authority to all mankind. "What therefore God hath joined together, let no man put asunder." He proceeds to adopt the statement of the Pharisees, that Moses gave the precept about the bill of divorcement, and explains that its nature was simply permissive, and designed to lessen and restrain evils which had their source in the hardness of their hearts. The design of the law was not to sanction capricious divorce, but to exclude a further and still more aggravated sin.

11. The actions and the teachings of our Lord during the earlier days of Passion-week abound in evidence of the same

truth. He sends his disciples for the colt with the message. "The Lord hath need of him," because it was needful that a prediction of Zechariah should be fulfilled. He condemns the sin of the Jews by a double reference to Isaiah and Jeremiah: "It is written, My house shall be called a house of prayer; but ye have made it a den of thieves." He silences their censure of the children by a still more pointed appeal to the Psalms. "Yea: have ye never read, Out of the mouths of babes and sucklings thou hast perfected praise?" In his answer to the question about his own authority, he accepts the principle that authority from God was required in such a message, and implies that John, like all the prophets, had this authority. After the parable of the vineyard, he makes his appeal to the written word once more. "Did ye never read in the Scriptures, The stone which the builders rejected, the same is become the head of the corner: this is the Lord's doing, and it is marvelous in our eyes?" He then reasons out the consequences of this Scriptural prophecy in the Psalm, and confirms them by a reference to two others in Isaiah and Daniel. "And whosoever shall fall on this stone shall be broken, but on whomsoever it shall fall, it will grind him to powder." The double allusion to two prophecies respecting Messiah is plain. "He shall be for a stone of stumbling, and for a rock of offense, to both the houses of Israel: and many among them shall stumble and fall, and be broken, and snared, and taken." Isa. viii, 15. "Thou sawest till that a stone was cut out without hands, which smote the image upon its feet of iron and clay, and brake them in pieces. Then was the iron and clay, the brass, the silver, and the gold, broken in pieces together, and became like the chaff of the Summer thrashing-floors, and the wind carried them away." Dan. ii, 34, 35. We have thus, from the lips of our Lord, in this one passage, both a confirmation of the authority of three different books of prophecy, and a striking testimony to the secret unity of Divine wisdom, which runs through the whole range of these various messages of God. One verse in the Psalms is a Divine key, which expounds the mutual relations of two distinct warnings—one in Isaiah, to the Jews, and another in Daniel, to those Gentiles who were long afterward to be called in their room.

12. The answers to the Sadducees and to the lawyers are peculiarly instructive. And, first, our Lord ascribes all the religious errors of the Sadducees to one source—ignorance of their own Scriptures. "Ye do err, not knowing the Scriptures, nor the power of God." He appeals to the record in Exodus, as being truly a Divine message. "Have ye not read that which was spoken unto you by God?" He infers confidently the truth of the resurrection of the dead from a single title of God on the face of the record. "I am the God of Abraham, and the God of Isaac, and the God of Jacob. God is not the God of the dead, but of the living." It may be added that the same reply, which put the Sadducees to silence, ought equally, among professing Christians, to silence and condemn a vast amount of Sadducean criticism about Elohistic and Jehovistic documents; as if either Moses were not the author of the Pentateuch, or else the names of God were introduced by him haphazard, in a strange mosaic, according to the accidental character of materials ready-made to his hand.

The reply to the lawyer—Matt. xxii, 40—is not less instructive. "On these two commandments hang all the Law and the Prophets." Now, these two precepts, in the eye of sound reason, are pure, essential, and immutable moral truth. And yet all the Law and the Prophets, our Lord assures us, depend upon them. How can falsehood depend upon pure and eternal truth? or how can imperfect morality be any real corollary from the great commandments of perfect love?

Again, the question which silenced the Pharisees reveals, in a striking manner, the authority and Divine inspiration of the Psalms of David. One verse of Psalm cx convicts them of ignorance respecting the true character of the promised Messiah. It is a Divine enigma, our Lord indirectly shows us, of which the only solution is in the great mystery of the Gospel—the Word made flesh, of the seed of David— "of whom as concerning the flesh Christ came, who is over all, God blessed forever." Thus, one title of God in the Law, by our Lord's testimony, is an adequate basis for faith in the resurrection of all the faithful dead; and another clause in the Psalms is also a sufficient evidence for that glorious truth, the Incarnation of the Son of God.

13. The parting discourse against the Pharisees abounds with proofs of the full authority ascribed by our Lord to the written Word of God. The scribes and Pharisees, while sitting in Moses' seat, were to be observed and obeyed, even while their actions were condemned. Unless the law of Moses were truly of Divine authority, such an instruction could never have been given. Their guilt lay in urging its minuter requirements, and omitting "the weightier matters of the law, judgment, mercy, and faith." Yet our Lord does not set aside even its least commandments, but confirms them. "These ought ye to have done, and not to leave the other undone." They witnessed against themselves that they were the children of those who had killed the prophets. The aggravation of their guilt clearly lay in the fact that the prophets were truly the messengers of God. "Thou that killest the prophets, and stonest them which are sent unto thee," is the condemning charge against Jerusalem. In the next chapter the words of Daniel the prophet are quoted as a Divine prediction, with the caution, "Whoso readeth, let him understand." The history of the flood of Noah, and of the general destruction of mankind, is also referred to as

a solemn and undoubted reality, a warning for the days of his own return.

14. The allusions to Scripture during the time of the Passion are, if possible, still more impressive. Every step in the pathway of the Man of sorrows seems here to be guided by a chart, which he saw clearly laid down for his own guidance in the Word of God. "Ye know that after two days is the Passover, and the Son of man is betrayed to be crucified." For he was the true Passover, and the time of his sufferings must correspond with the typical service, which had prefigured them for fifteen hundred years. His betrayal was to be the fulfillment of an inspired prophecy. "The Son of man goeth, as it is written of him; but woe unto that man by whom the Son of man is betrayed: it had been good for that man if he had not been born." The type of the Nazarite was now to be fulfilled in him. "I will not drink henceforth of this fruit of the vine until the day when I drink it new with you in my Father's kingdom." The fear and dispersion of his disciples would be the fulfillment of Zechariah's prophecy. "All ye shall be offended because of me this night; for it is written, I will smite the Shepherd, and the sheep of the flock shall be scattered abroad." The treachery of Judas is referred to the truth of Scripture as its secret explanation. "None of them is lost, but the son of perdition, that the Scripture might be fulfilled." Our Lord's patient submission to his enemies was in reverence to the revealed predictions of the written Word. "Thinkest thou I can not now pray to my Father, and he shall presently give me more than twelve legions of angels? But how then shall the Scriptures be fulfilled, that thus it must be?" The Evangelist adds a brief commentary on the whole course of his betrayal: "All this was done that the Scriptures of the prophets might be fulfilled." Our Lord's reply to the high-priest is a quotation from one of

Daniel's prophecies. "Hereafter shall ye see the Son of man sitting on the right hand of power, and coming in the clouds of heaven." The indignities he received were the fulfillment of Isaiah's prediction: "I hid not my face from shame and spitting." The purchase of the potter's field with the price of treachery was the fulfillment of another prophecy. "They parted his garments, casting lots: that it might be fulfilled which was spoken by the prophet, They parted my garments among them, and upon my vesture they cast lots." The exclamation, Eli, Eli, lama sabachthani, was a plain appropriation by our Lord, in the hour of his agony, of the twenty-second Psalm, as one connected prediction of his sufferings, and of the glory that would follow.

15. The Gospel of St. Luke furnishes many other examples of this constant appeal to the Scriptures by our Lord, as an authority without appeal. It will be enough to select some of the more striking, first before, and then during, the time of his Passion.

In Luke x, 25, we read that a lawyer stood up and tempted him, saying, "Master, what shall I do to inherit eternal life?" To this weighty inquiry our Lord replies at once by the question, "What is written in the law, how readest thou?" The second reply is a confirmation of the law's authority, and a virtual quotation—"Thou hast answered right: this do, and thou shalt live." In the next chapter the truth of the history of Jonah is affirmed, and its typical character is declared. "For as Jonas was a sign to the Ninevites, so shall also the Son of man be to this generation." The two narratives of the queen of Sheba and of the Ninevites are both confirmed, and a moral is derived from each of them. A further testimony follows to the Divine mission of all the prophets of the Old Testament, and a promise that others would soon be sent forth, gifted with the like authority. The words of Micah are presently quoted

(Luke xii. 51–53; Micah vii, 6,) as a true prophecy of the divisions to be occasioned by the Gospel. The prophets are again referred to, Luke xiii, 27–34, as the chosen messengers of God, and our Lord ranks himself among their number. "It can not be that a prophet perish out of Jerusalem." In chapter xvi we have the two emphatic declarations: "It is easier for heaven and earth to pass, than for one tittle of the law to fail;" and again, "If they hear not Moses and the prophets, neither will they be persuaded, though one rose from the dead." The short and earnest caution, "Remember Lot's wife," puts a seal of truth and inspiration on the histories of Genesis; for it is founded on a single verse, never alluded to elsewhere in the later Scriptures for fifteen hundred years. The address to the disciples on the approach to Jerusalem is also peculiarly impressive: "Behold we go up to Jerusalem and all things that are written by the prophets concerning the Son of man shall be accomplished. For he shall be delivered to the Gentiles, and shall be mocked, and spitefully entreated, and spitted on, and they shall scourge him and put him to death, and the third day he shall rise again."

16. The words of St. Luke, xxii, 37, deserve especial notice. "For I say unto you that this which is written must yet be accomplished in me, and he was numbered among the transgressors: for even the things concerning me have their fulfillment, ($\varkappa \alpha i \ \gamma \grave{\alpha} \rho \ \tau \grave{\alpha} \ \pi \varepsilon \rho i \ \dot{\varepsilon} \mu o \tilde{\upsilon} \ \tau \acute{\varepsilon} \lambda o \varsigma \ \ddot{\varepsilon} \chi \varepsilon \iota.$)"

Here our Lord not only applies to himself the words of Isaiah liii, 12, but gives this prediction the foremost place among the reasons why he was content to suffer. The Word of God must not fail. It would fail unless the Messiah were reckoned among the transgressors. It might seem strange and unseemly that the Son of God should submit to so deep an indignity, but the truth of God's Word must be maintained at any sacrifice, "for even the things which relate to me," the promised Messiah, the Son of God, "have their fulfillment." The incarnate Son of God himself, by his own testimony, must be subject to the authority of the written Word, and its announcements of his own sufferings were laws which even he must obey.

The conversation with the two disciples, after the resurrection, repeats the same lesson. "O fools, and slow of heart to believe all that the prophets have spoken. Were not these the things it behooved the Christ to suffer, and to enter into his glory? And beginning from Moses, and from all the prophets, he expounded to them in all the Scriptures the things concerning himself."

No statement can be more clear and express than that which our Lord has here made in the first bright dawn of his resurrection glory. He tells his disciples that Moses and all the prophets contained predictions of his own sufferings; that it was the dullness of their hearts alone which hindered them from perceiving their true application; and that this reference was so real as to create a moral necessity, beforehand, for the Messiah to suffer the very things which he himself had suffered. In other words, by refusing to suffer, and thus to fulfill these inspired predictions, he would have forfeited his claim to be the true Messiah of God. The truth of Scripture, in its prophecies, is thus made the moral basis of the whole work of redemption; and a refusal to see the reference to our Lord and his deep humiliation in these predictions of the law and the prophets, is declared to be a sure proof of folly and blindness of heart.

The same doctrine forms the substance of his parting address to his disciples, in the same Gospel, and is rendered still more striking by its connection with the gift, then bestowed upon them, of a clearer and spiritual vision. "And he said unto them, These are the words which I spake unto you, while I was yet with you, that all things must be fulfilled, which were written in the Law of Moses, and in the Prophets, and in the Psalms, concerning me. Then opened he their understandings, that they might understand the Scriptures, and said unto them, Thus it is written, and thus it behooved the Christ to suffer, and to rise from the dead the third day; and that repentance and remission of sins should be preached in his name among all nations, beginning at Jerusalem." Here our Lord gives his sanction to each of the three main divisions of the Jewish canon, the Law, the Prophets, and the Hagiographa; affirms that each contained prophecies concerning him, which the Divine veracity made it needful for him to fulfill; that these predictions included not only his sufferings which were now past, but that preaching of the Gospel which was shortly to begin; and, in short, that the whole Christian dispensation rests upon a moral and imperative necessity, that the Word of God in the prophecies of the Old Testament must inevitably be fulfilled.

It is needless to quote in detail the passages to the same effect in the fourth Gospel—John i, 17, 21–23, 29; (comp. Gen. xxii, 8;) verse 45; ii, 17, 22; iii, 14, 15; iv, 5; v, 37–39, 45–47; vi, 14, 31–35, 45; vii, 19, 22, 23, 37–39, 40–42; viii, 17, 18, 44, 52; x, 34–36; xii, 14–16, 37–41; xv, 25; xvii, 12; xviii, 4; xix, 24, 28–30, 35–37; xx, 9—or the numerous references to the authority of the Old Testament in the apostolic writings. In the book of Acts we have ten quotations from the Psalms, five from Isaiah, and others from Genesis, Exodus, Deuteronomy, Joel, Amos, Habakkuk, 1 Kings. In St. Paul, thirty-seven from the Psalms, fifteen from Genesis, ten from Exodus, one from Numbers, thirteen from Deuteronomy, one from Joshua, one from 2 Samuel, two from 1 Kings, one 'rom Job, three from Proverbs, twenty-seven from Isaiah, three from Jeremiah, from Hosea, and Habakkuk, and one from Joel, Haggai, and Malachi. In every instance the appeal to the Scriptures is made by the apostle as to the sure fountain of heavenly truth. Their titles are, Scripture, the oracles of God, the words of the Holy Ghost. Both in the Gospels and the Epistles, "It is written," is the decision for every doubt; and "Have you not read in the Scriptures?" is the rebuke for every form of ignorance and error.

The conclusion which every sincere disciple of Christ must draw from these sayings of his Lord and Master, confirmed by those of his apostles, is clear and self-evident. It is summed up for us in three general declarations of our Lord himself, and two of his chief apostles. "The Scriptures can not be broken." "All Scripture is given by inspiration of God, and is profitable for doctrine, for reproof, for correction, for instruction in righteousness." "Prophecy came not at any time by the will of man, but holy men of God spake as they were borne along by the Holy Ghost." The flaws which have been contracted in the transmission of these messages, we may infer safely from these multiplied quotations, are so few and slight, that for every practical purpose they disappear from view. They may be detected here and there by a strong microscope of minute criticism; but our Lord and his apostles, in hundreds of quotations, bearing on the most vital points of doctrine, and on the most weighty facts of Old Testament history, never find it needful once to allude to their existence, or to utter one caution against undue confidence in the Sacred text. No contrast can be more total than between the unbelieving, flippant criticisms on the Old Testament, practiced in our days by some learned men, who still "profess and call themselves Christians," and the tone of their divine Lord and Master, before whose judgment-seat they will stand, when deep reverence for their authority led him to renounce all angelic aid in the hour of his sorest conflict and deepest sorrow. "Thinkest thou that I can not now pray to my Father, and he will presently give me more than twelve legions of angels. But how then shall the Scriptures be fulfilled, that thus it must be?"

CHAPTER XI.

THE INSPIRATION OF THE NEW TESTAMENT.

The Scriptures of the New Testament, from their later origin, are not capable of receiving that direct proof of their Divine inspiration and authority from the lips of Christ himself, which the Law, the Prophets, and the Psalms have received in such ample measure. Since they began to be composed, several years after the ascension, and the latest of them were not written till near the death of the oldest apostle, at the close of the first century, they could scarcely receive a collective attestation even from the apostles themselves. There is also, in the historical Scriptures of both Testaments, a remarkable reticence on the part of the writers, with regard to their own especial claims. The Lord of the prophets, when on earth, amid the wonder caused by his miracles, "withdrew into the wilderness." The sacred historians, in like manner, seem to withdraw their own personality from our view, and are content to be simple witnesses of the facts they record; and seldom reveal their own names, or speak of any special guidance and direction of the Spirit they might have received. In the case of the Old Testament histories, this silence is amply compensated by the full testimony borne to their authority by our Lord himself. But in the parallel case of the Gospels and the book of Acts, no such compensation could occur. We are thrown, for the proof of their Divine inspiration, upon the combination of three different kinds of indirect evidence—the analogy of earlier

Scripture, the promises of Christ, and scattered intimations in the later books of the New Testament.

I. First, the inspiration and Divine authority of the Old Testament, established so firmly by the words and actions of our Lord himself, are a strong and almost irresistible presumption that the writings of the New Testament have the same especial character, and share the same authority. All the reasons which explain the first gift of written revelation at the time of the Exodus, in the growing number and importance of the facts of God's providence, which called for lasting memorial, and in the increasing fullness of the precepts, promises, and doctrines revealed, apply with equal, or even superior force, to the times of the Gospel. They form a most weighty presumption, from the precedent already given, that the facts of the Gospel history, and the new and higher doctrinal teaching of our Lord and his apostles, would not be left to chance and human error for their transmission to later times, but would also be embodied in writings of Divine authority, stamped, like those of the older covenant, with the signet of Heaven. The teaching to be preserved was equally complex and various. The importance of keeping it free from adulteration was at least as great as in the earlier messages of the Law and the Prophets. A written revelation was no doubtful innovation, but was now become a kind of standing law of the providence of God. The higher dignity of Christ compared with Moses, and of the Gospel compared with the Law, made its careful transmission, pure from human error, still more plainly expedient and desirable. So that every reason, drawn from the existence of the Old Testament, would seem to make it certain that inspired writings, of similar authority, would be given to embody in a permanent form, for the use of later ages, the oral teaching of Christ and his apostles, and the wonderful truths of the incarnation, atonement, resurrection, and ascension of the Son of God.

II. This general reason, from the precedent of the Old Testament Scriptures, becomes doubly powerful from the special character of the new dispensation of the Gospel. The authority of the Law and the Prophets is continually referred to one cause—that the writers were guided and actuated by the Spirit of God. Thus we read of Moses: "I will take of the Spirit that is on thee, and will put it upon them. . . . And the Lord took of the Spirit that was upon him, and gave it to the seventy elders; and it came to pass, when the Spirit rested on them, they prophesied, and did not cease. . . . And Moses said to Joshua, Enviest thou for my sake? Would God that all the Lord's people were prophets, and the Lord would put his Spirit upon them!" (Ex. xi, 17, 25, 29.) So David, as the sweet psalmist of Israel, describes his own messages: "The Spirit of the Lord spake by me, and his word was on my tongue." So, more generally, all the prophetic writings are called "the words which the Lord of Hosts sent in his Spirit by the former prophets." (Zech. vii, 12.) One of the most usual forms of quotation from the Old Testament in the New, is under the title of "the words," or "utterance," of "the Holy Ghost."

The gift, then, of written revelation in the Law, the Prophets, and the Psalms, is distinctly and expressly referred to the Spirit of God. But the Gospel is eminently the dispensation of the Spirit. His presence, after our Lord's ascension, was to be so much more fully manifested, that by comparison it is said to be vouchsafed for the first time. "For the Holy Ghost was not yet, because that Jesus was not yet glorified," John vii, 39. The apostles were ministers "of the new covenant, not of the letter, but of the Spirit, for the letter killeth, but the Spirit giveth life." "How shall not the dispensation of the Spirit be rather glorious?"

Now, since the one main work of the Spirit, even before the coming of Christ, was the gift to the Jewish Church of the written revelations in the Law of Moses, the Psalms, and the Prophets, and a much fuller manifestation of his presence was distinctly promised under the Gospel, it seems inconceivable that the writers of the New Testament should not have enjoyed at least an equal measure of his Divine teaching and guidance, have been equally preserved from error, and their messages have an equal claim to be called "the words of the Holy Ghost." We must else allow that the new dispensation, while in other respects an advance on the old, in this most important and vital element, underwent a strange retrocession, from the Divine to the simply human, from the teaching of the Spirit to the words of men; from pure truth, sealed with God's authority, to a mixed and imperfect record, subject to innumerable doubts, uncertainties, and abatements. This double presumption, though it rests in part on *a priori* grounds, and our natural sense of consistency and harmony in the ways of God, is still so simple and powerful that very few thoughtful minds can resist its force, or view it as less than decisive. It does not help us to decide what books of the New Testament should be reckoned canonical. But it makes it almost impossible to resist the conclusion, that some inspired records would be given under the Gospel, unless we reject the truth of our Lord's own repeated testimonies to the authority and inspiration of the Jewish Scriptures. In point of fact, scarcely an example can be found among Christians of a full admission of the Divine inspiration of the Old Testament, and of a denial that the same character is shared by the Gospels, and other writings of the New Testament.

III. A third presumption may be drawn from the same comparison with the earlier Scriptures, to confirm, not only the authority of the New Testament writings in the abstract, but the general outline of our actual canon. For the Old Testament, both by the Jews in general and by our Lord himself, is ranked under three divisions—the Law, the Prophets, and the Psalms. Or, viewing the whole in the order of time, it consists of a series of histories, forming three-fifths of the whole; of devotional and didactic books, belonging chiefly to the later part of the middle period of the history, and of prophecies, growing out of its latest portions. The histories reach from Creation to the return from Babylon. The Psalms and Proverbs, the chief books of the Hagiographa, belong to the reigns of David and Solomon. The written prophecies range from Isaiah to Malachi, or in time from Jonah to Nehemiah, through the latest portion of the history.

Now, the New Testament canon, as it now stands, exhibits the same threefold division, and in the same order of time. We have, first, an historical portion in the Gospels and Acts, reaching from the incarnation, the beginning of the new creation of God, to the planting of the Gospel in Rome, the capital of the Gentile world. We have, secondly, a doctrinal and practical portion, in the twenty-one Apostolic Epistles, all of them parallel in time with the later half of the book of Acts. We have, last of all, one book of prophecy, the Apocalypse, dating from a little beyond the close of the Sacred history, but within the limits and on the extreme verge of the apostolic age. The proportion of the history to the other portions is also precisely the same in the two Testaments. This close analogy of structure is a further presumption, not only that the Gospel has its own inspired writings, but that these are represented faithfully, with no serious excess or defect, in the actual canon.

IV. The promises of our Lord to his apostles form a second branch of evidence, which serves, in a more direct way, to prove the inspiration and authority of nearly the whole of the New Testament. Out of the twenty-seven writings of which it is composed, all, with three important exceptions, have sufficient and full historical evidence of an apostolic authorship. They are the writings of those divinely-commissioned messengers of the Gospel, one of whom has described their credentials in these words: "Truly the signs of an apostle were wrought among you, in all patience, in signs and wonders, and mighty deeds." They were fully-attested embassadors of the words of Christ. And this evidence must confirm their written as well as their spoken messages, and even, if possible, in a higher measure. For speech is sudden and momentary, and far more liable to the intrusion of error, through haste or negligence. But a written message is deliberate; it is open to revision, if the messenger were conscious of any negligence on his part, any intermission of the guidance of the Spirit of God, or any failure to abide in the light of his high commission. St. Barnabas, at least, and perhaps St. Paul, too, may have erred in feeling or judgment, when the contention was so sharp between them, and hasty words may have been spoken on either side; and St. Peter erred in act, if not in speech also, at Antioch, when his brother apostle "withstood him to the face, because he was to be blamed." Gal. ii, 11. Two, if not three, of these chief apostles, were thus liable to error in act, and probably in speech, even in practical questions, closely linked with the due fulfillment of their message. Even in their case the consent of two or three witnesses, or the absence of protest or correction from a brother apostle, seems required for the full assurance that, in special cases, their own infirmities had not mingled with their oral teaching, and impaired the practical fulfillment of their great commission. But in these very cases no trace of human weakness appears in their writings. St. Paul's allusion to Barnabas and Mark are as full and cordial as if no dissension had ever arisen; and St. Peter stamps with a title of Divine authority those very letters of St. Paul, which contain the mention of his own error, and of the rebuke he had justly received. So that, while a general promise of Divine guidance would apply to all the oral teaching of the apostles of Christ, it must be conceived, from the nature of the case, to be doubly emphatic and full, when applied to writings deliberately composed by them in the fulfillment of their solemn trust.

Now, the promises of our Lord to the apostles are very full and strong, both in their first commission, and in its later renewal at the time of his own death and resurrection. First, he says to them in allusion to their testimony before rulers: "It shall be given you in that same hour what ye shall speak. For it is not ye that speak, but the Spirit of your Father which speaketh in you." It is true that the promise has direct reference to one kind of special emergency. But if this guidance of the Spirit was promised so strongly for a personal and temporary purpose, how much more must we conceive it to apply to an occasion still more important, when they were making provision for the lasting transmission of their message, and for the guidance and comfort of the whole Church, in every succeeding age! At the close of the same discourse we have the emphatic words: "He that receiveth you, receiveth me; and he that receiveth me, receiveth him that sent me. He that receiveth a prophet in the name of a prophet, shall receive a prophet's reward." By the use of this title our Lord places their authority on a level with that of the earlier prophets. And since these writings are called "the oracles of God" and "words of the Holy Ghost," we may infer that the writings of the apostles, in the fulfillment of their commission, would claim to be received with the same submission and reverence by all the true disciples of Christ. It would not be they who should speak their own words, but "the Spirit of their Father would speak in them." The words at the last supper repeat the same promise, and include in it the gift of prophetic illumination: "When he, the Spirit of truth, is come, he will guide you into all truth; for he will not speak from himself, but whatsoever he shall hear that will he speak, and he will show you things to come." This solemn declaration that the Spirit would teach the apostles truth only, because he would not speak from himself, but by commission from the Father and the Son, would lose all its practical meaning, if the Spirit left them in their writings, to "speak from themselves," and thus to mix an indefinite amount of human error with the messages of God.

V. The higher rank of the apostles, compared with the prophets, both of the Old and New Testaments, is a further evidence of the same truth. The writings of the Old Testament prophets, our Lord himself bears witness, were the words of the Holy Spirit speaking by their mouths. He affirms, also, that a greater prophet than the Baptist had not appeared, and still, he that was "less," or "inferior," in the kingdom of heaven, would be greater than he. The natural meaning seems to be, that even those prophets who held quite a secondary place under the Gospel were really higher than the Baptist in spiritual honor and dignity. So we read that "God hath set in the Church, first, apostles, secondarily, prophets;" and that Christ gave "some apostles, and some prophets," when he ascended on high, and received gifts for men. We find in the book of Acts, Agabus, Judas, Silas, Simeon, Lucius, and probably Stephen,

Philip, and others, companions of the apostles, who belonged to this second class or order in the Church of Christ. The higher authority and dignity of the apostles, by whose hands alone the gifts of the Spirit were conveyed, is implied in the whole history.

The conclusion from this comparison is simple and clear. The writings of the prophets of the Old Testament were under the guidance of the Spirit, and of Divine authority. Much more must we believe that, under the dispensation of the Spirit, the same guidance would be vouchsafed to the apostles in their writings, since they rank still higher than the others in spiritual dignity and honor. If we receive, then, as historically true, the statements of our Lord with regard to the apostolic office, confirmed by the mutual testimony of the apostles themselves, then the inspiration of the New Testament, three books alone excepted, seems a clear and unavoidable inference. Accordingly, it seems that the early Churches were guided mainly by this principle in the formation of the canon; since the relation of Mark to Peter, and of St. Luke to St. Paul, gave their writings an indirect sanction, equivalent to immediate authorship by one of the apostles.

VI. In the historical books the character of simple testimony is most prominent, and a direct assertion by the writers of their own inspiration might seem out of place. The direct evidence chiefly applies, then, to the two other main portions of the New Testament, the Epistles and the Apocalypse. The apostles, in the Epistles, bear witness to their own inspiration, along with that of the Evangelists, and of the Old Testament; while the Apocalypse, besides claiming Divine authority for itself, puts a parting seal upon all the prophetic writings of the Word of God.

In the earliest epistle of St. Paul, the first to the Thessalonians, he makes this remarkable statement: "For this cause thank we God without ceasing, because, when ye received the Word of God, which ye heard of us, ye received it, not as the word of men, but as it is in truth, the Word of God, which effectually worketh in you that believe." He enforces his commands to them by the declaration, "He that despiseth, despiseth not man, but God, who hath also given unto us his Holy Spirit." His written and spoken messages bear the same title, the Word of God. "For this we say unto you, by the Word of the Lord, that we which are alive, and remain to the coming of the Lord, shall not prevent them which are asleep." He adds, at the close, the sanction of an oath to enforce the public reading of his message. "I charge you (with an oath) by the Lord, that this epistle be read unto all the holy brethren." The same tone of Divine authority runs through the second epistle to the same Church; and he adds a token at the close, by which his genuine epistles might be discerned from every counterfeit that might falsely assume his name. "The salutation of Paul with mine own hand, which is the token in every epistle; so I write." He joins together his oral teaching when among them, and his former letter, in the same rank and description, as "not the word of man, but the Word of God." 1 Thess. ii, 13; 2 Thess. ii, 15.

In the Churches of Galatia his authority had been questioned by the Judaizing teachers. He is thus led to affirm it strongly in the opening verse, and indeed through two whole chapters. The same tone of authority continues throughout the letter to the close.

In 1 Corinthians we have a distinct appeal to the teachers of that Church, who ranked highest in their spiritual gifts. "If any man think himself to be a prophet, or spiritual, let him acknowledge that the things I write unto you are the commandment of the Lord." In the Second Epistle to the same Church he directly compares himself with Moses, as one who had received like authority, with a still higher message, styles himself an embassador of Christ, reminds them that Christ spoke by him, and that both in his letters and when present he was intrusted with direct authority from the Lord for the edification of his people. In Romans he speaks of "the grace given to him that he should be the minister of Christ to the Gentiles, ministering the Gospel of God," and of the "mighty signs and wonders," with which, in the fulfillment of the same commission, he had preached the Gospel of Christ. Both at the opening and close of the letter he associates himself with the prophets and their writings, as now fulfilling the like office, and completing and unfolding their earlier messages, while no less than fifty quotations from Old Testament Scripture are embodied in this one epistle alone. In Ephesians he refers them to his own letter as a proof of his "knowledge of the mystery of Christ, which in other ages was not made known, as it was now revealed unto his holy apostles and prophets by the Spirit." He speaks throughout as God's messenger, filled with the Spirit, and armed with complete authority to utter precepts, doctrines, and promises, in the name of the Lord.

The same claim of full authority runs through the Pastoral Epistles. The glorious Gospel of the blessed Jesus was committed to his trust. Hymeneus and Alexander were delivered unto Satan, that they might learn not to blaspheme. He was "ordained a preacher and an apostle, (I speak the truth in Christ, I lie not,) a teacher of the Gentiles, in faith and verity." In the fulfillment of this office he gave commands to the men, to the women, to the bishops and deacons, and to Timothy himself. He predicts coming evils under an express voice from the Spirit, (iv, 1.) He gives in succession thirty distinct commands, referring to a large variety of ministerial duties and arrangements within the Churches. He enforces these commands by an appeal to God and Christ, and the elect angels, and calls his own teaching "wholesome words, the words of the Lord Jesus Christ, and doctrine that is according to godliness." He repeats a most solemn admonition to Timothy, "before God and the Lord Jesus Christ," to keep the commandment in his epistle, "without spot, unrebukable, until the appearing of our Lord Jesus Christ." In the Second Epistle, the last which he wrote, he declared solemnly, in the prospect of death, that "he was appointed a preacher and an apostle, and a teacher of the Gentiles;" and even associates his own teaching with the Old-Testament Scriptures, as of equal authority. "Continue thou in the things thou hast learned, and been assured of, knowing of whom thou hast learned them; and that from a child thou hast known the Holy Scriptures, which are able to make thee wise unto salvation, through faith which is in Christ Jesus."

VII. These testimonies in St. Paul's epistles are not confined to this part of the New Testament alone. They include three further statements, which apply directly to those books which have not apostles for their authors.

1. First, in 1 Cor. viii, 18, 19, we have a direct allusion to St. Luke as the writer of the Gospel we possess under his name, and already honored by the use of it among the Churches. This early view of the text, held by Origen, and embodied in the prayers of the Church, for many ages—coll. St. Luke's Day—has been disputed by several modern critics, from Grotius onward, on very weak and insufficient grounds. A comparison with the book of Acts proves clearly that St. Luke is the person designed. But the words, "whose praise in the Gospel is in all the Churches," are used by way of definition, or as a distinctive title, equivalent to a personal name. There were, how-

ever, scores of prophets and teachers, whose names must have been widely known as oral teachers of the Gospel. But St. Luke and St. Mark alone, among those inferior to the apostles, were honored to compose a written Gospel; and of these St. Luke alone was well known to have accompanied St. Paul in his first entrance to Macedonia, from which country the letter was written. On this view the whole passage is clear and consistent, and the Gospel of St. Luke receives here a direct sanction from the great apostle to the Gentiles, as an honorable portion of the writings of the new covenant.

2. The second passage—1 Tim. v, 18—in a later epistle completes and confirms the evidence derived from the first. "For the Scripture saith, Thou shalt not muzzle the ox that treadeth out the corn. And, The laborer is worthy of his reward." The former clause is a quotation from Deuteronomy, or the Law of Moses; the second is written verbatim in St. Luke's Gospel—x, 7. Both of these alike are called by the name of "Scripture," and appealed to as decisive authority. This is more remarkable in the second case, because they are the words of Christ himself. Yet they are referred to by the apostle simply as Scripture, or a saying of the written Gospel, and not in their distinctive character, as words spoken by the Lord himself. No fuller testimony could be given, in few words, to the inspired authority of the third Gospel; the very same which some might imagine, from the words of its own preface, to be more open than any other part of the New Testament, to doubt and reasonable contradiction. The words are further noticeable, because they furnish a proof how early this Gospel had acquired currency and full authority within the Church of Christ.

3. The third passage—2 Tim. iii, 16—affirms directly the inspired authority of the Scripture of the Old Testament,

which had been familiar to the beloved Timothy from his childhood. But there is no warrant for confining their testimony to these alone. On the contrary, the expression, "all Scripture," following the more general phrase, "the holy writings," requires us to take these words in their widest sense. Now this was the last of St. Paul's epistles, and all the others were written earlier; and Timothy was present when most of them were composed, and shared in the superscription of more than one of them. Again, in the previous epistle, to the same beloved companion, the Gospel of St. Luke has been already quoted under this very name of Scripture; and their internal relations are a strong proof that the two others, of St. Matthew and St. Mark, had been written still earlier. St. Paul had visited Jerusalem thirty years after the Ascension, and the Gospel of St. Matthew must, therefore, without a question, have been actually known to him. He had been, still later, at Cesarea, the Roman seaport of Judea, for whose converts internal evidence would lead us to believe that the second Gospel was written; and he was writing from Rome, to which place tradition has often referred to, and hence it is almost beyond a doubt that it must also have been known to him. If St. Matthew's Gospel claimed the title of Scripture, it is plain that St. Mark's, from its close resemblance of contents and style, must have done the same. So that these words of St. Paul, addressed to Timothy, would naturally, in the view of the latter, include these three Gospels, and the earlier letters of St. Paul himself. They are thus a direct association of the greater part of the New Testament, with the Law, the Psalms, and the Prophets, under the common title of "Scripture given by inspiration of God."

The testimony includes, not only the three earlier Gospels, and the other epistles of St. Paul, but the book of Acts also. For St. Luke was now with the apostles, as he had been during the voyage, and at the beginning of the first imprisonment. The book closes with the mention of that imprisonment, and of its two years' continuance, but says nothing of St. Paul's release. St. Luke was still present with the apostle, when he wrote to Colosse—Col. iv, 14—but not when he wrote, still later, to Philippi, to which place he had probably returned—Phil. ii, 19, 20; iv, 3. It is thus highly probable, and almost certain, that the book of Acts was written before the date of the Second Epistle to Timothy. But since it professes to be a continuation of the Gospel, which St. Paul has twice commended, and once referred to under the name of Scripture, it must evidently have been known to him, writing with St. Luke at his side, or in daily intercourse, and be therefore included in his declaration, that "all Scripture is given by inspiration of God, and is profitable for doctrine, for reproof, for correction, and for instruction in righteousness." The testimony, therefore, really applies to the whole of the New Testament, except the General Epistles, and the Gospel and Apocalypse of St. John.

VIII. The two epistles of St. Peter supply further testimonies of the same kind. First of all, the inspiration of the Old-Testament prophets is clearly and fully affirmed. The Spirit of Christ, St. Peter tells us, "was in them, and testified beforehand of the sufferings of Christ, and the glories that should follow." Twelve or thirteen quotations from the Old Testament, or direct allusions to it as the "oracles of God," occur in the course of this short letter. But he proceeds at once to make a similar statement concerning his fellow-apostles, that they had preached the Gospel "with the Holy Ghost sent down from heaven," and that their Gospel message was "the Word of the Lord which endureth forever." The mention, also, of St. Mark, at the close, as the apostle's son in the faith, if the second

Gospel were already written, for which we have strong internal evidence, would be an implied attestation of its character, and would agree with the tradition that it was written by St. Mark, chiefly from materials with which St. Peter had supplied him.

The Second Epistle contains three most important passages, on the authority both of the Old and the New Testament. First, the apostle lays down a fundamental law for the study of the Old Testament, based on the doctrine that all was Divine. "No prophecy of Scripture is of self-interpretation: for the prophecy came not ever by the will of man; but holy men of God spake, as they were moved (or borne along) by the Holy Ghost." Since all proceeded from the same Spirit, to regard them as independent human compositions, which some of late would propound for a first principle of true interpretation, is, according to St. Peter, a mischievous error. They must, on the contrary, be compared with each other, as parts of a greater whole, if we would understand their true and full meaning.

In the second passage, these inspired words of the Old-Testament prophets, and the commandments of himself and his fellow-apostles, are joined together, as equally binding on the conscience of Christians. The common object of both epistles was this—"that ye may be mindful of the words spoken before by the holy prophets, and of the commandment of us, the apostles of our Lord and Savior." The earlier message of the prophets, and the later one of the apostles, is thus equally sealed with full authority from God.

The third passage is more specific, and refers directly to St. Paul's writings. "Account that the long-suffering of our Lord is salvation; even as our beloved brother Paul also, according to the wisdom given unto him, hath written unto you. As also in all his epistles, speaking in them of these things; which they that are unlearned and unstable wrest, as they do also the other Scriptures, to their own destruction."

There are here two distinct assertions, both of them highly important. First, there is a reference to one epistle of St. Paul, written to these Christians, and in which the doctrine that the long-suffering of the Lord was salvation, was set before them. Now, as Galatia is mentioned in the opening of the First Epistle, and St. Peter was the apostle of the circumcision, either the Epistle to the Galatians, or that to the Hebrews, must naturally be intended by this reference. The former contains, however, no such statement as that to which St. Peter alludes; but the latter does in several places—Heb. ii, 1-3; iv, 1-3; iii, 14; vi, 9-12; x, 23-25, 35-39. The conclusion seems evident, that St. Peter ratifies, as the work of St. Paul, the only one of his epistles which does not bear his name, and of which the authorship has been consequently disputed, even down to our own days. Secondly, the apostle includes all the epistles of St. Paul under the sacred name of Scripture, "which they that are unlearned and unstable wrest, as they do also the other Scriptures, to their own destruction." This testimony is the more striking and weighty, when we remember that one of these letters contains the only mention of St. Peter's fault at Antioch, and of the reproof which he received from his brother apostle. There seems no good reason to doubt that the first three Gospels, no less than the Old Testament, are meant by the other Scriptures, with which the epistles of St. Paul are here united; as sharing the same title, and forming along with them one harmonious body of Divine truth, perfect in its own nature, though liable to be perverted by the ignorance and rashness of sinful men.

The short Epistle of St. Jude, besides six or seven

allusions to leading facts of the Old Testament, and one supernatural revelation, and the revival of an ancient and long-forgotten prophecy of Enoch, the seventh from Adam, seems distinctly to ratify the Second Epistle of St. Peter, as this had confirmed and ratified all the epistles of St. Paul. "But, beloved, remember the words which were spoken before by the apostles of our Lord Jesus Christ: how that they told you there would be scoffers in the last time, who would walk after their own ungodly lusts." There seems here a distinct allusion to the words of St. Peter—2 Pet. iii, 3—with this difference, that the evil is predicted as near in one case, and described as present in the other. And this view is confirmed by the other resemblances—Jude 6; 2 Pet. ii, 4; Jude 7; 2 Pet. ii, 6–9; Jude 8; 2 Pet. ii, 10; Jude 9; 2 Pet. ii, 11. There is thus a series of testimonies, by which St. Paul bears witness to the canonical authority of St. Luke's writings, and the two earlier Gospels, St. Peter to all St. Paul's epistles, and St. Jude to the epistles of St. Peter in their turn.

IX. The writings of St. John form confessedly the latest part of the New Testament, and they belong to all its three divisions. They complete the historical and epistolary, and constitute alone the prophetic portion, thus binding the whole into one complete system of Divinely-revealed truth.

Now, first, the Gospel, besides witnessing directly to its own apostolic authorship, as the work of that chosen and beloved disciple, who leaned on the bosom of the Lord, and thus claiming, in the highest degree, the faith and reverence of Christians, bears strong indirect testimony to the three earlier Evangelists. For the more closely it is examined, the clearer are the signs that it is, in its outline and conception, a supplemental narrative; designed to record, not merely a distinct aspect of our Lord's character, but portions of his ministry, and especially his visits to Judea, which had been purposely omitted in their works. These Gospels, it is evident from history alone, must have been well known to St. John; and a tacit reference to them, though an opposite statement has sometimes been paradoxically made, may be easily traced through the whole narrative. Thus, i, 6, refers plainly to Matt. iii, Luke iii, and its abruptness is best explained by the fact that a fuller account of the Baptist's ministry was already on record. Again, i, 15, refers to Matt. iii, 11, and then expounds it by a brief and noble commentary. John i, 32, 33, has a like reference to Matt. iii, 16, 17. The mention of Andrew, Simon, two other brothers, namely, James and John, Philip and Nathanael, implies that the list of the twelve apostles had been already put on record; since the Twelve are afterward mentioned in this Gospel, but their names are not given, and no account appears of their ordination to their office. In iii, 19, there seems a reference to the account in St. Mark of the false witnesses. In iii, 24, is a direct reference to Matt. iv, 12, and in iv, 44, to Matt. xiii, 57, and Luke iv, 24. In xviii, 11, we have a similar reference to Matt. xxvi, 38–44, and Luke xxii, 42, and there are several others. The visits to Jerusalem, and the notice of the Passover, about the time of the miracle of the loaves, dovetail remarkably with the other Gospels, and serve at the same time to fix the chronology of our Lord's ministry. Thus the fourth Gospel not only, by the mention of its author, attests its own inspiration, but confirms by an apostolic sanction those which were already in being.

The epistles of St. John supply no direct materials for the confirmation of the other New-Testament Scriptures; but two ideas pervade them in every part, that they are the teaching of the Holy Spirit, and the truth of God.

The Apocalypse, as it forms the latest portion of the New Testament, and its only book of prophecy, is peculiarly full both in the statement of its own inspiration, and in its testimony to all previous Scripture. It opens with its high title—"the revelation of Jesus Christ, which God gave unto him, to show his servants the things which must shortly come to pass." It pronounces a blessing on those who read and hear "the words of this prophecy." The beloved St. John names himself as the messenger of Christ. He says that he "was in the Spirit on the Lord's day," and that he wrote by the express command of the risen Savior. "I heard behind me a voice, as of a trumpet, saying, What thou seest, write in a book." There was thus the same voice of authority in its publication, as when the ten commandments, the earliest written message of God, were proclaimed, with "the voice of a trumpet exceeding loud," from the top of Sinai. Seven commands to write attend the seven epistles to the Churches, besides the double command already given. What is not to be written is enjoined—x, 4—as well as what is to be written—xiv, 13. Twice at the close the seal is put upon the message, "Write, for these are the true sayings of God." "Write, for these words are true and faithful." Lastly, the truth of this message is joined with a Divine title, which is like a seal on the authority of all the earlier Scriptures. "These sayings are faithful and true, and the Lord God of the holy prophets hath sent his angel to show unto his servants the things which must shortly be done. Behold, I come quickly: blessed is he that keepeth the sayings of the prophecy of this book." At the very close a double curse is pronounced on those who shall add to, or take away from "the words of the book of this prophecy." The Pentateuch and the Apocalypse, in this respect, stand alone. As to the earliest and the latest portion of written revelation, they alike contain a solemn caution against adding to them or taking away; and stronger internal declarations, than in any other

Scriptures, of their own Divine authority. Nine or ten times the writing of the Law by Moses is affirmed in Deuteronomy; and twelve times, or upward, the Apocalypse is declared to be written by the command of Christ, and to consist, throughout, of the true sayings of God.

Thus the inspiration and authority of the New Testament, though not capable of the direct evidence given to the earlier Scriptures, by the lips of our Lord himself, upon earth, has other evidence, from plain analogy with the Old Testament, from the character of the Gospel dispensation, from the revealed rank of the apostles, as even higher than the prophets, from the direct averments of St. Paul concerning his own epistles, and his indirect testimony to St. Luke's writings, and the earlier Gospels, from the cumulative testimonies of St. Peter and St. Jude, from the statements of the fourth Gospel, and the full and emphatic declarations of the Apocalypse, like a keystone to the whole—which leaves those Christians without excuse, who treat it as mingled and imperfect utterances of fallible men, and refuse to own that it is, in reality, "the true sayings of God," the last and highest portion of that Word which will assuredly judge them at the last day.

CHAPTER XII.

THE INTERPRETATION OF SCRIPTURE.

The Bible has been received by the Church of Christ from the first ages, as the Word of God, the great fountain of religious truth. It has thus been the object of wider, deeper, more earnest, and more assiduous meditation and study, than any other book whatever, and even more than all other books combined. Thousands on thousands of works have been written, to unfold its truths, and apply them to the hearts of men. The amount of Biblical literature, during the three centuries since the Reformation, is prodigious. The labor of a lifetime would not suffice for a bare perusal, much less for a careful study, of all its manifold varieties, in criticism, history, doctrine, ethics, and practical applications to the religious life. It has been translated, also, into near two hundred languages, and circulated in more than fifty millions of copies; and hence has arisen a still further amount of critical labor and learned industry, altogether unique in the history of the world.

Now, this immense accumulation of Biblical literature, although its source is the reverence the Bible has received for so many ages from the whole Christian world, may supply a skeptical spirit with large materials for casting doubt and suspicion on the Divine message. For this end it is only needful to view it from without, instead of within; and to trace the multiplied divergence and contradiction at the circumference of this mighty world of thought, instead of discerning its central unity, and its growing fullness from age to age. Man touches nothing which he does not defile. The gift of revelation to a fallen world implies that men are prone to go astray, and lose themselves in the thick mists of religious error. The world was full of Gentile idolatry when the Gospel appeared. Its presence brought light into the thick darkness; but it did not seal up the sources of delusion in the human heart. The course of Divine truth, in every age, has been a constant warfare, and not a triumphal progress; and its fullest victories are still to come. The interpretation of the Bible, then, has had a checkered course. Much precious truth has been unfolded; but no slight amount of human error, in various and divergent forms, has mingled with these expositions. The stream, however pure the fountain, has become turbid in its progress, and stained by the soil from the river-bed in which it had to flow. It is easy to dwell on this human side of the literature of the Bible, till the real excellency of the Word of God is quite obscured from our view. The trifling of mere verbal critics and grammarians, the strifes of interpreters, the dreams of mystics, the subtilties of schoolmen, the confusing influence of the mental parallax, in ten thousand minds, of different ages, countries, and modes of thought, may produce a feeling of almost hopeless perplexity. We may then be urged to cast the whole aside, as mere heaps of misdirected and useless learning; and to commence the study anew on a simpler principle, which sees nothing more, in these inspired oracles of God, than curious and interesting specimens of religious feeling, and valuable productions of human genius, in the earlier youth or earlier infancy of mankind.

The time is not distant, when a loud warning was raised, within the English Church, against the dangers of private judgment, and the maxim of Vincentius, on Catholic consent, was praised as the guardian angel of Christian orthodoxy. No private Christian was reckoned able to interpret, with safety, even the simplest messages of the Bible, unless sustained and protected by a catena of authorities, and some approach to "a unanimous consent of the fathers." The pendulum seems now to have swung violently the other way. The latest voice from the same cloisters assures the youthful and ingenuous student, that all the past labors of Christian divines are a hinderance, and not a help to the attainment of Scriptural knowledge; that they are stumbling-blocks in his path, and not way-marks, to guide his steps in the pathway of Divine truth. He has only to renounce them, and study the Bible for himself, like any other book, and he will enter more fully into its meaning than all the controversial writers of former ages put together.

Now, there can be no doubt that much evil has arisen from reading the Bible with preconceived opinions, and through the colored spectacles of human systems. Christians have thus often robbed their souls of the rich diversity of doctrine, precept, and example, and all spiritual wisdom, which is found in the unforced and genuine teaching of the Word of God. But there may be an equal danger on the opposite side. To despise human aids is no less dangerous than to exaggerate their value. If young students, with unfurnished minds and unprepared hearts, rush to the study of the Bible, as to that of Sophocles or Cæsar, in the conviction that by their solitary research, and dealing with it as the mere work of human authors, they will outstrip at once all the divines of past ages, they will soon illustrate one of its most elementary truths, that "pride goeth before destruction, and a haughty spirit before a fall."

The maxim lately propounded as the master-key of theology, to interpret the Bible like any other book, is one of those half-truths, which have often the mischievous effect of entire falsehood. For the Bible is like other books, and it is unlike them. It resembles them in being the work of various human authors, whose circumstances, tastes, and habits of thought and language, tinge and color each separate portion. But it differs from them, because it is the Word of the Holy Ghost, and a Divine unity of supernatural truth and wisdom animates the whole, and makes it instinct throughout with the mind of that Spirit, who "searcheth all things, yea, even the deep things of God." To insist on the former truth, and to deny the second, which is higher and more weighty, is not to simplify, but to falsify its interpretation. Unbelief is the starting-point of such a mode of study, and therefore unbelief is its natural and necessary consummation.

There are four main principles which form the key to the right study of the Scriptures. Two of these depend on the character of the Bible, and two others on the circumstances of those to whom it is given. We must study it *intelligently* and *naturally*, as composed of works written by human authors, and molded, in each part, by the circumstances which occasioned its composition. We must study it *reverently*, as the inspired Word of God, endued with a fuller meaning, and a deeper unity of truth and wisdom than the separate writers could supply. In the words of St. Paul, we must receive it, "not as the word of man, but as the Word of God, which effectually worketh in those who believe." We must read it *with a direct, honest exercise of our own judgment* on its contents, joined with prayer for the promised teaching of the Spirit. But that teaching is no where promised to mere self-will and presumption. We must read it, therefore, *in the diligent use of all those helps which the providence of God may put within our reach*, through the labors of the servants of Christ, the written or spoken ministry of the Word of God. It is mainly by these "joints and bands" that the mystical body of Christ is nourished with Divine truth, as its heavenly food, and "being knit together, increaseth with the increase of God." Lastly, the recognition of the Bible as Divine, and full of deeper meaning than the earlier writers of it attained to know, is far from leading, as some have untruly affirmed, to endless doubt and uncertainty. On the contrary, it is the only way by which the soul can ever gain a footing on the solid rock of eternal truth. Even if we could revive, in all their first freshness and youth, which is impossible, the thoughts and feelings of certain good, but imperfect and ignorant Jewish patriots, who lived long ago, this would still leave us as far as ever from any sure knowledge of the truth of God. It is only when we read the Bible as "the lively oracles of God," and the "words of the Holy Ghost," and thus discern the outlines of redemption, by an incarnate and atoning Savior, reaching through all its messages, from Genesis to Revelation, from Paradise to the Last Judgment, that our feet are truly planted upon firm ground. We know *what*, and we know also *in whom*, we believe; and instead of being carried to and fro, with every wind of false doctrine, we grow up, with steady and continual progress, into the full unity of the faith and the knowledge of Jesus Christ our Lord.

I. The first maxim of sound interpretation is to read and study the Bible, in the truth of its human character. It is a book composed of many books, each having its own distinct author, and wearing the marks of its human authorship in every page. This maxim, in one of the recent Essays, is a nucleus of truth, around which have crystallized many and dangerous errors. But the truth itself is not the less important and needful for the Christian student to bear in mind.

There is a mechanical view of Bible inspiration, which

shuts out, and practically denies, the human element in its composition. It reduces the whole process, so mysterious, and, possibly, so various in its nature, by which the Spirit of God overruled and guided the sacred penman, to one dull monotony of mere verbal dictation. In its rigor this has seldom been held by theological writers, at least of late years; but whenever stress is laid simply on the result of the inspiration in writing, irrespective of the thoughts and feelings of the sacred writers, there is a close approach to this view. An element, which is made unimportant, and quite superfluous, is in reality set aside. But in popular Christianity, this is the view entertained, wherever traditional orthodoxy and spiritual idleness make a league together. To realize the human features of the books of Scripture, and through them to reach the full sense of its Divine unity, requires patient diligence and persevering thought. It is much easier and simpler to receive all simply as the Word of God, and then to expound it by our own preconceived tastes, feelings, and habits of thought; without caring to inquire into its original meaning, or to realize those aspects of it which carry us out of ourselves, and place us amid the wonders of Providence in distant ages.

The simple truth is, that in reading the Bible, we can not get rid of a human element. We may fail to apprehend those which properly belong to it, from the character and circumstances of the sacred writers themselves; but we are sure, in this case, to replace them with others, borrowed from our own circumstances and mental associations. To travel out of ourselves, and to rise above ourselves, are the first steps in attaining the mind of God. We can not know God in his absolute being, but only as revealed, and revealed in his Word. Even in his Word, we can not apprehend the Divine elements, except through the human. We must pass out of ourselves, first of all, into sympathy with the "holy men of God," by whom the Scriptures were written; and, through communion with their testimonies, thoughts, and feelings, must rise into fellowship with that Spirit by whom they spoke, and that Lord to whom they all bear witness. All systematic theology, all conventional phraseology, and all limited and local forms of Christian experience, tend to contract an element of unreality in their use of Scripture, which can only be remedied by a perpetual return to the living fountains. The student who would retain the simplicity of faith, must so far obey the advice to "transfer himself to another age, imagine that he is a disciple of Christ or of Paul, and disengage himself from all that follows." He must have no theological "theory of interpretation, but a few rules guarding against common errors." His object must be "to read the Scripture with a real and not merely a conventional interest; to open his eyes, and see and imagine things as they truly were." For just as it was through the human actions of our Lord—his hunger and thirst, his fasting in the wilderness, his sleep on the pillow, his tears over Jerusalem—that his Divine glory slowly revealed itself to his first disciples, till they saw it to be "the glory of the Only-Begotten of the Father;" so it is through a more vivid sense of the human elements of the Bible, that we rise most safely and surely to the sense of its Divine unity, its wondrous fertility of goodness, wisdom, and love. When we lose sight of these elements it runs the risk of being mechanized and degraded into a mere school-book, or a string of texts without order or cohesion. It is only as they are restored, and come fully into view, that we realize it as one vast scheme of revelation, overarching, like the bow of heaven, all the six thousand years of the history of the world.

II. The Bible, then, must be read and studied, first of all, as a collection of authentic human writings, through fifteen centuries, from Moses to the beloved St. John. This will add new life and freshness to the fulfillment of the Christian duties of Scripture reading and meditation.

But must we read it as a merely human work? Must we forget or deny, because it had various human writers, that the whole is due to one higher Author, the revealing Spirit of God? This is the great question really at issue between the Christian Church in all ages, and a limited number of modern critics, who aspire to represent the progress, and really herald the predicted unbelief, of these last days. Must we, with "Confessions of an Inquiring Spirit," flout at the practice of bringing together texts, "a whole millennium apart," in illustration of doctrinal or practical lessons; though justified by the clear example of St. Paul, and of our Lord himself? Or shall we not allow that, amidst the human diversity, a Divine unity reigns in these sacred Scriptures; because every part is the Word of that God to whom all his works are known from the beginning, and with whom a thousand years are as one day? This, in brief, is the main question at issue, and one to which it becomes every Christian to give a clear and distinct reply.

In the first place, the principle which an unbelieving criticism would cast aside, is laid down in the New Testament itself, as the first and most essential law of Bible interpretation. St. Peter, in that Second Epistle, which would-be critics reject as spurious, but one sentence of which far outweighs, in solid worth, all their disquisitions, propounds this doctrine in the plainest and most emphatic terms. "Know this *first*, that no prophecy of Scripture is of self-interpretation; for prophecy came not at any time by the will of man, but holy men of God spake as they were moved by the Holy Ghost."

The reasoning here is simple, and easy to understand. The ἰδία ἐπίλυσις, or "private interpretation," denotes the construction of each separate portion of Scripture by itself alone, as if it formed a complete whole, proceeding from some human author. This is a false view of its nature. It is one out of many messages of the Holy Ghost. It is one component in a great series of utterances of Divine truth, from Adam and Enoch down to the last of the apostles. To attain its full meaning and purpose, therefore, it is absolutely needful to bear in mind its true character. Read it merely as an independent voice of man, and you will fail to interpret it aright. Read it as one out of many messages, given by the same Holy Spirit, though under special circumstances, and with features due to the character of the messenger he has chosen, and you have a key to its true and just interpretation. We must, therefore, exactly reverse the false maxim which has been lately propounded, and affirm, on the authority of the inspired apostle, that "illustration of one part of Scripture by another, must *not* be confined to the writings of the same age, and the same authors, far less to the same author, in the same period of his life." It is not true, in spiritual any more than in natural astronomy, that the planets move in orbits wholly independent, that they exercise no mutual influence, and have no common law of relation to that central Sun of righteousness on whom they absolutely depend.

But this great truth, which rests firmly on the authority of the inspired apostle, is confirmed still more fully by the sayings of our Lord himself, and the constant practice of all the writers of the New Testament. We have been told that "the new truth introduced into the Old Testament, rather than the old truth found there, was the conversion and salvation of the world."* This is a corollary which f llows unavoidably from a purely human view, in which

---

* Essay vii, p. 406.

we interpret the Scriptures "like any other book;" that is, with a steadfast refusal to own in it the presence of a Divine element, or the real voice of the Spirit of God. But this view, however gentle the phrase in which it may be conveyed, really gives the lie direct to our Lord and his apostles. Their constant, emphatic testimony is, not that they are putting new truths into the Old Testament, or palming on it a new sense foreign from its genuine significance; but that they simply unfolded its true meaning and reference, when the Spirit of Christ in the prophets "testified beforehand the sufferings of Christ, and the' glories that should follow." Those who reject this constant doctrine of our Lord, and of the whole New Testament, may be learned and ingenious speculators in Christian literature; but it is hard to see in what sense they can be disciples of Christ, while they contradict the Lord of glory in one main and conspicuous part of his teaching, on which his claim to submission and reverence is made, by his own lips, to depend. "Had ye believed Moses, ye would have believed me; for he wrote of me. But if ye believed not his writings, how shall ye believe my words?" "O fools, and slow of heart, to believe all that the prophets have spoken! Ought not the Christ to have suffered these things, and to enter into glory? And beginning at Moses and all the prophets, he expounded to them in all the Scriptures the things concerning himself." He, whose name is the Truth, did not, in the hour of his resurrection, enact the part of a spiritual juggler, and foist a reference to himself into texts, of which the true meaning was wholly different; in order, by this pious lie of representing the "new truth introduced" as "the old truth of the New Testament," to effect the conversion and salvation of the world. The supposition is little short of a monstrous blasphemy. No, he rebuked the blindness of his disciples; who, like many modern critics,

THE INTERPRETATION OF SCRIPTURE. 271

could not see, and were too foolish to believe, what those Scriptures really contained. He opened their understanding, to see the landscape which was there already, but which the scales of their spiritual ignorance had previously concealed from their view. Then all was plain to their opened eyes and quickened hearts; and through reproach, affliction, and martyrdom, they bore witness to Christ in the midst of malicious adversaries, "saying none other things than those which the prophets and Moses did say should come; that Christ should suffer, and that he should be the first that should rise from the dead, and should show light unto the people and to the Gentiles." Acts xxvi, 22, 23.

The same great truth, which is confirmed by the uniform consent of all the writers of the New Testament, and by the plainest sayings of our Lord himself, has also a negative proof in the confusion and perplexity of those critics, who venture to contradict it, and cast it aside. If the Old Testament be in truth the Word of God, it must be clear that no consistent explanation of it can be given on the contrary hypothesis, that it is a series of purely human writings. Our Lord was a Jewish peasant; but whoever strove to account for his words and works, on the hypothesis that he was a Jewish peasant only, must have plunged himself at every step into contradiction and absurdity. Even the officers of the Pharisees were forced to own—"Never man spoke like this man;" and unbelievers, under the momentary impression of his miracles, were led to confess—"This is of a truth that Prophet that should come into the world."

Now, the case is precisely similar with the Scriptures of the Old Testament. A learned school of naturalist critics have labored to expound and analyze them, on the negative view of their character. And what is the result of labors conducted on such principles? The authenticity and integrity of the books of Moses, of the prophecies of Isaiah and Daniel, of Joshua and Judges, in short, of all the main portions of the canon, in spite of the full external evidence in their favor, melt away and disappear. The facts, as they stand, will not agree with the hypothesis, and must be tortured and transformed, in order to obtain some decent show of consistency. That holy and perfect law, honored both by our Lord and his apostles, and all the prophets, as the gift of God, by his servant Moses, and placed from the hour of its completion beside the ark of the covenant in the holy of holies, has to be dissolved into a cento of fragments, a patchwork of imaginary documents, which the names of the Most High God are profaned in order to describe, due to some unknown and obscure compilers in the time of the kings. The very first chapter of Genesis must be degraded into a piece of unscrupulous guess-work, by some "Hebrew Descartes or Newton," who affirmed in the dark what he had no means of knowing, because he had not been trained in the modesty of modern science! The blessing of Jacob on his sons is turned, from a sacred prophecy, into a legendary fiction, of the time of Samson—in other words, into a manifest lie. The blessing of Moses, in like manner, is transferred to some mendacious author, in the times of David or Solomon. The book of Judges is turned from plain history into a new and singular Epos, of which the only poetical feature consists in the substitution of false dates for true ones. One-half of Isaiah's prophecies are wrested from the author to whom all antiquity, and the words of our Lord and his apostles assign them, and are referred to Baruch, or some apocryphal hand, to make the task rather less unmanageable, of stripping them of all their prophetic character. In the same way the writings of the beloved Daniel, referred to by our Lord as the words of "Daniel the prophet," and appropriated and applied to himself in the most solemn act of his public testimony before the high-priest, are turned into a base imposture of the time of the Maccabees; that prophecies plainly Divine, if genuine, may be expounded as meager summaries of past history, which have been impiously disguised by a preface of angelic visions, in order to make the imposture more complete.

Now, these results, however hateful and abominable in the eyes of the devout Christian, are only the natural fruits of that negative criticism, which labors to expound the Old Testament as a series of merely human writings. The Divine element in them, wherever it comes plainly to light, must then be got rid of by some critical violence or other. And this violence reveals itself by endless inconsistency and vacillation. The false witnesses against the authority and Divinity of the written Word, frame successively plausible hypotheses, in which charges of untruth are expressed or implied, "but neither so doth their witness agree together." Mythicism and naturalism, supplementary hypotheses, crystallization hypotheses, documentary hypotheses, a twofold, a threefold, a fourfold, a fivefold authorship, have all been applied to the Pentateuch alone, but still the witness does not, and will not agree. Many picklocks have been tried in turn, but the wards are obstinate. Those who refuse to see in the Word of God a Divine authorship, are compelled to set aside Moses, Isaiah, and Daniel; but they can not tell how to replace them, or frame any consistent view of the human authorship, which will enable them to expunge the miracles and prophecies, and thus to reduce the whole to the level of common history.

Let us take one or two examples, in detail, of the general truth. The Bible begins with a professed narrative of the creation of the world, and the first formation of man on the sixth day. Interpret like any other book, and one of two conclusions must follow. We have here either an open imposture, or a supernatural revelation. A "Hebrew Descartes or Newton," who, in total ignorance, should guess for himself what might have happened before the first man was in being, and then publish it as part of a Divine message, would simply prove himself a profane and dishonest liar. Thus, at the outset, every middle hypothesis is swept away. We must either interpret the Bible by moral rules, unlike those applied to any other work, or choose at once between branding it as a vile imposition and accepting it as Divine. But when once accepted as a Divine message, the attempt, by a series of critical artifices, to weed out of it all supernatural elements, is a course no less irrational and senseless than profane.

Let us take one other instance—the three verses in Genesis, Psalms, and Hebrews, which refer to Melchisedek. On the humanist view, the first of these was a mere accident, in the contents of some "Elohistic document," an early "monogram" on Chedarlaomer, which happened to get inserted by the last compiler of the Pentateuch. The verse in Psalm cx, 4, which introduces the name of Melchisedek, in an oath ascribed to Jehovah, must have been a mere poetical fiction of David, or some unknown writer, who ventured to take the name of God in vain, and ascribe to him a solemn oath, of which the writer knew nothing. The whole chapter, again, in Hebrews, must be a piece of laborious trifling, in which the weightiest conclusions are based on the premise of a mere accidental omission of names in Genesis, and a mere fiction of the Psalmist; while the forms of reasoning are abused to give an appearance of argument, where there is nothing more than the wildest caprice of fanciful interpretation. And still the upshot of this accident in Genesis, this profane fiction in the Psalmist, and 'his capricious folly in the apostle, is to bring out one of the noblest utterances of Christian doctrine, and one of the most cheering messages of comfort and promise to the weary heart. "Wherefore he is able also to save them to the uttermost that come to God by him, seeing he ever liveth to make intercession for them. For such a highpriest became us, who is holy, harmless, undefiled, separate from sinners, and made higher than the heavens..... For the law maketh men high-priests which have infirmity; but the word of that oath, which was since the law, maketh the Son who is perfected for evermore." Is this a hypothesis credible? Can we believe that such glorious issues of truth and holiness, such beautiful and lovely forms of comfort, hope, and promise, are the results of chance and caprice, of profane fiction, and childish folly?

Now, let us reverse the picture, and contemplate the same passages in their true light. "All Scripture," from Genesis to Revelation, "is given by inspiration of God." In every part, "holy men of God spake as they were moved by the Holy Ghost." To this revealing Spirit the remotely past and the remotely future are equally open, for "known unto God are all his works from the beginning," and "the Spirit searcheth all things, yea, even the deep things of God." It was the Holy Spirit, who, more than three thousand years ago, guided Moses, in his inspired narrative, to make this brief mention of Melchisedek, and his blessing on Abraham, and to omit purposely, all mention of his father, or mother, or genealogy; and introduce him suddenly into the scene as a mysterious person, a priest of the Most High God, standing above the father of the faithful, in dignity and honor, aloof and alone. It was the Spirit, nearly three thousand years ago, who taught David to give the title of Lord to his own son, as a pledge of Messiah's Divine glory; and revealed to him that oath of God concerning this unborn son of David, which could never else have been known—"The Lord sware, and will not repent, Thou art a priest forever after the order of Melchisedek.' It was the same Holy Spirit, who, eighteen hundred years ago, taught the apostle to expound to the Church the significance of the original history, two thousand years after it had occurred, in which the silence concerning Melchisedek's parentage and genealogy rendered him a type of the heavenly priesthood of the risen Son of God; to unfold the meaning of the oath in the Psalm, as the prophecy of a higher priesthood than that of Aaron, which the true Messiah would fulfill, and over which mortality had no power; and, last of all, to apply the whole in a glorious message of comfort to the Church of Christ. And it is the same Spirit, who now, in these our own days, has caused these his own words, by his wonderful Providence, to be diffused in millions of copies, and in countless languages, throughout the tribes of the earth; and then applies them, by his secret power and grace, to quicken the faith, and cheer the hearts of millions of believers, by the vision of their Great High-Priest, who intercedes for them perpetually before the throne in heaven.

III. Another question must now be answered. Private judgment, there can be no doubt, must be exercised, with prayer and humility, by every real student of the Word of God. A mere blind reception of the dicta of human authority, without thought or personal inquiry, is a superstitious counterfeit, and widely different from real Christian faith. But is it the wisest and safest course, in the acquirement of true spiritual knowledge, for every novice to start anew? Ought he to approach the Bible, like Sophocles or Plato, as a human work, to be mastered by "the plain meaning of words and their context alone," and to discard all the Christian writings of the last eighteen hundred years, and all the criticism and theology to which they have given birth, as a mere incubus and troublesome burden, which must be wholly cast aside, in order to gain insight into the true meaning? Such a view involves a strange inversion of the lessons of humility and true wisdom.

The contempt for human helps in the knowledge of Scripture, may assume two opposite forms, one of intellectual pride, and the other of fanatical presumption. It is hard to say which is the more dangerous. The former neglects or denies the promise of the Spirit, and professes to rely on human industry alone. The latter abuses the promise of the Holy Ghost, in order to justify a neglect of helps which he himself has graciously provided for the people of Christ, and to disguise a rash confidence in the hasty and unripe conclusions of one's own private understanding.

The Bible is a rich treasury of Divine truth. But the nature and purpose of this record, as designed for the instruction of the Church, in every age, requires the truth to be given in its most condensed form. It is perfect for the object for which it was really given, but not for other objects, for which distinct and collateral provision was also made. One of the chief of these is the expansion of the truth contained in the Scriptures, and its application to the varying circumstances and characters of individuals, and to the multiplied changes and experience of the whole Church of Christ. For this end a living ministry was expressly ordained, both under the Law and the Gospel, and its importance for the instruction and guidance of believers is commended in the strongest terms. A nursery full of seeds does not exclude, but requires, the labor and care of many gardeners, if its own purpose is to be really fulfilled, and countless landscapes are to be adorned with the fruits of Autumn and the flowers of Spring. The Bible is such a spiritual nursery; and the answer of the Ethiopian eunuch to Philip's inquiry, "How can I understand, except some man shall guide me?" expresses the usual law of God's providence in the use of human agents and ministers, to convey the clear knowledge of its truths to their fellow-men.

It would be most unwise, it is true, for the youthful student to begin his course by collecting a cumbrous apparatus of human authors, instead of coming directly and simply to the words of Scripture, with the honest desire to learn from them their true meaning. Such a plan would hedge up his way with thorns, and render very difficult any real access to the truth of God. But it is hardly less unwise to imagine that he will advance most safely and rapidly by rejecting all the labors of critics and theologians, and relying on his own skill and industry alone. Theology is the first and noblest of the sciences. The Bible supplies the materials, in rich variety, by which alone that science can be attained. But it needs much patient thought, much meditation on Divine things, the comparison of spiritual things with spiritual in prayer and humility, in order to "wax ripe and strong" in the knowledge of Christ, and to pass out of spiritual infancy into the firm intelligence of full manhood, or the ripened wisdom of the "fathers in Christ." Where, in the providence of God, other helps are denied, it may be hard to assign a limit to the Christian light and wisdom, which may be attained by solitary meditation on the Scriptures alone. But such circumstances, and such a Baptist-like calling, are exceptional and rare. In most cases it is either laziness or pride, which leads a young Christian to dispense with the aid derivable from human teachers and writings, and either heresy, or great spiritual barrenness, is the only result which can be expected to follow. Direct meditation on the Word of God ought ever to take precedence of the study even of the best human critics or commentators. Direct comparison of truth with truth, and Scripture with Scripture, far more than a perusal of the soundest system of divinity, must be the basis of a living and real theology. But contempt for the aid of theological writings is always an unhealthy sign, whether it arises from the mere self-conceit of intellectual pride, or disguises itself under a vail of spiritual phrases, and a claim to a simple dependence on the promised guidance of the Spirit of God. It is not the lazy or the self-conceited, but the humble and diligent, to whom the promise belongs, of being guided by teaching of that blessed Spirit into all truth.

IV. The question with regard to the single and double, or triple sense of Scripture, its types and symbolisms, and real or supposed hidden meanings, is far too wide to enter upon at the close of this chapter. But a few remarks seem required, on that charge of total uncertainty, which has been brought against the whole mass of received Biblical interpretation. "The book," it is asserted, "in which we believe all religious truth to be contained, is the most uncertain of all books, because interpreted by arbitrary and uncertain methods."

Is this a true and just accusation? The heart and conscience of every devout and intelligent Christian will answer at once, that it is a monstrous inversion of the truth. No doubt if we collect in one mass, all that has been written on the Bible, in criticism, commentary, and controversy, for eighteen hundred years, and seek to winnow out all the chaff of error, ignorance, heresy, and folly, we may be almost choked and stifled by its vast amount. But this is due to the immense variety of the Biblical literature, reaching through so many ages and countries of the world, and encountering a thousand tendencies to delusion and error in the hearts of men. If we take, on the one hand, those views of Christian doctrine and duty, which tens of thousands of humble and earnest disciples are receiving daily from their study of the Word of God, though tinged and colored, here and there, by the influences of education, personal feeling, and local or ecclesiastical tradition; or single out those works of theology, which have formed and molded the main current of our Christian literature, there will be found a great and even marvelous unity, both in the simpler outlines of Divine truth, and in its fuller and more scientific development. The impression of complexity, disorder, and confusion, of which such complaints are made, and which are used to terrify the young students into a total rejection of Christian theology, is like the result which would be produced if we were to collect all the mistakes of astronomical theories and calculations, from the time of the Chaldeans downward, mingling them with all the dreams of astrology, and then should advise the young astronomer to reject all instruments, and all mathematical theories of the solar and starry systems, with the copious accumulation of facts in so many observatories, and to betake himself, with the naked eye alone, to direct the study of the heavens. This would be no progress into clearer light, but a backward plunge into childish ignorance again. Astronomy is the most certain of all the sciences. But this certainty is not gained by resting in the first impressions of the senses on the motions of the stars, but by using them and multiplying them by assiduous observation, increasing their accuracy by instrumental aids, and thus rising through them, and beyond them, to a knowledge of the true system of the starry universe.

The same law applies to Christian theology. It can not be gained by neglecting the letter of the Scriptures; but it will never be reached by a superficial, self-confident approach to them, in the neglect of all aid from Christian teachers and guides, as human writings to be scanned by critical industry alone. The Bible is the most certain of all books, and its theology the surest and highest of all sciences, when it is read with prayer, with humility, with perseverance, in dependence on the promised teaching of the Spirit of God, and in the use of all the varied helps which he has provided for his Church, comparing spiritual things with spiritual, searching for heavenly wisdom as for hidden treasure. And this certainty rests upon the firmest ground, the direct promise of God himself, given to every humble and sincere inquirer—"If thou criest after knowledge, and liftest up thy voice for understanding; if thou seekest her as silver, and searchest for her as for hid treasures, then shalt thou understand the fear of the Lord, and find the knowledge of God."

CHAPTER XIII.

ON ALLEGED DISCREPANCIES OF THE BIBLE.

The apparent discordance between different statements in the histories of the Bible has often been made a powerful objection to the doctrine of its inspiration. The subject is one which naturally branches out into many details, impossible to compress within narrow limits. I shall, therefore, in the present chapter, confine myself chiefly to some general remarks, on some of the main difficulties which have perplexed the minds of many inquirers, and obscured their faith in the Divine authority of the Word of God.

1. Every word of God is pure, and, when it proceeds from its Divine source, must be free from all error. Such is the instinctive conviction of every devout and intelligent mind. On the other hand, the Bible is not strictly and absolutely free from all error, in the shape in which it actually reaches the great majority of its readers. Translations, however trustworthy, are not completely perfect. The transmission of the text, by copyists, may introduce a small amount of deviation from the first original. In so large a work, numbers and names in the genealogies are peculiarly liable to suffer from successive transcriptions. It is thus admitted fully, by all well-informed critics and divines, that the inspiration of the Bible does not require or secure theoretic and mathematical freedom from error, when it reaches the great bulk of its readers, and fulfills its great practical object, as a revelation to mankind at large. Slight errors of transmission and translation may

intrude, and have intruded, without destroying its authority and inspiration, or detracting in any perceptible degree from its practical worth.

2. Some writers, starting from this admission, have been disposed to proceed a step further. While admitting, perhaps, an ideal perfection of the Divine messages, before they are clothed in words, they suppose them to contract a degree of error and imperfection, as soon as they are embodied in human language. The substance of the thought, or doctrine, is owned to be Divine, but all the details, the phrases, the form, the historical circumstances, are supposed to be liable to mistake, and partial falsehood. In this way all difficulties, arising from apparent contradictions and historical discrepancies, are, in their judgment, easily and entirely removed. In the Gospels, for example, harmonists are rebuked for striving to establish an agreement which does not exist, and for refusing to see numerous contradictions between the different narratives; and when they ought rather to have owned freely this human imperfection in the Evangelists, and only to have seen in it a proof of their honesty, and of the substantial truth of the message so variously given.

This view, however simple and plausible it may appear at the first glance, is open to two grave and insurmountable difficulties. First, it evacuates the force of all those passages in which our Lord and his apostles appeal to the written Word, not only in the mass, but even in the separate clauses, reason upon the force of single words, and affirm that "it is easier for heaven and earth to pass, than for one tittle of the law to fail." And next, it seems to annul, to a great extent, the main purpose for which the messages of God were recorded in a written form. This purpose was evidently to secure at once the purity and the permanence of revealed truth, which, in mere oral tradition, is liable either to be corrupted by false additions, or to fade away into gradual oblivion. Now, so far as human error was permitted to intrude into the original writing, this object would be precisely reversed. As far as this intrusion extends, error would be imposed with the sanction of truth on every later age, would receive a wider currency, and acquire a greater permanence than it could otherwise have attained.

This view, then, of an intermittent, imperfect inspiration, which would leave room for an undefined amount of historical error, and maintain a substantial truth of doctrine alone, removes seeming difficulties, by abandoning the double evidence, *à priori* and *à posteriori*, from reason and from the express testimony of our Lord, on which the doctrine itself depends. It must therefore be, in almost every instance, a mere landing-place, either in the departure from traditional faith, into an entire rejection of the Bible, or in the upward progress to a fuller and firmer acceptance of its truth, and of its entire authority over the consciences of men.

3. Let us inquire, then, whether the difficulties which have seemed so formidable to some critics and divines, retain their force on a closer examination; or whether they are not really phantoms which disappear before a rigid and exact inquiry.

Here, first of all, it is needful to get rid of an ambiguity, by which the true question has often been obscured. Discrepancy may be used in the sense either of simple divergence or of positive contradiction. Differences of the former kind can create no real difficulty. When two or three inspired accounts are given of the same general series of events, there is no reason, but quite the reverse, why one should simply repeat the other, without any variation. By this means, in reality, nearly the whole benefit of a double and triple testimony would be lost. It was a maxim of the law, that "in the mouth of two or three witnesses every word should be established." But, to fulfill this law, it is needful that the testimonies should be really distinct. Some partial divergence in the details recorded, or in the molding of the narrative, is plainly desirable, and almost essential, that this main object of a plural testimony may be fully attained. It is only such divergence as implies a direct and real contradiction, or the partial falsehood of one statement, which can furnish a real argument against plenary and complete inspiration.

4. Again, one statement of the true doctrine of inspiration is found in those words of the apostle, that "God at sundry times, and in divers manners, spake in time past to the fathers by the prophets." Here three truths are contained, with a gradation in their importance, which complete the true and full idea of Divine inspiration. First, it was God himself who spoke by the prophets. The messages are truly and properly the words of God. Next, he spoke by the prophets, not by copying machines, but by living men, who were also "holy men of God." 2 Pet. i, 21. This teaches us that the human faculties of the messengers were not superseded, but fully employed. St. Luke wrote after having gained "perfect information of the facts from the beginning;" and St. Paul's epistles were written "according to the wisdom given unto him." The first phrase excludes a lax and partial inspiration; and the second, a mechanical dictation, in which the natural and spiritual endowments of the messengers, instead of being perfected, are set aside. Thirdly, it was "in many parts and many modes or forms." One feature in the Scriptures, thus prominently stated, is the freedom and variety of the types or molds in which various portions of it are cast. There is here implied the retention, in each case, of special

and individual characters, arising from the form of the communication—as history, Psalm, proverb, or prophecy—and also from the distinct position of every writer. The diversity arising from the human authorship is here recognized as one part of the truth, side by side with the unity of their common character as being alike the messages of God. But this principle will clearly have the fullest application to parallel histories; since here the distinctness and concurrence of testimonies must be one chief object implied in the very form of the revelation. Sameness would thus defeat one main purpose for which the parallel histories are given. In these cases, of which the chief instances are Kings and Chronicles in the Old Testament, and the four Gospels in the New, it is most reasonable, even on the view of their plenary inspiration, to expect the fullest measure of diversity, which is consistent with the general sameness of the narrative, and with the avoidance of positive contradiction.

5. The Scriptures, again, are a selection of truth in its most condensed form, to suit their purpose as a comprehensive and permanent record, which, if it became too voluminous, would fail of its main object, and cease to be generally accessible. This character runs throughout the whole of the Bible. Within one volume of moderate size we have a sacred history, ranging through four thousand years, copious patterns of devotion, proverbs of wisdom, sacred dramas, meditations on human life and its vanity, prophecies of the events of distant ages, four biographies of our Lord, a brief and full history of the apostolic Church, and various letters containing an ample outline of Christian doctrine, duty, and experience. The contrast between the brevity of Scripture and the ample material out of which the selection is made, is expressed at the close of the fourth Gospel: "And there are many other things

which Jesus did, which, if they should be written every one, I suppose that even the world itself could not contain the books that should be written." So, in the last book of Scripture, the prophet, in one case, is expressly restrained from writing what he has seen and heard, while in other cases a repeated command to write is given him.

Now, this remark sets aside at once a frequent source of false reasoning and critical illusion. The silence of a sacred historian about certain facts, is no proof, and even no presumption, that they were unknown to him. It is quite enough to account for their absence, if they did not fall within the special scope of his message. To take one instance, it has often been said that St. Matthew knows nothing of Joseph's original home being Nazareth, and that St. Luke knows nothing of the flight into Egypt, or of the visit of the wise men. There is no warrant whatever for either statement. Silence is here no proof of ignorance; and the range of the narrative of each writer is no reasonable measure of the extent of his knowledge. None of them professes to write all that he knew. The last of them affirms the exact opposite in the strongest terms. It is clear, from the fourth Gospel, that St. Matthew must have been present at the resurrection of Lazarus, and still the name never occurs in the first Gospel. A similar remark applies to the two others. This great miracle belonged to the visits to Judea, which are systematically left out in the earlier accounts of the Galilean ministry. So, again, the mission of the Seventy must have been well known, both to St. Matthew, St. Mark, and St. John, who make no allusion to it whatever. In like manner, St. Matthew's special object, which was to show the fulfillment of the prophecies in the person of Christ, made Bethlehem, his predicted birthplace, the natural starting-point in his statement; while the historical character of St. Luke made it equally natural to record the place where Mary received the promise of the incarnation, and explain how a decree of the Roman Emperor led to the temporary removal to Bethlehem, and thus was the means of securing the fulfillment of Micah's prophecy.

6. Once more, the truth of history does not preclude, in its own nature, all variety in the order of arrangement. Events, it is true, can only happen in one succession; but all history implies a grouping of actions and discourses by a reference to other links than those of sequence alone. The two main laws of history are these, that events shall be grouped together according to the intimacy of their connection, and that each group shall be placed as nearly as possible in the order of time. The larger and fuller the groups that are formed, and the wider will be the deviation from a single chronological series. And thus histories often become less strictly chronological, as the historian discerns more clearly the causes of events, and has the skill to arrange them by a deeper law than that of mere sequence in time. All discrepancies, then, in the Gospels, which consist only in differences of arrangement, are of no force to imply contradiction or falsehood, unless the true order of occurrence has, in both cases, been plainly affirmed.

7. Historical statements, again, have something which they assert, and something else which is merely probable inference, but will commonly be inferred in the absence of fuller evidence. Each of them is like a planet, with its solid nucleus of fact, and an attached atmosphere of probable conclusions. Let two planets come into contact, and the mass will be unaltered, but their atmospheres will be completely changed, and melt into one. So, when two testimonies concur, though equally true, each will usually modify the conclusions that would have been drawn from the other, while it stood alone. We might conclude, for

instance, from Num. xvi, that Korah, Dathan, and Abiram, all perished with their families; but Num. xxvi, 11, correct this hasty inference, for it tells us plainly that "the children of Korah died not." From Matt. xxi, 18, 21, we might easily suppose that the fig-tree cursed by our Lord withered at once under the eyes of the disciples; but from St. Mark's account it is plain that a day and a night intervened before the result was noticed, and led to that impressive conversation. Again, from Luke ii, 39, we might infer that the return to Nazareth was immediately after the legal rites had been performed; but we find from St. Matthew that the flight into Egypt came between. In each case there is no real contradiction. We have only to correct, by fuller evidence, natural but unproved inferences from the original statement. There is contact, but no collision. The atmospheres only are altered, and two sets of mere inferences, that were incompatible, have been harmonized together.

When these truths are borne in mind, there will be left only a few discrepancies, comparatively, in the pages of the Bible, which bear any signs of involving a real contradiction. It would be needless to trouble ourselves, in these cases, to discover probable or possible modes of reconciliation, from any inherent importance of these variations. They affect the practical worth of the Bible as little as floating specks in the air can lessen the brightness of the sun at noonday. It is simply the proneness of men to find excuses for escaping from the authority of God's messages, and the reverence due to the clear and full statements of him whose name is the Truth, which give importance to the inquiry It should ever be remembered that the authority of the Scriptures over the conscience of the Christian does not depend on their reaching us in a form absolutely free from the least trace of error, or on our ability to decide the exact point in the course of transmission, where any slight error, if proved to exist, has found entrance. It depends on the fact that these are the words of prophets, and apostles, and evangelists, messengers whose commission has been ratified by the voice of Christ himself, or by signs and wonders, and supernatural gifts of the Spirit of God. This authority attaches directly to their whole contents, and must belong to every part, till we have some direct and positive reason to except it from the rest; whether because it can be shown to deviate from the original text, or because it involves some form of provable inaccuracy and contradiction. This negative evidence, also, can only serve to prune off the particular text, or passage, where such a contradiction is found; unless the cases were so numerous, and so inwrought into the texture of the work, as to make it unreasonable to refer them to a corruption of the copies, or to some momentary negligence, at the first, in recording a perfect Divine message.

It would require a volume to enter in detail into the various cases in which a charge of inconsistency has been brought against the Bible histories. I will confine myself to a brief notice of those which have been alleged by two very different authorities, and different schools of thought; first, in the Seventh Essay, which seems almost entirely to set aside all the authority of the Bible as the Word of God, and a fountain of certain truth; and, secondly, in Dean Alford's able work on the New Testament, where a lax and lowered view of inspiration is joined with a firm and full maintenance of all the great outlines and doctrines of the Christian faith.

I. The following are the chief grounds alleged in the Seventh Essay, for refusing to the Evangelists the character of "perfect accuracy or agreement."

1. First, one supposes the original dwelling-place of our

Lord's parents to have been Bethlehem, another Nazareth. Matt. ii, 1, 22; Luke ii, 4. Eleven or twelve pages in Strauss's "Leben Jesu," are occupied with a laborious development of this objection.

This difficulty arises solely from a neglect of the fifth previous remark. St. Matthew says nothing about Bethlehem as the "original dwelling-place" of Joseph and Mary, but introduces it simply as the place where Jesus was born. Nay, on looking closely, we have a clear sign that he did not regard it as the original dwelling-place. Why else should the mention of it be delayed till the visit of the magi, and not given at once on the first mention of Joseph and his vision? Why not have said, "When his mother Mary was espoused to Joseph at Bethlehem," if Bethlehem, in the first passage as well as the second, were supposed to be the true scene of the occurrence? The argument from Matt. ii, 22, is equally destitute of real force. For the natural conclusion that Joseph and Mary would draw from the signal wonders at Bethlehem, and from their own views of the expected Messiah, would make them infer that Judea, and the city of David, were the proper place for the education of the infant Jesus. This is confirmed by John vii, 42, which shows the popular impression to have been precisely what Matt. ii, 22, implies in the mind of Joseph, that Bethlehem was not only to be the birthplace of Messiah, but also the scene of his life before his public work began.

2. "They trace his genealogy in two different ways." This is the old difficulty, which has been so often answered. When we remember that our Lord's birth was supernatural; that he had a real mother and a reputed father; that the genealogy by his reputed father, which would naturally be assigned to him, though his in a legal and improper sense, was not that by which he really took on him our nature,

but that he was "man of the substance of his mother," and of her alone; the presence of two distinct genealogies, one improperly his, but properly of Joseph, and the other improperly Joseph's, but his in strictest propriety, instead of a real difficulty, is in direct harmony with the great doctrine of the incarnation.

3. "One mentions the thieves' blasphemy; the other has preserved the record of the penitent thief."

Two steps are here wanting, to form a real contradiction. First, if St. Matthew had distinctly affirmed that each of the two malefactors had blasphemed our Lord, this could not prove an after-repentance on the part of one of them to be impossible and untrue. We might then have expected some allusion to his own more recent offense; but it would not be essential for St. Luke to mention every word of his penitent confession. In the next place, St. Matthew does not make the statement separately, concerning each of the two thieves, any more than each of the passers-by, or each of the chief priests, the scribes, and elders. He describes the conduct of three classes, using in each case the same plural term. In the two former cases, where the individuals are many, no one infers that the general statement belongs separately to each individual. Of thousands who passed by, there might be only a few who used the words, "Thou that destroyest the temple, and buildest it in three days, save thyself." The same is probably true of the chief priests, scribes, and elders. The rest of the class, even by their silence, were involved in a common guilt, and included in a common description. The case of the two thieves may have been, and probably was, exactly similar. The malignant conduct of three classes, the multitudes, the chief priests and scribes, and the malefactors, are given in St. Matthew; and the exceptions of remorse and pity, the wailing of the women, the people who beheld and smote their breasts, the confession of the penitent thief, the half-hidden under-currents of natural or godly sorrow, are recorded by St. Luke. There is thus unity of character in each account, and a real consistency between them.

4. "They appear to differ about the day and hour of the crucifixion." This objection may be answered in the words of another essayist, that "if it be merely one of appearances, and not of realities, it can teach us nothing." An objector, who states his difficulty in this manner, can not be very sure of his own ground.

In what sense do they "appear to differ" as to the day? No event could be more deeply graven on their memories. In none could a mistake of the day be, in itself, more incredible. They all refer it to the Friday in the week of the Passover. The supposed difference is not in the day of the crucifixion, for the weekly cycle is fixed and certain, but in the week-date, that year, of the Jewish Passover. Even this diversity, I believe, is an "appearance," and not a reality. The misunderstanding of one text in the fourth Gospel, is the only reason for supposing that it contradicts the consenting evidence of the three others, which all represent Thursday as the evening of the Paschal Supper, and Friday as the holiday, or great festal day. The difficulty about the hour is equally an appearance. For a comparison of John xviii, 28; xix, 14, with the few incidents between them, seems decisive in favor of Townson's view, that the hours in St. John date from midnight, like our own; and on this supposition all the statements agree fully with each other.

5. "The narrative of the woman who anointed the Lord is told in all four, but each has more or less considerable variations." It is here assumed that the event, in all the four Gospels, is the same. But the account in St. Luke differs in every particular, excepting the anointing only.

It was in a city of Galilee, while the other was in Judea, in the village of Bethany. It was before that circuit of Galilee, at the close of which our Lord began to speak in parables; and the other was a few days before the crucifixion. The woman, in one case, was a notorious sinner; in the other, the sister of the mistress who entertained our Lord, and of one of the guests who sat by his side. The motive, in one case, was gratitude for special sins forgiven; and in the other, for loving intimacy, and a brother raised from the dead. The objector, the objection, the reply, the promise, are all entirely distinct, and even plainly incompatible. Even the parting words alone, "go in peace," which prove the woman to have been a stranger in the party, and could never have been applied to Mary in her sister's house, with Lazarus at the table, are enough to prove that the two events are wholly different. When the blunder of confounding them has been rectified, the three accounts of the later anointing at Bethany have no contradiction whatever. There is only some uncertainty, whether St. John has placed it a little earlier, or the two others a little later, than its exact time. The latter opinion seems rather more probable, since it forms a parenthesis in both Gospels; but either view implies no real contradiction.

These are selected examples of inaccuracy in the Gospels; and there is not one of them, when fairly examined, which justifies the least charge of real contradiction. But we are instructed to make a catalogue "with the view of estimating their cumulative weight; since it is obvious that the answer, which might be admitted in the case of a single discrepancy, will not be the true answer, if there are many." Here there is a neglect of the principle in the third of the previous remarks. Discrepancies, in the wider sense of the word, are not contradictions. On the contrary, a real diversity to the full extent that truth will allow, is one essential feature of the Gospel narratives. It is the way by which they could fulfill the main purpose for which the history was given in this form, so as to satisfy the legal requirement—"In the mouth of two or three witnesses shall every word be established." For automata, however high the influence that directs their movements, are not, and can not be, witnesses. This supposes an intelligent person, who uses his own senses, consults his own memory, and describes or narrates occurrences which he has seen, or which have been told him by others, from a point of sight peculiarly his own. We have just seen six or seven discrepancies, involving no single case of contradiction. Multiply such cases a hundredfold, and the truth of the Scriptures will remain unimpaired by their "cumulative evidence."

II. The same general hypothesis, of partial inaccuracy and contradiction in the Gospels, has obtained of late a wider currency through Dean Alford's valuable work, in connection with a reverent and Christian tone of thought, and critical labors worthy of high esteem. The high reputation of the author, and the extensive use of the work among theological students, appear to justify a few remarks in this place. If the view be supported by strong evidence, there would be a sinful want of candor in refusing to accept it through any fear of consequences, since truth alone is safe, and error of all kinds is dangerous. But if the reasoning is misty and obscure, and the view a groundless concession, without evidence, to superficial criticism, it must be like a dead fly in precious ointment; and some caution against its acceptance, even on such authority, belongs clearly to the object of the present work.

1. The real discrepancies, according to this able writer, "are very few, and nearly all of one kind. They are simply the results of the entire independence of the accounts. They consist merely in different chronological arrangements."

Such are the transpositions of the passage to the Gadarenes Matt. viii, 28; Mark v, 1; Luke viii, 26; and the difference of position of the incidents in Matt. viii, 19–22; Luke ix, 57–61. The way of dealing with such discrepancies has been twofold. Enemies of the faith have recognized them, and pushed them to the utmost, often attempting to create them where they do not exist. Equally unworthy of the Evangelists has been the course of those who are called the orthodox harmonists. They have usually taken upon them to state that such narratives do not refer to the same incidents, and so to save, as they imagine, the credit of the Evangelists, at the expense of common fairness and candor. "The fair Christian critic, with no desire to create discrepancies, will candidly recognize them where they unquestionably exist. . . . If the arrangement itself were matter of Divine inspiration, then we have no right to vary it in the slightest degree." (Prol., pp. 12, 13, 19.)

There is here, I think, no little confusion of thought. First, accounts written under the common guidance and especial control of the Spirit of God, can not possibly be "entirely independent." Such a description, rigorously taken, excludes inspiration altogether. It makes them of self-interpretation, because they have come solely by the will of man; and would set aside their higher character, as parts in one harmonious and Divine scheme of revelation, in which "holy men of God spake as they were moved by the Holy Ghost."

Next, differences of arrangement involve contradiction and error, only in cases where every event is fixed by clear notes of time, or where the writer has professed his purpose to adhere throughout to the exact chronological succession. But this does not apply to the case of the Gospels. St. Luke is the only one who expressly states his purpose to write $καθεξης$, or "in order," and we have clear proof that in the whole book of Acts, and at least one-half of the Gospel, the design has been fulfilled. The inversions that have probable evidence belong mainly to St. Matthew, and except perhaps in one or two instances, wherever there is likelihood of such an inversion, there is no direct note of the true sequence in time. Thus in Matt. ix, 2, the words, "And behold," may very well introduce a new incident, though its true date, as we learn from the two other Gospels, was before the return from Gadara.

The idea that inspiration would forbid a historian to arrange his materials, except by mere sequence, like the writer of an almanac or annual register, has no show of reason or common-sense in its favor. Events have other laws of connection than simple sequence, and narratives, whether inspired or uninspired, have other objects to fulfill than those of a table of chronology. In the first Gospel there seems a plain reason for a partial departure from the strict order of time, in order to bring together, early in its course, two or three cardinal discourses of our Lord, the Sermon on the Mount, and the commission of the apostles. No one has a right to alter the arrangement of the Gospels as inspired narratives; but no one has a right to assume, invariably, that the order of mention was conceived by the writer to be the order of time, and then to impute falsehood and error to the words of inspiration, because of an assumption destitute of all reason.

The censure which has been freely thrown, here and elsewhere, on the orthodox harmonists, is due mainly to some mistiness and confusion of thought. If these harmonists advanced their own conclusions as absolutely certain, and not merely as the most probable view at which they were able to arrive of the true succession of the events, they would be worthy of real blame. But this the best and wisest of them have not done. On the other hand, it is no slight inconsistency, into which some critics who censure them have fallen, to maintain that distinct narratives are not really inconsistent, and still to decry, one by one, every possible alternative of their harmony, as strained, improbable, and incredible. This clamor against harmonies is, in reality, a slight infusion of the mythical theory, which has tainted unconsciously the views of some critics, otherwise orthodox and sound. If our Lord's life be a reality and not a fiction, then all the events in the four Gospels must have had a real sequence in time. The four narratives, if they furnish materials, on the one hand, for a full conception of our Lord's spiritual character, furnish them, also, for a definite biographical outline in the true order of succession. It may not be easy to attain the full ideal conception, or the precise historical reality, but we may approach to each of them. The limit, on either side, is a perfect doctrinal christology, and a perfect chronological harmony. But if we aim at one, and proscribe and defame all attempts to reach the other, then we sacrifice the historical reality of our Lord's life to the spiritual idea, and are taking the first step toward the Straussian or mythical pole of infidel delusion.

2. "It is more consistent with the fair interpretation of the text, to suppose that Matthew himself was not aware of the events, Luke i, ii, and wrote under the impression that Bethlehem was the original dwelling-place; certainly, had we only his Gospel, his inference would be universally made."

Now, since it is owned that his narrative contains "nothing inconsistent" with St. Luke, this supposition implies no contradiction. It would rather prove a special control of the Spirit of God, whereby the writers, though in partial ignorance, were still kept from all real inconsistency. But the inference has really no warrant but a superficial view of the history. Once let us realize the natural effect of the special revelations on the minds of Joseph and Mary, and compare them with the popular view of Micah's prophecy, as including the education of Messiah, no less than his birth—John vii, 46—and the need of a fresh message to induce a removal to Galilee will appear perfectly natural. In fact, the opposite view really implies that St. Matthew invented the incident recorded in ii, 22. For if the fact of Joseph's original residence at Nazareth is consistent with his need of such a message from God, then the Evangelist's knowledge of the fact must be equally consistent with his statement, that such a message was given.

3. "As the two accounts now stand, it is wholly impossible to suggest any satisfactory method of uniting them: whoever has attempted it has violated probability and common-sense. On the other hand, it is impossible to say that they could not be reconciled by a thorough knowledge of the facts themselves. If St. Luke had seen St. Matthew's Gospel, or *vice versâ*, the variations are utterly inexplicable; and the greatest absurdities are involved in the writings of those who assume this, and then proceed to harmonize. Of the presentation, etc., Matthew's account knows nothing; of the visit of the magi, the murder of the innocents, and the flight to Egypt, Luke is unaware."

These remarks are more difficult by far to reconcile with each other, and with the inspiration of both Gospels, than the two accounts themselves. First, if it were impossible for St. Luke to have written as he has done, if he had seen St. Matthew's account, how is it possible for the Holy Spirit, by whom his writing was controlled, and who certainly must have known the precise nature of the other record, to have allowed him to dispose it in such a form, or to make such omissions? Why should the very same fact, the existence of St. Matthew's account, be a decisive reason with the Holy Spirit, for directing the second narrative of the infancy into this particular form, and a decisive reason to the Evangelist, if it were known, rendering that form impossible? Is it essential to the character of a sacred historian, that his views on the choice and right disposition of his materials should be directly the reverse of those which the facts themselves require us to ascribe to the Spirit of God?

Next, it is a plain contradiction to suppose that every attempted union of the two accounts is a violation of common-sense and probability, and still to imagine that they may be reconciled by facts now unknown. The flight to Egypt, if a real fact, must have occurred after the Presentation, since the interval before it is plainly too short for the journey. It must either, then, come before the return to Nazareth in Luke ii, 39, or there must have been a later return to Bethlehem, and a later return to Nazareth again. The first is the simple and natural view, adopted by most harmonists—the latter a possible, but much less probable alternative. To style them both violations of common-sense, and still to hold that the two accounts are true and reconcilable, if other facts were known, is to overlook and contradict the very nature of the problem. The converse reasoning is clearly irresistible. If both accounts are true, the flight to Egypt must have occurred, either before the Presentation, or after it, and before the return to Nazareth in St. Luke, or else after that return. But the first is impossible from the limits of time, and the third is improbable. Therefore the second must be highly probable; and either the second or third, instead of violating probability, must be certainly true.

4. "The reconciliation of the two genealogies has never been accomplished; and every attempt to do it has violated

either ingenuousness or common-sense. The two genealogies are both the line of Joseph, and not of Mary."

Now, since almost every conceivable variety has been proposed, if both genealogies are inspired, some one of these solutions must not only be possible, but the very truth, designed by the Holy Spirit when both were given. The above remark is thus harder to reconcile with common-sense than the harmonies it condemns. It is even in direct contradiction with the remark which follows it. For if both the genealogies are Joseph's, since he could not have two real fathers, either the main principle of Grotius, that Heli was his natural and Jacob his legal father, or the opposite view, that Jacob was the real, and Heli his legal father, must plainly be true. But if one of two alternatives is clearly true, they can not, both of them, be violations of common-sense and probability. In fact, the usual view, that St. Luke has given the true genealogy, and that Heli was the father-in-law of Joseph, may be established alike by external and internal evidence; and the relapse from it into a different solution has created artificial difficulties, where simple-minded believers find only a deep harmony of Divine wisdom.

5. "A comparison of Luke iv, 16-24, with Matthew xiii, 53-58, Mark vi, 1-6, entered on without bias, can scarcely fail to convince us of their identity. That he should have been thus treated at his first visit, and then marveled at their unbelief on his second, is utterly impossible. That the same question should have been twice asked, and answered with the same proverb, is highly improbable. The words 'whatever we have heard,' must refer to more than one miracle. Here the order of St. Luke begins to be confused."

Now, since St. Luke openly professes his purpose to write "in order," and with perfect knowledge of all things from the very first, the view in this extract does imply a real inaccuracy and contradiction in the Gospels. For the visit to Nazareth in St. Matthew and St. Mark is plainly made to follow the parables, and the raising of the ruler's daughter, and comes shortly before the mission of the Twelve. Hence, if St. Luke speaks of the same visit, the very first event he names in our Lord's ministry is wholly out of its true order, is transferred from the later half of the period to its first beginning, and even fastened to a wrong place by the words at the close. For St. Luke plainly describes the course of teaching at Capernaum, and the cure of the demoniac, as results which followed our Lord's escape from the Nazarenes.

When we read the accounts, however, without bias, it seems impossible to avoid the conclusion that two different visits are described. The first, in St. Luke, instead of answering to Matt. xiii, 53–58, answers plainly to the brief notice in Matt. iv, 13—" And leaving Nazareth, he came and dwelt in Capernaum." A visit to his own city, at the opening of his ministry, is there evidently implied; and St. Luke simply gives us the full particulars of that conduct, which led our Savior to leave Nazareth, and choose another center for his Galilean ministry. The passage chosen, and the brief comment, evidently suit the public opening of his message in Galilee, and lose most of their force, if they are placed eighteen months or two years later. The words "as his custom was," agree with the same view. For he must have been accustomed, up to the opening of his ministry, to have frequented this very synagogue on each Sabbath day, which custom was now broken off by the conduct of the Nazarenes. But if referred to a later time, all the special force of the words is lost, and they would apply less to this synagogue than to almost any other. In the visit in St. Mark he wrought some miracles, even in Nazareth, on a few sick folks, but the account in St. Luke makes such a result of that visit clearly impossible. In fact the whole tone of the two narratives, their beginning, middle, and close, are quite different.

Two reasons alone are urged for confounding the visits in one. First, that our Lord could not possibly have marveled at their unbelief, if they had rejected him with violence already. But even viewing the facts in a purely human light, there is no force in this objection. Undeserved violence, and open wrong done to those whom it was a duty to honor, often produce a strong reaction. By comparing Mark iii, 31–35, it is probable that the second visit was at the request of some of the Nazarenes, who had become ashamed of their violence, when the miracles and fame of Jesus were past dispute. In this case their sullen persistence in unbelief would be more surprising, even to a human view, because the force of his miracles had made them ashamed of their brutal violence. But the true force of the words lies still deeper. They do not mean that our Lord was taken by surprise; but simply teach how strange a madness unbelief, in its more aggravated forms, must be reckoned in the eyes of One who is perfectly holy.

The other reason, from the repeated use of the same proverb, becomes a strong proof, on a closer view, of the distinctness of the visits, and not of their sameness. For when our Lord's ministry was hardly begun, and his name scarcely known in Galilee, he quotes it in the negative form: "No prophet is accepted in his own country." But when, after eighteen months of preaching, with constant miracles of Divine power, his fame was widely spread, and all Galilee looked up to him as a "great prophet," in whom "God had visited his people," the proverb is quoted in an opposite way, and exhibits the Nazarenes as the solitary exception in the midst of the general acknowledgment of his claims. "A prophet is not without honor, save in his own country, and kindred, and father's house." Thus every circumstance really conspires to prove the visits distinct, and the alleged inaccuracy of the Gospels resolves itself into a new example of perfect consistency and truth. We have merely an instance where the wise rule has been neglected, which the learned writer himself has laid down, "that similar incidents must not be too hastily assumed to be the same." (Prol., p. 13.)

6. "In the last apology of St. Stephen, which he spake being full of the Holy Ghost, we have at least two demonstrable historical inaccuracies." (Prol., p. 19.)

The first of these is thus explained, in Acts vii, 4: "The Jewish chronology, which Stephen follows, was at fault here, owing to the circumstance of Terah's death being mentioned—Gen. xi, 32—before the command to Abraham to leave Haran, it not having been observed that the mention is anticipatory." The real error, however, is that of the critic alone, who entirely overlooks the true explanation, adopted by Usher, Clinton, and most of the best chronologers, and which is confirmed by Gen. xi, 29, and the age of Sarah; that Abraham was not the oldest, but the youngest son of Terah. For Sarah, we are clearly taught, was the sister of Milcah and daughter of Haran, and was only ten years younger than Abraham. Gen. xi, 29; xvii, 17. The words of St. Stephen, then, instead of contradicting Genesis, fix its meaning, and establish the harmony of its separate statements; and the opposite view, while it charges him with error, is itself "a demonstrable historical inaccuracy."

The second asserted error is in Acts vii, 15, 16: "So Jacob went down into Egypt and died, he and our fathers, and were carried over into Sychem, and laid in the sepulcher that Abraham bought for a sum of money, of the sons of Emmor, the father of Sychem." Here there is, no doubt, an apparent confusion of two purchases and two burials. Abraham bought a burial-place at Hebron, from Ephron, in which Jacob and Leah were buried. Jacob, again, bought a piece of ground at Sychem from the sons of Hamor the father of Shechem, where the bones of Joseph were buried. We have no account of the burial-place of the other patriarchs.

Now, here it is important to remember when, and where, and before whom the words were spoken. It was at Jerusalem, where the study of the law was at its hight, before the hostile Sanhedrim, and the high-priest, and all the scribes, men accustomed to count the very letters of the law of Moses, that Stephen, full of the Holy Spirit, was making his formal defense against a charge of contempt of the law, after a controversy upon that law in the synagogues for many days, in which no adversaries "were able to resist the wisdom and the spirit with which he spake." Is it consistent with reason or common-sense, to impute to such a man, at such a time, and in the presence of such judges and adversaries, the double mistake of supposing that Jacob was buried in Sychem, in contradiction to the full narrative in the close of Genesis; and that Abraham lived in the time of Shechem, though his death and burial in Hebron are recorded in Gen. xxv, before mention of Jacob's birth; and the purchase of the ground in Shechem is stated in Gen. xxxiii, shortly before the death of Isaac, and eighty years after Abraham's death? Is it rational to expound this verse, so as to make Stephen, a learned Jew, full of the Holy Spirit, more ignorant of the sacred history, of which he is giving a rapid outline, than a well-informed Sunday school child in these days?

On the other hand, the explanation of Flacius and Bengel is simple and complete. St. Stephen, as being thoroughly familiar with the details of the two histories and speaking to the Sanhedrim, who were equally familiar with them, compresses the two into one by a series of mental ellipses, which his audience would at once supply for themselves. The two incidents are referred to by a regular alternation. Jacob is named, and not Joseph, of those who were buried; Sychem, and not Hebron, of the two burial-places; Abraham, and not Jacob, of the two purchasers; and the sons of Emmor, the father of Sychem, and not Ephron the Hittite, of the two parties from whom the purchase was made. There is here too much method in the seeming inaccuracy, to leave any reasonable doubt of its real source. Bengel has remarked, with his usual judgment: "In writing, omissions of this kind are usually marked by the pen; but they may be admitted in discourse, when, in a matter fully known, and present equally to the mind of the speaker and the hearers, merely what is enough is spoken, and the other words, which would hinder the flow of the discourse, are to be reckoned as if they were spoken also."

It would occupy too much space to enter here upon other alleged discrepancies, and especially those two main subjects, the last Passover, and the order of events on the resurrection-day. I believe that they both admit of an adequate solution, which changes them from stumbling-blocks to the faith into powerful confirmations of the Gospel narrative.

To conclude, the presence of a few slight inaccuracies in the Gospels, or in other histories of Scripture, would be no decisive argument for a lowered theory of their inspiration, consistent with the entrance of human error; unless these were clearly inwrought into the texture of the narrative, and were more than solitary specks on the surface, easily accounted for by defective transmission, and as easily removed. But while there is ample proof in the Gospels of the diversity of the testimonies, and the independent authority of the four witnesses, the attempt to establish a contradiction, whether by Christian critics, or skeptical adversaries of the faith, when submitted to a close examination, invariably fails. Its usual result will be to bring to light some undesigned coincidence, some delicate harmony of truth, which escapes the careless reader, and only reveals itself to a patient, humble, and reverent study of these oracles of God.

CHAPTER XIV.

THE BIBLE AND MODERN SCIENCE.

The discoveries of modern science have often been supposed to form a strong disproof of the inspiration and Divine authority of the Scriptures. Much has been written on both sides in this important controversy. The lines of argument have also been various, alike in the defenders and assailants, till the whole subject is involved, to many minds, in no slight perplexity and confusion. The chief topics in the controversy are the Bible Astronomy, the History of Creation, the History of the Flood, and the Unity and Antiquity of Mankind. In all these the main question to be answered is of this nature: Does the Bible, in its allusions to scientific truth, agree with the doctrine that its messages are the words of God, or betray itself to be the production of fallible Jewish writers, tinged throughout with undeniable and manifest error?

The contrast, arising from these opposite views of the Bible, may easily be exaggerated in their probable effect on its scientific allusions. Uninspired writers, who are content to adhere modestly to the teaching of the senses, and do not pretend to make discoveries, or to speculate on secret causes, may escape, almost entirely, the fault of the propounding scientific error. On the other hand, the great end of Divine revelation is not the diffusion of natural knowledge, but the moral renovation of mankind. Facts of a scientific character are plainly collateral, and not the main object of the work. Such messages would d'verge from their true purpose, if they anticipated the discoveries of a science in some distant age. A summary of modern astronomy, chemistry, or electricity, we feel instinctively, would be quite out of place, in such an early revelation of the will of God to men. It would, in fact, be a supernatural prophecy of a very peculiar kind, less instructive to mankind in general than those which have actually been given, and far more useless and perplexing to the readers of every intermediate age.

A just view of the subject will, therefore, produce great caution in our acceptance, either of objections to Scripture, or supposed confirmations of its truth, drawn from the scientific or physical allusions scattered through its pages. If its purpose were scientific, we might expect to find in it wonderful scientific discoveries, assuming that it is a true revelation from God. On the other hand, if its writers were not only uninspired, but rash, presumptuous impostors, who sought the credit of knowledge beyond their fellows, then scientific errors would be almost sure to abound. But the contrast, in this one feature, between good and fallible men, who write with modesty and reverence, and true revelations in which the Almighty suits his message to the actual wants and state of mankind, would be far less striking and conspicuous than many seem to assume. It is only on a few points that we may expect some intimation to be given, that the God of the Bible is also the Lord of nature, "in whom are hid all the treasures of wisdom and knowledge."

There is, however, one point of view, in which the negative presumption for the inspiration of the Scriptures has, even at first sight, no little force. For they do evidently claim to be a revelation from God. The account of creation itself, on any other view, is a manifest absurdity. If this claim be groundless, the writers can not be classed among modest and cautious men. Presumption in that which is the greatest must lead us to expect presumption in that which ranks far lower in importance. He who invents messages from the Creator, is not likely to be scrupulous in his claims to special acquaintance with the works of God. Hence, false revelations, almost invariably, involve some flagrant contradiction of true science. Hinduism, at this moment, is melting away under a system of secular education, which undermines and destroys the authority of its Shasters and Vedas, because of the false geography and physics interwoven with their theology. False religion and false science are there so inseparably united, that any scheme of instruction, in which the truths of science are taught, and the truths of God's Word are withheld, becomes really equivalent, in practice, to a direct propagation of irreligion and unbelief. And hence, conversely, the mere absence of false science, in a professed revelation from heaven, is no slight presumption in favor of its truth. The claim of Divine authority, on questions relating to man's moral state and future destiny, is only confirmed by the absence of pretended discoveries, with regard to the constitution and laws of the natural world, which have been committed to the slow and laborious decipherment of man's native intelligence.

I. The Astronomy of the Bible is the first and earliest of those topics, from which scientific assaults on its inspiration have been raised. It had nearly passed, indeed, into oblivion, when kindred questions in geology and physiology have revived it once more. The revival of science, we have been told, displaced the Ptolemaic by the Copernican theory. But the Hebrew records, the basis of our faith, manifestly countenance the opinion of the earth's immobility. Galileo was compelled, by the Inquisition, to sign the statement, that "the proposition that the sun is the center of the world, and immovable, is absurd, philosophically false, and formally heretical." But the brilliant progress of science subdued the minds of men. The controversy between faith and knowledge slumbered, and the limited views of the universe in the Old Testament ceased to be felt as religious difficulties. The progress of geology, a new science, has forced attention to the subject once more. The *prima-facie* view of the Bible narrative reverses, to a great extent, our present astronomical, as well as geological views of the universe.

This astronomical objection, now revived from a long sleep, has never had much weight with candid and thoughtful men. It is true that the Romish inquisitors, who condemned Galileo, have lent the whole weight of their scientific and theological eminence to the cause of infidelity, and their names naturally stand foremost in the proof that the Bible and modern astronomy contradict each other. But the authority of Newton himself, which many may be disposed to rank higher on such a question, is thrown decisively into the opposite scale. The immortal writer of the Principia, it is clear from his later works, did not share the perplexity which some smatterers in astronomy profess to feel, when they observe that the Bible speaks on these subjects in the common language of all mankind. When we are told, for nstance, that "the sun was risen upon the earth, when Lot entered Zoar," it is not Newton who complains that we do not read, in its place, a scientific statement such as this, "That Palestine had revolved, when Lot entered the city, until its tangent plane coincided once more with the solar azimuth." True science is cautious and modest, and is not easily betrayed into such absurdities.

In reality, the whole objection to the language of Scripture on this subject, arises from the influence of three errors—that scientific statements of the earth's motion are absolute, and not relative truth; that popular language is simply false, and not relatively true; and that the relation of matter to matter, in connection with the laws of force and motion, is of higher importance than its relation to the senses and universal experience of mankind.

First, the statements of modern science, after all, embody relative, and not absolute truth. All motion, and all action, so far as science can reveal it, is simply correlative. We can not conceive of a fixed position in absolutely empty space. Viewing first our own system as a whole, the planets do not, in strictness of speech, revolve around the sun, but the sun and the planets move alike around the common center of gravity. The doctrine that "the sun is immovable from its place" may not be "formally heretical" as the inquisitors affirmed, but there can be no doubt that it is "philosophically false." If popular language, then, were replaced by that of the Copernican theory, the result would be only, on the principles of the objection, to substitute one scientific mistake for another. But it is now ascertained, also, that the whole solar system is in movement toward a point not very far from the bright star of Lyra. The true nature, therefore, of the earth's pathway through space is not a circle or ellipse in a fixed plane, around the sun as its center, but a complex spiral, thirty degrees aslant from the vertical, in which the interval of the successive rounds is four-fifths of their diameter. And we have no assurance that this result is absolute and final. For most of the stars from which the motion of the sun is deduced belong to the great system of the milky way, and it is by no means impossible that these may partake of a common motion with regard to other sidereal systems. There are thus four or five modes of conception, all equally relative, as the observer is on the earth, on the sun, in a fixed position with regard to the center of the solar system, a fixed position in the sidereal system, or one still more remote and independent.

Again, it is a great mistake to conceive that the language of common life, adopted also in Scripture, is the expression of simple falsehood, and not of a most important variety of scientific truth. Thus we have been told that the account in Genesis "does not describe physical realities, but only outward appearances; that is, it gives a description false in fact, and one which can teach us no scientific truth whatever." There is, however, no ground at all for this fancied contrast between facts and appearances. Appearances are simply those facts, in relation to the senses of men, by which alone we come to the knowledge of other facts not immediately observed, and in some cases not observable. Every sunrise and sunset, and every meridian transit of a star, is as much an astronomical fact as the Newtonian theory, the rotation of the earth, or the elliptic shape of its annual orbit. In reality, it is facts of this kind which form the whole material of modern astronomy in its most advanced form and scientific language is not used to disguise them. Practical astronomers have been compelled to introduce a large variety of technical terms, all framed on precisely the same principles, and molded by the same laws of thought, as the phrases of Scripture and of common life. Such, for instance, are the transits of Venus and Mercury, the occultation of stars behind the moon, the contact of the sun and moon in an eclipse, the immersion and emersion of Jupiter's satellites, the transit instrument for observing the transit of stars across the meridian, their elevation by refraction and depression by parallax, the preceding and following side of the heavens, right and oblique ascension, the entrance of stars into the field of the telescope, the upper and lower culmination of circumpolar stars, when they either pass the zenith, or graze the horizon. These are a few conspicuous examples of a fixed and constant law of scientific language, which runs through the whole range of practical and instrumental astronomy. The maxim which charges the Bible with scientific falsehood because of its astronomical phrases, fastens the same charge on the "Nautical Almanac," and the "Connaissance des Temps," and indeed on every record whatever of the materials or the results of modern astronomy.

Still further, the relations of matter to matter, or to an observer perched in the ideal center of our solar system, are far less important, in a practical sense, than its relations to the experience and daily observation of mankind. Bulk, mass, and lifeless magnitude, are not things of supreme importance, especially in a moral message designed for the spiritual recovery of a fallen world. The double purpose of all revealed truth is to restore man to his dominion over nature, and his allegiance to God. Whenever one is renounced, the other is lost, and the rebel against Divine authority becomes the victim of some form of conscious or unconscious idolatry. But if the earth be held quite subordinate to the sun, simply because of its inferior bulk and weight, then man must be immensely inferior to the ground on which he treads, and the rhinoceros and hippopotamus, the oaks and cedars, the volcanoes and their streams of lava, must rank far above him in the scale of being. Pride tempts man, in the consciousness of mental power, to forget both his moral weakness and physical insignificance. Pantheistic fatalism sets aside all moral distinctions, and degrades him into a mere passive atom in the vast machine of the universe. The Bible alone reconciles and harmonizes the contrasted truths of his actual condition, his physical insignificance, his moral frailty and corruption, and the dignity of a nature framed in the image of God, and made to have dominion over all the works of his hands.

The motions of the heavenly bodies depend on laws of force, which relate to quantity of matter and distance alone. Men of science have thus to make abstraction of their other qualities and relations, however important, to place themselves in thought somewhere in empty space, and to contemplate their motions, either from that fixed point, or with reference to that body which has the greatest mass, so that complex relations may be more simply conceived. Yet, even in abstract science, the same motive requires them sometimes to forsake these foreign points of view, and return to the earth again. In the lunar theory, the earth. and not the sun, is the center to which the motions have to be referred. The sun is treated as revolving round it, only more slowly than the moon and at a greater distance, and as deranging the lunar ellipse by this revolution. By no other means can the complex inquiry be duly simplified, and the lunar perturbations clearly ascertained. How much more, when the message relates entirely to the present duty and future hopes of mankind, must all the outward works of God be viewed in relation to this great object, and not with relation to mass and mechanical force alone! One soul is far nobler than millions on millions of cubic leagues of empty space; and even if these were filled with nebulous mist, or this mist condensed into a vast globe of fire, it could never rival the dignity of one rational and immortal creature, formed in the image of God, capable of knowing its Creator, and enjoying his love forever.

The Bible, therefore, in describing physical changes with direct reference to the constant experience of mankind, or terrestrial observers, adopts the only course which agrees with the scope and purpose of a moral revelation. For it would violate its own character, and one of its own chief doctrines, unless the material works of God were treated as subordinate to the life, happiness, and moral welfare of mankind. The lesson which it teaches on its first page, is the only sure antidote to every form of degrading idolatry—that man is the lord of nature, because he is the subject and child of the living God.

II. The history of Creation, in Genesis, has given rise to more serious difficulty, from its alleged contrast with the lessons of geology. The discordant nature of the expositions offered by various Christian writers has been turned into an argument that no satisfactory solution can be found. The spectacle, we are told, of able and conscientious writers employed on this impossible task, is painful and humiliating. They shuffle and stumble over their difficulties in a piteous manner, and do not breathe freely, till they return to the pure and open fields of science again.

Now, what is really painful and humiliating is that men, who still call themselves Christians, should venture to compare the first of God's messages, confirmed as Divine by Christ and his apostles, to a stifling and mephitic cavern, from which we must escape with all speed, and take refuge with mammoths, mastodons, and the skeletons of extinct monsters, in order to breathe more freely, and avoid the risk of suffocation. It may be unwise to affirm that "geological investigations all prove the perfect harmony between Scripture and geology in reference to the history of Creation." But the opposite assertion, that they are plainly irreconcilable, is still more unreasonable on the side of science alone, and adds the guilt of degrading the Word of God into the presumptuous guess-work of some Hebrew impostor, who dared to propound his own ignorant fancies as revelations from the Almighty.

The statement in Genesis is to this effect: that man was created and placed on the earth, in Asia, in the Garden of

Eden, six or seven thousand years ago; that his creation took place on the last of six successive days, during which the earth was changed from a dark, waste, and unformed condition, to a well-furnished habitation, by signal acts of creative energy; and that a seventh day followed, or a Sabbath of rest, which God appointed for a lasting ordinance, because on this first seventh day he rested from all his work which he created and made.

Now, geological science discloses a long series of changes, through which our earth had passed before any traces are found of man's presence, and a distinct fauna and flora in each of these eras, amounting to many thousand extinct species. The question is, how these two statements are to be reconciled, or whether they are wholly incompatible. Some writers, as Hugh Miller, MacCausland, and Macdonald, expound the days of Genesis to be long periods, in the order of which they trace some resemblance to the main outlines of geological discovery. A few others, as Dr. Pye Smith, restrict the whole narrative to local and limited changes in Central Asia alone; which must strike every one at once, as falling very short of the natural scope and force of the description. But many writers of eminence, as Chalmers, Buckland, Sedgwick, Dr. Kurtz, and Archdeacon Pratt, in his able pamphlet on Scripture and Science, hold that the days of Genesis are literal days, that the ages of geology are passed over silently in the second verse; and that the passage describes a great work of God, at the close of the Tertiary Period, by which our planet, after long ages, was finally prepared to be the habitation of man. This, I have no doubt, is the true and simple explanation. I shall now endeavor to show that the objections brought against it in the Fifth Essay are entirely worthless, and that it is the assailant, and not the eminent writers assailed, who exhibits a strange confusion of thought, along with a lamentable determination to disparage the truth of Scripture, and set aside its Divine authority.

1. The first and main question relates to the mode of representation employed in the sacred narrative. The Christian interpreters, who hold the day-periods or the literal days, agree in the view that the events are optically described, that is, as they would appear to a spectator placed on the surface of the earth. This is a principle common to their two expositions, which afterward diverge from each other. And this, accordingly, is the first object of assault in the recent Essay. The objection runs as follows:

"Both these theories divest the Mosaic narrative of real accordance with fact; both assume that appearances only, not facts, are described; and that in riddles, which would never have been suspected to be such, had we not arrived at the truth from other sources. It would be difficult for controversialists to cede more completely the point in dispute, or to admit more explicitly that the Mosaic narrative does not represent correctly the history of the universe up to the time of man. At the same time the upholders of each theory see insuperable objections in detail to that of their allies, and do not pretend to any firm faith in their own. How can it be otherwise, when the task proposed is to evade the plain meaning of language, and to introduce obscurity into one of the simplest stories ever told, for the sake of making it accord with the complex system of the universe which modern science has unfolded?"

This whole objection, urged in so contemptuous a tone, rests plainly on that gross and fundamental error which has been already exposed. Appearances and facts are no real antithesis. Appearances are themselves facts. They are precisely the facts, on which all science depends, as the materials from which it is derived, and to which it must return, in order to confirm its discoveries, or yield any practical benefit to mankind. What is an eclipse but an appearance? And yet what is the proof, above all others, by which modern astronomy has established its claim to be a real science, but the marvelous accuracy with which eclipses are foretold, even in their minutest details? Scientific speculation is like the balloon, which carries the observer into the upper sky, and enlarges the sphere of his vision. Phenomena are like the ground, from which it must ascend, and to which, after a short journey, it must soon return; though with a knowledge enlarged beyond the limits of its first horizon, or perhaps alighting in a country never visited before.

The Mosaic narrative, then, if it be a faithful record of appearances, is also a record of facts, and stands on a level, in scientific truthfulness, with the daily register of any modern observatory. For these consist entirely of appearances, whether of stars in the field of a telescope, or of the mercury in a barometer or a thermometer, or of the index in the anemometer or galvanometer, or of the clouds in the sky, only noted down with mathematical precision. They are appearances from first to last. The flippant censure, aimed against the first chapter of the Bible, would sweep away in a moment the records of all our scientific observatories as equally false and faithless, and with them would destroy all the materials on which science itself depends.

The second falsehood in this objection is the assertion that the optical view of the Mosaic narrative turns a simple story into a riddle, the true meaning of which could never be suspected unless we gained it from other sources. This, it will be plain on a little reflection, exactly reverses the real truth. Any other view of the passage would turn it into a riddle to the readers of all early ages of mankind; and even to the great majority in our own days, who have not abused the discoveries of science so as to falsify the daily and hourly experiences of human life.

There are four plain reasons why the narrative in the first of Genesis should be optically given, or describe changes as they would appear to a terrestrial observer. First, it is the constant and habitual language of daily life. Secondly, it is the equally-invariable style of all our scientific observations. Thirdly, it is the constant usage of all historians, without exception, ancient and modern. Fourthly and lastly, it is the idiom of the Bible itself, in every other part of the sacred narrative. The claim of modern sciolists, that this chapter alone should be put in masquerade, and describe changes as they would appear from Sirius, or the center of gravity of the sun and the planets, is just as reasonable as to require that it should have been written in some language used by angels, instead of being given, like all the rest of the Bible, in the language of men. The passage just quoted is more than a simple error. It is a direct and total inversion of the real truth. If it were wished to turn the first page of Scripture into a riddle, unintelligible to all former ages, and hardly to be understood, except by one person in a thousand, even in our own days, we might frame it according to the recipe of those assailants of its truth. It would then run pretty nearly as follows:

"In the beginning God created the heavens and the earth. And first, God said, Let there be immense oceans of nebulous matter, scattered throughout all space; and it was so. And God said, Let the nebulous matter condense slowly, under the law of universal gravitation; and it was so. And God said, Let the central portion of each heap of mist condense into a sun, and the smaller portions condense into planets, and let the planets revolve each around its own sun; and it was so. And God said, Let one planet of one sun condense into solid matter, and become liquid with intense heat; and it was so. And God called the planet earth, and the central body it revolved around he called the sun; and it was so. And God said, Let the earth, after long ages, cool down, till solid strata can be formed upon its surface; and it was so. And God said, Let plants and living creatures grow upon the earth, and be destroyed again; and it was so. And the period of their birth and destruction was a second day. And God said, Let ferns and other plants grow in great abundance, and then be buried, and reduced to coal in the crust of the earth; and it was so. And the period of these plants was a third day. And God said, Let oolite and sandstone strata be formed, and other races of plants and animals be buried in them; and it was so. And the period of these strata and the animals entombed in them was the fourth day. And God said, Let mighty lizards be created, and then destroyed and buried; and it was so: and the lizard period was a fifth day, etc." Such an account of creation, whatever might be its measure of scientific accuracy, would have been an unmeaning riddle to all past generations of mankind. We should have a meager summary of physical changes, wholly unintelligible to common readers, instead of the simplicity, beauty, and grandeur of a Divine message.

It is urged, however, that if the description be one of appearances, it can teach us no truth whatever. If this remark were correct, the late expedition to Spain, to observe the total eclipse of the sun, though planned with so much care by astronomers of eminence, must have been an unmingled folly. They could only describe appearances, not realities; and what could science gain by all their observations? Why, then, may not the Bible narrative be equally instructive, equally definite in its teaching, though it be a record of appearances alone? Appearances are, in truth, the only materials from which every science is derived, and the medium by which alone it is applicable to the use of mankind.

The objection, then, to the optical construction of the sacred narrative, that it deprives it of all definite meaning and gives it a non-natural sense, exactly reverses the real truth. The record of visible appearances is quite as definite, in its own nature, as a statement of physical causes, and is far easier to understand; and no simple reader, in the age when Moses wrote, could attach any other meaning to the words than that which is so rashly condemned.

"The difficulties arise," it is said, "for the first time, when we seek to import a meaning into language, which it certainly never could have conveyed to those to whom it was originally addressed. Unless we go the length of supposing the simple account of the Hebrew cosmogonist to be a series of awkward equivocations, in which he attempted to give a representation widely different from the facts, without trespassing against literal truth, we can find no difficulty in interpreting his words." This remark is strictly true. But it justifies the interpretation it is supposed to condemn, and condemns that which it is supposed to justify. The meaning of light, to the early Hebrew, could not be the undulations of a subtile ether, diffused through infinite space, but simply a state of the earth, air, and sky, in which objects were clearly visible to the senses of men. The sun, moon, and stars, to the same readers, could never be supposed to mean immense balls of solid matter, luminous, or non-luminous, floating at large in the depths of space, but visible discs of light, seen daily revolving through the sky. The whole force, then, of this first objection to the sacred narrative, is due simply to a denaturalization of some minds, through dwelling amidst the mechanical relations of physical astronomy, till they reverse the laws of criticism and the facts of history, and put light for darkness, and darkness for light, in their attempt to fasten error and contradiction on the Word of God.

2. The second maxim, implied in that view of the narrative, which retains the literal days, and accepts also the facts of geology is the distinctness of the absolute creation, in the first verse from the six days of creation that follow. The result, indeed, is much the same, if we suppose the Hebrew word *bara* to be taken in a looser sense, and that the first verse is merely a summary of the whole account that is afterward given. On this view nothing whatever would be said of the absolute formation of matter, but the whole would begin with the chaos or confusion before the first day.

Assuming, however, that the first verse relates to the absolute beginning of creation, or the first origin of things, an objection is started from the mention of the heavens on the second day. It is inferred that "during those indefinite ages there was no sky, no local habitation for the sun, moon, and stars, even supposing them to have been included in the original material."

This difficulty would be real, if the heavens in Scripture meant always the lower firmament alone. But this is quite untrue. The apostle speaks of being caught up into "the third heaven," which certainly was not the region of the clouds. Hence, although the lowest heavens were made on the second day, the first verse may still retain a very clear and definite meaning. The first heaven is that of sense, or the visible firmament. The second heaven is that of science and philosophy, or the depths of the starry universe. The third heaven is that of faith and spiritual vision, or that immediate unvailing of the Divine presence to pure and sinless spirits, which answers to the Holy of Holies in the Jewish Temple. The opening words of the Bible, then, may refer immediately to the third heavens of glory, and the heavens of sidereal astronomy; while the mention of the lower heavens, or visible arch of the sky, comes in its natural place, in connection with terrestrial and atmospheric changes, among the steps by which our earth was prepared to be the dwelling of man.

3. The third principle involved in this view of the passage, when compared with the facts of geology, is that the darkness and confusion in the second verse refers to a state which intervened between the Tertiary and Human period. And here a double objection is urged. First, on the authority of Hugh Miller, it is affirmed that such a break "is by no means supported by geological phenomena, and is now rejected by all geologists whose authority is valuable." And next, it is said that such a construction falls short of the natural meaning of the text, and reduces the third verse from a noble description, the admiration of ages, to a pitiful *caput mortuum* of empty verbiage.

The course of thought pursued in the Fifth Essay, in its labored assault on the truth of Scripture, is here singularly perplexed and illogical. Dr. Chalmers and Hugh Miller, and all others who accept either the view of literal days or day-periods, agree in affirming that the optical construction of the narrative, with reference to a human observer, is the only one historically natural, or critically possible. This their unanimous consent is cast aside on the strength of naked assertions, which directly reverse the manifest truth, the experience of every observatory, and the constant usage of the whole Bible. Both these classes of writers agree in the firm conviction that the narrative in Genesis and the facts of science do agree, though they vary in their conception of the precise nature of their agreement. This their consent is equally cast aside, as the effect of scientific ignorance or of theological prejudice, and no scruples, either of modesty or of pity, lessen the confidence with which their consenting judgment is denounced and condemned. But Hugh Miller, after holding once the view of literal days, renounced it for that of day-periods, on the ground that geology allows of no gap or break between the Tertiary and Human periods. His argument is founded on eight animals, and two kinds of shells, which he believed to be common to the two eras. On the other hand M. D'Orbigny, in a work on fossil geology, of which a summary is given in two volumes of Lardner's Museum of Science, and which includes an examination of eighteen thousand species of radiata and mollusca alone, has deduced conclusions diametrically opposite. He shows that there are twenty-nine eras, in each of which the genera are partly the same as in the preceding one, and partly different; but that the species, except only one or two per cent. in a few cases, are all distinct, and imply a new creation. Even in respect to genera, the contrast between the Human and Tertiary periods is the widest of the whole—these two forming, in Hugh Miller's theory, part of the same day—since only five hundred and forty are old genera, or common to the Tertiary, and one thousand, three hundred and twenty-seven are new. But according to the same writer, the species are entirely new, and "the entire fauna and flora of the last Tertiary period were destroyed."

In the Christian Observer, January, 1858, this argument has been developed, in disproof of the fundamental assertion, on which Hugh Miller's theory depends. The essayist quotes a reference to it in Archdeacon Pratt's able pamphlet on Scripture and Science, in which he speaks of it as conclusive, and gives a summary of the facts, and the necessary inference to which they lead. He does this, however, merely to show "the trenchant manner in which theological geologists overthrow one another's theories," and carefully abstains from touching either the facts or the argument.

On the contrary, he proceeds to observe that "Hugh Miller was perfectly aware of the difficulty involved in his view of the question," and proceeds to give the details of his theory; when those details have nothing whatever to do with the argument thus dismissed; and, instead of Mr. Miller being aware of the difficulty, his theory is based on a conclusion drawn from the supposed sameness of eight species, in direct opposition to this large induction of M. D'Orbigny, from twenty-nine successive eras, and nearly twenty thousand species; and from eighteen hundred genera in the Human and Tertiary periods alone. What is still more strange in the presence of such an extract, Hugh Miller's assertion, thus largely disproved, is accepted for a sufficient proof of the untenability of the theory of Chalmers, and that its abandonment was "not without the compulsion of irresistible evidence; and that the view which results from the large induction of M. D'Orbigny, after cataloguing twenty thousand species, and which is summed up in two volumes of the Museum of Science, as the latest and ripest conclusion of geology, "is now rejected by all geologists whose authority is valuable."

Such a style of argument, where the truth of Scripture is in question, can hardly be too strongly condemned. It betrays, if not a settled purpose to damage the authority of the Bible by any artifice of special pleading, at least a total incapacity to discern the really-vital points of the controversy, the true limits of authority, and the results of a wide and genuine induction of geological evidence. All that is true and beautiful in Hugh Miller's writings is cast aside; and a solitary error, since disproved by the evidence of thirty eras and twenty thousand species, is stolen from him, and dipped in poison, that it may inflict a deadly wound on the faith which was dearest to his heart.

Let us now inquire whether the other objection has more

weight. Does this view reduce a noble and sublime description to "a pitiful *caput mortuum* of empty verbiage?" It supposes that, after the Tertiary period, and by the convulsion which gave birth to the mountain-chains of the Alps and Andes, our planet was wrapped in a sea of vapor, and buried for a long period in midnight and impenetrable gloom. This chaos, optically and physically complete, it assumes to be the starting-point of the inspired description. After an unknown period of total darkness "upon the face of the deep," light broke out suddenly, on the first day, at God's command, over the whole surface of the globe. Now, it is self-evident that such a fact is all that Moses and his cotemporaries, and all readers of the Pentateuch down to our own days, could naturally or reasonably understand by the words. They could never suppose it to mean the creation of luminiferous ether, filling infinite space, nor the commencement of certain undulations, regulated by unknown mechanical laws. The light has distinct reference to the previous darkne s. The darkness was "upon the face of the deep," and the deep is no synonym for infinite space, but for the earth's surface, while mainly covered with water, before the dry land appeared. The instantaneous breaking forth of light over our world, where all before had been wrapped in utter gloom, is one of the noblest images which can enter the human mind; and those who can call it empty verbiage seem to need themselves a similar process of mental illumination.

4. The omission of the long eras of geology, which the same view of the passage implies, can furnish no real objection to its truth. On the contrary, it seems to result inevitably from the character of this Divine message. It describes a brief work of God's almighty power, by which our planet was fitted to be the abode of man. All the objects which man sees around him are referred in it to their

Divine Author. His power is shown in the swift completion of so great a work, his wisdom in its orderly progress and a moral character is infused into the whole, when six days of creative energy are seen to be followed by the Divine Sabbath of rest, a precedent for the use of mankind in every later age. Nothing is wanting, nothing superfluous. A description of the earth's fluid nucleus, of primary rocks, of the flora of the coal measures, or of the extinct animals of the Secondary and Tertiary periods, would have been only a strange and unnatural excrescence in such an early message from God to man.

5. The objection to this view, from the break which it requires, has been thus stated.

"The hypothesis was first promulgated at a time when the gradual and regular formation of the earth's strata was not seen or admitted so clearly as it is now. Geologists were more disposed to believe in great catastrophes. Buckland's theory supposes that previous to the appearance of the present races of animals and vegetables there was a great gap in the globe's history; that the earth was completely depopulated, as well of marine as land animals, and that the creation of all existing plants and animals was coeval with that of man. This theory is by no means supported by geological phenomena, and is now, we suppose, rejected by all geologists, whose authority is valuable."

Now, let us compare with this positive assertion the statement of Dr. Lardner—"Museum of Science," xi, 71, 1856—based on the labors of Murchison and D'Orbigny.

"The anticipations of Sir R. Murchison have been more than realized by the subsequent researches of M. D'Orbigny, founded on his own observations, which extended over a large portion of the New as well as Old World; and upon the entire mass of facts connected with the analyses of the crust of the earth, collected by the observations of the most eminent geologists in all parts of the world It appears from these researches that, during the long periods of geological time, from the first appearance of organized life on the globe to the period when the human race and its cotemporaneous tribes were called into existence, the world was peopled by a series of animal and vegetable kingdoms, which were successively destroyed by violent convulsions of the crust, which produced as many devastating deluges. The remains of each of these ancient creatures are deposited in a series of layers; and it has been found that each successive animal kingdom was composed of its own peculiar species, which did not appear in any posterior or succeeding creation, but that genera once created were frequently revived in succeeding periods; that many of these genera, however, became extinct long before the human period."

"By careful analyses of the strata and the animal remains, geologists have ascertained with a high degree of probability, if not with absolute moral certainty, that subsequently to the first appearance of the forms of animal life, which took place after the fourth great convulsion of our globe, there were at least twenty-eight successive convulsions of a like nature, each of which was attended with the complete destruction of the animals and plants which existed on the globe. In fine, after the latest of these catastrophes, when the last strata of the Tertiary period were deposited, *the most recent exertion of Creative Power took place, and the globe was peopled with the tribes which now inhabit it, including the human race.*"

"The disruption of the earth's crust, through which the chain of the great Alps was forced up to its present elevation, which, according to M. D'Orbigny, was simultaneous with that which forced up the Chilian Andes, a chain which extends over three thousand miles of the western continent.

terminated the Tertiary age, and preceded immediately the creation of the human race and its concomitant tribes. The waters of the seas and oceans, lifted from their beds by this immense perturbation, swept over the continents with irresistible force, destroying the entire fauna and flora of the last Tertiary period, and burying its ruins in the deposits that ensued. By this dislocation, Europe underwent a complete change of form. Secondary effects followed, which have left their traces on every part of the earth's surface. When the seas had settled into their new beds, and the outlines of the land were permanently defined, the latest and greatest act of creation was accomplished, by clothing the earth with the vegetation that now covers it, peopling the land and water with the animal tribes which now exist, and calling into being the human race." (xii, p. 552.)

It is clear, from this comparison, that the statement in the objection exactly reverses the real truth with regard to the latest conclusions of geology. With the failure of its foundation, the whole fabric of skeptical inference reared upon it falls at once into ruins.

6. But another objection has been drawn from the events of the fourth day; though in reality it is only the first difficulty with regard to the optical style of the narrative, in one special application. "What," it is asked, "were the new relations which the heavenly bodies assumed to the newly-modified earth, and to the human race? They had marked out seasons, days, and years, and given light for ages before to the earth, and to the animals which preceded man as its inhabitants."

The reply is evident. With those previous ages and their condition, and the plants and animals that lived in them, man and his cotemporaries had no more to do than if their theater had been some wholly different world. It was out of the ruins of these former creations that the present arose. To man himself, or any of the creatures living on the earth, and which have enjoyed the sunshine to the present hour, that fourth day was the first on which sun, or moon, or stars appeared. It was the earliest of those appearances to the eyes of the present creation, which have lasted to this day's sunrise, or to the shining of the stars this night in the firmament of heaven.

If any doubt could remain of the adequacy of this explanation, it will be removed at once by the comparison of other passages in the Word of God. Thus we read in St. Peter of the world before the Flood, that "the heavens and earth which were of old, being overflowed with water, perished; but the heavens and earth which are now, are kept in store, reserved unto fire." Here it is plain that the present heavens and earth are described as distinct from those before the Flood, and succeeding in their room. This plainly can not refer to the substance of the earth, or of the heavenly bodies, but to their relations to the senses of man; so that the vault of the sky, and the surface of the earth, are constantly compared to a robe or vesture which may be rolled away. The interpretation, then, which refers—Genesis i, 14–19—to the solid globes of the sun, the moon, and the stars, as they exist in space, and hence infers a contradiction between the Bible and modern science, does no less violence to the rules of sound criticism than to the reverence due to the Word of God.

7. Another supposed contradiction to the truths of science has been found in the mention of the firmament. The word, in Hebrew, means simply an expanse. But it is urged that the context requires us to admit that the writer viewed this expanse as a solid vault, since it is said elsewhere to have pillars, foundations, doors, and windows; and

here separates waters which are above from those which are below. To insist on the derivation, it is said, is mere quibbling, in the face of these clear proofs that the Bible ascribes to it a real solidity.

There is something really amazing in the self-confidence with which such charges of ignorance and folly are brought against the sacred writers. A little modesty and common-sense would have shown that an argument which proves too much proves nothing, and that the sacred writers could never have thought that rain came down, literally, through square openings in a solid vault of the sky; nor that the sun, moon, and stars, if set in a solid vault, supported by pillars, could revolve daily from east to west, and reappear in the east again. The same passage of noble poetry which tells us, in magnifying the power of God, that "the pillars of heaven tremble and are astonished at his reproof," also tells us that "He stretcheth out the north over the empty space, and hangeth the earth upon nothing." If one phrase, taken alone, seems to imply solid supports, the other seems just as plainly to anticipate the views of modern science, and represents our world as self-supported in empty space. If windows are ascribed to heaven in one place, as a figure to represent the descent of rain from above, their existence seems just as strongly denied in another. "If the Lord would make windows in heaven, might this thing be?" Once admit the principle that all these phrases are vivid metaphors, to express great truths which were evident to the senses of mankind, and all is consistent, easy, and natural. The foundations of the earth, the pillars of the sky, denote simply the firmness and steadfastness of these two main objects of the knowledge of man, the wide landscape spread around him, and the blue vault every-where above his head. The opening of the windows of heaven denotes the descent of rain from that upper sky, where no water could before be seen to exist, and is a metaphor plainly drawn from the skylights of some human building. The placing of the sun, moon, and stars in the firmament has no reference to a solid structure, in which case they would be fixed and immovable, but to their permanent manifestation, as moving daily through the azure vault of the heaven.

The only phrase which gives the least countenance to the gross, material view of the firmament, a view which plainly is refuted, rather than confirmed, by the etymology, is the mention of the waters above and below it, which it separates from each other. But a very little patient thought will suggest at once the true meaning. The blue vault or expanse is a result relative to human vision. Its existence depends on the mutual relation of the eyes of men and animals, and the optical properties of the earth's atmosphere, through which alone we obtain a knowledge of objects beyond the reach of our other senses. It is, in short, the sensible limit between the visible and the invisible. All water, then, which is visible to the senses, either in the seas or in the clouds, is described as being under the firmament; and all which is invisible, and concealed from the senses, with equal propriety of phrase, is described as above the firmament. It is out of this state of invisibility, that it reappears continually in rain, to fertilize the earth. This change, from the invisible to the visible, is the opening of the windows of heaven, by which the waters above the firmament descend and mingle with those below.

The relation, then, between the latest conclusions of modern science, and the Bible history of creation, is one of independent truth, but of perfect harmony. Science reveals a long series of changes, once unsuspected, by which the strata of our planet were formed, and a succession of nearly thirty vegetable and animal creations, which were suited no doubt, to the state of the earth in which they appeared, but were successively destroyed by volcanic convulsions on the largest scale, by which new mountain chains rose into being. The most complete separation of species, an immense preponderance of new genera, and the rise of the most stupendous mountains—the Alps and Andes—separate the last of these from the present human creation. Science proves that, before man appeared, the earth must have been waste and desolate; all previous forms of life were destroyed and entombed; and though its strata might be completed, its whole surface was covered with mighty inundations, and its atmosphere loaded with the vapor from the seas and oceans, which such a vast volcanic eruption could not fail to send up in immense and enormous volumes, wrapping the whole surface of the planet, perhaps for years or centuries, in thick impenetrable darkness. But science, while it may reveal the fact that man, and existing planets and animals, are cotemporary in the geological sense, is far too dim-sighted to disclose the times, the order, and the details of that last creation in which all these had their birth. For any thing which its most skillful interpreters can tell us, this work might have lasted through thousands of years, or Almighty Power might have compressed it into a single day. It is here that the Word of God steps in, and beginning its narrative with that creation which now exists, and with which alone man has any thing to do, at least till these recent discoveries were disentombed, reveals to us the order, the swift fulfillment, and the moral grandeur of this great work of God. The fourth commandment pronounced on Sinai, by the lips of Jehovah himself, gives us the sublime fact, and its application to the instruction and guidance of mankind. "Six days shalt thou labor and do all thy work, but the seventh day is the Sabbath of the Lord thy

God. For in six days the Lord made heaven and earth, the sea and all that in them is, and rested the seventh day; wherefore the Lord blessed the seventh day, and hallowed it."

CHAPTER XV.

THE BIBLE AND MODERN SCIENCE, CONTINUED.

In the previous chapter a brief reply has been offered to modern arguments against the inspiration and authority of the Bible, and its supposed contradiction to the truths of astronomy and geology. The other topics, the History of the Flood, the Unity of the Human Race, and the conclusions of Ethnology, have not been so prominent in the most recent attacks, and their treatment would lead too far from the main purpose of the present work. But it seems desirable to clear up some difficulties of a more general kind; and to point out the line of truth and wisdom, between that superstitious abuse of Scripture, which leads to "a fantastical science," and that undue confidence in imperfect science, and contempt for the authority of the Divine oracles, which leads inevitably to "a heretical religion."

The Bible, in the view of the Christian Church, consists of a series of inspired records, or messages from God to mankind. "All Scripture is given by inspiration of God." It "can not be broken." It is God himself who "spake in time past to the fathers by the prophets." It is the Holy Ghost, who spoke by Moses, by David, by Isaiah. "Prophecy came not at any time by the will of man, but holy men of God spake, being moved or borne along by the Holy Ghost." It is "the Lord God of the holy prophets," by whom these various messages of Divine truth were given to men. The Son of God himself suffered on the cross, "that the Scriptures of the prophets might be fulfilled." And he has told us himself that "it is easier for heaven and earth to pass away, than for one tittle of the law to fail."

Such statements as these, from the lips of the Savior and his apostles, might be expected to secure the Scriptures from imputations of contradiction, error, and falsehood, at least on the part of those who profess to be disciples of Christ. They do not require us to believe that these messages are absolutely perfect, without the least speck or flaw, in the form in which they reach the hands of every individual, after translation and transcription have been at work for thousands of years. They do not, perhaps, require us to decide how near to the fountain-head some minute, microscopical faults, from the infirmity of copyists or amanuenses, may have been permitted to come. But they do seem clearly to imply that the gift was perfect, and free from all error, as first communicated from the God of truth to his chosen messengers, or curiously and wisely fashioned, by the use of their faculties, within their minds, whether in history, precept, doctrine, devotion, or spiritual meditation. The whole, therefore, comes to us plainly stamped with a Divine authority. And this authority must extend to every jot and tittle of its contents, till some adequate evidence, external or internal, shows it to be a fault of translation or transmission; a slight flaw, in whatever way occasioned, which has become attached to the original and Divinely-perfect message.

The Bible, again, is marked throughout by the unity of a great and moral purpose. Its design is not to interfere with the slow and silent progress of natural science, but to make sinners wise unto salvation. It was written for the use of every age, from the time when its earliest messages were given, and not to gratify the scientific curiosity of our own busy generation. A treatise on astronomy, geology, chemistry, electricity, or botany, would evidently be quite out of place in these lively oracles of God. They would, by such an excrescence, renounce in part their own true character, and descend from their sacred hight into a lower sphere. We have no right to expect in them a premature relation of the law of gravitation, and the Newtonian theory of the heavens, or of the undulatory theory of light, or of the chemical constitution of matter, or a thousand other natural truths, which the progress of science may, perhaps, in future ages, make known to men. The allusions in Scripture to all these subjects, we might reasonably infer, would be incidental, secondary, and collateral.

On the other hand, the Bible is not a message to pure, disembodied spirits; but is addressed to man in his actual character, as a being composed of body and soul, born in the weakness of infancy, placed in the midst of this lower, visible creation, and trained through his senses to the knowledge of himself, of nature, and of God. A revelation designed for such a being must inevitably include within it many facts that belong to almost every field of scientific inquiry. All nature must be laid under contribution, like the treasures of Egypt for the tabernacle, to form this marvelous and complicated structure of heavenly wisdom. Facts, which belong to geography, chronology, botany, zoölogy, astronomy, civil legislation, and political history, meet us, and must be expected to meet us, in almost every page of the Sacred narrative.

These simple remarks are enough to clear away two great errors, on opposite sides, by which Christian faith has been clouded with a dangerous skepticism, or loaded with a superstitious excrescence. They show at once how vain must be the attempt to maintain a doctrinal authority in Scripture, and still to impute to it a merely human character, wherever it touches on questions of natural science. For the two elements are blended throughout no less intimately than body and soul are united in man himself. Let us take, for instance, the leading truth of Christianity, the resurrection of our Lord. No truth can be more central to the revelation, or more intensely spiritual in its true significance. Yet it contains points of intimate connection with a dozen different sciences. It is a geographical truth; for he rose from the tomb at Calvary, and ascended from Olivet. It is a chronological truth; for he rose the third day, during the procuratorship of Pontius Pilate, and on the first day of the week, which begins the long, unbroken series of Christian Sabbaths. It is a physiological truth; for the body which was laid in the grave, was raised on the third day, before it had seen corruption. It is connected with a truth of botany; for that sacred body had been embalmed with myrrh and aloes, a hundred pounds in weight. It is a truth of political history, for crucifixion was a Roman and not a Jewish punishment, and a Jewish watch, by permission of a Roman governor, had been set over the tomb. It is connected with important facts of mental philosophy; for the disciples believed not for joy, and wondered. It is connected equally with the science of jurisprudence, and the laws of evidence; for he appeared openly, "not to all the people, but to witnesses chosen before of God, who did eat and drink with him after he rose from the dead." And hence the idea of retaining the authority of the Bible, as in any sense Divine, and making an exception for parts into which there enters some scientific element, is utterly delusive and impracticable. The doctrines and the facts, the precepts and the histories, are joined inseparably by the Spirit of God himself, and man, with his most laborious efforts, can not put them asunder. Deny the authority of the facts, and you destroy the whole revelation.

But the same truths will serve equally to shut out an opposite error, which would make the Bible, because of its Divine origin, a substitute for the researches of human science, and would strive to extract a complete system of natural philosophy from its pages. The Bible, from its nature as a true and Divine history, must contain valuable materials for many branches of science, but not the sciences themselves. In speaking of natural objects, it deals with facts, patent to the senses of men, and not with secret causes that lie hidden from general view. It speaks of earthquakes, but not of the volcanic heavings of a fluid nucleus, or of the internal combustion out of which they may arise. It speaks of sunrise and sunset, of the waxing and waning of the moon, but not of the earth's revolution, or the laws that guide the motion of our satellite, and determine its phases. It speaks of hail mingled with fire, sent from heaven, but propounds no theory of electricity to account for the violence of the thunder-storm, and the strange contrast of heat and cold in the same phenomenon. It alludes to trees and plants, from the cedar of Lebanon to the hyssop on the wall; but no formal classification of them, as endogens and exogens, or in any other way, is found in its pages. Thus, while it furnishes rich materials, in various ways, to men of science, it speaks a language intelligible to all mankind. It is mere folly and ignorance to tax the Scriptures with falsehood because of this popular character, which is one mark of their Divine wisdom. The contrast between scientific and popular statements is not a contrast between truth and falsehood; but between truth in its simpler and alphabetic forms, which lie within the reach of a child, and in those deeper combinations which lie remote from the surface, and are gradually disclosed by a patient induction from multiplied observations and experiments. Every sunrise and sunset, observed in every spot on the earth's surface, is a separate truth of astronomical science, no less than material for poetical description. But the revolution of the earth on its axis is a wider and more comprehensive truth, which sums up and explains thousands of sunsets in ten thousand spots on the surface of the earth, and reveals, with scientific accuracy, the order and interval of their succession from day to day. It is thus equally an error to deny that the Scriptures furnish, on Divine authority, facts which constitute the partial materials for various branches of natural science; or to suppose that their statements embody and define any scientific theory, teach any particular cosmogony, and supersede the labors of patient induction by a physical theory of nature revealed from heaven.

Another form, in which the attempt has been made to restrict the authority of Scripture, is by exempting from the range of Divine revelation all those departments of truth "for the discovery of which he has faculties specially provided by his Creator." A general charge of ignorance or negligence has been brought against the whole body of Christian divines, because they have overlooked this great axiom, or adopted it with such limitations as destroy its value. This doctrine is the starting-point of the Essay on the Mosaic Cosmogony, and the goal to which it returns. Under its friendly guidance, the Divine record of creation, to which the Son of God appealed with holy reverence, is to resume the dignity and value which it had lost while esteemed to be the Word of God, by ranking as the speculation of some Hebrew sciolist, who had never learned the modesty of modern science, and made a bold, but mistaken guess at the origin of the world. Men have regarded it, for ages, as the inspired truth of God; but it is cheering to be assured, that their respect for it need not be in the least diminished, when they come to regard it as the blind and ignorant conjecture of some unknown pretender to Divine communications.

Let us see, first, how far this maxim will carry us on the road of unbelief. We have the faculty of memory, specially provided to teach us the facts of history, or of human testimony. Therefore no facts of history can be included in a Divine message. We have the faculty of imagination, specially provided to make us capable of poetic feeling and thought. Therefore poetry and its high imagery must be excluded also. We have a conscience, designed and adapted to teach us moral truths. Therefore a Divine revelation must pretend to teach no morality. We have reason and judgment, specially designed and adapted to combine facts and truths together, and derive inferences from their union. Therefore all reason and argument, and all appeals to the understanding, must be banished from the messages of God. By the moral sense, combined with the faculty of reason, we can gain some general conceptions of the First Cause and his moral attributes. Therefore the knowledge of God himself, his nature, attributes, and will, must form no part of Divine revelation. The principle, so highly praised, is thus a simple and effectual expedient for getting rid of all revelation whatever, by leaving it no single subject, within the range and compass of the human faculties, which it is permitted to reveal.

The maxim, then, which theologians are blamed for being slow to receive, is grossly and manifestly absurd. No truth can possibly be revealed, unless there be a faculty fitted to receive the revelation. A landscape can be unvailed only to the seeing eye, and melodies of music only made known to the hearing ear. Where the faculties have been obscured by sin, the work of revelation may be twofold, and include the opening of blind eyes, and the unstopping of deaf ears, as well as the exhibition of visions of heavenly truth, or melodious utterances of Divine love. But a faculty which is fitted to receive, and if to receive, then by diligence and care to discover, moral and spiritual truth, is not a substitute which excludes Divine revelation, but the previous condition on which its possibility depends.

But the context in which this maxim appears, and the purpose to which it has been applied, makes its error doubly conspicuous. It is used to justify the degradation of the first chapter of Genesis from a Divine message into a mere human speculation. Now, if there be one part of the Bible history which is beyond the reach of a merely human knowledge, it must be a record of the steps of creation before the first existence of man. All later events named in the Bible might have been handed down, without a Divine inspiration, by the ordinary processes of human tradition. Here alone such a tradition was plainly impossible. Even modern science must here be completely at fault. Astronomers might sooner be able to give us a chart of the bays and islands of the lost Pleiad, or of a planet of Sirius, than geologists, by their own researches, to recount in detail the events of the six natural days which immediately preceded the first appearance of man on the face of the globe. Yet this is the chapter out of the whole Bible, which it has been labored to deprive of a Divine origin, on the plea that what man can learn by his unaided faculties can never be the object of supernatural revelation.

Let us examine the maxim more closely. It is not uncommon, with Christian writers, to assume a wide contrast between truths which man might learn without Divine communication, and those for which it is indispensably required. They do not restrict the authority of the Bible to truths of the second class alone; but still, it is their presence on which the value of the gift is supposed mainly to depend The same contrast, however, has been borrowed by skeptical writers, and worked out on its negative side. It then becomes a powerful engine to destroy the authority of revealed religion. Every fact of history and every moral truth, since it might be learned by the right use of our natural powers, is exempted from the province of revelation. Nothing is left to revealed religion but a few mysterious doctrines, which are to be blindly received, because it is impossible to understand them, and they are unfit, in their own nature, for any exercise of the human conscience or reason.

It will be found, I think, on closer reflection, that there is no ground for this line of rigid demarkation. All truth is mutually related and harmonious. In the mind of Omniscient Wisdom, all things past, present, and future, and all truths of every kind, must be united in one vast scheme of Providence, in which there is no flaw. "He is the Rock, his work is perfect." Every reasonable creature, whose powers are not impaired by sin, has some partial knowledge of this mighty scheme, though it is only like a drop in an immeasurable ocean. But he has also a capacity of progress. He can observe more and more, himself; and he can learn more and more from the testimony of other observers. He can combine, more and more fully, these elements of knowledge, and thus discover slowly the laws of Providence, both in the natural and spiritual world. There seems to be no essential separation between truths attainable in course of time by the use of our natural faculties, and others quite unattainable. But the contrast is almost infinite, in the degree of facility with which particular truths may be learned by observation alone, by the help of human testimony, or by direct revelations from the Fountain of all truth and wisdom.

Let us take, for example, the science of astronomy. A single student, if his life were indefinitely prolonged, might multiply his observations, perfect his instruments, and enlarge his attainments in analysis, till the discoveries of thousands had all been equaled and surpassed by himself alone. He might thus amass larger and more exact materials than we now possess, and combine them by a profound analysis which should throw the Principia and Mécanique Céleste, and the labors of Plana, Struve, Airy, Herschel, Adams, and Leverrier, completely into the shade. But before this pinnacle could possibly be reached, long, interminable ages must have rolled away. Facts, which he might have learned in a moment from the simple testimony of another observer, would have become immensely remote, before he could rediscover them, if at all, as inferences from his own discoveries and observations.

Now this, which is true of astronomy, must be still more true of our human knowledge of the character, works, and ways of God. Even apart from the effects of sin, our lifetime is far too short for any large advance, by our own unaided wisdom, in a science so glorious. This knowledge is too wonderful for us: it is high, and we can not attain unto it. The discoveries of a lifetime would be the merest atom in this boundless ocean of truth. Even the help of our fellow-men could do only a very little to facilitate our progress in this pathway toward clearer light. But if our Maker himself were to condescend to become our teacher, and out of the stores of his infinite wisdom to select the truths most helpful to our progress, and still within the range of our actual capacity, then would our progress be far more rapid and easy. In the humble use of this Divine aid, we might soon leave far behind us, in the low and misty valley, those who had never received, or who had neglected and despised it, and travel, with swift and hopeful steps, up the mountain side toward the summit of the everlasting hills.

But the debasing influence of sin on the human faculties, renders this contrast between the attainments possible in the use of natural powers alone, and by the aid of Divine revelation, far more complete. Men need not only to be taught, but to be made willing to learn. It is not enough that a wide landscape of heavenly truth is spread out before them. The eye of the soul must undergo a healing process, before they can gaze upon it undazzled, and without confusion. When the last glorious vision was revealed to the beloved Daniel, its brightness overwhelmed him, and he fell senseless to the earth. The same Person, who was the great object of prophecy, and the Revealer of what was noted in the Scripture of truth, needed also to act the part of a Divine Physician, and to strengthen the faculties of the prophet, as well as to provide a glorious vision on which his eyes might rest. He touched him once, and the swoon passed away, and he stood trembling, but mute with deep astonishment. He touched him again, and the dumbness was removed, and he was able to utter a confession of his weakness, and to plead for further succor and grace. He touched him a third time, and strength was given, and the prophet could hearken to the message, and gaze, even to the last, upon that glorious vision. We have here a picture of the constant law of all Divine revelations to a world of sinners. The Revealer must also himself become the Physician; or else the most glorious revelations of unseen things, and the largest disclosures of the ways of Providence, will be offered in vain, while a death-like stupor settles down upon the souls of men.

Again, there are truths in the spiritual, just as in the natural world, which, from our actual position, must become known to us as facts, long before we could attain, by any process of reasoning, to deduce them from other truths, or to discover their secret laws. It is possible, for instance, that the luminosity of the sun, in contrast with the planets, may result in some way, now unknown to us, from its immensely-superior mass. In this case, the solar mass would be a physical cause, and the solar light a scientific corollary. But every inhabitant of the earth must experience the light of the sun, long before they could deduce the mass of the sun and planets from their observations, or obtain any glimpse of a scientific relation between two facts apparently so independent. In like manner, unfallen spirits must have distinct communion with the persons of the Godhead, long before they could possibly obtain any glimpse of the Trinity as an essential corollary from the perfection of the Divine Being; and fallen sinners must have learned the atonement, and felt its recovering power, long before they can be expected to gain any deep insight into its mystery, as reconciling the attributes of the Godhead in the infinitely-wise counsel of redeeming love.

These truths, duly weighed, will fully explain the use and need of Divine revelation, without resorting to any broad separation of truth into two kinds, of which the first may be attained by human faculties alone, and the others need a miraculous interference. The question is not what men might possibly learn, supposing no moral averseness from Divine truth, and that their lives were prolonged indefinitely, to give them space for growing discoveries. This is the real question, how, within the limits of a very short probation, unwilling hearts may be bowed into the attitude of willing disciples, and dull and backward scholars may, within a few years or days, become wise to salvation, and gain a firm hold on those great doctrines of God's holiness, their own corruption and guilt, and that way of acceptance through a divine atonement, on which all light, peace, holiness, and comfort depend. Every child, who consults an almanac to learn the time of a coming eclipse of the sun, has faculties, which might perhaps, in the course of some thousands or myriads of years, enable him to discover for himself the laws of the heavenly motions, to reproduce the Newtonian theory, and calculate the eclipse from his own observations. But an abstract capacity, loaded with such conditions, can not in the least diminish the worth of the almanac to such a child, as a ready and sufficient source of the information which he requires. Nay, the same is true of the most advanced astronomer. He may add, by his own labors, to the domain of science; but still he needs, both in his daily life and for the wants of his own observatory, to depend on the ready-made ephemeris, no less than the merest peasant or the youngest child.

The maxim, then, that Divine revelation must be restricted to those subjects which lie entirely beyond the reach of human faculties, and which man could never possibly learn without some direct aid from above, is no less opposed to sound philosophy than to the actual features of the Christian religion. If the Bible teaches little, comparatively, on matters of physical science, it is because it moves on a higher level, and refers to spiritual objects; and still more because, in the secondary use which it makes of the works of nature, its purpose is best fulfilled by dwelling on those aspects of them which lie nearer the surface, and are open to the observation of all mankind. On the other hand, we have plainly faculties by which we can observe or acquire historical facts; and more than one-half of the Bible consists of history. We have a conscience by which we can discern right and wrong. Our Lord himself appeals to the unbelieving Jews—"Yea, and why even of yourselves, judge ye not what is right?" The faculty was present, and, if used aright, there may have been no absolute limit to its possible attainments. And yet the largest portion of the Bible, next to simple narrative, consists of moral precepts, examples, and exhortations. It is not to supply the absence of a missing faculty, but rather to heal the sickness of a faculty that is diseased by sin, and to quicken its slow and halting progress in the pathway of truth and wisdom, that Divine revelation is really given. Its authority, then, is stamped alike on every part of the truth which lies within the compass of its actual message. It is not a map of the world, but its statements of the places where sacred events occurred are accurate and true. It is not a system of optics or astronomy; but its mention of the visible work of the fourth day, of the sunset when Abraham received his vision, or the sunrise when Sodom was destroyed, or the darkness at the crucifixion, is accurate and true. It is not a system of chronology, but the ages and the dates it records, when its true text has been ascertained, are, like the Gospel itself, worthy of all acceptation. It has a holy anointing from the Spirit of truth, which runs down to the very skirts of its garment. Its sayings, whatever their subject, when cleared from specks and flaws that may have been contracted here and there in the transmission of the message, are "faithful and true;" for it is "the Lord God of the holy prophets" by whom these lively oracles have been given to mankind, "to give light to them that are in darkness and the shadow of death, and to guide our feet into the way of peace."

CHAPTER XVI.

THE BIBLE AND NATURAL CONSCIENCE.

The relation between the authority of the Bible and the claims of conscience is one of the most fundamental questions in the whole range of practical theology. Any serious mistake on this point strikes at the foundations of Christianity. If conscience be silenced, and external commands, through human interpreters, are blindly imposed on the whole Church, the way is open for the fatal inroad of all kinds of superstition. If private conscience be made the supreme authority, and the Word of God be allowed no other force than it borrows from the choice or caprice of the individual, we accept a principle which is the root of all infidelity, and anarchy will be enthroned under the imposing titles of a spiritual religion and a reasonable faith.

Statements, which have lately been made, seem clearly to present this later view as characteristic of the full manhood of the individual Christian, and of the whole race of mankind. With the age of reflection, the spirit of conscience comes to full strength, and assumes the throne. As an accredited judge, invested with full powers, he sits on the tribunal of our inner kingdom, decides on the past, and legislates on the future, without appeal except to himself. He is the third great Teacher, and the last. He frames his code of laws, revising, adding, abrogating, as a wider and deeper experience gives him clearer light. The law of the child or the youth may be an external law, in making, enforcing, and applying which we have no share; which governs from the outside, compelling our will to bow, though our understanding be unconvinced and unenlightened, and cares little whether you reluctantly submit or willingly agree. But the law which governs and educates the man is internal; a voice which speaks within the conscience, and carries the understanding along with it; which treats us not as slaves, but as friends; which is not imposed by another power, but by our own enlightened will. This law of conscience marks the last stage in the education of the human race. We are now within the boundaries of this third period. The Church is left to herself, to work out by her natural faculties the principles of her own action. In learning this lesson she needed a firm spot, and has found it in the Bible. Had this contained precise statements of faith, or detailed precepts of conduct, we must either have become subject to an outer law, or have lost the highest instrument of self-education. But the Bible, from its form, is exactly suited to our wants, for even its doctrinal parts are best studied by viewing them as records of the highest and greatest religious life of the times. Hence it is to be used not to override, but to evoke, the voice of conscience. When the two appear to differ, the pious Christian immediately concludes that he has not really understood the Bible. Its interpretation varies always in one direction, and tends to identify itself with the voice of conscience. From its form it can not exercise a despotism over the human spirit. If so, it would become an outer law at once, and throw back the world into the stage of childhood. But its form is such that it wins from us all the reverence of a supreme authority, and yet imposes on us no yoke of subjection. The principle of private judgment puts conscience between us and the Bible, and makes it the supreme interpreter, whom it may be a duty to enlighten, but never to disobey.*

These statements, by a large amount of friendly violence, may perhaps be explained away into the simple truism, that the Gospel, in contrast to the Law of Moses, is a dispensation of liberty, and includes very few external ordinances. But in their natural meaning they go much further, and involve three principles, which evacuate and destroy the whole authority of the Word of God. They teach, first, that the Scriptures have no authority, and impose no obligation, unless they have been indorsed and accepted by the individual conscience; and then only in that particular construction which each one puts upon them in his own mind. Secondly, that private, individual conscience is a supreme judge, whom, however faulty or imperfect his decisions may be, it is always a duty to obey. And thirdly, that in the present manhood of the world, whenever public opinion, or the prevailing impressions of educated men, and the apparent teaching of Scripture, diverge from each other, the voice of Scripture must be fitted to the independent conclusions of man's natural conscience, and not the general conscience rectified, purified, and enlightened, by submission to the authority of the Word of God.

I. The first main question which needs decision, is the nature and limit of the authority due to the Scriptures. Are they a revelation from God, which claims obedience and submission in virtue of its Divine origin? Or, are they simply a rich treasury of materials, which our conscience, the supreme law, may employ in forming its own conclusions, and which impose no obligation, till each particular person adopts and applies them in the exercise of his private judgment? On the answer to this inquiry it must depend

---

* Essays and Reviews, pp. 31, 34, 44.

THE BIBLE AND NATURAL CONSCIENCE. 353

whether the Church and the world are still under moral government; or, under the plea of magnifying the rights of conscience, we are given up to a state of spiritual anarchy, where no law is binding on any Christian, but just whatever he chooses to receive and obey.

Let us first consider what are the express statements, on this subject, of the Scriptures themselves. We find, in the very front of our Lord's teaching, the impressive sentence, "Think not that I am come to destroy the Law and the Prophets; I am not come to destroy, but to fulfill. For verily I say unto you, Till heaven and earth pass, one jot or one tittle shall in no wise pass from the law, till all be fulfilled. Whosoever therefore shall break one of these least commandments, and shall teach men so, he shall be called the least in the kingdom of heaven; but whoever shall do and teach them, the same shall be called great in the kingdom of heaven." It seems plain that our Lord speaks here as the great Lawgiver. He denies that he has come to set aside the authority of commands already given. On the contrary, he had come to clear them from pernicious glosses, and to develop their full meaning. His purpose was not to abrogate, but to enlarge and complete the code of Divine morality; and those who taught the exemption of his disciples from even the secondary and inferior precepts, would lose all claim to spiritual eminence, and be called "least in the kingdom of heaven." At the close of the discourse we have a renewed warning of the guilt and danger of disobedience, and the most prominent feature in the whole sermon is declared to be its tone of Divine authority.

If we pass from one of the earliest of our Lord's discourses, to one of the last, the same feature stands out in clear relief, amid all the rich fullness of its grace and compassion: "Ye call me Master and Lord, and ye say well, for so I am." "I have given you an example, that ye shall do as I have done to you." "If ye know these things, happy are ye if ye do them." "If ye love me, keep my commandments." "He that hath my commandments, and keepeth them, he it is that loveth me." "He that loveth me not, keepeth not my sayings." "If a man love me, he will keep my words." "If ye keep my commandments, ye shall abide in my love, even as I have kept my Father's commandments, and abide in his love." "This is my commandment, that ye love one another, as I have loved you."

The lesson of the Epistles is precisely the same. More than three chapters of the Epistle to the Romans are composed of distinct apostolic commands, addressed with authority to the Roman Christians. The laws of the second table are all reimposed, with a Gospel commentary on their mutual relation. xiii, 8–14. The apostle declares, at the close, that the aim of his whole ministry was "to make the Gentiles obedient by word and deed;" and that the Gospel he preached was the commandment of God, and made known to the nations for the obedience of faith. In 1 Cor. xiv, 37, we have the impressive caution—"If any man think himself to be a prophet, or spiritual, let him acknowledge that the things which I write unto you are the commandments of the Lord." In the Second Epistle he tells them, "To this end did I write, that I might know the proof of you, whether ye be obedient in all things," and he distinguishes in one case between simple advice and direct apostolic precept. 2 Cor. viii, 8–10. One-half of the Epistle to the Ephesians is made up of such precepts, given in the most direct and imperative form, while the fifth commandment is recognized as still binding on Christians—"Honor thy father and mother, which is the first commandment with promise; that it may be well with thee, and thou mayest live long on the earth." In the

Epistle to the Philippians, the same truth is taught in plain terms, that Christian disciples were bound by the authority of apostolic commands: "Wherefore, my beloved, as ye have always obeyed, not in my presence only, but now much more in my absence, work out your own salvation with fear and trembling." In every other epistle of St. Paul, the same truth appears. St. James is even more explicit, and says to the Christian believers, "Whosoever shall keep the whole law, and yet offend in one point, he is guilty of all. For he that said, Do not commit adultery, said also, Do not kill. Now, if thou commit no adultery, yet if thou kill, thou art become a transgressor of the law." And, again, "Speak not evil one of another. He that speaketh evil of his brother, and judgeth his brother, speaketh evil of the law, and judgeth the law; but if thou judge the law, thou art not a doer of the law, but a judge. There is one Lawgiver, who is able to save and to destroy." St. Peter fills his First Epistle with precepts of the most pointed and authoritative kind; while in his Second he states the object of both his letters in these words: "That ye may be mindful of the words which were spoken before by the holy prophets, and of the commandment of us, the apostles of the Lord and Savior." St. John's Epistle abounds in declarations of the same kind: "Hereby we do know that we know him, if we keep his commandments." "I write no new commandment unto you, but an old commandment, which ye had from the beginning. Again a new commandment I write unto you." "Whosoever committeth sin, transgresseth also the law, for sin is the transgression of the law." "Whatsoever we ask we receive of him, because we keep his commandments." "This is his commandment, that we should believe on the name of his Son, Jesus Christ, and love one another, as he gave us commandment." "This is the love of God, that we keep his commandments, and his commandments are not grievous." "This is love, that we walk after his commandments." In the last book of the canon, though mainly prophetic, this same truth enters into the repeated description of the faithful, that "they keep the commandments of God, and have the testimony of Jesus Christ."

Now, in all these passages, which are only specimens out of a large number, we are taught that every Christian is distinctly placed under the authority of God's commands, given by Christ and his apostles, and recorded in the New Testament; and the duty of obedience is made to depend simply on the fact that such commands have been given. They can not be rightly obeyed, unless they are first understood, and their Divine authority recognized. But these are conditions of actual obedience, and not of the obligation to obey. So far is this from being true, that neglect of the message is itself ranked among the most dangerous and deadly sins.

This great truth, that the commands of Scripture are binding by their own authority as the words of God, and not simply when indorsed by the private conscience, results further from the distinct mention, in the Bible, of sins of ignorance, and of presumption. Now, if no command were obligatory on the Christian, but such as his own conscience has previously recognized, this distinction must be set aside. Sins of ignorance would then be impossible, and all sins would be those of presumption, or committed with the present knowledge that they were sins. But this contradicts equally the Old Testament and the New. The law made distinct and full provision for the pardon of sins of ignorance, and of those alone. Num. xv, 22–31. The Psalmist offers the petition, "Keep back thy servant from presumptuous sins, lest they get the dominion over me." But it is only after the confession and prayer, "Who can understand his errors? cleanse thou me from secret faults." And the prayer of our Lord upon the cross, for his murderers, places the contrast in the clearest light: "Father, forgive them; for they know not what they do." On the principle now examined, these sinners must have been guiltless, because their own conscience had never pronounced sentence against them for their great and aggravated crime.

But this notion, that moral obligations depend simply on the impressions of the individual conscience, and not on the true relations between each person and his fellow-creatures, and the glorious Creator, is no less opposed to the lessons of a sound philosophy than to the plain and repeated statements of the Word of God. Moral commands are in their own nature as unchangeable as the being of God, the relations of sovereignty and dominion, which he bears toward his intelligent creatures, and their own capacities for receiving and imparting happiness. Add to these relations a power of choice, and nothing more is required to create moral obligation. The office of conscience is not to create new duties, but to discern those which do exist, and bring home to us their imperative claim on our obedience. The atheist is bound to love his Maker with all his heart and mind, no less really than the most devout Christian. The man steeped in selfishness, till he has come to reckon worldly prudence his sole duty, is bound to love his neighbor as himself, no less than a Howard or a Wilberforce, a St. Paul or a St. John. The most ignorant idolater, who bows down with sincere reverence to his idol, and says, "Deliver me, for thou art my God," is bound by the second commandment, no less than Moses, or Isaiah, or Daniel. For the command is based on a Divine attribute, which is unchangeable, and not on the slippery and uncertain impressions or fancies of sinful men. No doctrine can be more dangerous to society than one which exempts from the laws of the second table the disobedient child, the revengeful duelist, or assassin, the abandoned sensualist, the thief, and slanderer, whenever they have seared their own conscience, and lost the feeling of their own obligation. And none can be more fatal to true religion than one which pronounces atheism and idolatry to be blameless, whenever the fool has really said in his heart, "There is no God;" or a deceived heart has turned the idolater aside, "that he can not deliver his soul, or say, Is there not a lie in my right hand?"

II. Again, is Conscience a supreme judge, invested with full powers, who legislates without any appeal but to himself, and whom it may be a duty to enlighten, but can never be a duty to disobey? Are the Scriptures merely an exciting cause to awaken the independent voice of this judge, and must their teaching be accommodated to it, whenever they seem to diverge from each other?

The answer to this question is partly implied in the reply to the former. If the laws of God are of binding authority in their own right, then a mistaken conscience can never reverse the true law of duty. It may render acts relatively sinful which are lawful in themselves, because a person would thereby run counter to his own sense of what is right; but it can not make that lawful which in itself is wrong. The law of God does not prescribe mechanical acts, irrespective of the temper and spirit in which they are done. "He that doubteth is condemned, if he eat; because he doeth it not in faith; for whatsoever is not of faith is sin." A diseased conscience introduces a moral discord, so that actions against the conscience, even when materially right, become morally wrong. But this, far from proving that conscience is a supreme judge without appeal, proves exactly the reverse. It shows the moral discernment of right and wrong to be so essential a part of the moral being that, when this is perverted, sin is inevitable, whether we obey its lessons, or disobey them. Men can not render God a fit and acceptable service, when "their own heart and conscience are defiled."

The true question is not, whether a mistaken conscience can render acts sinful to the individual which are lawful in themselves, but whether it can render actions lawful, which, apart from its erroneous decision, are morally wrong. Such a doctrine is a direct proclamation of moral anarchy. It strikes at the very foundation of the dominion of God.

Let us test it, first, by one or two statements in the Scriptures themselves. Our Lord gave the warning to his disciples: "The time will come when he that killeth you will think that he doeth God service." Were these persecutors of the first disciples innocent, when they carried out their sincere convictions of duty by murdering the saints of God? If private conscience be a supreme judge, and without appeal, they were innocent. But the Scriptures pronounce them deeply criminal, and their voice is confirmed by the deepest instincts of every Christian heart. Again, was Saul of Tarsus innocent when he "verily thought with himself that he ought to do many things contrary to the name of Jesus of Nazareth?" Was his conduct blameless when he consented to the murder of Stephen, and held the raiment of them that slew him? Was he a pattern of moral uprightness when he "made havoc of the Church, entering into every house, and haling men and women committed them to prison," when he "punished them oft in every synagogue, and compelled them to blaspheme?" What is his own sentence, when recovered to a sounder mind? He declares himself, on account of these conscientious acts, to have been "the chief of sinners." He proclaims himself a marvelous example of the riches of God's long-suffering, that the most guilty, in later ages, might not despair of the Divine mercy because of the greatness of their crimes. He alludes to the ignorance under which he then labored, but never dreams that it had power to turn his sins into virtues, and to free them from blame. Its only effect, in his view, was to avert a still deeper measure of guilt, so as to leave his case just within the extreme limit of Divine forbearance. "Who before was a blasphemer, and a persecutor, and injurious; but I obtained mercy, because I did it ignorantly, in unbelief." "Howbeit for this cause I obtained mercy, that in me first Jesus Christ might show forth all long-suffering." Nothing can be more decisive and clear than this judgment of the great apostle in the deliberate review of his own history. A perverted conscience can not alter the nature of sin, and make it lawful. It merely frees it from that deeper aggravation, in which men sin presumptuously against the light, and their own convictions, and thus load themselves with a more dangerous and almost hopeless condemnation.

The same conclusion results equally from a direct consideration of the nature of conscience. It may be allowable, as a figure of rhetoric, to speak of it as a judge which holds its court within the soul, and pronounces its judgment on all the lower faculties. But such metaphors, when constantly used, are liable to create a serious delusion. When it is said that conscience comes in between the Bible and ourselves, as a mediator and interpreter, the metaphor has been mistaken for a fact, and leads to dangerous consequences. For conscience is simply the mind itself, exercising its judgment on the moral relations of right and wrong in its own actions, and the actions of others. Its supremacy over other faculties is merely a varied expression for the truth, that the relations the mind contemplates, when its acts receive this name, are in their own nature of binding authority, and claim allegiance and submission. In its other actings, the mind contemplates things equal or inferior to itself, or superior beings, irrespective of any claim to actual dominion and supremacy. But the laws of moral duty are royal laws in their own nature, and speak with the voice of a king; and the judgments of the mind, in which it recognizes them, partake of the same character. Thus the supremacy of conscience depends entirely on the distinctive nature of moral truth; but its defects, weakness, and error are due to the mind itself, and are one form of its moral guilt and infirmity. Its dictates are binding, therefore, so far as they are the true reflection of eternal truths, or of real moral relations perceived by the soul. But the mistakes of conscience have no more real authority than any other kind of error. They have this peculiar feature, that they make sin inevitable. In obeying them the man sins against laws of God; and, in disobeying them, against his own convictions of duty, and the internal harmony of his own moral being.

Conscience, then, is no mediator, which private judgment can interpose between the mind of the Christian and the Word of God, so as to shield him from the weight of the direct authority of the Scriptures. It is simply the mind itself, recognizing the control of moral obligations, whether dimly taught by the light of Nature, or more clearly by the voice of Divine revelation. If the Bible be the Word of God, then its moral precepts must be received by the conscience at once, so far as they are understood, and owned to be obligatory. If it be viewed as a human production, a double process will be required: first, to discover what it enjoins; and next, to discern how far its precepts are confirmed by the moral judgment, which may be formed on other grounds. In this case, natural conscience may be said to come between the soul and the Bible, because its revealed commands are not held to be binding of themselves, and require to be ratified by some further and more decisive authority. But this plainly involves an entire denial of its Divine character. On the other hand, when its authority is allowed, there can be no middle party required, to render its precepts of direct and immediate obligation. They bind, because they exist, and are the voice of God. They can be felt to be binding, and guide the practice, only so far as their authority is accepted, and their true meaning is discerned. A personal conviction with regard to our own duty must accompany the acting of the mind upon the moral lessons in the Word of God; but it neither adds to their authority, nor creates the obligation to obey; just as an image on the retina does not really intervene between the eye and the landscape, and is only a necessary result, from the optical structure of the eye, during the act of vision.

III. A third question remains to be examined. Is it one feature of the present advanced age of the world, that whenever Scripture and private conscience appear to diverge, we must suit our construction of Scripture to the supposed lessons of conscience, instead of molding the conscience into submission to the truth of God? This is a very momentous inquiry. It has been affirmed that "when conscience and the Bible appear to differ, the pious Christian immediately concludes that he has not really understood the Bible." In other words, his conscience may be assumed to be infallible, but his interpretation may be wrong, and the latter must be revised and varied till the discrepancy is removed.

Now, such statements as these involve a double error. They assume that conscience, in the case of the pious Christian, can give decisions independent of the moral teaching of the Scriptures, and unaffected by it; and also, that its decisions are less fallible, and more trustworthy, than the conclusions drawn with regard to the true meaning of the Word of God.

First, it is untrue that the conscience of the pious Christian can give decisive judgments, while he is still uncertain whether they agree with the Word of God, and even suspects some contradiction between them. For since he believes that the Bible is a Divine revelation, he must believe that what God really commands in his Word is just, right, and true, and that moral judgments contradicting that Word must be deceptive and erroneous. An infidel, of course, may form moral judgments in entire independence of the Scriptures, and when they differ from his impression of the Bible precepts, he will at once impute the difference to the moral immaturity of the sacred writers. But with the Christian this is impossible. So long as he remains uncertain what the Scriptures really teach on a question of morals, so long the voice of conscience must remain in suspense, because he dare not pretend to set up his own guesses above the express revelations of the living God. The mere assertion, then, of the power and right of the natural conscience to form a fixed moral judgment on cases mentioned in the Scriptures, before the voice of Scripture itself has been heard, is a virtual rejection of Christianity. Such a claim is consistent and natural in the lips of the unbeliever alone.

It is plain, however, that the natural conscience may form impressions on laws of moral duty, or the character of particular actions, of a provisional kind, which diverge from the first impressions left on the mind by the teaching of Scripture, without any formal rejection of its authority. And the second question which arises must be, how these are to be reconciled together. Must our interpretation of Scripture always give way to the supposed voice of natural conscience? Or must conscience always submit to the apparent meaning of Scripture? Or, again, must each, in turn, be modified and revised by the help of the other?

The true answer is here very evident to a thoughtful mind. Our interpretations of the Bible are liable to error, especially with regard to its indirect moral teaching, by examples, or in exceptional circumstances; and so also are the first impressions of natural conscience. The disciples needed their eyes to be opened, that they might understand the Scriptures; and they, whose heart and conscience are defiled, will be sure to form erroneous conclusions on moral right and wrong, till they have been cleansed and renewed by the Spirit of God. To claim infallibility for crude and hasty inferences from Scripture, so as to quench deep moral instincts of the soul, is the high road to all superstition. To set up natural conscience for an infallible rule, and either to reject the voice of Scripture, or violently to distort it, in order to get rid of a felt discordance from that rule, is the very essence of infidelity. The path of true wisdom lies between these extremes. It will use the plainer lessons of conscience to correct and remove gross and careless misconstructions of the lesson conveyed in isolated narratives of Scripture. But it will also use the voice of Scripture, especially when derived from the comparison of many passages, to correct the superficial and erroneous teachings of natural conscience; and thus to raise it, from the low level of a spurious charity, a mere counterfeit of true benevolence, into communion with the Divine holiness, and the solemn, as well as the tender and gentle features of heavenly love.

IV. Is there no difference, then, it may still be asked, between the liberty of the Christian and the rigor of the Jewish dispensation? Are we now, in the times of the Gospel, no less under the dominion of an external law, than the disciples of Moses under the elder covenant? Are we

THE BIBLE AND NATURAL CONSCIENCE. 365

not taught by the apostle, in most emphatic language, that Christians are "not under the law, but under grace?" Are we not charged to "stand fast in the liberty of Christ, and not to be entangled with a yoke of bondage?" Do not these and similar passages lend some countenance to the idea, that in former ages there were commands binding on the conscience, simply in virtue of their publication; but that now, under the Gospel, no command is of authority till received and digested by the conscience itself, as a kind of spiritual moderator, and thus engraven on the tablets of the heart? Perhaps the simplest and clearest reply to these questions will be found in a brief review of those foundations of Christian morality and Christian faith, on which their right solution must depend.

First of all, moral truth is not a mutable and variable thing. It is no chance product of human opinion, no capricious and arbitrary creation of the Divine will. It is the reflection of God's own moral perfection, in its relation to the responsible creatures he has made, and is thus unchangeable in its principles and grand outlines, like the attributes of the Most High. Moral perfection is in reality the Divine image retained in the spirit of angels, and restored in the souls of men. "God is love," and the full resemblance of that love is the perfection of the rational creature, the great and supreme law of moral duty. But since all being is twofold, the Creator and his creatures, this law parts at once into two great commandments, the love of God and the Supreme Goodness, and the love of God's creatures. It thus forms the double precept, in its wide and full meaning, "Thou shalt love the Lord thy God with all thy heart," and "Thou shalt love thy neighbor as thyself." Each of these admits of further divisions, according to the attributes or states of the object loved, and the capacity or state of the moral agent himself. To dwell on the second only—love to our fellow-creatures may assume three fundamental varieties. They may be viewed simply as creatures capable of happiness; and love to them under this character is simple benevolence, which extends even to lower forms of irrational life. They may be viewed, next, as moral creatures, loving or selfish, holy or unholy. Love toward them in this second aspect assumes two opposite forms—the love of the good, and the hatred or abhorrence of the evil; and this constitutes moral righteousness or holiness. Again, sinful and unholy creatures may be viewed as still capable of moral recovery. Love to them, under this character, constitutes the last and highest element of true Christian morality, or that grace which is the distinguishing lesson of the Gospel of Christ. Still further, the complex nature of man, as composed of body and soul, and his own condition, as a dying creature under moral probation, and a sinner encompassed by acts and messages of Divine grace, vary these fundamental outlines, and multiply them into an immense diversity of moral obligations.

Conscience is simply the mind itself, viewed in its capacity for discerning the truth and authority of these obligations, and for passing judgment, by the aid of this knowledge, upon all the various actions of men. It is an enlightened conscience, when these relations are seen clearly, and felt in all their real power. It is a dark and ignorant conscience, when they are ill understood, and the mind seldom awakens to the sense of their surpassing and supreme importance. It is a perverse and defiled conscience, when the love of sin in the heart warps and falsifies the judgment, so that men call evil good, and good evil, put light for darkness and darkness for light, bitter for sweet and sweet for bitter. It is a seared conscience, when the soul becomes reckless and willfully desperate in sin, and refuses altogether to own the unchanging authority of the eternal laws of right and wrong.

The conscience of man, since the fall, is darkened and defiled, but neither wholly seared and insensible, nor totally blind. His sense of his duty toward God is the most grievously obscured, and in a lower degree, but far less completely, his sense of obligation toward his fellow-men. By the mere light of nature, in favorable circumstances, he attains some partial knowledge of the duties of truth, justice, and benevolence. But, without teaching of revelation, all the higher lessons of moral obligation, the holiness of the law, and the grace of the Gospel, remain almost, or altogether unknown.

Now, in using the higher help, and fuller teaching, which Divine revelation supplies, men are exposed, from a double cause, to the risk of serious error. Mere intellectual dullness, or haste and rashness, form one source of misinterpretation; and moral disease and darkness are another, still more dangerous. Through dullness or haste, men may mistake beacons of warning for moral examples, or the absence of express condemnation of wrong actions for a virtual approval; or the praise of mixed actions, because of some element of faith and piety, for a sanction to all the accessories of human infirmity and sin; or duties, resulting from rare and exceptional circumstances, may be taken for normal examples, given for general imitation. In all these cases a conscience, moderately enlightened, may serve to correct the too hasty inferences of a superficial judgment.

But the other source of error is wider in its operation, and far more dangerous. The sinful heart shrinks from the holiness of the Divine law, and seeks by a natural instinct to elude its authority. The severity of God's anger against sin grates painfully upon ears that are in love with worldly pleasure; and it is striven to set the truth aside, as a contradiction to the Divine benevolence. The laws of the first table, as most obnoxious to the fallen heart, are wholly rejected, or robbed of all the fullness of their meaning; and those of the second table are pruned and lowered, till grace is turned into moral indifference, and holiness defamed as a Jewish superstition. All that remains is then a wretched *caput mortuum* of sickly, sentimental, unreal benevolence, degenerating by degrees into selfish prudence alone. Thus, instead of conscience being an infallible guide, to whose independent decisions our interpretations of Scripture must be compelled to bow, the exact reverse is true. The diseases and obliquities of conscience, in sinful men, are the most fruitful cause of laborious perversions of the Word of God. Men love darkness, rather than light, because their deeds are evil. They shrink, with instinctive shuddering, from the holy severity and stern authority of the Divine Law, and too readily corrupt and pervert the grace of the Gospel itself, by confounding it with the doctrine of indiscriminate mercy, and a message of universal impunity to sin.

The authority, however, of the commands of God does not and can not depend on the unwilling submission of men. A diseased conscience may shrink from the light, and close the eyes against it. A sinful heart may send up thick vapors, like the smoke from the abyss, to obscure this upper firmament. But the stars abide in their everlasting courses, and never cease to shine, nor to rule over this night-season of moral darkness, till the full Dayspring shall arise. Whether known or unknown, whether obeyed or disobeyed, the great law of love, along with all the corollaries that flow from it, is always binding upon the souls of men. They can not, by any willful darkness, escape from its power. They can hide themselves in no cavern, where its presence does not overtake them, and pronounce them guilty, so long as they refuse, or **even** neglect to obey.

This law of duty, in its higher and nobler aspects, applies to man simply as an immortal spirit, and requires the obedience of the heart alone. But in its lower and more practical forms, it applies to man both in soul and body, and requires the obedience of the outward act, as well as in the affections of the heart. Under the earlier dispensation of the Law, these outward requirements were greatly multiplied, and were needed to train and discipline the inner man to the free service of love. Out of the corruption of this system arose the self-righteousness of the Pharisees, which worshiped the outward form, and stifled or denied the inner meaning of the Divine commands, and in which the weightier matters of the law—judgment, mercy, and faith—were completely set aside.

The contrast, then, of the Gospel of Christ with the Law of Moses does not consist in the abrogation of the Divine commands, or in making them dependent, for their authority, on the previous indorsement of man's natural conscience. That would indeed be a fatal error, and pave the way for the great antichristian apostasy of the last days. In this nobler astronomy, the earth must revolve around the sun, not the sun around the earth. The conscience of man, a dependent and subordinate gift of the Creator, must submit to the firm and eternal laws of his moral government. It is a planet which derives all its light, and order, and beauty, not only from the enlightening beams, but from the controlling authority, of the Sun of Righteousness. Once let that control be withdrawn, and it becomes indeed a "wandering star," which must travel further and further into the depths of error and delusion, till it loses itself in the outer darkness. Such was the state of those Jewish persecutors, in early days, of whom our Lord warned his disciples—"The time will come, when he that killeth you will think he doeth God service." Such was the state, in later times, of those importers of ascetic superstition into the Church of Christ "speaking lies in hypocrisy, seared in their own conscience as with a hot iron, forbidding to marry, and commanding to abstain from meats, which God hath created to be received with thanksgiving." Such is the inspired description of those selfish apostates of the last days, who "walk after the flesh in the lust of uncleanness, and despise government," and "whose own heart and conscience are defiled" with the love and practice of sensual sin. It is only when the conscience bows with reverence and full submission to the authority of God's written Word, that, like a planet obeying the central law of gravitation, it abides in the light which streams from Him whose word it obeys. It then receives and reflects the pure light of Divine truth, and its innumerable applications to every field of moral duty, and to all the varied relations of human life, and the hills and valleys of earth are bathed with the brightness and the sunshine of heaven.

CHAPTER XVII.

THE HISTORICAL UNITY OF THE BIBLE.

The Bible combines within itself various characters. It is a sacred history, a code of religious doctrine and morality, and a message of peace and hope, or a prophecy, to successive generations, of a redemption to come. If truly inspired, it will bear, in every one of these characters, some impress of its Divine Author. It will be pure, for God is pure, and holy, for God is holy. It will be marked by historical unity, for "known unto God are all his works from the beginning;" by doctrinal consistency, and fullness, for "the Spirit searcheth all things, yea, even the deep things of God;" by practical power over the hearts of men, for the Word of God is a word of power, and "effectually worketh in them that believe;" by harmony in its prophetic announcements, for its Author is that Spirit to whom all the secrets of the future are disclosed, whose messages are of no private interpretation, but a consistent revelation of the good things to come. Let us examine the Bible, first, as a Sacred History, and see whether, in this aspect, it does not yield abundant evidence of its Divine authority and inspiration.

The historical books of Scripture form three-fifths of the whole. They are composed by nearly twenty writers, in two different languages, during a space of more than fifteen hundred years. If merely the works of men, it would therefore be vain to expect in them any marked unity of plan, outline, and moral purpose, running through the whole. Such a unity, if it be found to exist, must evince the presence of a higher author, the Spirit of God.

I. Now, first, the historical character of the Bible is in itself a mark of the Divine wisdom, by which it has been suited to its professed office, as a public revelation from God to man. By this alone it is widely distinguished from nearly every case of pretended revelation. Facts and imposture do not agree together. There is no history, properly so called, in the Koran; none in the Shasters and Vedas of Hinduism; none in the Zendavesta; none in the sacred books of Egypt, so far as they are recovered, or their contents are known. But the Bible is, first of all, a sacred history. It professes to be God's own record of the leading facts in the course and progress of the moral government of our world through successive ages. It mounts upward to a period so remote, that no parallel testimonies exist, with which to compare it. But it reaches onward through all the later periods of ancient history; while it closes, in the first century of the Christian era, amid the fullest blaze of Greek and Roman civilization. Three-fifths of each Testament are purely historical. In either case the histories take precedence of all the other sacred books, and form the basis on which they rest, and out of which they evidently spring.

This historical form of the message fulfills many important objects. It is, in the first place, a convincing pledge for the reality of the whole. Men are prone, by nature, to flee from their Maker's presence, and hide themselves in the dark caverns of their own unbelief. Purely-doctrinal messages, or spiritual truths presented in an abstract form, would have little power to meet and overcome this great evil. Men need to be taught that the Almighty is a God nigh at hand, a real, living Governor, whose authority, like the blue sky, bends over all, and, whether

THE HISTORICAL UNITY OF THE BIBLE. 373

they choose or refuse, embraces them continually on every side.

A revelation, couched in a history of mankind from the creation downward, meets this temptation of the fallen heart, desirous to escape, if possible, from the sense of the Divine Presence. Men can not escape from the history of the Bible. Its facts encounter them on every side. If they go back to creation, the Bible is there, and if they trace out the dispersed families of mankind, the Bible is there also. If they take the wings of the morning, to visit the lands of the East; there, in the land of Egypt, or the plains of Chaldea, amid Arabian deserts, or the hills and valleys of Canaan, the ever-present hand of God, revealed in these histories, holds them in on every side. The obelisks of Nineveh are brought suddenly to light, after a burial of two thousand, five hundred years, and Bible facts are found engraven upon them. The monuments of Egypt are deciphered, and Shishak, So, Tirhakah, Necho, and Hophra, all the Pharaohs whose names meet us in the Bible, meet us there also, and dovetail at once into their places in the sacred history. In later times the remains of antiquity bring before us, in the coins of Herod the Great, and Herod Antipas, in the guild of dyers at Thyatira, the corn ships of Alexandria, the title of the Roman chief of Melita, and inscriptions by the "temple-keeping Ephesians" to the great Artemis, and her heaven-descended image, ever multiplying coincidences with the New Testament history. The plains east of Jordan are explored; and in Bashan, the Bible "land of giants," after thousands of years, buildings worthy of a race of giants are brought to light once more. The voices from the half-deciphered tombs of the old Pharaohs, even though fulsome adulation, royal pride, and foul idolatry, have left on them a triple stamp of falsehood, seem still, in many parts, like dim and muffled echoes of the true sayings of God. Their divergence from the Bible, where they seem to diverge the most, resembles the difference between the same landscape seen dimly through a sea of mist, and in clear sunlight. In proportion as we emerge out of obscure antiquity into a historical age, their harmony with the Bible becomes apparent. Where the divergence seems wide in the view of some investigators, amid the twilight of the world's infancy, there are still such important points of agreement with Genesis and Exodus, as to force the suspicion, even on the least religious minds, that, after all, the defect may belong to the blunders of interpreters, or to the falsehoods of pride and flattery in the heathen sculptures themselves, and leave the truth of the Bible unshaken and unimpaired.

But there is a further benefit in the historical form of the Bible, besides the evidence which it forces, even on reluctant hearts, of the reality of God's moral government. The Divine message is brought into greater harmony with the weakness of mankind.

The view has been lately advanced, that precept, example, and internal conscience, form three successive stages, both in the training of the individual and of the world. But the hypothesis, even apart from the conclusions which have been rested upon it, seems very questionable. Example comes even earlier, perhaps, than precept, in the real order of moral training. The child imitates out of mere instinct, even before it has learned to obey. It seems a truer description, that example is the means by which mere instinct is gradually transformed into conscious and intelligent submission to moral law. Its influence is not by any means delayed till childhood is passing into youth. It begins with the first hours of infancy, and is then, perhaps, relatively the most powerful; though its absolute power may increase with the growth of thought and reason, and become still more conspicuous, when the years of childhood are passing away. Moral tales have a mighty power over children, long before a code of ethics would have any great influence. Even with the majority of educated men, biographies and travels are more attractive, and do more in molding the heart, than didactic treatises of a moral kind.

Now, the Bible, by the large proportion of direct narrative it contains, and the precedence of these historical books over the rest, is wisely adapted to this instinct of our nature. It deals with men, as truly children in the sight of God, who need training by examples and simple narratives, before direct precepts can exercise their due power, or mysterious truths and doctrines be usefully revealed. The sacred histories form thus the larger portion of each Testament. They are the stem on which all the other parts depend. Plain, real fact, blossoming out into high and holy truth, is the character, throughout, of the Word of God. It stoops, first of all, by its narratives, to the condition of men, as dwelling in the outward world of time and sense, that it may raise them to the knowledge of their Maker, and the vision of unseen and eternal things.

II. The unity of purpose, in all the sacred histories, is a further token of their Divine origin. The Bible is a history of redemption. It begins with a brief account of the Creation. But after its mention of the Temptation and the Fall, it announces the coming of a Redeemer, who would subdue the deceiver and adversary of mankind. The expansion of this hope is the one object of all the later histories. They reveal the main steps of Divine Providence, by which this first great promise was to be at length fulfilled. Amid the rank and luxurious growth of lust and violence, of unbelief and idolatry, truth and righteousness are kept alive in the earth by ceaseless acts of Divine power and wisdom; till at length the Seed of the Woman is born, and a new and brighter era of Gospel hope dawns upon the benighted nations, which had long been sitting in darkness, and the shadow of death.

All the main features of the Bible history are simply explained by a reference to this great object of the whole message. It determines what is said, and what is left in silence; what is briefly touched upon, and what is unfolded more at large. A few chapters are the sole record of two thousand years from Adam to Abraham. The work of redemption was then in its first infancy. The Spirit of God, like the dove when it first returned to the ark of Noah, seems to flee away from those ages of dim light and abounding wickedness; and to await, in silence and hope, the abating of the floods of ungodliness, and the arrival of brighter days.

With the call of Abraham a new era in the scheme of Divine mercy plainly began. Here, also, the history evidently begins to expand, and becomes far more copious. Still, it passes by in silence the rise of idolatrous empires, and confines its narrative, almost entirely, to the lives of the three chosen patriarchs, whose names were to be linked inseparably, through all later ages, with the name of the true and only God. Two hundred years from the death of Jacob to the Exodus, are dismissed in three chapters only. But with the Exodus itself began a fresh stage of Divine revelation, and two whole books, mainly historical, are occupied with the great subject, accompanied by two others, filled with the Divine laws, which were given to the people of Israel. Another whole book is given to the narrative of the Conquest, the historical basis of the Jewish polity for fifteen hundred years, and itself the type of a greater deliverance. But three centuries that follow, in which there was no fresh revelation, are compressed into a single book, with one short episode in the history of Ruth. The line of inspired prophets began with Samuel, and that of kings with Saul and David; and the history expands once more, and is on a larger scale. It attains its greatest fullness in the reign of David, the center of a new era of Divine promise; and then contracts into a more rapid sketch of the later reigns. Three short books, after the Captivity, are marked by the entire absence of miracles, by the continuation of the history of Judah alone, by a remarkable, preservation of the chosen people, and by a definite prediction of the time when Messiah would appear. The history is then suspended, till the time of the Incarnation. It resumes with a short account of our Lord's infancy, and a fuller record of his public ministry, death, and resurrection, by four different witnesses. One of these continues his earlier narrative of our Lord's lifetime by a history of the early Church, till the Gospel is firmly planted by St. Paul himself in the metropolis of the heathen world.

Now, in all these histories one great purpose is conspicuous. Hope in a Savior still to come is the leading feature of the Old Testament; and faith in a Savior who has actually appeared is the animating principle of the New. Facts are omitted, which have only a remote bearing on this great hope of the Church; and those are unfolded most fully into which it enters with the greatest clearness. The Bible history, from first to last, is instinct with life and hope. Every-where it reveals the Spirit of God, brooding over the dark and troubled waters of a sinful world, and preparing the way for a great and blessed regeneration still to come.

III. Continuity of outline is another main feature of the Bible history. It does not resemble, in the least, the independent workmanship of twenty writers, the earliest separated from the latest by fifteen hundred years. It wears the marks of one continued narrative, carried on uniformly through four thousand years, from the days of Paradise to the preaching of St. Paul to the Jews at Rome, with one single break, where the Law and the Prophets are parted from the higher message of the Gospel of Christ.

This continuity is seen in the whole series of the Old Testament histories. The Book of Genesis reaches from the Creation, in one unbroken descent, to the death of Joseph. Exodus begins with the death of Joseph and his brethren, and carries us through the deliverance itself, till the tabernacle is finished, at the opening of the second year, and filled with the cloud of glory. Numbers resumes from the same time, or rather earlier, before the second Passover, and reaches to the conquest of the land on the east of Jordan. Deuteronomy, besides a review of the journeys in the wilderness, closes with an account of the death of Moses. The Book of Joshua reaches from the death of Moses to that of Joshua and of Eleazar. The Book of Judges resumes with some details of the conquest, and reaches to the death of Samson, after the long strife with the Philistines had begun. The First Book of Samuel begins with the birth of the prophet, in the days of Samson, and extends through the reign of Saul to his overthrow and death. The Second begins with the accession of David, and reaches nearly to the close of his reign. The two Books of Kings continue the history, in unbroken order, to the Fall of the Temple. Three short books recount the restoration after the Captivity. The Books of Chronicles contain simply genealogies from Adam to David, and a fuller narrative of the reigns of the kings of Judah only, from David to Zedekiah. The New Testament resumes the history, after a pause of four centuries, and continues it from the Incarnation, till the Gospel was planted in Rome, the great center and metropolis of the heathen world.

A series of histories, so continuous through four thousand years, from the Creation to Nero, could not be the chance work of twenty writers, fifteen centuries removed at the two extremes. A higher wisdom must surely have been present, and molded every portion into harmony with the common design of the whole. The single break between Malachi and the Incarnation only strengthens the proof of design. Stars wane before the sunrise. The gift of prophecy was suspended, and sacred history was withheld for a season, before that dawn of the Sun of Righteousness, after which both of them were to reappear in richer splendor and beauty than before. The words of the heathen poet, in reference to the works of creation, must apply here with equal force, "*Mens agitat molem, et magno se corpore miscet.*" One mind, the mind of the Holy Spirit, must have brooded over this wide range of history, evolving deep harmonies of truth and wisdom out of the seeming chaos of confusion and spiritual darkness, through the long and weary course of these four thousand years.

IV. Simplicity of style is another feature of the sacred histories by which they are distinguished from common narratives. There is no comment, and no rhetorical amplification. Where genealogies are given, there is no attempt to relieve their barrenness by digressions and arts of composition. The most startling miracles are mentioned in the same quiet tone as the most commonplace occurrence. The writer seldom pauses, even for a moment, to direct the attention of his readers to the wonders he has to record. A calm, quiet, solemn, earnest tone marks the whole narrative. The writers never turn aside to deprecate suspicion, never pause to amplify what is marvelous, and seldom allude for a moment to collateral testimony. However rich in materials for reflection their narrative may be, they abstain from all moral commentary. The history is left to supply its own key. There is no condemnation of Lot, in his ready acceptance of Abraham's offer, but the results of his choice, too selfishly made, speak for themselves. There is no direct censure of Jacob's deceit in the case of the blessing, but his whole life is one tale of silent retribution. He is deceived, in turn, in all that is dearest, with reference to his flocks, to his wife, to his best-beloved son. Thus the histories of the Bible, while they are simple beyond all others, are also the most profound. The youngest child reads them with lively interest; and the most experienced Christian, the moralist, and the divine, return to them continually, and find them rich with unsuspected treasures of moral truth and heavenly wisdom.

What can be more simple than the history of Joseph? Its truth and pathos find their way irresistibly to every heart. But what can be more profound than the lessons it conveys, on the laws of duty, the ways of Divine Providence, and the character and work of the promised Redeemer? It follows abruptly after a dry, unadorned genealogy of the sons of Esau, and is closed by a list, almost equally dry in appearance, of the sons and grandsons of Jacob. It bursts upon us at once with the completeness of a perfect drama, where every part conspires, simply and naturally, to the issue designed from the first. The dreams of Joseph are fulfilled through the envy of his brethren, in spite of their settled purpose to falsify them; and the deep reality of human character and feeling, in every step of the narrative, renders doubly conspicuous the unfailing truth of God's promises, and the sureness of his counsel, who sees the end from the beginning. Amid the darkness of heathenism, and the sinful perverseness of the chosen seed, there dawns a bright earnest of the promised redemption; and the Christian, who compares it with the New Testament, is compelled to feel, in all the main steps of the narrative—Behold, a greater than Joseph is here!

This simplicity of the Bible history is one out of many marks which strongly attest its Divine inspiration. We feel, even when we are not able to explain, the stamp of Divinity which rests upon it. Skeptical critics may strive to persuade themselves, or their readers, that the early narratives of the Bible are epic poems or mere legends. We read them once more, and the illusion disappears. In every sentence we hear the tones of truth and reality. The impression they leave on the mind, and have left on every candid and thoughtful reader since the hour when they were written, is like that made on our senses, when we gaze on the blue vault of heaven. They are inimitably simple, and still they are unfathomably profound.

V. The condensation of the Bible histories is not less striking than their simplicity. This was required, indeed, by the practical object for which they are given. A history of the world through four thousand years, in which the main steps of God's moral government should be recorded for the lasting guidance of his people, required the utmost condensation, or it would fail to be accessible to the vast majority of believers. The structure of the Bible fulfills this necessary condition in the highest degree. It is full, every-where, of the seeds of things. Its minutest incidents, on close examination, are found to be rich with a large variety of spiritual truth. They are like the images on the human retina; and every speck contains, in miniature, a condensed landscape of heavenly wisdom.

This condensation of the Bible narratives is doubly striking, if we compare them with the earliest heathen records, the lately-deciphered monuments of Egypt. Let us hear the description of these, which Baron Bunsen has given, who still regarded them as a lever which must overturn our faith in the truthfulness of the early histories of the Bible. "Where," he asks, "is there an instance of so many and such magnificent monuments, which sometimes tell us little, frequently nothing at all? . . . The written character is prolix; the repetition of fixed phrases makes it still more so. Little is lost by occasional *lacunæ*, but comparatively little advance is made by what is preserved. There are few words in a line; and what is still worse, little is said in a great many lines. Inscriptions on public buildings were not intended to convey historical information. They consist of panegyrics on the king, and praises of the gods, to each of whom all imaginable titles of honor are given. Historical facts are thrown into the shade, as something paltry, casual, incidental, by the side of such pompous phraseology as—Lords of the World, Conquerors of the North, Tamers of the South, Destroyers of all the Un clean, and all their Enemies. The case of the papyri is certainly different. But written history, such as the historical books of the Old Testament, so far as our knowledge of their writings goes, was certainly unknown to the old Egyptians."

The early books of the Bible are a total contrast, in this respect, to the previous description of the most ancient heathen records. The object seems to be, in every part, to condense into a small compass the largest possible amount of real information. Simple facts, condensed and multiplied, seem here to constitute the basis on which the whole superstructure of moral, prophetic, and doctrinal messages was to be reared. And this feature which marks the earliest Bible histories, remains equally striking to their close. The Book of Acts stands preëminent above all classic histories, for the variety, the condensation, and the fullness of its narrative. It links itself with the whole range of the Old Testament Scripture, with all the facts of the Gospels, the cotemporary messages of the Epistles, and an immense variety of the facts of classical antiquity; while it records the successive steps by which the Gospel was transferred from Jerusalem to Rome, and the way prepared for long ages of Gentile privilege, and Jewish desolation.

VI. The Pentateuch, or the Law of Moses, forms the first of four main divisions of the Bible history. Its historical unity is a most conspicuous feature of the whole. Instead of permitting us to resolve it, as some modern skeptics have labored to do, into a clumsy and imperfect patchwork of three or four different authors, it requires us to see in it the work of a higher mind, and a deeper wisdom than even that of Moses, by which the course of the whole narrative must have been secretly and powerfully controlled.

First of all, in its general character it stands alone, and has no counterpart in any human production whatever. It is a code of national law, inwrought into the texture of a regular history. Again, it is a history of mankind from the earliest times, briefly and comprehensively given, and blossoming into lessons of moral duty, and institutes of national wisdom. It roots itself in the soil by innumerable details, in its earlier portion; and rises, at its close, into a most earnest and impressive series of Divine commands and exhortations. Thus it stoops to man, as to a little child, takes him by the hand, teaches him to look upward, and leads his footsteps, gently, along the steep hill-side of eternal truth. Through a simple record of facts it rises gradually into the region of moral duty, of precepts, doctrines, and promises. It begins with the loss of Paradise through man's transgression; and ends with a description of God's own prophet, from the hight of Pisgah, looking out upon a glorious vision of an inheritance, like Paradise, still to come.

This double character, of facts passing into doctrine, command, and promise, runs through the whole Pentateuch, but with a manifest progress and gradation. The first book is almost wholly historical, since it ends before Moses, the great prophet and lawgiver, was born. But it is not mere history. Its leading facts are made the basis of distinct commands and ordinances, which form essential parts of the law of the Lord. The history of the Creation, in the first chapter, is closed by the institution of the Sabbath, the first, in order, of all the revealed commands of God; and its repetition, with details, in the second chapter, closes with the law of marriage, the grand basis of all social and domestic obligations. The third chapter, again, closes with a double appointment of human labor and conjugal obedience. The fourth chapter implies the institution of animal sacrifice. The ninth puts a seal upon the sacredness of man's life, by a public appointment of death to be the penalty of murder. The rite of circumcision is enjoined to Abraham by a distinct covenant, while a law of tithes, and another ceremonial observance, are indirectly imposed, in the later course of the patriarchal history, on the people of Israel.

The laws, however, in Genesis, though of high importance, are comparatively few in number. In Exodus they form rather less than one half of the whole book. In Leviticus there is only a very slight intermixture of narrative: it consists almost entirely of the ordinances of the tabernacle worship, and of other national institutes. The first and last chapters of Numbers have the same character, but the middle is chiefly historical. Deuteronomy, on the other hand, is mainly a rehearsal and repetition of Divine laws; but its first chapters are a review of the history in the wilderness, and it closes with an account of the parting words, and of the death of Moses. There is thus a plain organic unity from first to last. The two elements of facts and laws are present throughout the Pentateuch: but the facts, in Genesis, are the main substance of the work, with only a few laws interposed; while Deuteronomy is a book of laws and Divine ordinances; but it is firmly anchored, both at its opening and its close, upon the great series of events which compose the sacred history.

Again, the Book of Genesis, in its first chapters, must either be a supernatural revelation, or a mere legendary fiction. But every feature of legendary composition is here precisely reversed. There is no trace of a desire to amplify doubtful and marvelous narratives. because the account goes back to the most distant ages, the birthday of the world. On the contrary, one short chapter alone is given to a general history of the Creation, a second to the state of man before the fall, a third to the fall itself, a fourth to the first example of God's moral government over a world of sinners, a fifth to the genealogy of sixteen hundred years, from Adam to Noah; and three others to the Flood, where a new covenant of grace began. Three chapters more complete the whole account to the call of Abraham; so that eight chapters travel rapidly over more than two thousand years.

With the call of Abraham a new dispensation of mercy began. Here, therefore, the history expands at once into larger proportions. Forty chapters unfold rather less than three centuries of the patriarchal history. A further expansion ensues at once after the call of Moses, and fifty historical chapters are occupied with an interval of forty years only, till his death. There is thus an evident harmony and proportion of historical development in the whole Pentateuch, which severs it widely from all the heathen legends; and is a clear sign that it "came not by the will of man," but that Moses composed it under the guidance of a higher wisdom, and "spake as he was moved by the Holy Ghost."

Let us contrast it, for example, with Manetho and the Egyptian monuments. The history of that famous Egyptian priest has perished, except two or three short fragments in Josephus. But we learn, from an extract in Eusebius, that it professed to begin with reigns of the gods, occupying 13,900 years, and four dynasties of Manes, or souls of the dead, and Heroes, who reigned over Egypt for 11,000 years more, and were followed by Menes, the first mortal or human king. All these are described as Egyptian reigns. They were designed evidently to flatter the national vanity and pride. There is no trace of any message in the history, to remind the Egyptians of their brotherhood with the foreign races they were accustomed to hate or despise. What a total contrast to the simple record in the first chapter of Genesis! The very first lesson taught to the Jews in their national law, the immediate gift of the God of Israel, was their brotherhood with the whole race of mankind; with whom they shared, in Adam, a common sentence of guilt and shame; and, both in Adam and Noah, a common message of hope and coming redemption.

The historical interweaving of the whole narrative is another feature, which shows the Divine wisdom by which it was framed. Every device of skepticism is baffled when it strives to rend asunder the seamless robe of this fundamental record of patriarchal history. In the latter half of Genesis, for example, from the birth of Isaac onward, we find not less than a hundred retrospective allusions to the previous portion of the narrative, and most of them of a distinct and specific kind. Some are direct, others indirect and comparatively latent. Some refer to a single passage, and others to the combined result of several statements.

The same character of retrospective allusion runs through the four later books, and compacts the whole Pentateuch so firmly together, that no critical artifice can succeed in parting it asunder. It would need little more, to disprove every variety of the document hypothesis, than to print separately the different alleged documents; when it would be seen at once that they were merely torn and broken fragments of the Pentateuch, and could have no claim to form a complete and independent whole. The firmness of structure, in these early books of Scripture, is like that which the skillful architect gives to the lowest courses of the lighthouse, which has to resist the incessant surging of the waves of the ocean, and to bear aloft, on its summit, the beacon-light, by which ten thousand mariners may be rescued from fatal shipwreck, and find it a star of hope and peace amidst the darkness and the storm.

VII. In the later books of the Old Testament, from Joshua to Nehemiah, the historical unity, though rather less conspicuous than in the Pentateuch, is not less real. The diversity of the writers, and the interval of more than a thousand years from the first to the last, make this feature, in some respects, even more striking than in the books of Moses, and compels us to read in it the result of a higher wisdom.

The Book of Joshua is a history of the conquest, the fulfillment of the prophecies in the law, and the basis of all the later history of the chosen people. It contains every thing essential to such a record, and nothing superfluous. First, we have the passage of Jordan, and the renewal of the national covenant. This is followed by four main steps in the Conquest, the fall of Jericho and of Ai, and the defeat of a great southern and a great northern confederacy of the Canaanites. There is, next, a formal catalogue of the kings and districts that were subdued.

The record of the Conquest is followed by the division of the land. And first, there is a repeated summary of the allotment by Moses to the trans-Jordanic tribes. Then we have the fulfillment of the promise to Caleb, and the allotments to the two leading tribes of Judah and Joseph. Next follows the supplementary allotment to the seven remaining tribes, with a list of the towns and villages in each portion, closed by Joshua's own private inheritance. The ecclesiastical arrangements follow, the appointment of the cities of refuge, and those of the Levites. The eastern tribes are then dismissed to their inheritance beyond Jordan. Last of all, Joshua, before his death, solemnly recounts to the people the mercies of God, and twice renews with them the national covenant.

The last chapter illustrates, in a striking manner, the way in which the whole series of sacred history is bound together. It goes back, in its review of the past, to the days of Terah, the father of Abraham, and mentions his idolatry, which is only implied in Genesis, in the land of Chaldea. It mentions next, in succession, the call of Abraham, the birth of Isaac, and of the sons of Isaac, Esau and Jacob, the inheritance of Esau in Mount Seir, and the descent of Jacob and his sons into Egypt, forming a brief summary of four-fifths of the Book of Genesis. In three verses more it gives an abridgment of Exodus, and in the last clause, of the Book of Numbers. In the eighth verse we have a brief repetition of the twenty-first of Numbers, and in verses 9, 10, of the striking episode of Balak and Balaam. Three other verses describe the Conquest itself, and the fulfillment of the promises in Deuteronomy. The mention of the oak or pillar, and of the sanctuary in Shechem, refers us to the history, in Gen. xxxiii, of Jacob's purchase from the Shechemites; the burial of Joshua, to the previous mention of his inheritance in the middle of the book; and that of the bones of Joseph, to three passages in Genesis and Exodus—Gen. xxxiii, 18-20, 24-26, Exod. xiii, 19—so as to bind together, by these retrospective allusions, the whole series of the sacred history.

The Book of Judges, which reaches from the death of Joshua to the Book of Samuel, when a new era of the Theocracy began has a distinct unity of its own. The successive relapses into idolatry, and the captivities to the heathen, showed the need of a righteous king, and that the true rest was not yet come. The book begins with a review of those failures in obedience to the Divine commands, which contained the seeds of later degeneracy and rebellion. Then follows a general summary of the whole period, in its double aspect of repeated apostasy and renewed help and deliverance. These periods are then briefly recorded in the order of time, from the first captivity under a king of Mesopotamia to the partial deliverance wrought by Samson at his death. The history then reverts to two main illustrations of the national sins of Israel in the next generation after Joshua and the elders, and closes them with a remark which contains the intended moral of the whole history, and made it a virtual prophecy of the national revolution which was soon to follow—"In those days there was no king in Israel: every man did that which was right in his own eyes."

The First and Second Books of Samuel have a similar unity of design. They contain the steps of the great transition from the earlier form of theocracy, under judges, to the permanent choice and establishment of the royal line of David. The former contains the successive steps, by which their judicial honor was taken from Eli and his priestly house, and transferred, first to Samuel, then to Saul, and finally to David, the center of a new era of promise and blessing. The Second Book is occupied with the forty years of his reign, just as that of Numbers with the forty years in the wilderness. The kingdom was settled by covenant in David's line: the ark, which the sin of Eli's sons had betrayed to the Philistines, was brought to Jerusalem; and preparation was made, on the site where the pestilence was arrested, for building the temple of God.

The Books of Kings continue the history through the reign of Solomon, and the division of the two kingdoms, down to the reign of Zedekiah, and the Fall of the Temple. In their opening chapters we have the building of the Temple, and the reign of Solomon, when the queen of the South came from the ends of the earth to hear his wisdom. The Theocracy, or typical kingdom of God, then reached its climax of strength and beauty, and began quickly to reveal its imperfection, and hasten into decay. The rest of these books contains the history of the schism, which rent Israel from Judah, and continued till the ten tribes were led away captive to Assyria, and Judah to Babylon. There is a clear unity of style in this portion of the history. It is also the stem which supports the greater part of the prophecies of the Old Testament. Three of the greater and nine of the minor prophets belong to this period. To make the connection still more intimate, three chapters of the Second Book of Kings are repeated, with very slight change, in the midst of Isaiah's prophecies, and two others are repeated in the book of Jeremiah's prophecies, at its very close.

The history is continued still further, in a second series, on the return from the Captivity. The Books of Chronicles begin from the Creation, and reach to the Captivity of Babylon. They are then continued by the Books of Ezra and Nehemiah, the last two verses of Chronicles and the first two of Ezra being the same. The nine chapters of genealogy from Adam to David, though they contain no history, supply copious materials to confirm the Mosaic narrative, and the actual truth of the later records. The remainder of the First Book gives fuller details than the Books of Samuel with regard to the last years of David, and the whole priestly economy. The Second Book confines itself, almost entirely, to the kingdom of Judah. In the first and leading series of sacred history, the prominent feature is the course of national sin, by which the kingdom of David sunk into ruin. But in Chronicles the main subject is the mercy of God to the people of Israel, and to the chosen line of David, issuing at length in that decree of Cyrus, by which the prophecies of Isaiah and Jeremiah were fulfilled.

The three short Books of Ezra, Nehemiah, and Esther, which continue this supplementary history, and bring it down through a whole century after the Return, have a character of their own. The grandeur of the old covenant has ceased. It has decayed, and grown old, and is ready to vanish away. No miracle is recorded in this last period of the sacred history. The unfinished air of the Books of Ezra and Nehemiah must strike every thoughtful reader. They are a little promontory, jutting out from the earlier times of the Law and the Prophets, and nearly severed from them by the Captivity—where hope might plant its foot more firmly, and look forward, across generations of delay, to the promised coming of Messiah. The prophetic books, which belong to the same period, contain some of the clearest predictions of his Advent. Side by side with Ezra and Nehemiah, as if to show that their unfinished character is the result of design, we have a history, in the Book of Esther, which has never been surpassed, in dramatic unity and power, by any fiction which human fancy has devised. It has a marked resemblance of character to the history of Joseph at the close of the Book of Genesis. In each of them the inspired narrative rises into a sacred drama, complete and harmonious in every part, of which the main purpose is the deliverance and preservation of the chosen people. In the Book of Nehemiah, again, we have a summary of the whole course of Jewish history through fifteen hundred years, from the call of Abraham to the time when the covenant was renewed after the return from captivity. Thus, in two cotemporary books, wholly opposite in character, and in two opposite ways, a signal unity is impressed on the whole series of Old Testament histories, from the times of Abraham and Joseph, and the old Pharaohs, to those of Nehemiah, Esther, and Mordecai, under the Persian kings.

The break in the history, after Nehemiah, only completes the proof of this all-pervading unity of design. The waning of the elder dispensation, and the withdrawal, through four hundred years, of sacred history and prophecy, was adapted, in the highest degree, to render the dawn of the Gospel more impressive.

VIII. The four Gospels are the next main division of the sacred history. And here the marks of Divine wisdom are still more conspicuous than in the narratives of the Old Testament.

The life, death, and resurrection of our Lord, are the central object of Old Testament prophecy, the sum and substance of the Christian faith. The great end for which all written revelation is given required that these should be placed in clear and full relief. Here, therefore, and here only, in the whole range of inspired messages, we have four parallel and collateral histories. In the Old Testament two is the highest number of such parallel series, or a bare sufficiency under that rule of the law—"In the mouth of two or three witnesses shall every word be established." But here, in the Gospels, the legal provision is exceeded. Four testimonies have been provided, and not two or three only; so that they fulfill the description of our Lord, and give to us "good measure, pressed down, shaken together, and running over."

But the same rule of the Law, when compared with the Gospels, yields a further sign of the deep wisdom which presided secretly in their composition. Two witnesses are barely sufficient, but three are ample, for confirmation alone. When a first record, then, has been made, and one testimony given, a second would naturally have, for its chief purpose, to confirm, and not to amplify and extend it. A third would be less needful, though still desirable, for mere confirmation of the others, and might reasonably be expected to ratify and to supplement their statements, almost in equal measure. A fourth, if given at all, plainly exceeds the limit named in the Law. Its main object, we may infer, would be to supplement and enlarge the previous narratives, since it would be almost superfluous for mere confirmation of them alone.

Now, if we take the Gospels in the order in which they now stand, and in which they have been placed from the first, such is precisely the relation which exists between them. St. Mark, the second, has only two or three incidents not recorded by St. Matthew, though the different arrangement in one large portion, and the far greater fullness of the details, preserve it from all suspicion of being a mere summary. Its aim, throughout, is to confirm St. Matthew, and not to supply facts wholly new. The Gospel of St. Luke combines both objects in almost an equal proportion. In the account of our Lord's infancy, it supplements the narrative of St. Matthew, and hardly one incident is the same. In seven chapters that follow, it confirms the evidence of its two predecessors, and agrees further with St. Mark in the arrangement. Ten chapters after these are mainly a supplement to the previous narratives; six others are in the main confirmatory, and the last chapter, again, is supplementary, and consists mainly of new matter. The Gospel of St. John, on the contrary, is supplementary from first to last. Except in the account of the miracle of the loaves, and some leading events in Passion-Week, it contains information wholly new, which is not to be found in any of the three earlier Gospels. This gradation of character, in fulfilling the double object of confirming earlier testimonies, and of giving further information, is a secret but powerful evidence of the deep wisdom which molded the separate narratives, so as to fulfill most effectually the end for which they were given.

The silence of the Gospels with regard to our Lord's infancy, and the interval before his ministry began, is another mark of that secret wisdom of the Holy Spirit which controlled the Evangelists. Apocryphal writings have many legends of this obscure period; but the Gospels themselves pass it over in reverent and expressive silence. They seem thus to echo the words of that prophecy, which Isaiah had given concerning our blessed Lord—"He shall not strive, nor cry, nor lift up his voice in the streets." A lesson of quietness, humility, and reverence, most alien from the tone of religious forgeries, is hereby inwrought into the whole texture of the sacred history.

The harmony and apparent discrepancies of the Gospels are another proof, when rightly viewed, of their common inspiration. Two things are plainly required, in order that they might fulfill in the highest degree the great object for which a Divine revelation is made. There must be, on the one hand, such a substantial and manifest unity, as to give them the force of concurrent evidence. On the other hand, there needed such a measure of distinctness in each testimony, as to clear their general consent from all suspicion of being artificial and collusive.

Now, the four Gospels satisfy this double condition in a singular manner. The history of criticism, and of the theories of their origin, which have divided the opinions of the most learned and diligent students, is alone a sufficient proof of the fact. One large class of critics, induced by the features of close resemblance, have labored to complete a theory of the formation of the first three Gospels from a mechanical combination of six or seven earlier documents. Others, again, from the multiplied diversities between them, have strongly maintained a view diametrically opposite, that they grew, quite independently, out of oral tradition, and that no one Evangelist had seen the work of any other. The zealous maintenance, by many learned writers, of both of these opposite views, is a clear sign that the Gospels combine, in the fullest measure, the marks of a plural and of a concurrent testimony. Had they differed more widely, they would have failed to confirm each other's evidence, and their authority would have been weakened and destroyed by the presence of undeniable contradictions. Had their agreement been more complete, and free from all divergence, they would have lost their character of a fourfold testimony, and have failed to satisfy one main purpose for which the history was conveyed to the Church in this peculiar form.

Again, the unity of the whole Bible history may be seen in the frequent allusions made in the Gospels to the facts of the Old Testament. Among those which are referred to, and incidentally confirmed by their testimony, are the creation of Adam and Eve—Matt. xix, 4—the first institution of the Sabbath, the ordinance of marriage, the guilt and crime of the first tempter, the murder of Abel, the wickedness in the days of Noah, the Flood, the law of ribution for murder, after the Flood; the genealogy of patriarch, the destruction of Sodom, the history of

Lot's wife, the covenant of circumcision, the expulsion of Ishmael, the oath of God to Abraham, the vision of Jacob, his purchase of ground at Shechem, the birth of Pharez and Zarah, all within the Book of Genesis. In Exodus, the words to Moses at the bush, the appointment of the Passover, the gift of manna from heaven, the Divine communication of the Law by Moses, the ordinance of cleansing for the leper, the sacrifices in the tabernacle on the Sabbath day, are all the object of direct mention, or plain allusion. We have also two genealogies, one of which reaches back to Abraham, and the other even to Adam, and nearly a hundred distinct quotations from the Old Testament.

But while the Gospels are thus linked, retrospectively, with all the earlier histories, they are united in the closest manner with the later narrative in the Book of Acts, and with the Apostolic Epistles, and the Book of Revelation. St. Matthew is especially the means of securing an intimate relation between the Old and the New Testament. St. Mark unites together St. Matthew and St. Luke; since the incidents, with three slight exceptions, are entirely those of St. Matthew, and the order, with hardly an exception, the same as in St. Luke. The third Gospel, again, is continued by St. Luke himself in the Book of Acts, and thus forms a link with the later history; while St. John's Gospel unites the Evangelical history with the Epistles and the Prophecies, because three epistles, and the only prophetical book of the New Testament, like the Gospel itself, have the beloved disciple for their common author.

Besides these more technical characters of the Gospels, in which they may be seen clearly to carry on one great, consistent scheme of sacred history, there are others of a still deeper kind, which never fail to impress the humble and reverent reader. There is a calmness and quietness of tone, a transparent, unadorned simplicity, which makes us forget the writer in the contemplation of the glorious object he sets before us. Like Moses and Elias on the mount of Transfiguration, the Evangelists themselves disappear from view, and are lost, that Jesus their Lord may be seen alone. No where can we see more plainly the force of those words, which belong to all the inspired messages of God, that "the testimony of Jesus is the spirit of prophecy." Every chapter and every verse converges here on one great object, and seems to repeat the words of the Baptist to his disciples: "Behold the Lamb of God, who taketh away the sin of the world!"

IX. The Book of Acts, the last of the four main divisions of sacred history, and by far the shortest in extent, retains the same character, and exhibits no less clearly the historical unity which pervades the whole.

And first, the book has a remarkable unity in its general outline, from its beginning to its close. Its subject is the planting of the Gospel in the heathen world. It opens, accordingly, with the promise of Christ to his apostles—"Ye shall be witnesses unto me, both in Jerusalem, and in all Judea, and in Samaria, and unto the uttermost part of the earth." And it closes with the most definite point in the completion of this great work, when the apostle of the Gentiles arrived at Rome, the metropolis of heathenism, and after summoning the Jews to a conference, denounced their national unbelief, and announced the transfer of the rejected blessing to the heathen—"Be it known, therefore, unto you, that the salvation of God is sent unto the Gentiles, and that they will hear it." Every part concurs in describing the steps by which this great change was fulfilled. We see the Gospel spreading, first, from the Hebrews to the Hellenists at Jerusalem; then, on the murder of Stephen, from Judea to Samaria, and the first step taken toward a national conversion from heathenism by the baptism of the Ethiopian eunuch. Then follows the conversion of Saul, the destined apostle of the Gentiles, and that of Cornelius of Cesarea, the first Gentile Roman convert, in whose case the partition wall began to be broken down. There is mention of the reverent submission of the Jewish believers to this unexpected change, and the formation of the first Gentile Church at Antioch. After the murder of the apostle James by the Jews, there follows at once the first missionary journey of Paul and Barnabas to Cyprus and Asia Minor. And then, after their return, and the decree of the council, affirming the freedom of Gentile believers from the Law of Moses, the transition is complete. The Church of the Jews, and the other apostles, pass entirely out of sight. We have the regular course of St. Paul's ministry, in Asia, in Macedonia, and Achaia, and at Ephesus; till the persecuting malice of the Jews completes the work his zeal had begun, and transfers him, a prisoner for the Gentiles, from Jerusalem and Cesarea to the imperial city, which was to form the center of the Church's history, for good and for evil, through the whole course of the Gentile dispensation.

The book is called familiarly the Acts of the Apostles. But the mention of the apostles is kept subordinate in every part to the one design of the whole. After the list in the first chapter, no mention occurs, in its whole course, of any other among the Twelve than Peter, John, and the elder and younger James. The foremost of them, St. Peter, disappears silently from view after his miraculous rescue from the malice of Herod. No light whatever is thrown upon his later journeys and labors; and the last sentence concerning his travels and labors is merely this: "He departed, and went to another place." He appears again in the council of Jerusalem; but after its decision, a vail is drawn over his labors, and those of the other eleven; and St. Paul alone, the apostle of the Gentiles, becomes the subject of the whole narrative. This marked exclusion of events which were not essential to the main object, is a proof of the Divine wisdom which controlled the sacred penman in the composition of the work, and rendered it, by its simplicity, condensation, and unity, a worthy completion of the long series of inspired history.

But this unity of design is no less perceptible in the connection between this book and the rest of the New and the Old Testaments. And here we may notice, first, its subordination to the Gospels. We have four distinct narratives of the life and death of our Lord, but one only, little more than one-fourth of their combined length, to record the later history of the Church for more than thirty years. The three years of our Lord's ministry occupy more than three times the space, in the New Testament narrative, of the thirty years which follow. For Christ himself, his life, death, and resurrection, are the great sum of the whole Gospel message, and the history of the Church is kept in strict and beautiful subordination to the history of the heavenly Bridegroom.

Again, the book divides naturally into two main portions of nearly equal length, the second of which begins with the first council at Jerusalem. The first of these abounds in references to the earlier portions of Scripture. In the first four chapters alone, there are eight or ten quotations from the Old Testament, or allusions to its statements, in direct confirmation of their truth. The words of two Psalms are declared to be the words of the Holy Ghost. The ordinance of the first-fruits, on the day of Pentecost, receives its figurative fulfillment; and the confusion of tongues at Babel finds its New Testament contrast and Divine antidote in the gift of tongues at Jerusalem. Four different prophecies are quoted in the first sermon of St Peter, and declared to be then receiving their fulfillment. His next discourse appeals generally to "all the prophets, which have been since the world began," and again to the words of Samuel and the later prophets; but more distinctly to the covenant with Abraham after the sacrifice of Isaac, and to the prediction of Moses in Deuteronomy, shortly before his death. In the next chapter we have a quotation from Psalm cxviii, an allusion to the first record of Creation, and a further quotation from the second Psalm. Besides these, two distinct summaries of the Old Testament are embodied in the narrative, the first in the apology of St. Stephen at Jerusalem, and the second in St. Paul's discourse at Antioch in Pisidia. The truth of the Old Testament is the common basis on which the first martyr, full of the Holy Spirit, and the greatest of the apostles, equally rest their appeal, when contending earnestly for the truth of the Gospel. Thus the Book of Acts, by the whole character of its earlier history, is dovetailed inseparably with all the previous histories in the Word of God.

The second or later division has an entirely different character. Only two quotations from the Old Testament are found in it; one of them from Amos, quoted by St. James in the council at Jerusalem, and the other from Isaiah, quoted by St. Paul to the Jews at Rome, like a mournful key-note at the close of the sacred history. But on the other hand, the points of comparison with general and classical history are here greatly multiplied; and the coincidences with the historical allusions in the writings of St. Paul are so abundant, as to form a most convincing and irresistible proof of the genuineness of the epistles, and the truth and fidelity of the sacred narrative. These chapters form thus the outmost boughs of the inspired history, and bear upon them most abundantly the golden fruitage of

THE HISTORICAL UNITY OF THE BIBLE. 401

heavenly truth, unfolded in the didactic and doctrinal portions of the New Testament.

These facts point clearly to one conclusion. This connected series of history, with one single break, constructed on one uniform plan, and almost on the same scale, from the Creation onward through four thousand years; confirmed by all foreign evidence in its later portions, where alone heathen records yield any clear light, and self-sustained in all the rest by its own truthfulness and transparent simplicity of style; expanding itself in that generation when the Law was given, and in a less degree when the forefather and type of Messiah came to the throne, and most of all, during the three years of our Lord's ministry; but in all the other parts moving calmly, swiftly along, indulging in no comments, recording the minutest details and the most startling wonders in the same tone of simple dignity and unadorned plainness of speech, and interwoven, from first to last, with innumerable mutual references, is a fact wholly unique in the literature of mankind. The Bible, in its historical unity, stands alone, and without a rival. One Mind may be clearly seen in its whole course, by whose wisdom its various writers were guided and controlled, so as to furnish, at the long interval of fifteen hundred years, a simple and connected outline of the moral government of the world—a scheme of mercy which began in Paradise, but first blossomed out, and began to yield more abundant fruit in the resurrection and ascension of our Lord, the Pentecostal gift of the Spirit, and the spread of the Gospel throughout the moral wildernesses of the heathen world.

CHAPTER XVIII.

THE DOCTRINAL UNITY OF THE BIBLE.

The doctrinal, even still more than the historical unity of the Bible, bears evidence to its inspiration and Divine authorship. Thirty-nine books in the Old Testament, and twenty-seven in the New, the work of forty different writers, are here collected into one volume, though their first composition is spread over the long interval of fifteen hundred years. They were all composed in times of heathen darkness, when the most civilized peoples and mightiest empires of the world were bowing down to stocks and stones, or offering polluted worship to "gods many, and lords many," the impersonations of passion, strife, jealousy, and every impure and hateful lust. The language, the style, the character, the special object, no less than the date of these books, are all widely different. But the great outlines of truth are every-where the same. There is development, but no discrepancy. There are partial contrasts, adding life to the whole by the diversity of the parts, but no contradiction. A manifest and undeniable harmony of thought, tone, and doctrine, animates and pervades the whole. The view of man is every-where the same; that he is the creature of the living God, accountable to his Maker; fallen, but not hopeless, guilty, but not left in despair; the subject of a present curse, but still within reach of the richest blessing; corrupt and impure, but capable of restoration to the Divine favor and image; placed under a penal sentence of death, but capable of

THE DOCTRINAL UNITY OF THE BIBLE. 403

attaining a blessed immortality. The doctrine concerning God is every-where the same; that he is one, and there is no other than he; that all the gods of the heathen are idols, but the Lord made the heavens; that he is almighty, all-wise, good, perfect, holy, merciful, everlasting, the Maker of all things, and the Judge of all men; a pure, invisible Spirit, who must be worshiped in spirit and in truth. The revealed way of salvation is every-where the same, by faith in God, and in the promise of a great and powerful Redeemer, atonement by sacrifice, and the substitution of the guiltless for the guilty, forgiveness procured by the shedding of blood, and inward renewal of heart, the fruit of that forgiveness, by which the soul is renewed after the image of God, in righteousness, holiness, and truth. The practical lessons of duty are also the same in every part, faith in the promises of God's mercy through an atoning Savior, working by love—the love of God supremely, and the love of all mankind.

It would require a large volume to unfold thoroughly this unity of the Bible, from Genesis, through the Psalms, the Prophets, the Gospels, and Epistles, to the Apocalypse, in all the main doctrines of the Christian faith. It is only by means of a diligent and prolonged study of the Scriptures, that the full impression of this deep and real harmony can be received into the mind. I shall merely endeavor to show, by the selection of a few passages, how each main doctrine runs, like a golden woof, through the whole series of these Divine messages; and then illustrate the real harmony, amid partial contrast, or fancied contradiction, between the teaching of the Old and the New Testament.

I. The doctrinal harmony of the Bible, from first to last, may be traced clearly in its explicit statements on all the main topics of religious faith.

1. The first revealed truth is the fact of creation, **or** that all things were formed by the will and power of one true and living God. The Bible opens its message with these words: "In the beginning God created the heavens and the earth." This great truth had been entirely lost from view in the reign of polytheism and fable; and chaos, night, and Erebus, replaced the conception of the creative will of the Almighty. It is equally lost in the speculations of a pantheistic philosophy, of which there are too many specimens in modern times. But the testimony of the Scriptures to this great truth is consistent, **uniform, and unvaried**, from first to last.

First, when the judgment of the Flood was sent upon the world, it is announced in these words—"I will destroy man whom I have created from the face of the earth, both man and beast, and the creeping thing, and the fowls of the air; for it repenteth me that I have made them." And again—"In the image of God made he man."

In the first mission of Moses, the truth is indirectly taught, in the Divine expostulation: "Who hath made man's mouth, or who maketh the dumb or deaf, or the seeing or the blind? have not I the Lord?"

When the Law was given on Mount Sinai, this doctrine was publicly embodied in the fourth commandment: "For in six days the Lord made heaven and earth, the sea, and all that in them is, and rested the seventh day; wherefore the Lord blessed the Sabbath day and hallowed it." The statement is repeated in Exodus xxxi: "For in six days the Lord made heaven and earth;" and again in Deuteronomy, in two or three varied forms. It is found in twenty different Psalms, gives its tone to the Book of Job, and runs through all the Proverbs. It appears, in the most various associations, in the prophecies of Isaiah. "At **that day shall a man look to his Maker**," xvii, 7. "Ye have not looked unto the Maker thereof, nor had respect unto him that fashioned it long ago," xxii, 11. "Shall the work say of him that made it, He made me not? or shall the thing formed say of him that formed it, He had no understanding?" xxix, 16. "Lift up your eyes on high, and behold who hath created these things, that bringeth out their host by number?" "The everlasting God, the Lord, the Creator of the ends of the earth, fainteth not, neither is weary; there is no searching of his understanding." Isa. xl, 28. "Thus saith God the Lord, he that created the heavens, and stretched them out; he that spread forth the earth, and that which cometh out of it; he that giveth breath unto the people upon it, and spirit to them that walk thereon," xlii, 5. The voice of Jeremiah is the same in his earnest prayer: "Ah, Lord God, thou hast made heaven and earth by thy great power and stretched-out arm, and there is nothing too hard for thee!" And that of Zechariah: "The burden of the Word of the Lord, which stretcheth forth the heavens, and layeth the foundation of the earth, and formeth the spirit of man within him."

The same great doctrine runs through the New Testament. We find it in the opening of the fourth Gospel, applied to the Word, the only-begotten Son of the Father: "All things were made by him, and without him was not any thing made that was made." It appears in our Lord's thanksgiving, in the first and third Gospels: "I thank thee, O Father, Lord of heaven and earth!" and in his reply to the Pharisees: "Have ye not read that he which made them in the beginning, made them male and female?" In the Book of Acts it appears in every part. In the thanksgiving and prayer of the early Church: "Lord, thou art God, which hast made heaven and earth, and the sea, and all that in them is," iv, 24. In the words of the apostles at Lystra: "Sirs, why do ye such things? We are men of like passions with you, and preach that ye should turn from these vanities unto the living God, who made heaven and earth, and the sea, and all things therein," xiv, 15. And again, in St. Paul's discourse at Athens: "God that made the world and all things therein, seeing he is Lord of heaven and earth, dwelleth not in temples made with hands." And, not to multiply quotations from the Epistles, it meets us repeatedly in the closing book of the canon, in the song of the heavenly elders, in the oath of the mighty Angel, and in the proclamation of the everlasting Gospel by another angel to the idolaters of the last days: "Fear God, and give glory to him, for the hour of his judgment is come, and worship him which made the heaven, and the earth, and the sea, and the fountains of water."

2. The unity of God is another doctrine which stands out in full relief in every part of the Bible. In the earlier books it is doubly conspicuous when we contrast the Word of God with the monuments and remains of Egypt, and the wild and dark fancies of polytheism throughout the ancient world. "I am the Lord thy God, thou shalt have no other gods but me." "Thou shalt worship no other god, for Jehovah, whose name is Jealous, is a jealous God." "Unto thee it was showed, that thou mightest know that the Lord he is God, there is none else beside him." "Hear, O Israel, the Lord our God is one Lord."

The same truth runs through the Psalms and the Prophets, and forms a prominent character of their teaching. "All the gods of the nations are idols, but the Lord made the heavens." "Confounded be all they that serve graven images, that boast themselves of idols: worship him, all ye gods." "I am the Lord; that is my name; and my glory will I not give to another, neither my praise to graven images." "Before me there was no god formed, neither shall there be after me. I, even I, am the Lord, and beside me there is no Savior." "Is there a god beside me? Yea, there is no god, I know not any." "The Lord is the true God, he is the living God and an everlasting King: at his wrath the earth shall tremble, and the nations shall not be able to abide his indignation. Thus shall ye say unto them, The gods that have not made the heavens and earth shall perish from the earth, and from under these heavens."

In the New Testament, while the doctrine of three Persons in the Godhead is taught, the Divine unity, in contrast to the many gods of heathenism, is maintained with equal clearness. So the apostle writes to the Corinthians: "For though there be that are called gods, whether in heaven or in earth, as there be gods many, and lords many, yet to us there is but one God, the Father, of whom are all things, and we in him; and one Lord Jesus Christ, by whom are all things, and we by him." And again, to Timothy: "For there is one God, and one Mediator between God and man, the man Christ Jesus."

3. The fall and corruption of man is another truth which meets us equally in every part of Scripture. It is seen in the account of the world before the Flood. "And God saw that the wickedness of man was great in the earth, and that every imagination of man's heart was only evil, and that continually." It reappears in the blessing after the Flood: "I will not curse the ground any more for man's sake, for the imagination of man's heart is evil from his youth." We read it, further, in the growth of idolatry after the Flood, in the guilt of the Cities of the Plain, and their destruction, and the sentence pronounced upon the Amorites— Gen. xv—with the reason assigned for delaying the judgment. The history of the Exodus is one ceaseless illustration of its truth. Moses sums up his review of the conduct

of Israel in the words: "Ye have been rebellious against the Lord since the day that I knew you." David makes the penitent confession: "Behold, I was shapen in iniquity and in sin did my mother conceive me." Ezra exclaims in the same spirit: "O my God, I am ashamed and blush to lift up my face to thee, my God; for our iniquities are increased over our heads, and our trespass is grown up to the heavens." The last prophecy of the Old Testament is one ceaseless expostulation with the sin and stubbornness of the chosen people. The Gospels open with the warning of the Baptist: "O generation of vipers, who hath warned you to flee from the wrath to come?" and toward their close they reëcho the description in those solemn words of the Savior: "Ye serpents, ye generation of vipers, how can ye escape the damnation of hell?" The opening chapters of the Epistle to the Romans are full of the same truth. The apostle quotes evidence to confirm it from six different Psalms, and from Isaiah's prophecies, and then draws the universal inference—"Now we know that whatsoever the law saith, it saith to them who are under the law, that every mouth may be stopped, and all the world become guilty before God."

4. The doctrine of a Redeemer, by whom deliverance from the curse of sin would be given to men, is another truth, which runs through the whole of Scripture. "The testimony of Jesus is the spirit of prophecy." It meets us in the first account of the Fall, where the Seed of the Woman is announced, who should bruise the head of the serpent. It reappears in the promise to Abraham of that Seed, who should possess the gate of his enemies, and in whom all the nations of the earth would be blessed. It is announced by the dying Jacob, in the words—"The scepter shall not depart from Judah, nor the lawgiver from between his feet, until Shiloh come, and to him shall the

gathering of the people be." It is implied in the types of Isaac's sacrifice, and of Joseph's exile, sufferings, and exaltation. It is seen in the promise of the prophet like unto Moses, and in the types of the paschal lamb, the smitten rock, from which there flowed living water, the scapegoat, and the brazen serpent. It meets us in the Psalms and Prophets with growing clearness; and the titles, the King, Immanuel, the Prince of Peace, the Man of Sorrows, the Branch, Messiah the Prince, the Son of Man, the King of Zion, the Shepherd, Jehovah's Fellow, the Messenger of the Covenant, the Sun of Righteousness, reveal the various attributes of grace and holiness, which were to be manifested in the person and work of the Incarnate Son of God.

5. The way of salvation by faith is another doctrine in which all the sacred writers conspire with a striking unity. "By faith Abel offered unto God a more acceptable sacrifice than Cain." Heb. xi, 3. Abraham "believed God, and it was counted to him for righteousness." Gen. xv, 6. This fundamental doctrine, though specially unfolded by St. Paul, runs through all the intermediate books of Scripture. Trust in God, in the Old Testament, and faith in Christ, its equivalent in the New, is every-where proclaimed to be the pathway of life and salvation. Man fell through unbelief, and by faith alone he can be recovered. This great truth appears equally in the books of Moses, in the later Prophets, and in the Gospels, the writings of St. Paul, and the Epistles of St Peter and St. John. The eleventh of Hebrews is a divine commentary on the Old Testament histories, in which this aspect of them is brought into full relief; and the whole message of the Bible is summed up in the solemn contrast, "He that believeth on the Son of God hath everlasting life; and he that believeth not the Son shall not see life, but the wrath of God abideth on him."

6. The need of sacrifice and atonement is another truth, in which we may trace the all-pervading unity of Scripture. Abel's sacrifice was accepted when he brought the firstlings of his flock; and Cain's was rejected, who brought a bloodless offering, the fruits of the earth. When Noah had slain the victims in sacrifice after the Flood, "the Lord smelled a sweet savor," and a renewed covenant of mercy and promise was given. It was in the midst of such sacrifices that the covenant was again renewed to Abraham with special promises. After the sacrifice of Isaac, in a figure, and of the ram caught in the thicket in his stead, a still fuller blessing was given by a new covenant, and confirmed with the oath of God. The Law of Moses was full of sacrificial ordinances, from the Passover on the night of the Exodus to the latest ordinance of purification, in Numbers, by the spotless heifer that was to be slain, and whose ashes were to sprinkle the unclean. Isaiah transfers the types of the law to their antitype, the coming Messiah: "All we, like sheep, have gone astray: we have turned every one to his own way; and the Lord hath laid on him the iniquity of us all." "When thou shalt make his soul an offering for sin, he shall see his seed, he shall prolong his days. . . . By his knowledge shall my righteous servant justify many, for he shall bear their iniquities." The New Testament repeats the same truth in still clearer accents, and refers all the types in the legal sacrifices to their great Antitype: "The Son of man came, not to be ministered unto, but to minister; and to give his life a ransom for many." "Behold the Lamb of God, who taketh away the sin of the world!" "Without shedding of blood there is no remission." "God hath made him to be sin for us, who knew no sin, that we might be made the righteousness of God in him." "These are they which have come out of great tribulation, and have washed their robes, and made them

white in the blood of the Lamb." "Who his own self bare our sins in his own body on the tree, that we, being dead to sin, might live to righteousness, by whose stripes ye are healed."

7. The need of regeneration and holiness of heart in order to salvation is another truth which runs through the whole Bible. The contrast is drawn broadly, throughout, between the righteous and unrighteous, the believer and the unbeliever, the obedient and the disobedient. In the Flood, and the deliverance of Noah; in the destruction of Sodom and Gomorrah, the rescue of Lot, the intercession of Abraham, and the promise that the city should have been spared for the sake of ten righteous; and in the repeated contrasts of the Psalms, the Proverbs, and all the Prophets, the same doctrine every-where appears. "The Lord loveth the righteous, but the wicked, and him that loveth violence, his soul hateth." "The Lord preserveth all them that love him, but all the wicked will he destroy." "The Lord taketh pleasure in his people; he will beautify the meek with salvation." The prayers of the Psalmist teach the same lesson: "Create in me a clean heart, O God; and renew a right spirit within me." The Old Testament closes with a strong assertion of this moral contrast, and the opposite issue to which it leads: "Then shall ye return, and discern between the righteous and the wicked, between him that serveth God, and him that serveth him not."

The same contrast is revealed with equal clearness in the New Testament, and is there ascribed more plainly to its secret cause, the work of the Holy Spirit on the hearts of men. "A good tree," our Lord tells his disciples, "can not bring forth evil fruit, neither can a corrupt tree bring forth good fruit. Do men gather grapes of thorns, or figs of thistles?" Again, to Nicodemus: "That which is born of the flesh is flesh, and that which is born of the Spirit is spirit." "Except a man be born again, he can not see the kingdom of God." The apostles dwell much on the same truth: "They that are in the flesh can not please God." "To be carnally minded is death, but to be spiritually minded is life and peace." "If any man be in Christ, he is a new creature; old things are passed away: behold, all things are become new." "For if ye live after the flesh, ye shall die; but if ye through the Spirit do mortify the deeds of the body, ye shall live." "Follow after holiness, without which no man shall see the Lord." "Faith without works is dead, being alone." "As he which hath called you is holy, so be ye holy in all manner of conversation: because it is written, be ye holy, for I am holy." "He that doeth righteousness is righteous, even as He is righteous; he that committeth sin is of the devil." "Here is the patience of the saints: here are they that keep the commandments of God, and the faith of Jesus." All these, and many similar passages, teach the same lesson. They separate all mankind, morally and spiritually, into two opposite classes, believers and unbelievers; those who live after the flesh, and after the spirit; those who serve God, and those who serve him not; and teach that a well-grounded hope of salvation belongs to the former class, and to them alone. Repentance and conversion is the bridge by which the soul passes from one side to the other of this gulf of moral separation; and the message of our Lord is solemn and weighty, and sums up the voice of all Scripture: "Except ye repent, ye shall all likewise perish." "Except ye be converted, and become as little children, ye shall not enter into the kingdom of heaven."

II. This doctrinal unity of the Bible might easily be traced in many other particulars, and under every diversified topic of religious truth. But it may be well to confine

THE DOCTRINAL UNITY OF THE BIBLE. 413

our view to one aspect in which it has been controverted and denied, from the contrast between the Old and the New Testament. If it can be shown that, even where the apparent divergence is widest, the real harmony is complete, no further proof will be needed of that Divine Authorship which belongs to the whole, and which has provided for men, by prophets and apostles, a perfect and harmonious treasury of Divine truth.

The contrast in question has been stated by a modern skeptic in these terms:

"Here are two forms of religion which differ widely, set forth and enforced by miracles; the one ritual and formal, the other actual and spiritual; the one the religion of Fear, the other of Love; one finite, and resting altogether on the special revelation made to Moses, the other absolute, and based on the universal revelation of God, who enlightens all that come into the world. One offers only an earthly recompense, the other makes immortality a motive to a Divine life. One compels men, the other invites them. One half the Bible refutes the other half; the Gospel annihilates the Law; the Apostles take the place of the Prophets, and go higher up. If Christianity and Judaism be not the same thing, there must be hostility between the Old and the New Testament, for the Jewish form claims to be eternal. To an unprejudiced man this hostility is very obvious. It may indeed be said, Christianity came not to destroy the Law and the Prophets, but to fulfill them; and the answer is plain, their fulfillment was their destruction."

The self-confident and irreverent tone of this objection, in which the lie is directly given to our blessed Lord's own declaration, does not speak well for the practical power of that "absolute religion" by which the writer strives to replace and supersede historical Christianity.

And first, this objection, instead of being the result of

intellectual progress, is merely a relapse into an error which appeared very early, and from which it was one of our Lord's first lessons to deliver his own disciples. The difference of tone between his own teaching and that of the Law of Moses, or rather of the scribes and Pharisees who expounded it to the people, was soon observed, and led many hearers to suspect that his purpose was to set aside the authority of these earlier messages of God. But our Lord asserts the falsehood of this notion in the strongest and plainest terms: "Think not that I am come to destroy the Law and the Prophets: I am not come to destroy, but to fulfill. For verily I say unto you, Till heaven and earth pass, one jot or one tittle shall in no wise pass from the Law, till all be fulfilled."

The objection affirms that the fulfillment of the Law and the Prophets, under the Gospel, is their destruction. Our Lord affirms the exact reverse, that the fulfillment of them, which it was his object to secure, was the contrast and antithesis of their destruction: "I am not come to destroy, but to fulfill." It is no slight presumption in this reckless advocate of "absolute religion" to give the lie direct to the Son of God in one of his most solemn and deliberate statements.

But while the alleged contradiction between the Law and the Gospel is thus disproved by the highest authority, that of our Lord himself, so that no one can be his true disciple who affirms them to be hopelessly at variance, a partial and real contrast between them is clearly recognized in the New Testament. In the opening of the fourth Gospel we find it distinctly announced. "For the Law was given by Moses, but grace and truth came by Jesus Christ." So again, after the Baptist's message—"The Law and the Prophets were until John; since then the kingdom of heaven is preached, and every one is pressed into it." The

Epistles of St. Paul have this for their main subject. "The law made nothing perfect, but the bringing in of a better hope did, by which we draw nigh to God." "Therefore by the deeds of the law shall no flesh be justified, for by the law is the knowledge of sin." "Before faith came, we were kept under the law, shut up to the faith that should be revealed." "For if they which are of the law be heirs, faith is made void, and the promise made of no effect. Because the law worketh wrath; for where there is no law, there is no transgression." "For if the ministration of death, written and engraven on stones, was glorious, how shall not the ministration of the Spirit be rather glorious?" In these and many other passages a strong contrast is plainly allowed and affirmed between the earlier messages of the Law, with their holiness and severity, and the grace, tenderness, and freedom of the Gospel of Christ.

The contrast, then, between the Law and the Gospel is no modern discovery of unbelievers. So far as it is real, it is recognized fully and openly in the New Testament, and forms the basis of some of its most earnest appeals to the hearts and consciences of Christian men. On the other hand, the falsehood which exaggerates this partial contrast into a total contradiction is detected by our Lord, when it first began to arise in the hearts of his own disciples, and receives his earnest and indignant reprobation. He who maintains it must first claim to be wiser than Christ himself, and thereby forfeits at once the name and character of a Christian.

But let us examine the statement more closely. And first, is the religion of Moses and of the Old Testament ritual and formal only? Let Moses himself answer, in his earnest appeal before his death: "And now, Israel, what doth the Lord thy God require of thee, but to fear the Lord thy God, to walk in all his ways, and to love him, and to serve the Lord thy God with all thy heart and with all thy soul. . . . Love ye therefore the stranger, for ye were strangers in the land of Egypt. Thou shalt fear the Lord thy God; him shalt thou serve, and to him thou shalt cleave, and swear by his name. He is thy praise, and he is thy God." And our Lord himself, who alone, of all mankind, ever fulfilled the Law of Moses, assures us that its weightiest matters were not the tithe of mint, anise, and cummin, but lessons of a far higher kind, even "judgment, mercy, and faith."

Again, is the teaching of the Law a religion of fear alone? Is it finite, making no appeal to the unchangeable moral attributes of the Most High? Every religion must take its impress from the character of the object of worship. Cruel gods must create a fierce and cruel religion, and licentious divinities one of impurity and sensual lust.

Now, one part of the Law is plainly designed to reveal the true character of the God of Israel, in contrast to the superficial and hasty impressions which might be formed from a less thoughtful observation. When Moses offered the prayer in a time of distress and fear, "I beseech thee, shew me thy glory," the answer was given—"I will cause all my goodness to pass before thee, and I will proclaim the name of the Lord before thee." After special preparation, and with peculiar solemnity, the desired revelation was given. "And the Lord passed by and proclaimed, The Lord, the Lord God, merciful and gracious, long-suffering, and abundant in goodness and truth, keeping mercy for thousands, forgiving iniquity, and transgression, and sin, and that will by no means clear the guilty; visiting the iniquity of the fathers upon the children, and upon children's children, unto the third and fourth generation."

What was the effect of this message, this crowning revelation of the "religion of fear" upon him who received it? "And Moses made haste, and bowed his head toward the earth, and worshiped, and said, If now I have found grace in thy sight, O Lord, let my Lord, I beseech thee, go among us, for it is a stiff-necked people; and pardon our iniquity and sin, and take us for thine inheritance." Nor was this a transient impression on the mind of Moses alone. The Psalmist, four hundred years later, learned from the same passage a religion of hope and love: "He made known his ways unto Moses, his acts unto the children of Israel. The Lord is merciful and gracious, slow to anger, and plenteous in mercy. He will not always chide, neither will he keep his anger forever. For as the heaven is high above the earth, so great is his mercy toward them that fear him."

Does the Law, again, offer only an earthly recompense? Its fundamental promise is in the words to Abraham, "I will bless thee, and make thy name great, and thou shalt be a blessing." "Fear not, Abraham, I am thy shield, and thy exceeding great reward." "I will be a God unto thee, and to thy seed after thee." Since God himself is "the everlasting God," these promises clearly partake of the same character. The patriarchs desired "a better and a heavenly country." God was not "ashamed to be called their God, for he had prepared for them a city." In the hope of a better portion, they "confessed themselves strangers and pilgrims on the earth." The dying Jacob exclaimed, "I have waited for thy salvation, O Lord." Moses "had respect unto the recompense of reward," and therefore made mention of a book of life, in which his name was written. The Divine law enjoined the Israelites: "The land shall not be sold forever; for the land is mine, and ye are strangers and sojourners with me." The commandment set before them "life and good," and promised, on their obedience, that the everlasting God would be "their life, and the length of their days." The eternal God was to be their refuge, and underneath them were to be his "everlasting arms." They were to dwell in safety, as a people saved by the Lord; and their days to be multiplied as the days of heaven. To the Levites the further promise was given, when excluded from a distinct territory, that "the Lord God of Israel was their inheritance." In all these promises there was a direct reference to God himself, as their God by especial covenant; and to those who read them with faith they would be a sure pledge, not merely of temporal, but of eternal blessings.

Again, does the Law merely compel by force, and not invite by the power of moral suasion? No statement could be more opposed to the truth. The whole Book of Deuteronomy is one continued, earnest appeal to the conscience, the feelings, and the heart of the people of Israel. It is perhaps the longest, the most sustained moral invitation to be found in the compass of the Word of God. The voice also of the prophets is a perpetual expostulation, a series of earnest appeals to the conscience and heart of later generations.

Has the Gospel, on the other hand, no solemn messages, no appeals to fear, to temper the grace and tenderness of its invitations? Far from it; the warnings it contains are more severe than those of the Law itself, borrow from them their sharpest accents of rebuke, and infuse into them a tone of still deeper meaning. "I will forewarn you whom ye shall fear: fear him, which after he hath killed hath power to cast into hell: yea, I say unto you, Fear him." "Ye serpents, ye generation of vipers, how can ye escape the damnation of hell?" "If the word spoken by angels was steadfast, and every transgression and disobedience received a just recompense of reward, how shall we escape, if we neglect so great salvation?" "Of how much sorer punishment shall he be thought worthy, who hath trodden under foot the Son of God, and counted the blood of the covenant, wherewith he was sanctified, an unholy thing, and done despite to the Spirit of grace?" "It is a fearful thing to fall into the hands of the living God." "For even our God is a consuming fire." In the face of these and similar passages, it is indeed strange how the most superficial could venture to set up the imaginary contrast, that the Gospel is a religion of love only, without fear, and the Law one of fear only, without love. In each message both of the Divine attributes are distinctly revealed, though not in the same proportion. The righteousness and holy severity of the Law is tempered by rich revelations of Divine grace; while the fuller and clearer grace of the Gospel is guarded by warnings still more solemn than the penal sanctions of the elder covenant; and a still sorer punishment is denounced upon those who despise and disobey.

Again, the promises of the Gospel, while they relate mainly to the future, include the present also. It retains the lower promises of the Law, and only tempers them, by the knowledge of the cross, with a new element of patience and mingled sorrow. Our Lord lays down this law of hope clearly to his followers: "There is no man that hath left house, or brethren, or sisters, or father, or mother, or wife, or children, or lands, for my sake and the Gospel's, but he shall receive a hundredfold now in this time, with persecutions; and in the world to come, eternal life." The apostle repeats and confirms his Master's promise, and declares that "godliness is profitable for all things, and hath the promise of the life that now is, as well as that which is to come." The two dispensations, even where the seeming contrast is the greatest, interlace and overlap, like the folds of the curtains of the tabernacle, with a marvelous unity, and reveal, amidst their partial contrast, the one mind of the Divine Spirit, penetrating, molding, pervading, and harmonizing the whole.

But this deep unity between the Law and the Gospel may be seen more clearly when we look below the surface, and refer them to those Divine attributes which they are especially designed to reveal.

There are three successive forms of Divine goodness, ascending by a climax to its fullest and highest exhibition. The first is simple bounty, or love to creatures, as creatures, irrespective of every moral difference. This is the basis of natural religion in its simplest and most elementary form. It is implied and assumed in the Bible, and blends with its messages; but is like the court of the Gentiles, when compared with the higher lessons of written revelation. The second is righteousness and holiness, or the love of moral good, and the hatred of moral evil. This is the fundamental truth of the legal covenant. It reveals God in his holiness, in that hatred of sin, as well as delight in goodness, which finds its reflection in the double precept, "Thou shalt love thy neighbor, and hate thine enemy." It is this character of the Old Testament which makes it wear so forbidding and repulsive an aspect to all hearts that are still under the power of sin, and have attained no real sympathy with the Divine holiness. It is an aspect of perfect goodness, higher than simple, indiscriminate bounty, but less excellent than the grace of the Gospel. This is the third and highest form of Divine goodness—kindness to the unthankful and the unworthy; a love which does not flatter or indulge them in their sin, but uses all patience and wisdom to raise them from the depth of moral evil into the image of God, the recovered possession of purity, uprightness, and love.

There is nothing, then, arbitrary or capricious in this mutual relation of the Law of Nature, or the earlier stage of unwritten revelation, the Law of Moses, and the Gospel of Christ. They are three steps in the same series, an outer court, a holy place, and a most holy; and are all required in a complete and harmonious revelation of the Divine goodness to sinful men. The partial contrast between the Law and the Gospel is just as essential to the wisdom of the message as their secret harmony. It is only the severity of holiness which can prepare us for a just and full apprehension of Divine grace. Remove these preparatory teachings, and grace ceases to be grace. It soon degenerates into mere indifference to moral good and evil, the darkest form of a perverse fatalism, instead of the best and noblest form of goodness, tender compassion to the guilty, and redeeming love.

Contrast, however, is not contradiction. It is one element in the most complete and perfect unity. The hues of light in the rainbow are contrasted with each other, and still they are only pure light analyzed and separated into its varying elements. And so it is with the truths of the Law and the Gospel. In one we have types, in the other antitypes. In one holy severity is more apparent, in the other tender compassion and grace. But the contrasted truths interpenetrate the whole. The Gospel, with its richest grace, is virtually contained in the Law; and holiness, in its deepest and most solemn tones of warning, blends every-where with the rich harmonies of the Gospel promises. The God revealed in the Law is one who "careth for the strangers, and relieveth the fatherless and the widow;" who "giveth good to all flesh, because his mercy endureth forever." He is One who promises that he will hear the cry of the poor in his distress, "for I am gracious;" and commands his people: "Thou shalt not oppress a stranger, for ye know the heart of a stranger, for ye were strangers in the land of Egypt." He is One who forbids every grudge, and enjoins a perfect love; who cares for the safety of the poor, the deaf, the blind; and teaches lessons of kindness even to the child in his play, from the lost ox or ass, and the gleanings of the harvest field. On the other hand, the Gospel fences round its most gracious promises with terrors borrowed from the language of the Law, and the prospect of coming judgment. Its most gracious invitations follow close upon a warning to unbelievers: "It shall be more tolerable for Sodom and Gomorrah in the day of judgment than for you;" and its noblest descriptions of the future blessedness are linked with the solemn declaration, "For without are dogs, and sorcerers, and whoremongers, and idolaters, and murderers, and whosoever loveth and maketh a lie." Righteousness in the Law prepares the way for grace; and grace, in the Gospel, reigns "through righteousness unto eternal life." They are attributes of perfect goodness, contrasted, but still harmonious; revealed successively, that their true force and meaning may be more clearly seen by dull and earthly minds, and still blending ever with each other in their partial separation. Mercy is vailed, yet every-where present in the Law, but is revealed in the Gospel; and the grace of the Gospel, centering in the cross of Christ and his Divine atonement, is the highest, noblest, and most wonderful exhibition of the righteousness of God. Thus "mercy and truth meet together, and righteousness and peace embrace each other." "Truth springs" here "out of the earth" in the person of the incarnate Redeemer, and "righteousness looks down from heaven," while the Spirit, the reward of his suffering and agony, is poured out upon a sinful world.

CHAPTER XIX.

REDEMPTION A PROGRESSIVE SCHEME.

The Bible, if composed of true revelations from God to man, reaching through a space of fifteen hundred years, may be expected to throw some light on the scheme of Divine providence. Its first object may be to promote personal religion, to reclaim prodigals from their sin, to provide a firm ground of hope for sincere penitents, and instruct them in their present duty to God and their fellow-men. But since its professed aim is to renew the souls of men in the image of God, it must, in its higher lessons, give its disciples some real insight into the plans and purposes of the Most High. For its object is not only to convert rebels and slaves into servants, but to exalt servants themselves into the friends and the sons of God.

The Scriptures satisfy this reasonable expectation. A unity of living hope runs through the whole course of their messages. The histories, the doctrines, and the prophecies, all harmonize with each other; and reveal, under varied aspects, one consistent scheme of Divine wisdom, which moves on continually toward the redemption of a sinful world.

All skepticism, however unconsciously, has its root in the heart. Man must feel and own that he is a sinner, before he can feel his need of a Redeemer. He must own his guilt, before he can sue for pardon, or welcome the Divine atonement by which pardon is secured. He must learn his weakness in the inward conflict with selfishness and sin, before he will rest on a higher strength than his own, or seek the promised help of the Spirit of God. So long as he thinks that he needs education alone, without conversion or renewal of heart, the Gospel of Christ will remain to him a sealed mystery. If he attempts, in this state of mind, to interpret the scheme of providence, he will be almost sure to lose himself in a labyrinth of error. God's providence is not a course of education for a world of teachable, happy, sinless disciples of truth. It is a hospital for souls laboring under a sore disease, a scheme of redemption for the lost and guilty, procured through the dying agony of the Son of God. Whenever this idea of redemption is lost, then the key of knowledge is taken away, and providence becomes a hopeless enigma. The facts of history, and the testimonies of Scripture, have then to be set aside, or garbled and falsified, in order to reconcile them with the demands of some false and deceptive theory, some philosophical counterfeit of Christianity, from which all its distinctive features have passed away.

That view of providence, which sees in it simply a scheme for the world's education, denies the fall of man, and, by consequence, his need of a Divine redemption. It diverges, then, from the Bible at the outset, and this divergence increases, as we travel along the stream of time. The darker features of the world's history have to be explained away, in order to reconcile them with a sinless progress of humanity from infancy to perfect wisdom. The foulest abominations of heathenism, for thousands of years, have then to be softened down into the harmless and natural delusions of infancy, before human reason had ripened by the due exercise of its own powers. The later idolatries and sensual vices of Greece and Rome, and the self-righteousness of the Jewish Pharisees, to suit the same theory, must be taken for the generous and attractive impulses of opening youth; and the apostasies of the middle ages, or the feverish worldliness and intellectual pride of later times, must be termed the growth of manly strength, or the calm and mature wisdom of ripened and experienced age. Thus the testimony of the Bible has to be reversed and falsified in every point, both in its historical statements and its prophetical warnings; and the heady and high-minded are beguiled with the flattering notion that they are wiser than the wisest of former generations, from the happy accident of their being born in a later and more enlightened age of the world.

The comparison of the times of the Law to childhood, and of the Gospel to a riper age, has a direct warrant in the Scriptures themselves. But it belongs to the true disciples of the Law and the Gospel alone. When extended to the whole world, with its multitude of unbelievers, the comparison fails. Where there is no life, there can be no real growth. There must be repentance and conversion from sin to God, before the true education of the soul can begin. Unbelief may revolve in cycles of error from age to age; but only those who enter in at the strait gate can walk in the way of life, and thus advance nearer and nearer to that moral perfection, the recovered image of God, after which their souls continually aspire.

The Bible, alike in its histories and prophecies, is flatly opposed to those theories of mankind's gradual and universal progress in moral and religious truth, which have been propounded by unbelieving philosophy, and which sometimes labor, however vainly, to support themselves by an appeal to its own statements. The pictures it sets before us are widely different—a series of rebellions and apostasies, resisted, and partially overcome, by mighty acts of Divine grace; but continually repeated in new forms, till they issue, in the last times, in a solemn and fearful controversy between light and darkness, and in judgment on unbounding ungodliness, as well as in rich mercy and grace to those who know God and obey the Gospel of Christ. We are told, in the New Testament, that "in the last days perilous times shall come," and that "evil men and seducers shall wax worse and worse, deceiving and being deceived." And, however the views of Christians may vary with regard to the future course of Providence, and the final victories of truth, one thing must be plain, to all who read the Scriptures with reverence, that they are no where ascribed to a natural law of human progress, but to gracious acts of the Holy Spirit, or direct judgments of Christ, which will overcome and reverse the downward tendency of the human heart, and bind a reluctant and rebellious race, by mercy and judgment, to the footstool of the Most High.

But while the Bible is thus opposed to those spurious theories of progress, which are based on human pride, and contradict the facts of history, it exhibits a progress of a different kind, in the ceaseless unfolding of a scheme of Divine mercy for the redemption and recovery of sinful man. God, in his own nature, is unsearchable: he can be known only as he is revealed. A revelation of moral attributes, since it must consist of the successive acts of God's moral government, must plainly be progressive. Salvation, or the recovery of the soul from the power of sin, is by faith alone. The object of faith is Divine truth. It is by the knowledge of the truth that the souls of men are actually redeemed and renewed. And since the providence of God unfolds itself, from age to age, in new acts of judgment and of mercy, the materials of moral influence are thus increased and multiplied, which the Holy Spirit, the Lord and Giver of life, employs in his gracious work upon the hearts of men, both in their first conversion and in their later advances in heavenly wisdom. There is thus a double progress, which the Scriptures reveal to us. The first is that of the Divine counsel itself, or the acts of mercy and judgment, which constitute the moral government of the world, and the messages of revelation. This is unintermitted, ceaseless, and unfailing. It admits of no arrest, and no reverse. However dark the moral state of the world may be in special crises of Providence, the stars, even at midnight, move on in their everlasting courses, and prepare the way for a brighter sunrise to follow. The second kind of progress is that of the actual fruits of redemption in each successive age. And this resembles the apparent movements of the planets. There is a general progress, subject to temporary retrocession and decline. Seasons of Divine forbearance, through man's perverseness, lead to spiritual decay. "Because sentence against an evil work is not executed speedily, the hearts of the sons of men is fully set in them to do evil." That evil is permitted to reach a certain hight, and is then broken to pieces by new acts of judgment, followed by fresh and higher revelations of mercy. And thus, although by a checkered and seemingly-irregular course, the work of grace moves on continually, and truth prevails, by a slow but sure advance, from age to age. Even when it seems to decay, and "the faithful are minished from the children of men"—the time of fear and sorrow is only the season of travail before a joyful birth. Each fresh exhibition of the stubbornness and inveteracy of evil illustrates more brightly, in the result, the victorious energy of redeeming love.

Let us begin with the Book of Genesis. No sooner has man fallen from his original uprightness, and become the prey of death, than hope dawns upon him in the first promise. The Seed of the Woman, it is revealed, shall bruise the head of the serpent. The message, however dim at first, implied clearly a Deliverer to come, by whom the miseries of the fall should be repaired, and the power of the deceiver be overcome. This same promise runs, like a golden thread, through all the later Scriptures. In the very first chapter of the New Testament, the miraculous birth of the Messiah answers strictly to this his earliest title in the Old Testament. The words of our Lord himself announce the promised triumph as already begun. "I beheld Satan, as lightning, fall from heaven." "Now is the judgment of this world: now is the prince of this world cast out." The apostle renews the promise to the Christians of Rome, where Satan's seat was so long to be established: "The God of peace shall bruise Satan under your feet shortly." And its completion is one main subject of the last and crowning prophecy of the Word of God, where the old serpent is revealed in vision, first in the hight of his power and fiercest malice, and then in his downfall and final judgment.

The history of the world, before the Flood, is one of Divine forbearance carried to its extreme limit, till one righteous family alone was found on the earth. A darker and more gloomy season can hardly be conceived, than that which the sacred historian sets before us. "The earth was corrupt and filled with violence," and "all flesh had corrupted their way upon earth." Then followed a most solemn judgment, and a signal deliverance. Amidst the desolation, a new covenant of mercy was sealed with the future race of mankind, which implied that no judgment, so total, should ever be repeated, and no season of such utter darkness settle down again upon our sinful world.

When idolatry began to prevail once more, after the Flood, and threatened to renew the former calamities, a new course of redeeming mercy began. One people were set apart in the person of their forefather, by a series of miraculous visions, to be the special depositories of the truth of God, till the promised Redeemer should appear. The covenant with Abraham marks evidently a new era in God's providence. Special mercy and electing grace were to minister to the larger object of a world-wide redemption. "In thy seed shall all the nations of the earth be blessed."

This further promise, like the earlier one in Paradise, is repeated through the whole course of Scripture to its close. It is the ground of the promise made to Moses at the bush: "I will bring you into the land, concerning which I did swear to give it to Abraham, to Isaac, and to Jacob, and I will give it to you for a heritage: I am the Lord." It occurs continually, as the warrant of faith and hope, in the Psalms and the Prophets: "Thou wilt perform the mercy unto Abraham, and the truth unto Jacob, which thou hast sworn unto our fathers from the days of old." It meets our eyes in the very first verse of the New Testament: "The book of the generations of Jesus Christ, the son of David, the son of Abraham." It is repeated again in the song of Zacharias. After the day of Pentecost, St. Peter appeals to it once more: "Ye are the children of the prophets, and of the covenant which God made with our fathers, saying unto Abraham, And in thy seed shall all the families of the earth be blessed. Unto you first, God, having raised up his Son Jesus, sent him to bless you, in turning away every one of you from his iniquities."

Before the grace of God, however, could be clearly made known to men, there was needed a full revelation of his holiness. This was the great office of the old covenant. "By the law is the knowledge of sin;" and the knowledge of sin can alone awaken the desire for mercy, or discover to men the true meaning of the grace of the Gospel. During the times of the Old Testament this revelation became fuller and fuller, with every new display of sin and perverseness of the chosen people. Truth stood on the defensive amidst the gloomy reign of heathen idolatry, and the state of actual piety was often lamentably low, as in the days of Gibeah, or the reign of Ahab; but the materials were preparing, slowly and patiently, which the Spirit of God would employ in all later ages to help forward the promised victories of truth and righteousness. Every generation yielded its fresh contribution to the growing temple of revealed truth, till the last of the prophets announced the approaching advent of Messiah, and the rising of the Sun of Righteousness, with healing in his wings.

The birth of our Lord, and still more his death and resurrection, marked a new and nobler era in the development of this scheme of Divine mercy. The whole range of earlier prophecy, from the sentence on the serpent in Paradise to the parting words of Malachi, began to be fulfilled. Three great wants of mankind were supplied—a perfect Example, a Divine Atonement for sin, and a living Fountain-Head of heavenly grace. In the new dispensation of the Spirit, after the great sacrifice of the cross was complete, grace was to be as conspicuous as righteousness had been before; and the message of the Law to one favored race alone was replaced by a free proclamation of pardon, life, and immortality, through the atoning death and resurrection of Christ, to all the nations of the earth.

The New Testament, however, in proclaiming the sure triumphs of the Gospel, and the final establishment of the kingdom of God in the age to come, no where announced a smooth and easy progress of truth to its full victory. On the contrary, it foretold, under the Gospel, conflicts, reverses, and apostasy from the faith, like those which formed the history of the Old Testament. The earlier record of the sins of Israel was to supply descriptions for new forms of evil within the Church of Christ. Strong and repeated cautions are given against the superstitions of the latter times, and against the selfishness and open unbelief that would prevail in the last days. The sacred history teaches how the Law had been perverted into pharisaic self-righteousness, when the grace of the Gospel was revealed. The prophecies of the New Testament forewarn the Churches that the grace of the Gospel, in its turn, would be extensively abused, and turned into a plea for sensuality and unbelief, before that fuller display of righteous judgment which would break in pieces all the power of evil, and introduce a lasting reign of righteousness and peace.

The Bible reveals, then, a continual progress, in the ceaseless unfolding of the Divine attributes through successive ages, from the Patriarchs to the Law, from the Law to the Prophets, from these to the times of the Gospel, and from these again to a glorious triumph and reign of righteousness still to come. But while this objective progress is without intermission, it is not so with the actual prevalence of truth and holiness among mankind. This has its seasons of marked revival and progress, and its intervals of apostasy and decay. The abuse of earlier messages or degrees of light, when it has reached its climax, brings down the judgments of God, and these judgments are followed by new displays of mercy. All the analogies of Scripture, and its direct prophecies, confirm the hope that the next thousand years of the world's history will surpass the times of the Gospel, as far as these have surpassed the times of the Law and the early Patriarchs. But this hope is quite consistent with warnings of wide-spread apostasy from the faith, through intellectual pride, and a strong current of unbelieving worldliness in the last days. All theories of progress, which lead men to rely on their natural powers in dealing with the truth of God, and to look down on the Bible as a secondary and uncertain guide, in comparison with their own conscience and reason, instead of being the heralds of real advance, are ominous precursors of spiritual delusion and open apostasy from the faith. Men, without the guidance of the Holy Spirit, are just as liable to deadly and fatal error in our times as in any previous age. The louder their boasts of intellectual advancement and superior intelligence, the more plainly the snares of that great deceiver, who is "king over all the children of pride," are weaving around their path. It is only by returning to sit, with the docility of little children, at the feet of Christ, that they can avoid the danger which the prophet has described in such vivid terms: "Give glory to the Lord your God, before he cause darkness, and your feet stumble on the dark mountains; and while ye look for light he turn it into the shadow of death, and make it gross darkness."

The Bible is a history of redemption, but of a redemption still incomplete, and of which the full and open triumph is reserved for days to come. Viewed in the light of this great truth, a singular unity of prophetic hope runs through the whole, and becomes doubly striking when we compare its earliest and latest messages. No books of the Bible are more contrasted in their general character than Genesis and Revelation. The interval of time which separates them is more than fifteen hundred years. The first is a simple, unadorned history; the second, a series of highly-poetical visions. The first is the earliest variety of Hebrew prose; the second, in a language then unborn, embodies the main features of Hebrew poetry. The Book of Genesis records common events upon earth; the Apocalypse, to a great extent, is the description of heavenly wonders. One is a preface to the Law, the other a supplement to the Gospel. One was written by the adopted son of Pharaoh's daughter, learned in all the wisdom of Egypt; the other, by an unlearned fisherman of despised Galilee. The first abounds with innumerable details, names of persons, places, and domestic annals of the most minute and various kind; while the other scarcely stoops to set its foot upon earth, but dwells apart as on a mount of Transfiguration. When the former was composed, Israel had scarcely begun to be a nation; but when the exile received his visions in Patmos, their national history was closed for ages, and they were already outcasts and wanderers through the earth. All things on earth were changed in this long interval— Egypt, Canaan, and Babylon; only God and his redeeming grace remained unchangeable. Yet the latest book corresponds to the earliest, as the loops and curtains of the tabernacle, or the various parts of the Temple, with multiplied harmonies, partly of the most obvious, but in part of the most delicate and unobtrusive kind. Creation has its counterpart in the promise, "Behold, I make all things new." The uncreated light which fills the heavenly city; the successive revelation of the beast from the sea, the beast from the earth, and one like to the Son of man; the Sabbatic rest of a thousand years, the river from the throne, watering the heavenly paradise; the great river Euphrates, the gold and precious stones of the New Jerusalem, the tree of life in the paradise of God; the marriage of the Lamb, the Second Adam, and the clothing in which the Bride is arrayed; the old serpent, the deceiver of the nations, the woman and her mystic Seed, and sore travail; the removal of the curse, and the angel guards at the open gates of the heavenly paradise; the cry of the martyrs from beneath the altar of burnt-offering, and the rainbow around the throne, are all so many distinct allusions, in this closing prophecy, to the earliest chapters of the sacred history. The Old Testament here conspires with the New, and the history of the world's first infancy is seen to be stored with lessons of Divine wisdom, which were to be fully unvailed, after six or seven thousand years, in the final close of the mystery of God.

The Bible, then, amidst the large variety of its contents, which embrace an interval of fifteen centuries in their composition, and seven thousand years in the times to which they refer—in its histories, psalms, proverbs, prophecies, and epistles, earthly facts and heavenly revelations—exhibits, from first to last, the clear signs of a Divine unity which pervades and animates the whole. Its distinct parts are not of separate interpretation. Behind the human authors stood the Divine Spirit, controlling, guiding, and suggesting every part of their different messages. Their words "came not at any time by the will of man, but holy men of God spake, borne along by the Holy Ghost." As the Jordan flows underground in part of its course, so this Divine unity may be obscured from hasty observers by the multitude of intervening works of which the whole message is composed, by the variety of historical details, the diversity of manner and style, of age and local circumstance, in the sixty-six books which constitute the Bible. But its sunrise and sunset are equally glorious, and reveal clearly the hidden harmony of the whole revelation. It traces the course of Providence from that Creation in which our earth was prepared for the habitation of men, to the complete accomplishment of that new creation in which it will be the habitation of righteousness forever. It begins with the first bridal of Adam and Eve, the parents of all mankind, and closes with the heavenly bridal of the Second Adam, the Lord from heaven, and the Church of the Firstborn, in whom the great mystery of that ordinance is fulfilled. It begins with a vision of the earthly Paradise forfeited by sin, and the taste of the forbidden tree of knowledge. It closes with the revelation of a better and heavenly Paradise, where no tree of knowledge is seen, but the tree of life alone, and even its leaves are for the healing of the nations. It begins with the success of the old serpent in deceiving Adam and Eve, and ends with the vision of his overthrow by the Seed of the Woman, when he can deceive the nations no more, but sinks under the righteous judgment of God. It begins with man's exclusion from Paradise by the watching cherubim and the flaming sword; and ends with the revelation of the heavenly Jerusalem, whose gates are open continually, while an angel at every gate invites the nations of the saved to bring their honor and glory into the city of God.

The more closely, then, we examine the Bible, the more plainly it will appear to be indeed "the true sayings of God," "the Word of God, which liveth and abideth forever." In its width, its freedom, and its grandeur, it reflects the largeness of God's universal providence. Like that providence, it has its seeming discrepancies, and its real perplexities, much to exercise faith, as well as much by which it is nourished, parts which may appear trivial and superfluous, and depths which repel the frivolous with a sense of impenetrable gloom. Even those who sincerely embrace the Gospel may rest satisfied with a dim and imperfect measure of knowledge, and thus have their faith in it exposed to sore trial, whenever new temptations assail the Church of Christ. But in proportion as we search it with humble diligence and earnest prayer, fresh harmonies of Divine truth, new wonders of Divine grace and love, will disclose themselves to our view. One difficulty after another will slowly melt away, and resolve itself into a halo of heavenly beauty. Sixty generations of the Church have studied it unceasingly; but this incorruptible manna neither wastes nor corrupts, and they have never exhausted its stores of Divine wisdom. Sixty generations of unbelievers have assailed it on every side with winds of false doctrine, but it has only rooted itself the more firmly in the hearts of Christians, and in the history of the world. And still, after all these ages, there are deep mines of truth in it which have never been explored, harvests of spiritual food still to be reaped by coming generations, and healing medicines for countless evils that are still concealed in the depths of future time. The words of the prophet to Ariel of old will assuredly be fulfilled, soon or late, in all who assail this enduring Word of God: "And the multitude of the nations that fight against her and her munition shall be even as the dream of a night vision. It shall be as when a hungry man dreameth, and behold he eateth, but he waketh, and his soul is empty; or a thirsty man dreameth, and behold he drinketh, but he waketh, and is faint, and his soul hath appetite: so shall all the multitude of the nations be that fight against Zion." But those who draw near with reverence, and while they meditate, loose their shoes from their feet on this holy ground, will equally find the promise of the Psalmist fulfilled in their own experience: "They shall be abundantly satisfied with the fatness of thy house, and thou wilt make them drink of the river of thy pleasures: for with thee is the fountain of life, and in thy light we shall see light." The meteors of false philosophy blaze for a moment, and disappear; but the written Word of God is an effluence from the Uncreated Light, and must endure forever.

www.ingramcontent.com/pod-product-compliance
Lightning Source LLC
Chambersburg PA
CBHW051726300426
44115CB00007B/476